INTERNATIONAL ECONOMIC RELATIONS OF THE WESTERN WORLD 1959–1971

2 INTERNATIONAL MONETARY RELATIONS

INTERNATIONAL ECONOMIC RELATIONS OF THE WESTERN WORLD 1959–1971

Edited by
ANDREW SHONFIELD
assisted by
HERMIA OLIVER

VOLUME 2
INTERNATIONAL MONETARY RELATIONS
SUSAN STRANGE

with an essay on
FINANCE FOR DEVELOPING COUNTRIES
CHRISTOPHER PROUT

Published for
THE ROYAL INSTITUTE OF
INTERNATIONAL AFFAIRS

by

OXFORD UNIVERSITY PRESS
LONDON   NEW YORK   TORONTO
1976

Oxford University Press, Ely House, London W.1

GLASGOW NEW YORK TORONTO MELBOURNE WELLINGTON
CAPE TOWN IBADAN NAIROBI DAR ES SALAAM LUSAKA ADDIS ABABA
DELHI BOMBAY CALCUTTA MADRAS KARACHI LAHORE DACCA
KUALA LUMPUR SINGAPORE HONG KONG TOKYO

ISBN 0 19 218317 6

© Royal Institute of International Affairs 1976

PREFACE

A large number of people in and around Chatham House were engaged over a period of some four years in the project which is the subject of these two volumes. The volumes themselves represent only a portion of a considerably larger iceberg, the invisible part consisting of other ideas and pieces of preliminary research, some of them highly promising, which were connected with this exercise but could not, for one reason or another, be developed to the point where they could be fitted into the present framework of analysis. As may be readily imagined, the problem with a subject as variegated and wide-ranging as this was not one of amassing relevant material but of choosing what to exclude.

We reached a decision at an early stage not to attempt to produce a comprehensive history of the period under review. Our object was not after all to recount events, however interesting in themselves, but to test the degree of robustness of the system of international co-operation which *seemed* to have emerged in the Western world by the 1960s. Our aim was to conduct these tests in conditions which placed the system under maximum strain. We therefore deliberately chose for our case studies circumstances in which the impulse towards conflict was visibly vying with the impulse to collaborate. The kind of questions that we then asked ourselves were: How near was the system to some form of breakdown? At which points was it most vulnerable? What factors had been responsible for avoiding a threatened catastrophe? Had serious damage been done in the process to the prospect of future collaboration? It will readily be seen that our historical analysis had a certain practical intention: we were trying to find out how far the apparent successes achieved in the field of international economic relations could reasonably be expected to recur in other circumstances, when the underlying economic and political conditions might be less favourable than they were in the period under review. We deemed ourselves to be doing something like the work of one of those test drivers who chooses the roughest and nastiest pieces of ground to traverse in order to observe how the vehicle behaves when it gets close to stalling.

When we started out in 1970, with the support of a substantial research grant from the Social Science Research Council, the precise time-limits of the piece of history which we intended to cover were by no means clear. The aim of the research, which was spelt out in some detail in the outline to which the SSRC gave its approval, was simply to unravel the significant strands which appeared to give to international economic relations in the period that began with the end of the 1950s a distinctive character, different from that of any period that had preceded it. But the terminal point of our study only suggested itself—or better, imposed

v

itself—with the unfolding of the events surrounding the dollar crisis of the summer and autumn of 1971. Afterwards, we realized that this had indeed been a watershed: as such it provided the natural point from which to look back over the landscape.

The way in which that decision emerged reflects the characteristic *modus operandi* of the study. The study groups at Chatham House which were trying to make sense of different aspects of this recent piece of history were constantly referring forward to events that were occurring in the present. This was a natural, as well as sometimes a highly contentious, way of testing out some of the hypotheses that were being developed out of the historical analysis. It led to some highly productive, as well as passionate, arguments. We thus found ourselves to some extent monitoring present events as a guide to the interpretation of the past. Our procedure was to subject the various portions of the work to the scrutiny of one central study group at Chatham House, consisting of all the members of the research team who have contributed to these volumes, our rapporteur and research assistant, Ann-Margaret Willis, plus one or two people with special knowledge of the subject who acted in effect as standing advisers on the study. Among the latter particular mention should be made of Miriam Camps, who gave us the benefit of her exceptional knowledge of US and European policy-making. We were also fortunate in having Professor Richard Cooper of Yale as a member of the group during the year when he was a visiting research fellow at Chatham House, and in being able to make use of William Diebold Jr of the Council on Foreign Relations, New York, as a kind of corresponding member, especially in the early stages when he was writing his own work, *The United States and the Industrial World* (Praeger, 1972) which traversed a lot of the ground which we were trying to cover. Exchanging drafts with our sister organization in America proved once again to be a productive intellectual process.

The composition of the main research team changed over time. At an early stage we suffered a severe loss through the death of Professor Sidney Wells; he was one of the original group of three people, with Susan Strange and myself, who worked out the research strategy for the project. Thereafter we were acutely conscious of missing him on a number of occasions. We also suffered, as is inevitable in conducting a piece of research which tries to make use of people who are directly engaged in public affairs as well as of academics, from a certain depletion of our number through the successes of some of our researchers in other fields. This happened, for example, when Christopher Tugendhat, who was working on the role of international business corporations, became a Member of Parliament. Others who contributed as members of the research team at various stages of the project but were then called away to other tasks included Sidney Golt, Caroline Miles, and Stuart Holland.

A number of people assisted us greatly by giving us the benefit of knowledge derived from their personal involvement in the events which are analysed in these pages. They did this both by commenting on discussion papers and drafts of the text and also in some cases by joining directly in the mêlée of the study groups themselves. Needless to say, the responsibility for the interpretations that finally emerged from these discussions, in so far as they are reflected in these volumes, belongs exclusively with the authors. But the opportunity of testing out our ideas in this way was invaluable, and our thanks are due to a long list of distinguished people for their help: Sir Alan Bullock, Sir Frederick Catherwood, Mr William Clark, the late Sir Edgar Cohen, Mr Roy Denman, Sir Frank Figgures, M. Boyer de la Giroday, M. André de Lattre, Sir David Pitblado, Sir Richard Powell. Others who were consulted and to whom we owe a debt of gratitude include: Dr Fred Bergsten, Dr Guido Carli, Mr William Dale, Mr Michael Dealtry, M. André Dequen, Dr Otmar Emminger, the late Gabriel Ferras, Dr Milton Gilbert, Professor Charles Kindleberger, Mr John Kirbyshire, Dr Giovanni Magnifico, Mr Robert Roosa.

The index to volume 1 was compiled by Katharine Duff and to volume 2 by Zuzanna Shonfield, who also worked on the chronology. Among colleagues on the staff at Chatham House, I should mention in particular the contribution made by James Fawcett, when he was Director of Studies, to our examination of international monetary affairs during the 1960s. Margaret Cornell collaborated with me in the direction of the project in its early stages, before she became Administrative Director. The project owed a great deal over its four years to Eileen Menzies's organizing ability, in ensuring that the variegated membership of our numerous study groups managed to get together and that the arrangements for people and paper consistently worked.

In regard to volume 2, acknowledgment should be made to Alison Young who was a valuable research assistant to the Chatham House group in 1970–2.

Chatham House,   A. S.
  London.

CONTENTS

ix

FINANCE FOR DEVELOPING COUNTRIES
by CHRISTOPHER PROUT

INTRODUCTION: PAST TRENDS AND NEW FACTORS

by Andrew Shonfield

The period covered by this study runs from the formal restoration of currency convertibility by the main non-dollar currencies at the end of 1958 to the emergence of the inconvertible dollar in 1971. The rationale of this choice of opening and closing dates was discussed at some length in volume I, Part I, and need not be repeated here. 1959–1971 forms a distinct epoch in the history of international economic relations. It begins with the cautious return of the weakened European powers to a normal peacetime regime of free financial exchanges, after an interval of a quarter of a century, under the tutelage of the Americans. It ends after a sustained and unparalleled expansion of international financial transactions with the dramatic acknowledgement by the Americans that there has been a distinct shift in the balance of economic power between themselves and the rest of the world, to their detriment. The declaration of dollar inconvertibility by the United States in August 1971 was intended to be heard on the world public announcement system with the amplifiers turned on at full blast. It was an announcement to the effect that the rules of the game in international economic relations were going to be changed.

But changed how? The intention, as well as the constraints on it imposed by the facts of a greatly increased interdependence of the nations belonging to the Western economic system, remained ambiguous.

This volume, which is devoted to an analysis of the main developments in international finance during this period, complements the study of international trade in Parts II and III of volume I. It also attempts to provide some pointers to underlying trends in the conduct of international relations which seem likely to stretch into the future. These are summarized and considered in Susan Strange's concluding chapter (ch. 12). Various aspects of her analysis of international finance were taken into the first Part of this two volume work, entitled *An Overall View*, where the different strands in the structure of international economic relations, commerce, money, politics, were brought together. Rather than traverse that ground again, I think it may be of some value to supplement the interpretation by referring the reader briefly to certain developments which occurred subsequent to the terminal date of our history. Not that this will resolve the ambiguities about the meaning of the apparent watershed of 1971.

2 s.—1

The intention is simply to point to some significant events of the early 1970s which have a special bearing on our subject rather than to attempt a full analysis of them. It is at least worth reminding oneself of what happened to some of the proffered solutions which were current in the early 1970s, and also of the way in which the international economic system of the Western world, which had been shaped by the highly favourable conjuncture of events in the decade of the 1960s, faced up to the new and unfamiliar threats which were sprung upon it in the first half of the subsequent decade.

There was a marked tendency in the intellectual atmosphere surrounding the crisis of 1971 to look to the market mechanism to produce, unaided, a result far superior to anything designed deliberately by governments or central banks. There was a widely held belief, which had been given currency by some unusually articulate and persuasive economists of the monetary school, that the international financial system was breaking down because of a wilful refusal to allow a well-nigh perfect mechanism of monetary exchange to operate without hindrance. The automatic mechanism which was ready to hand to perform the task so much better than any man-made system of rules was a collection of floating exchange rates responding directly to the shifting demand for particular currencies.

The manifest failure of the Bretton Woods regime of fixed exchange parities created a mood in which the promise of benefits from a system of an opposite kind, in which the movement of exchange parities was subjected to no restraint whatsoever, was believed to be almost unlimited. For a start, nations would not need to bother any longer about the size of their currency reserves; indeed, if each of the national monetary authorities would simply abide by the market's decision about the appropriate price of its currency, foreign exchange reserves of any kind would be otiose. If only the Western nations would stop spending their energies on schemes to enlarge the pool of world reserves to keep pace with the advance of world trade and monetary transactions, and simply rely on the price mechanism to ensure that the demand and supply for all currencies was always automatically in balance.

In this climate of opinion the decision to suspend the convertibility of the dollar which led at one remove—the Smithsonian Agreement of December 1971 on a new range of parities—to a regime of fluctuating exchange rates, produced a kind of hallelujah chorus from the influential school of monetary economists and their spokesmen. US Secretary of the Treasury John B. Connally, whose activities had threatened political havoc within the Western alliance during the closing months of 1971, was hailed as the ' real professional '.[1]

There seemed to be no end to the good things which would flow from unleashing the exchange rates. Domestic economic management would simply follow the lines set by the international market in currencies. ' A flexible exchange rate would make an incomes policy unnecessary ', Professor Harry Johnson, probably the most sophisticated and persuasive exponent of the doctrine, promised.[2] As to the foreign exchange market itself, it was confidently predicted that freely floating currencies would produce more stability of exchange rates rather than less—once people engaged in international transactions got used to the basically simple idea that they had to hedge all their bets, and allowed the speculators to use their expertise to do the job for them.

It is worth noting that these arguments were given greater force through their coincidence with a deeper strain in political and economic thinking which came to strong expression at the time. In the early 1970s there was a widespread sentiment of disappointment with the results of the efforts that had been made over the previous two decades to apply economic science to the deliberate management of national affairs. The feeling of disillusionment was most marked in the United States and Britain, and these two countries still largely set the tone for the currently received wisdom of the economics profession. There were in fact good reasons, as the following chapters show, why these two countries in particular should have felt disappointed with their performance in economic policy-making. That was not, of course, the sole cause of the notable resurgence of what may be termed the ' robot school ' of economic management at this stage. The evidence of intellectual history suggests that there is a certain cyclical pattern in fashions in economic thinking. In this instance the modish message was that there had been altogether too much political interference with forces which were in reality beyond any form of political control. The moral that was persistently pointed up by Milton Friedman, the extremely articulate Professor of Economics at Chicago University and the acknowledged high priest of the movement, was that governments should just confine themselves to making one or two key decisions about the broad economic results which they sought, and then set the dials controlling the short-term management of the economy permanently in the chosen positions, promising never to move them. Even better if the control-box could be padlocked and the governments persuaded to go away and think about something else!

There had without doubt been an excessive confidence among the first generation of postwar economists about their capacity to manage the economy by means of small and frequent adjustments of the controls at the centre. The experiences of the 1960s and early 1970s made it very easy to demolish the pretensions of what was called ' fine tuning' of the economy. At the same time the rigid stance adopted by many governments in defending their fixed currency parities because of the ' political symbolism ' attaching to exchange rate adjustments [3] cried out to be remedied. But as we have seen, the would-be purveyors of the remedies produced their own characteristic excesses in making their claims. The actual behaviour of foreign exchange markets in the period following 1971, and most especially after the move to a general system of independently floating currencies in the spring of 1973, provided no empirical support for the contention that exchange rates would be more stable once they were set free. An analysis of the data up to the beginning of 1974 indicated clearly that fluctuations were both wider and wilder than they had been before. [4] The guardians of the main currencies were impelled on a number of occasions to move into the market in order to smooth out some of the more violent oscillations; as the survey by F. Hirsch and D. Higham concludes, ' exchange rates in the spot market surveyed have demonstrably needed management '. Nor have the innovations in the international currency system of the early 1970s lived up to their promise of simplifying the business of domestic economic management. Incomes policies which were initially eschewed by a number of governments, indeed treated by them as a contemptibly facile and ineffective device, have been increasingly resorted to by those same governments, as their countries have one by one fallen victim to the great inflation which built up from the second half of 1972 onwards.

The riposte of the advocates of international monetary mechanics was that it was precisely because governments could not rid themselves of the habit of interference that the market had been prevented from doing its beneficent work. Incomes policies, whatever their plausibility in the short run, were, they contended, doomed to irrelevance; but while the doomed attempt was in progress it was likely to affect the expectations of enough people to distort rational economic decision-making. Similarly, the proper functioning of a free market in international currencies, which would have made the holding of national monetary reserves unnecessary, was being impeded by the widespread vice of ' dirty floating '. [5] The phrase itself suggests a certain moral failure, if not actual degradation, in the very attempt of a national authority to manage a floating currency in such a way as to prevent its value from deviating too far from what it regards as its long-term norm. The implicit condemnation derived less from a dispute about economic theory than about political behaviour. On the one side, governments tended to see it as part of their business to use their currency reserves to ease the processes of economic adjustment, essentially by buying time—either to damp down the unsettling effects of too many short-term shifts in the value of their currency or in order to make a necessary long-term change in its value less abrupt. The monetarists for their part were sure that it was wrong even to make the attempt. First of all, governments were almost inevitably going to get it wrong; only the market could tell them what was the true long-term value of their currencies. Secondly, governments, with their built-in distaste for inconvenient changes, would in practice not use the time bought through their interventions to make any necessary adjustments easier, but to avoid them altogether.

The record of the United States and the United Kingdom during the years under review in this volume (see below, chs 5 & 11) amply confirms the grounds for the latter suspicion. Yet to seek a remedy for this kind of political weakness by requiring governments passively to accept whatever value the majority of market dealers happen to put on their national currencies, conscientiously refusing to be moved to any counteraction by their own views on the subject, appears to be a device which is almost wilfully deficient in political realism. The intermittent cowardice and self-deception of governments is proposed to be dealt with by demanding of these same governments a credible promise of permanent heroism and a guarantee of iron nerves. For it would not be enough that each of them would in practice leave the market to determine the value of its currency; to make the system work in the way intended it would have to be known in advance that all of those concerned could be relied upon to abstain from interfering with the process. Otherwise the market would be seriously diverted from its task of registering the probable shifts in the supply and demand for particular currencies on the basis of its knowledge of trading and financial transactions, into the anticipation of political decisions by governments and their monetary authorities. Even though a government had announced its intention of not intervening, the wise speculator would surely make a judgement about the political circumstances in which the leaders of that government would feel that they had to.

As Keynes pointed out long ago, an efficient speculative market is one in which the promise of gain is largely based on good short-term guesses about what other speculators will do. Success, he showed, depends not on ' superior long-term forecasts ' but comes from ' foreseeing changes in the conventional basis of valuation a short time ahead of the general public. . . . The professional investor is forced to concern himself with the anticipation of impending changes, in the news or in the atmosphere, of the kind by which experience shows that the mass-psychology of the market is most influenced.' [6] In a foreign exchange market the professional is bound to be guided by an assessment of how this or that government will react to the often complex consequences for its domestic policy of a given change in its exchange rate. It would be an extremely reckless person who believed in the promise of total abstention from the market by the party most interested in it. The history of foreign exchange markets is littered with firm government guarantees discarded during crises.

None of this is intended to suggest that the movement away from fixed exchange rates in the period after 1971 was anything but a benign process. Obsession with the fixity of the rates had come to interfere seriously with rational political behaviour on the part of a number of Western governments. But there was a certain exaggeration accompanying the first stages of this revolutionary change—both on the part of the revolutionaries and on that of the advocates of counter-revolution. Mr Jeremy Morse, the chairman of the 'Committee of Twenty' set up by the International Monetary Fund (IMF) to work out a scheme for the reform of the international monetary system, described, from the vantage-point of mid-1974, how the expectations of both sides had been modified as a result of a quite short experience of the actual operation of a system of floating exchange rates. ' If one looks back over the exchange market experience of the past fifteen months, one would have to be a naive fixed-rater to believe that par values could have been made to work over that period and, equally, one would have to be a naive floater to be complacent about the size of the fluctuations in rates...'.[7] Morse described how the reformers had begun by looking for very precise and automatic mechanisms of international monetary adjustment, but had gradually come to realize that the system would require to be *managed*—and then to notice that effective management would mean leaving a considerable degree of authority in the hands of some international authority. This brought them straight back to the politics of the problem.

The Committee of Twenty decided that the uncertainties affecting the international economy were at that stage too large to allow it to complete its task and come up with a comprehensive set of proposals. The fortunes of individual countries were changing with extraordinary rapidity, under the impact of the worldwide inflation and the oil crisis of 1973–5. The United States, having been in a position of extreme financial weakness, seemed suddenly, with the new bargaining power acquired as a result of the oil crisis, to be stronger than ever. The attempt of the European Community to manage a concerted monetary policy had resoundingly broken down, leaving Germany as the leader of a group of small European countries which hinged their currency values on the D-mark. Meanwhile Germany itself had emerged, unwillingly, as an international monetary reserve centre; there were now more D-marks held in national reserves than pounds sterling.[8] In this turmoil it had become clearer than ever that what the nations of the

Western world required was a reinforced international institution with some of the functions of a world central bank; that was the burden of the report issued by the Committee of Twenty in mid-1974. It was only that the politicians were not yet ready to design the institution which they needed. But they were even more unready to accept the beguiling arguments advanced by the ' robot school ' of monetarists, that the acceptance of their alternative scheme would make the whole laborious enterprise of international monetary collaboration, with the implied surrender of national sovereignty, entirely unnecessary.[9] It had become apparent that the system of managed floating exchange rates required more, rather than fewer, internationally agreed rules than the old regime of fixed parities. What was essentially a political problem could not be bypassed by a technician's rule of thumb.

It could of course be argued that the disorder in the international economic system, brought on by the worldwide inflation which took over progressively from the second half of 1972 onwards, made the monetary reform more, not less, urgent, in view of the way in which the uncontrolled expansion of the world's monetary supplies had contributed to the result.[10] Total international monetary reserves doubled in value in the four years up to the end of 1973. The expansion in the whole of the decade previous to that had been about 25 per cent. The main source of the great upsurge in reserves during the early 1970s derived from the outflow of dollars from the United States. It was an unfortunate accident that the first issue of SDRs (Special Drawing Rights) by the IMF reinforced the vast increase in world liquidity caused by the US dollar deficit, even though it was only a small fraction—some 10 per cent—of the total. It threatened to bring one of the outstanding enterprises in international collaboration of the 1960s into disrepute (see below, ch. 8).

However, the great inflation of the early and middle 1970s was something more than a purely monetary phenomenon. There were other deeper sources of the trouble, and some of these were not man-made. The failure of harvests in 1972 and the panic buying of cereals which it provoked happened to coincide with a sudden spurt in production and business in almost all the Western industrial countries. The background to this latter movement was that several Western countries had suffered from a small-scale business recession during 1970 and 1971. In the United States industrial production actually fell below the level of the late 1960s; in Britain it stagnated over a period of nearly three years. A deliberate effort was then made to stimulate business activity in a number of different places at the same time. This happened in the early part of 1972; and in the subsequent twelve months the combined industrial output of the OECD countries suddenly increased by an extraordinary 12 per cent.[11] The combination of the exceptional increase in the pressure of industrial demand with the failure of agricultural supplies was enough to fuel a very steep increase in prices.

Whether this was the whole or even the major part of the explanation for what followed was, however, a matter of deep disagreement. The argument about the precise character of this particular inflation, much the most extreme and widespread that the Western world had suffered during any peacetime period in the course of the twentieth century, was not resolved by the time that the brief boom which began in 1972 gave way to the severe recession of 1974–5. Governments for the most part reacted to the former according to a pattern of fiscal and monetary behaviour learnt during previous inflations within their experience. There was a general tendency to see the spectacular surge of prices from 1972 onwards as a continuation, in an accelerated form, of the inflationary trend that had been allowed to establish itself in earlier years. That analysis had the effect of inclining governments strongly towards the adoption of especially sharp deflationary measures to counter the price rise, as if by adding to the rigours of the later treatment they would make up for their failure to attack the problem with sufficient vigour earlier on. Yet the evidence suggested strongly that the 1972–3 inflation in its initial phase had little in common with the milder variety of essentially wage-induced inflation of the 1960s. Wage increases played a relatively small part in 1972–3; it was the upsurge in world commodity markets which was the chief cause of the havoc which overtook consumer prices in the Western industrial countries.[12] There was an equally powerful adverse effect on the balance of payments of those Western countries which were heavily dependent on imports of food and other primary products. Several of them, including notably Britain and Italy which had both suffered a massive deterioration in their terms of trade, were in an extremely vulnerable position when they were struck by the rise in oil prices in the autumn of 1973.

To begin with, the oil crisis was seen as the great equalizer. All Western countries would henceforth find themselves in balance-of-payments deficit on their current account—because they could not collectively sell enough goods and services to cover the immediate increase in the cost of their oil imports—and would have to rely on the help of those who controlled the international supply of capital. It did not prove in the event to be quite like that. Germany managed by dint of a remarkable increase in its export sales to remain in overall surplus on its current account; its problem was that it attracted more capital from the Middle East oil producers than it wanted. At the same time the gathering recession which caused a fall in domestic demand in a number of Western countries made it possible for them to reduce their oil deficits faster than had been anticipated. The up-shot was that the differentiation between the weak and the strong economies in the international system was, if anything, sharpened.

But there was no doubt about the decisive effect in improving the position of potential exporters of capital in a world full of rich nations anxious to borrow the wherewithal to pay their bills. It was plain that the United States was going to be the chief financial intermediary for the Western world; in one way or another it would be able to control a large part of the flow of funds from the surplus oil producers, who kept their unspent earnings in dollars, to the deficit countries. The crisis served to remind the Western world once again of America's uniquely powerful position in the international economic system. This fact had been overlaid by the monetary disorder of the early 1970s and the sharp decline in the international value of the dollar. The matter was now brought sharply into relief; almost overnight all the previous talk about the problem of getting rid of the ' dollar over-hang '—the vast funds which had flowed out of the United States into the reserves of the Western world from 1970 onwards—ceased. Most of the nations concerned expected to need all the dollars that they could lay their hands on in order to pay their oil bills.

US economic diplomacy in the wake of these events became more openly political than it had been before. It seemed that the change of mood which had been registered in the dollar crisis of 1971 was in this respect an enduring one. The United States aggressively took the lead in mobilizing the Western alliance to meet the challenge of the oil-exporting countries. US diplomacy overshadowed the Middle East. The promise of opening up vast additional energy resources in the United States overshadowed the future. And the immediate offer of an emergency sharing of the available oil supplies, together with the capital funds to provide a safety net for any one of the Western nations which got into serious balance-of-payments trouble, dominated the present.

Relationships with the Third World

The upsurge of world commodity prices and the oil crisis of 1973–4 brought into prominence a number of anxious questions about the long-term relationship between the Western industrial nations and the less developed countries of Asia, Africa, and Latin America. It had come to be accepted in the course of the previous two decades that the terms of trade tended to move more or less continuously against the primary producing countries of the Third World, and that the odds were that their proportionate share of international trade would go on gently declining. The prosperity of the Western capitalist system seemed to have less and less connection with the destinies of the areas which comprised its former colonial dependencies. Were the events of the early 1970s to be interpreted as a permanent reversal of these well established trends? Was the Third World demonstrating a hitherto unsuspected capacity to force the Western countries to sacrifice some of their own material welfare to the interests of poorer peoples? Some of the fighting talk of the radical oil-producing states, like Algeria and, in the different South American context, Venezuela, indicated a serious . intention to challenge the West in this way. The producers' cartel was to be the weapon which would carry forward the work left unfinished by the wars of colonial independence.

The present study does not address itself to this wider aspect of international economic relations. Its focus is on the interrelationships between the advanced capitalist countries which have been the main influence in shaping the international economic system that emerged in the course of the 1960s and early 1970s. The affairs of the developing countries as they appear in these two volumes therefore have something of the quality of ' noises off '. That does not, it need hardly be said, reflect a judgement by the authors about their relative importance. We are concerned in this study with an analysis of where and how the decisions affecting the main bulk of international economic transactions are made. That has led us to concentrate our study on the narrow band of countries bordering the North Atlantic area, with an extension in the North Pacific to Japan. We are not suggesting that the most significant underlying forces which will determine the form and content of the world economy in the long run are necessarily to be found here.

Even during the relatively short period covered by our history the affairs of the developing countries have exercised a certain influence on the economic relations between the members of the group of capitalist countries on which our attention is centred. The question of development policy was itself a relatively new one at the start of our period in the late 1950s. That nations should seek to establish international rules and conventions about it was an unfamiliar idea. The colonial empires were still in the last stages of being dismantled, and the natural answer seemed to be to leave it to each of the Western nations concerned to take the lead in looking after its colonies or ex-colonies. It was the United States which insisted that the issue was a serious international problem. Its practical aim was to induce other nations, particularly those without colonial ties and traditions, like Germany, to share with the Americans the burden of providing aid for development. The establishment in 1961 of the Organization for European Co-operation and Development (OECD)—to replace the OEEC, whose title did not go beyond Co-operation—enshrined the objective officially as part of the agenda of diplomacy among the Western group of nations.

Most of the developed countries would probably have preferred to keep the issues connected with aid and development separate, isolated from the main subject-matter of international economic relations. But the problem kept coming back at them, boomerang fashion, threatening to disrupt the arrangements and rules which they were laboriously constructing for managing their financial relations with one another. This story provides the underlying theme of the final chapters of this volume, by Christopher Prout.

It was, as he shows, a search for *order*, rather than for any major expansion of the development effort of the poor countries, which supplied the main impulse for the initiatives taken by the Western capitalist countries. That is not to say that the quantity of aid disbursed by any individual country was a matter of indifference to the others. The regular provision of a certain level of aid was, in some measure, a badge of respectability. This was a point which seems to have been reflected first in the behaviour of the Germans during the early 1960s and subsequently in that of the Japanese, when they increased their contribution to development finance in spectacular fashion towards the end of the period under review. However, it was not a matter of setting precise targets—a given percentage of the national income or product of the rich to be transferred to the less developed countries by official aid and other means—in the manner of the UN Conference on Trade and Development (UNCTAD). When the OECD referred to such targets, it was in order to employ them as a device for nudging any outstanding laggard in the right direction. They were not norms which members were seriously expected to fulfil.

The more important matter, where norms were the subject of serious examination by the OECD group of countries, was the terms on which aid was granted. The prime object was to ensure that these terms did not vary in such a way as to introduce an element of unfair competition into the business of supplying goods and services to developing countries. Concessionary terms accorded by suppliers had to be monitored—not because there was any desire to impose a limit on the generosity of the rich countries towards the poor, but because of an anxiety to prevent the less generous from obtaining commercial advantages by pretending to be more generous than they really were. Christopher Prout traces the process by which the donor countries came to look for increasingly refined criteria of their comparative performance. To do this effectively they found that they needed to identify the ' aid element ' in any transfer of resources to the developing countries. It was an extremely useful by-product of their desire to keep tabs on one another, which proved to have a wider application in the strategy of development.

In this enumeration of the practical motives of the advanced industrial countries, it is important not to down-grade the philanthropic purpose out of existence. It is too easy to fall into a facile kind of *Realpolitik* in the analysis of development policy. Without the powerful support of an influential minority of the citizens of Western societies for the effort of amelioration in the Third World, governments would not have been able to continue to levy the annual contribution towards development, in the face of the increasing resistance of taxpayers to good but expensive causes, during the epoch under review. It was certainly a philanthropic effort of modest dimensions. However, it was sufficient to prompt a desire to monitor the output, as well as the input, of the aid-giving process. Ministers of development were appointed in a number of countries, and their task was to devise means to ensure that the resources made available were efficiently used by the receiving country. It became a common object of policy in the donor countries to be able to demonstrate that the resources transferred had made a significant difference to the developing country receiving them—or if not, that a critical examination was being made of the development programme itself.

It was out of this kind of political motivation that the international consortia of aid-giving countries organized by the World Bank and the other joint development organizations emerged (see below, p. 370). Sharing the responsibility for surveillance not only made it somewhat easier to operate but also provided each minister of development with some presumptive evidence, against domestic critics, that he was not wasting resources on uncertain projects which would not have passed muster if subjected to critical examination by other, more demanding, donor countries. It seems to be commonly assumed that one's neighbours are more rigorous and severe in matters involving charitable sentiments than one is oneself.

Collective management of the debtors

A different and powerful motive which has played a consistent, though little analysed, part in the behaviour of Western countries is the desire to prevent poor nations facing a crisis of external debt from dropping out of the international system altogether. This has probably given rise to more concerted endeavour than almost any other matter in the field of development policy. One is led to ask what becoming a drop-out really means and why the advanced industrial countries are so anxious to avoid its happening. They have of course the simple desire to collect the debts owing to them. But as the narrative shows, the results of their forbearance are often, in financial terms, meagre (see below, pp. 399ff). The evidence suggests that it is the symbolic effect of debt repudiation which is most feared. It tends to have reverberations elsewhere, and perhaps to put dangerous thoughts into the minds of people who now patiently accept the uncomfortable constraints on their economic activity imposed by the requirements of debt servicing. The creditworthiness of many other developing countries might well suffer, through the general loss of confidence among lenders, if one of them were seen openly to default.

These considerations seem at any rate to provide the only plausible explanation for the mounting of the remarkable series of debt rescue operations described by Susan Strange in chapter 5. Creditors do not want the conventions governing the international borrowing system to be too blatantly disturbed. And behind this sentiment there is often a deeper anxiety, which is felt especially by the officials who run foreign ministries and their political masters. This is that the drop-out nation, having engaged in financial hostilities with its creditors, is likely to proceed to establish a siege economy at home, place its citizens under severe controls, and try to sever its relationships with the rest of the world. The removal of external constraints tends to make its behaviour much less predictable; it may also become less inhibited about using violence towards its neighbours. Drop-outs, in other words, have less to lose by kicking over the traces. They may too easily develop into an explosive element within their geographical regions—as Cuba, for example, became in the 1960s—with a capacity for producing sympathetic detonations.

Thus the Western collaboration in this aspect of policy towards the developing countries was ultimately based, as so much else in the story of international economic relations recounted in these two volumes, on the collective desire to reduce the risks of costly international disorder. The Western nations behaved like rich financiers who agree to put up the money to save a fringe bank, of which they disapprove, from bankruptcy, simply in order to avoid even a temporary shock to the confidence of the general public. The rules were too uncertain to risk any gross deviation from them.

It would be an error however to press the financial market parallel too far. Relations with the developing countries do not rank among the major policy concerns of the Western nations and have not been endowed with an importance comparable to other aspects of international economic relations described in this study. That is one of the reasons why the OECD was admirably designed as an international institution to provide the modest degree of policy co-ordination which the Western nations were seeking in this field. The chief aims of these efforts at co-ordination were firstly to make the aid-giving activities of the donor countries more transparent, and secondly to apply gentle, though persistent, pressure to conform to certain standards of behaviour, which became as time went on marginally more demanding. It was a device for securing small incremental improvements on a matter which, though not regarded as insignificant, was accepted as being of a secondary order of importance, and doing so by the technique of polite mutual examination of national performances carried out inside the club of rich countries. It was the opposite of the vision of UNCTAD. There were no confrontations between opposing interests and no scope for great disputes on issues of principle. But within its incremental limitations, the technique worked.

It even contributed something to the making of American policy at a time, during the late 1960s and early 1970s, when domestic sentiment in the United States on the subject of development aid became increasingly soured. The American government, which had originally internationalized the responsibility for development through the OECD, was by the end of the 1960s itself carried on the tide which it had generated. At any rate it was able to show that its aid-giving —which was bitterly fought over each year in Congress where the appropriations requested for American spending on development were systematically, and sometimes savagely, cut back—now had acquired some of the character of an act of solidarity with its partners in the Western alliance. The roles of the two sides had been reversed: the Americans who had originally been so keen on the idea of minimum standards of performance among the rich countries in providing assistance to the poor, were now being chivvied by fellow members of the OECD to raise the proportion of their gross national product spent on development aid towards the higher average that the others had established. There were indications that some of the US officials concerned were not entirely displeased to be a little embarrassed in this way. But there was no sign in the mid-1970s of any readiness on the part of the American administration to resume its earlier leadership in the effort to set the terms of a common Western policy aimed at the developing countries.

The oil crisis gave the question of Western relations with the Third World a new urgency at this stage. There were two issues which were thrust upon the attention of the industrial countries. One was the exceptionally severe effect of the increase in oil prices on the developing countries which were poor in natural resources. These were outstandingly located in the regions of extreme over-population in South Asia. The second issue was the general threat of the primary producing countries of the Third World to use the occasion presented by the successful coup of the oil producers' cartel, OPEC, to shift the terms of trade decisively in their favour.

With regard to the first of these matters, the Western nations were above all concerned to limit the secondary effects on world trade of a sharp decline in the real income of less developed countries, caused by the rise in the cost of their oil imports. The initiative was taken by the IMF early in 1974, to establish a special source of additional finance for poor countries to help them cover part of the oil deficit in their balance of payments. Since, however, the funds for the purpose were to be derived from loans subscribed by the surplus oil exporting countries, no additional burden was placed on the Western industrial nations. The main threat at this stage was in fact that the latter, faced with a sudden collective deficit in their own balance of payments on account of oil, might attempt to cut down their external expenditure on development aid. Here the OECD served its by now established function of formulating minimum standards of performance of the rich countries towards the poor: its member countries were persuaded to give a joint undertaking that they would not try to deal with their own problems by reducing their aid programmes. That of course secured only the money value of the existing programmes; it did not prevent the real value of the resources transferred for the purposes of development from declining.

The effect of the decline on the fortunes of the developing countries was aggravated by the world-wide business recession, which cut the demand for their exports. That in turn exercised an influence on the second issue—the possible attempt to force a shift in the terms of trade in favour of the primary producing countries of the Third World. A recession in a number of world commodity markets, which by the mid-1970s had brought some prices down as fast as they had risen during the earlier boom, did not offer a propitious climate for launching a series of commodity cartels. Nevertheless, as was noted earlier, certain of the radical members of OPEC, who saw their organization as the spearhead of an advance by the whole of the Third World, energetically urged this course.

There were noticeable differences in the reactions of the Western nations to the somewhat diffuse threat from the commodity producers. The American response was one of indignation, followed by counter-threat. It was not that the United States was more at risk than other industrial countries if the primary producers formed cartels; rather the contrary. There was a deeper ideological reason for the sharp American reaction. Any suggestion of deliberately holding back supplies in order to rig the price, as OPEC had done, offended deeply against the anti-trust principles which had acquired something of the character of the established commercial religion of the United States since the start of the twentieth century. It was in keeping with this mood that US policy concentrated almost obsessively in 1974–5 on forcing a break in the solid price front of the members of the oil cartel. More practical political motives reinforced these sentiments. A new group of countries, the owners of scarce natural resources in the Third World, were purporting to change the established balance of power between themselves and the Western capitalist system; it was not surprising that the leader of the West should take the lead in resisting the attempt. What was striking, however, was how little enthusiasm the other members of that system evinced for this leadership. The US government was eager to insist on the point of principle. The new US Trade Act passed at the end of 1974, which was to provide the basis for the extended multilateral GATT trade negotiations of the so-called ' Tokyo Round ', went so far as to withhold the proferred commercial concessions from nations which impeded access to their supplies, that is those which organized a restrictive export cartel.

That the Europeans and Japanese seemed to be less deeply affronted by the threat tended to be interpreted only as more evidence of a lack of spirit on their part. In this phase of international economic relations among the Western countries, an overtone of American moral condemnation of its European allies in particular was intermittently in evidence. The fact was that the Europeans found the behaviour of the would-be perpetrators of the proposed wickedness less than wholly shocking. They were readier than the Americans to parley with them.

However, the difference which showed up so clearly in the rhetoric of the different members of the Western alliance had little practical impact on the economic relationship with the commodity exporting countries of the Third World. When it came to the point, none of the industrial countries were prepared to pay significantly more in real terms for their imports of primary produce. They were interested in varying degrees in promoting schemes for the stabilization of prices, following the experience of the sharp commodity boom and slump of these years. But they were not ready to contemplate a shift in the commercial balance of power between the Third World and the industrial nations, in the form imagined by the radicals of the Organization of Petroleum Exporting Countries (OPEC) and their allies. Nor was there any evidence that world markets could be successfully managed by the developing countries so as to impose this change upon the West.

Rather, the problem as it presented itself to the latter was how best to proceed in order to absorb the relevant oil surplus countries into fully fledged membership of *its* economic system. The possibility did not apply to all OPEC countries; some of them, like Nigeria and Indonesia, were, and would remain for some time, poor developing nations which would use their oil wealth to develop rather faster than would otherwise have been feasible. But a few of the most liberally endowed oil producers, notably those in the area of the Persian Gulf, would be, to an increasing extent over a number of years, the owners of surplus funds on a scale which introduced a new factor into the international financial system. Bringing them as rapidly as possible into an active role in the IMF and into the organized development aid business through the World Bank were the first moves taken by the West in the process of absorption.

How much further could the absorption go without a parallel political process? This was the question which underlay the differences in the approach of the US and some of its Western allies. The Americans were inclined to insist on the politics right from the start; for them this was part of the very stuff of international economic relations. The Europeans and the Japanese tended to be more lax and to believe, perhaps too readily, that the political commitment would emerge of its own accord out of the practice of doing business together. But the issue was one of tactics only; it was not a question of whether, but of how and when the newly rich oil-producing nations would take their place in the caucus of Western countries, which together determine the rules of the game of the international financial system.

Notes

[1] Peter Jay, *The Times*, 22 Oct 1971.

[2] *Further essays in monetary economics* (London, 1973), p. 221.

[3] Ibid., p. 217.

[4] See F. Hirsch & D. Higham, 'Floating rates—expectations and experience', *Three Banks Review*, June 1974. The increased volatility was most in evidence in the spot market, but the performance of the forward exchange market, too, disappointed the hopes of the advocates of floating exchange rates.

[5] The epithet was, it seems, first used by Professor Karl Schiller, the German Minister of Economics and Finance, to describe the management of floating currencies by monetary authorities which set themselves to oppose the verdict of the foreign exchange market (see below, p. 352, n. 10).

[6] J. M. Keynes, *The general theory of employment, interest and money* (London, 1936), pp. 154–5.

[7] 'The evolving monetary system', *Finance & Development*, Sept 1974.

[8] See F. Boyer de la Giroday, *Myths and reality in the development of international monetary affairs* (Princeton, 1974), p. 16.

[9] Johnson, *Further essays in monetary economics*, pp. 205f. He argues that the effective harmonization of national economic policies required for 'a single world currency system' would mean a surrender of sovereignty, and that 'the main argument for flexible exchange rates at the present time is that they would make this surrender of sovereignty unnecessary . . .'.

[10] See Robert Triffin, 'Focus on gold', paper delivered to RIIA, 13 Jan 1975.

[11] See *National Institute Economic Review*, May 1974, p. 48. The output increase occurred between the first quarter of 1972 and the first quarter of 1973.

[12] Cf., for example, the analysis of the US inflation of 1972–3 with that of 1970–1 in W. Nordhaus & J. Shoven, 'Inflation 1973: the year of infamy', *Challenge*, May 1974, which indicates that about two-thirds of the rise in the US wholesale price index during the period November 1972–August 1973 was due to price increases in agricultural products.

INTERNATIONAL MONETARY RELATIONS

by Susan Strange

1

RATIONALE: PURPOSES AND QUESTIONS

A simple enough purpose—to write the story of international monetary relations in the 1960s—proved the source of many more problems than at first appeared. It was conceived as a straightforward complement to the story, told in volume I, of trade negotiations between the leading industrial states in the world market economy. Together, they were to supply the missing economic dimension to much conventional international political history. This book was to deal with the special forms, matter and methods of diplomacy in monetary affairs that in the course of a decade had been developed by those rich countries to whom money and monetary relations mattered a great deal, and who assumed (without ever being challenged) the responsibility for managing the monetary system on which the world market economy depended. It was to be a study of a more or less self-contained network of official dealings between a restricted group of states.

But it became increasingly evident that this state-to-state focus made for serious areas of omission and inadequacies of treatment—by no means all of which it has been possible to make good. For this is one of these areas of international studies where the actions of governments in their role of steersmen to national economies are much more subject to domestic political pressures than they are in conventional ' foreign policy ' matters. A rickety coalition government or one about to face an election is more apt than others to change its monetary policies and thus to affect the course of monetary diplomacy within the group. Compared with conventional diplomacy, too, where changes in status are usually gradual and foreseeable, monetary diplomacy is subject to much more sudden changes of fortune, unpredictably and quite quickly relegating a strong currency to the ranks of the weak, and vice versa.

To tell the story of international monetary relations properly, therefore, really requires a much fuller account than it has been possible to give in a book of this size of both the political and the economic situation in each of the countries, and of the policies chosen to deal with them. There has been space, too, only briefly to describe the mushrooming international money markets, the vastly expanded international banking network which was the dynamic background to the official negotiations. And while the main concern of the study and of the protagonists was with monetary relations amongst themselves, the threats to the system they were managing did not come only from within the developed world. Its stability could be jeopardized either by wholesale stagnation or breakdown of the economies of the developing and semi-developed countries, or by their involuntary exit from it through bankruptcy and default on borrowed credit. The decision to invite Christopher Prout to add a study of the rich countries' treatment of the debt problems of poor countries is a partial recognition that the main study is by no means the whole story of the international monetary system in these years.

For the restriction of the study to a specific period I make no apology. Although Andrew Shonfield, in his introductory essay, has tried to indicate some of the ways in which the trends that emerged in this period might be interpreted in the light of later events, December 1958 and December 1971 were the defining milestones of the piece of history that we undertook to explore. And despite the ever present temptation to carry on with the story, I have thought it best in the main body of the study to stick to this.

A main purpose of this study is to try to use a political approach to material usually assigned to international economics. And conversely, to introduce economic material into the field usually assigned to international politics. I will not repeat here my criticisms—often reiterated—of international relations scholars for avoiding (or worse still, treating as summarily and distastefully as they can) the facts of the international economy; or of international economists for ignoring or wishing away the political context, domestic no less than international—within which the market economy must operate.[1] But if the two divorced dimensions of academic study of the world's political economy are ever to be reunited, it is most unlikely that it can be done by dealing in abstractions or by trying to marry together their mutually incompatible methods of constructing general theories. Rather it will be by laying a firm foundation of specific research projects. These must be well defined and require to be ' bilingual ' in the sense of attaching equal attention to the economic and the political. It may be slow and hard, but it is, I am sure, the only practical way to proceed.

At the present time, for instance, both international politics and international economics have built into them a bundle of conventional, accepted theories about the functioning of the international system that too often go untested by pragmatic study. The economists make assumptions about political processes and political choices and motivations and the political scientists do the same about economic processes and economic motivations. Key concepts about the exercise of economic power or the definition of the national interest are easily taken for granted but never too precisely defined. A specific study of international monetary relations should offer material by which these conventional theories can be tested and by which familiar but vague concepts can be more sharply and usefully defined.

The big central question about which both international economics and international politics try to theorize concerns the functioning of what we loosely call the international system—the relationship and roles of actors in it, and the nature and courses of change affecting it. In international monetary relations, we have an issue-area that is self-evidently part of the international political system, since it is governments which are the main actors; and which is equally self-evidently part of the international economic system, since the subject of their deliberations is money. In this issue-area therefore, theories concerning the world market economy must assimilate somehow the reality of the inequality of power among the states and the asymmetry of costs and benefits among them when it comes to creating the collective good of international monetary order.

Equally, theories concerning the international political system must take into account far more than they have done the threat of economic disorder and the possibility that it is unequally perceived and feared. The study shows that this threat is both a motivation for co-operation and a source of dissension between states. Sometimes, as we shall see, this dissension can be more influential on state behaviour than the patterns of alliance and the calculations concerning national security that are sometimes held to be the core of international politics. In recent years particularly, a good deal of attention in international politics has been given to various polar models; using the analogy of magnetic fields, international politics has been likened to a bi-polar system in the postwar period, changing more recently to various supposed kinds of multipolar systems. This could be one of the theories that is due for rethinking—or even relegation—in the context of the real world.

What, then, brings about change in this system that is neither purely ' political ' nor purely ' economic '? And in which it is quite wrong— certainly misleading—to talk of monetary diplomacy as a ' sub-system ' of the major system. It may be permissible to talk of geographical or cultural sub-systems, but monetary relations are no more a sub-system than are the strategic relations between states. The inseparability of money from politics—so well recognized in political science when applied to the unitary state—is equally true of the international system. This, surely, is what is meant by the fashionable cliché that money and trade have, in the last ten years, ceased to be ' low politics ' and have become ' high politics '.

Here again, where change is concerned, theory demands some challenge. Economics students are still taught—some economists even still believe—that exchange rate changes are the consequence and reflection of altered trade flows and of the increased or diminished competitiveness of an economy's exports. Does the history of international monetary relations in the 1960s bear this out? Similarly, international political students are still taught that states seek above all to maximize power in their relations with other states. Does the history of international monetary relations bear this assumption out, or do we need to re-examine critically this conventional concept? It has been argued by Richard N. Cooper and many others who have followed him that national interest now comprehends an expanded coincidence with the international welfare.[2] We should consider whether economic interdependence demands, as the price of continued wealth and stability in economic life, the increased subordination of narrow short-term national interests to enlightened long-term interests. Does national interest now actually require not the assertion but the suppression of economic sovereignty and, if so, where and to whom? And what, anyway, do we understand by this ' economic sovereignty '? Is it not, after all, a concept which never could be defined in any absolute terms, and which in contemporary conditions is increasingly drained of meaning?

Even more fundamental questions concern the nature of economic power in international monetary relations. Economists are sometimes inclined to scorn the state that accumulates gold in its reserves instead of enjoying the imports it might have purchased, and to dismiss this neo-mercantilist behaviour as an irrational and atavistic response to outworn shibboleths and bygone customs. Are they right? Or does the history of monetary diplomacy show the strength and relative independence to be derived from the accumulation, either of large gold reserves or of foreign exchange assets? Small reserves, or reserves inadequate to the demands which could be made upon them have been shown in recent years to be a real source of political weakness. Britain and France have both at times had to accept multilateral surveillance as the price for supplementing owned reserves with borrowed ones. Germany and Japan, by contrast, have incurred no penalties for accumulating large surpluses in their reserves. And if there has been an economic ' cost ' involved, it does not seem to have irked them.

Indeed, the more questions one asks about international monetary relations, the more apparent it is how little we really know or can agree on. Not only are we unsure how powerful the United States—

as the economic leader, top currency state, the most affluent member
of the group of rich states, and the military protector of the Western
alliance—really is when it comes to directing the course of the international monetary system. We are also not even sure what is the real
source of whatever power it is that the United States has. Is it in the
last resort a political power, as the holder of the nuclear trigger? Or
does it rest on the cornucopia opened up by US enterprise overseas?
Once the capital that flowed out was American; now it is largely non-
American in origin. Does this mean that the real economic power of
the United States lies in the technological or managerial leadership
possessed by US companies over most others? Or is it that, having
grown through the opportunities offered by so large and well-supplied
a capital market as that in the United States, American corporations
are then poised to expand, unchallenged, across the non-communist
globe and even, recently, into the Soviet Union itself? More specifically for international monetary relations, is the US negotiating position strong because of, or in spite of, its position as the owner of an
international reserve currency? Notwithstanding a great deal of
expert academic debate on the costs and benefits of a reserve currency,[3] no one has paid much serious attention yet to the question of
the political effects on US foreign relations, especially on its relations
with its political allies. All that has been established, it seems, is that
the dollar's role gives the United States a greater capacity to influence
the development of the international economy, and the freedom to
run a recurrent deficit with impunity. But the other side of the coin, no
less significant, is the greater involvement of the United States in the
international economy, through its foreign investments and foreign
banking operations more than its foreign trade. This new American
involvement suggests that the United States now may be not only
more influential in the system, but may also feel more responsible for
its welfare. As it becomes more vulnerable to the threats of instability
and disorder that may afflict the international monetary system, will it
become readier to make short-term sacrifices to maintain monetary
security as it has done to maintain military security?

These are some of the questions which I have had in mind in
undertaking this study. It will be apparent that I am concerned in
it with two broadly distinguishable kinds of international action. One
has been the continuing process of revision of the ' rules of the game ',
by the relatively small oligarchy of monetarily important states. The
original rules drawn up at Bretton Woods had to be constantly re-
drawn and reinterpreted, stretched and supplemented. Nor was it
only a rule-making function: sometimes the instruments of rule-
making enforcement, such as they were, also had to be changed and
improved.

In short, I am concerned in large part in this study with the system by which, in the absence of a world central bank, the chief monetary states have tried to work through collective agreement a limited form of credit and monetary management for the international economy. They have tried, as a group—a kind of syndicate or consortium—to do the job which each government now undertakes for its own national economy. Much the greater part of this rule-making and rule-supervision has been conducted in the IMF, some of it, mainly directed at developing countries, by the World Bank. Some subsidiary part has been played by smaller ad hoc groups forming themselves into aid consortia or creditors' clubs to deal with problem areas or weaker brethren in the international economy. Some of the work of substituting for a world central bank has been left to quite obscure bodies, like the Berne Union of Credit Insurers, through which was negotiated such agreements as could be reached on the regulation of trade credit.[4] Some very embryonic rule-making for international capital markets has been conducted altogether outside the official network of intergovernmental organization. And just as governments have sometimes left the job to professional associations, such as the Stock Exchange Council or Lloyd's brokers, to lay down the working rules for national financial markets, so governments have so far left it to private bodies like the International Association of Bond Dealers to draw up such rules as may be needed for the new market in Eurobonds.

The other kind of action described in this study has been much more in the nature of improvised crisis-management. It has been directed less to the drawing up of rules for the management of the international economy than to the devising of arrangements necessary to maintain a minimum stability and certainty of outlook in it. Most of it has been through co-operation between national central banks of the same international oligarchy, or affluent alliance, of rich states, important in international financial relations, that were engaged in the rule-making and supervising business. These central banks found themselves, increasingly in the 1960s, in two roles, both of which became more difficult as they came into mutual conflict. One role, the original one, was as monetary manager for the national economy over which they had varying degrees of power and responsibility. And this was made more difficult as a result of growing economic interdependence and the easier transmission of monetary influences from one country to another. The newer role was as members of a consortium of monetary agents all engaged—though perhaps with different degrees of commitment—in maintaining the stability of the sometimes unruly world market economy. In this task of international monetary management, they were, in turn, often frustrated or handicapped as a result of domestic policy measures taken by member states.

Each kind of international action, when the parties have been at their most co-operative (and perhaps have been most frightened), appears to have opened up new possibilities for international co-operation in the future. Can we infer from this that ultimately people and governments will develop a real sense of international collective responsibility for the general welfare? The vision of an international economic community outgrowing the confines of the national state has often seemed to beckon at the rainbow's end. But rainbows quickly fade, and sometimes gusty storms have often followed these brief glimpses of future peace, brotherhood, and harmony in the world. An important question to be asked of all kinds of financial co-operation concerns the nature of the limiting factors, the reservations and qualifications which were attached on various occasions to international co-operative action, no less than to its positive content.

These are the sort of broader analytical questions that a study like this ought to be able to illuminate, however partially and tentatively. In the following chapters the reader will find that a number of hypotheses are advanced in response to these broad analytical questions about the system and how it works. Some will be rejected in the light of the evidence, some will be modified, and some will be provisionally endorsed. It is not seriously suggested that these hypotheses can really be tested in any properly scientific sense and it must be admitted that the choice of hypotheses in the social sciences is always and necessarily a subjective business. But it may nevertheless be helpful to examine for probability the different alternative interpretations of known events in international monetary diplomacy, leaving it to the reader to give the final verdict.

The source material on this subject is of the sketchiest. All central banks, however they may differ in other ways, tend to share a preference for silence, secrecy, and stealth, and to shun the glare of publicity. Official accounts given, for example, by the Bank of England, in its *Quarterly Bulletin*, of the Basle Agreements or of the setting up of the Gold Pool, are laughable in their brevity and baldness. The international organizations, whose officials have the advantage of a front seat for most of the action and are often able to see more than one point of view, are, however, almost as inhibited as the central banks. Fund officials who have given their own account of these events have usually tended to avoid any nasty political questions, and to pretend they do not exist—or at least that disagreement must not be mentioned in polite society. The Bank for International Settlements (BIS) at Basle has a valued status as a Swiss bank incorporated under Swiss law, and this, and its own functions as a commercial operator in the monetary market, incline it to concentrate on the operative and technical aspects of any situation rather than on the complex and insoluble political aspects.

The only other observers with at least back stall seats have been the financial journalists, and some of these have already made brave attempts to tell the story as they see it. To them I am greatly indebted, in their books and throughout in their dispatches. Without press cuttings this history could never have been written. In time, no doubt, much additional evidence will emerge from the memoirs and biographies of those concerned. One must certainly hope so. If M. Wilfrid Baumgartner, or Dr Otmar Emminger, or William McChesney Martin, for instance, were to publish reminiscences as detailed as those available for the 1920s from Benjamin Strong or Emile Moreau, then much that is misty and vague in the narrative which follows would become clear. The Per Jacobsson papers, of which some extracts have already been published by his daughter, Dr Erin Jucker-Fleetwood, must contain much useful material about the early years of the 1960s when newspaper attention was a tithe of what it was even five years later. Perhaps, too, one day M. Pierre-Paul Schweitzer will give his version of the middle and later years without fear or favour of finance ministers who will long have vanished from the scene. For surely this is a subject just as deserving of a full record as the minor battles and parochial political conflicts that are the subject of so many published memoirs.

Notes

[1] See my 'International economic relations: the need for an interdisciplinary approach', in R. Morgan, ed., *The study of international affairs* (London, 1972).

[2] *The economics of interdependence* (New York, 1968). See esp. his final chapter.

[3] Notably by Herbert Grubel, Robert Aliber, Henry Aubrey, Charles Kindleberger, Walter Salant, Emil Despres, and Fred Bergsten: less conventionally by Harry Magdoff and Michael Hudson.

[4] See Christopher Prout, below, p. 378.

THE HISTORICAL PERSPECTIVE

Every historian, every storyteller, has the same problem. How much, or how little, to tell the reader of ' the story so far ', whether to describe the characters or to let them speak for themselves; to explain, or to take for granted the context of ideas and social pressures within which they have to resolve their difficulties and conflicts.

The reason for opting for a slightly Shavian historical introduction to the story of international monetary relations in the 1960s rather than launching directly into the action is, first, that most readily available histories of international affairs in recent times have been overwhelmingly political in their emphasis. And although economic historians are (and economists ought to be) familiar with the background before 1960, many students of international affairs who are now profoundly concerned with the problems of the international monetary system will not be. The present chapter is therefore intended mainly for these readers.

But there is another reason for giving more than perhaps the bare minimum of ' the story so far '. It is that the story has two interrelated, interwoven plots, and the historical perspectives of these plots are by no means the same. One plot is, basically, an international organization story, the story of how the states who had set up the International Monetary Fund (IMF) in 1944 to provide some minimal law and order between independent national monetary systems adapted, extended, and supplemented the rule-book and authority of the Fund. It was never as efficient or as orderly as the order which a world central bank would have imposed on the international monetary system. But in a world divided by national sovereignties, it was all that could be conceived, and it had to adapt as best it could to changing circumstances. In this plot, the main scenes are played by the states who are the leading members of the Fund, and their lines to each other are spoken by finance ministers or their officials. The historical perspective begins for all practical purposes with the Bretton Woods Conference of 1943.

The other plot—no less important—centred in the international co-operation practised by national central banks and most often undertaken for the collective management of crises that arose, not between states, but when international financial and money markets became threateningly nervous and unstable. The purpose was not so much to make up for a non-existent international monetary order, substituting the Fund's rule-book for a world central bank, as actually to simulate such a bank. By acting together—even if only at times of crisis—the central banks of the affluent countries were trying in the 1960s to impose, on behalf of public authority and in the general public interest, some order and restraint over the more unruly and disorderly activities of private enterprise; or, if this were impossible, at least to cancel them out. The growing interdependence of the world market economy and the expanding volume of international financial transactions and the markets in which they took place made this all the more necessary.

In this plot, the chief actors were again states but to the extent that their opponents were financial markets, those markets must also be counted as actors—though perhaps like gods, angels, devils and fairies in fiction-drama, actors of a different order from mortals. If they did not speak, they still mimed their lines most effectively by means of price movements and the shifting of funds. In this plot, the lines for states were spoken by Governors of central banks and their officials; and the focus of the historical perspective for this kind of international co-operation is more on the 1920s and 1930s than on the 1950s.

In the 1960s the two plots constantly interacted—as they had not done, or not so evidently, in the 1950s. Now the problems of organization between states—and most notably the adjustment problem and the confidence problem—were multiplied and complicated by pressures emanating from the continuing and unsuppressed turbulence in the private sector. At the same time, the more noticeable the conflicts (and consequent collective indecision) between governments about the rules governing the international monetary order (e.g. on matters like the price of gold and the obligations of reserve-currency states) the more nervous and unruly the markets with which the fire-brigade service provided by the central bankers had to deal. This is why neither aspect of the story of international monetary relations is complete without the other, and why some historical perspective explaining the earlier non-convergence could be helpful.

The major players in both plots also need introduction. Who were the leading members of this managing oligarchy of states at the start of the 1960s and what were their perceived concerns and national interests? How high, in their respective orders of political priority, did the development of international monetary co-operation come? How did the foreign policy and security interests of states affect their behaviour in this issue-area? Or, since here they spoke either through Finance Ministries or central banks, were they more apt to be affected by their responsibility for developments in their respective domestic economies and by their responsibility for promoting growth and maintaining employment, order, and justice nationally? Did their roles alter with the variations in the status and power of the central bank in the national political system?

Finally, whether regarded (as suggested above) as a special kind of actor or, more conventionally, as the dynamically influential environment within which the states operated, there were the international capital and money markets. After 1958, these markets expanded with phenomenal rapidity and exerted powerful pressures on governments, chiefly via their exchange rates. The circumstances surrounding and shaping this expansion also deserve some brief introduction.

The Fund and the development of international authority up to 1960

Much of what has been written about the IMF has been concerned with the methods and mechanism of its operations, and much of what was said at its inauguration and has been written since about its intentions and objectives laid greater stress on its negative rather than its positive aims. Everyone could see what it was designed to avoid—the postwar instability of exchange rates, in Europe especially, the financial chaos that accompanied the World Depression, and the protective controls and restrictions, and the competitive devaluations that followed World War I. These negative aims had such a strong appeal that the Fund, although it was so predominantly Anglo-American in conception, proved generally rather readily acceptable to other governments. The converse, positive image of these negative aims was undoubtedly perceived by many of those engaged, as delegates or officials, in the Bretton Woods enterprise. But when translated into terms comprehensible to laymen, it did not always seem very coherent or consistent—as witness the level of parliamentary or Congressional debate in 1944 when it came to ratifying the agreement. One of the most articulate and ambitious expositions of its positive purposes, was that written by Robert Triffin. Writing in the later 1960s just before the Stockholm Agreement of 1968 on Special Drawing Rights (SDRs), Triffin condensed his philosophy in a prediction.

I boldly predict that the historical trend toward the national displacement of commodity money by fiduciary money and toward the increasingly centralized orientation and management of the latter by national authorities will be duplicated in the international field by a similar displacement of gold reserves by fiduciary reserves and by an increasing subordination of the latter to joint orientation and management ... The inadequacy of the agreements that may be reached in the present phase of the negotiations and the new crises that may be unleashed thereby upon the world economy would probably reverse this trend in the short run ... They will not however permanently arrest a movement that is part and parcel of a far broader evolution which only the blindest of so-called realists are unable to read in our world's history. The displacement of commodity money by fiduciary money and of commodity reserves by fiduciary reserves reflects the effort of man to control instead of being controlled by his environment in the monetary field as well as in others.[1]

In more specific terms, the effort to control the monetary environment required of the international organization entrusted with the task a triple aim: to maintain it in a healthy balance between monetary stability and growth, to impose so far as it could the necessary rules on the national currency areas in the system, and to ensure that the frontiers dividing these areas were as ineffectual in monetary terms as possible. Put another way, the positive aims were the imposition of order and stability on the system and the preservation of its unity as a single working system. The latter aim required monetary liberalization, the counterpart to GATT in the trade field and the removal of all kinds of restrictions on financial transactions across frontiers, the ending of non-convertibility and the abolition of administrative exchange controls or multiple exchange rates that acted to penalize certain types of transactions or transactors. That was one part of the Fund's role. The other part, the imposition of order and stability, was more complex. The stabilization role—uppermost in the mind of its chief American author, Harry Dexter White—required the Fund to act (so far as it could) to maintain equilibrium, maintaining a balance in the world economy between depression and inflation, and to that end using its resources as a regulatory influence on the world money supply and giving warning and advice when its own power to achieve expansion or restriction appeared inadequate to the task. But maintaining order, in monetary terms, means rather more than just holding a balance. What the market demands—now on the international scale as it once did on the national scale—is protection from arbitrary change and interruption. The operators wanted to be sure that contracts could, by and large, be depended on, that the terms under which they were made would not, by and large, change without warning, and that the rules governing competition—who could deal and who could not—would not be subject to sudden major changes. Nor was this all. To produce order in a market it is not always sufficient to satisfy the demands of the dealers for certainty and fair dealing; the market authority, or its substitute, has to interpose itself between creditors and debtors, sometimes insisting on mercy and patience from the former, sometimes imposing discipline on the latter. When market authorities are well developed and seek to manage as well as to order a market, there is also often some capacity to support or assist the market, either as lender of last resort or as the ultimate buyer or seller.

The significance of the Fund, as a political instrument in the international economy, was that it had been directed to undertake these functions and that it had been given some of the means to do so. It was the first organization specifically designed for these tasks, and was set up in order to carry them out.

There had been earlier attempts that failed, plans that had been pigeon-holed, proposals set aside. One was that of Britain at the Genoa International Monetary Conference of 1922. The scheme was for a gold exchange standard that would have had some resemblance to the Bretton Woods system in that it would have laid down 'rules of the game' for national monetary authorities. The British proposals, seeking a way out of the postwar monetary chaos, provided that all central banks should regulate their credit policies so as to maintain fixed parities and to prevent undue fluctuations in the purchasing power of gold.[2] As to settlements within the system, the 'centre' countries (what Professor John Williams later called the 'key currencies')[3] would hold their reserves in gold and maintain free but stable gold markets. Other countries would be encouraged to supplement their gold holdings with short-term assets provided by the centre countries. Despite its evident advantages for Britain, this plan—effectively for a gold exchange standard—was readily accepted by European central banks. But it failed primarily because of fundamental disagreement over political priorities between the French and the Americans. Benjamin Strong, Governor of the Federal Reserve Bank of New York (FRBNY), was convinced that little progress towards fixed stable exchange rates could be made until the German mark—already labouring under accelerating inflation—was stabilized. But the French would not consider the necessary loan for this purpose until the vexed question of reparations had been settled to their satisfaction. And even if this impasse had been avoided, it was by no means certain that the Americans would have gone along with the British plan. Strong saw it as demanding a surrender of American sovereignty in monetary policy-making: 'I think you realize,' he wrote to Sir Montagu Norman, Governor of the Bank of England, '. . . that *the domestic functions of the bank of issue are paramount to everything.*'[4]

The United States, through Strong, also made it clear that it realized that these proposals implied a radically new departure in international monetary management and that it wanted to take no responsibility for 'impoverished nations of the world . . . especially . . . those whose government finances are in complete disorder and quite beyond control'.[5]

Renewed attempts to achieve some measure of international monetary order came in 1933 at the World Economic Conference held in London and were undertaken with the admirable intention of substituting co-operation for nationalism as a means to general economic recovery after the world depression. One plan, inspired by Keynes's thinking and put forward by the British government, was for an international monetary fund of $1½-2 billion from which countries could draw on condition that they stabilized exchange rates and removed exchange controls and other impediments to international trade. A less ambitious idea which at one time looked to have some practical possibility was for a tripartite fund that would stabilize the British, French, and US currencies by co-ordinated market intervention by the three central banks concerned to maintain stable rates between themselves. But as the ill-fated London Conference broke up in disarray, neither idea came to anything. Each of the governments—and especially that of the United States—had no doubt at the time that its political life depended on putting domestic policy objectives before all else.

In the conditions of 1933 few countries, certainly not the United States, could have accepted the delays and uncertainties of a major co-operative recovery effort. The need for leadership and action—almost any action—was too pressing. The test—in America at any rate—was whether a policy brought prompt increases in prices, spending, and employment. Measures that met this test were accepted and squeezed for all they were worth. Others were rejected.[6]

By these criteria a stabilization programme that would have taken time and effort to negotiate could not qualify. The rich industrialized countries then split into the French-led gold bloc, the sterling area, and the United States. The consequence of these failures was that much then depended on the network of inter-central bank co-operation built through the joint efforts of Norman and Strong around the dollar-sterling axis, and on such influence on the governments of lesser countries as could be exerted by this monetary condominium. This was most successful when it was done through the medium of the League of Nations.

Although it figures rather small in the histories of the League, and economists at the time did not find it particularly interesting, the organization and management of the League's monetary rescue operations, first for Austria and Hungary and then for a number of Baltic and Mediterranean states, seems from a longer perspective worth recalling as a significant beginning in international monetary co-operation. It was not that 'creditors' clubs' had not existed before, but they had not been legitimized by operating through a permanent international organization. These ventures in multilateral surveillance not only indicated clearly a growing sense of collective responsibility—though at first this was limited to countries in the special political category of potential candidates for Bolshevik revolution. They also set important precedents not only for the developing countries, who later found themselves the wards of the Bank and Fund and international aid consortia, but also for Britain and other beneficiaries of the General Arrangement to Borrow (see below, ch. 4).

Funds for the Austrian loan of 1923 were provided by the Bank of England and the Banque de France, but the supervision of Austrian fiscal and financial policies was entrusted to a League commissioner. A similar procedure was followed for Hungary and the other League clients. In an earlier period—one recalls the European ' rescue operations ' and the subsequent ' surveillance ' of Morocco or of Egypt, and the comparable US ' Customs-house takeovers ' in the Caribbean— the creditors were responsible to no one but themselves, and their surveillance was understandably regarded by the victims as indistinguishable from imperialist annexation.

After such tentative and trivial beginnings, the Bretton Woods Agreement of 1944 and the two institutions derived from it (i.e. the IMF and the World Bank) were without question a great leap forward. It is perhaps worth recalling the extent to which the power of the Fund—which may have been inadequate to its tasks but was still a tremendous advance on any previous international organization—was increased by the linking of the Bank and the Fund as twin-membership bodies and of the resources of both with the legal authority of the Fund. The result of this was that no state could gain access to the financial resources of the Bank without joining the Fund, and had no right to financial assistance from either unless it subscribed to the legal obligations imposed by the Fund.

The membership of the Fund (which by 1971 had risen to 120) was only 68 in 1960. Of these 32 were original members; 17 had joined in the first five years of its existence, and 19, including Argentina, the Federal Republic of Germany, and Japan, joined between 1951 and 1958. Poland had left and Czechoslovakia had been expelled; the Soviet Union (though present at Bretton Woods) had never joined. China had never bothered to contest its representation by Taiwan. Switzerland and New Zealand were other absentees. Two-thirds of the Fund members already ranked as what are now called developing countries, and the proportion was to increase. In the IMF Annual Report of 1960, they are described as ' less industrialized countries ' and as being in most but not all cases exporters mainly of primary products. They were the principal targets of Fund appeals for monetary discipline, and they had hitherto exerted little influence on its development. Since most of them maintained Article xiv restrictions on the convertibility of their currencies they were obliged to have annual consultations with the Fund aimed at the reduction and elimination of these restrictions. The conditions attached to standby credits arranged for them were often tougher than for richer countries.

The multiple exchange rates, which were the administrative device which many of them preferred for national economic protectionist purposes, were more harshly frowned upon than the no less protectionist tariffs and other barriers devised by the industrialized countries. And only a small minority of them had been able so far to get much help from the Fund.

One reason for this lay in the structure of the Fund and the voting arrangements in its most important body, the Executive Board. The two decision-making bodies in the Fund were the Executive Board and the Board of Governors. The Governors met only once a year, and though each member was represented, voting was weighted according to members' quotas. Certain important decisions (changes in membership, quotas, or price of gold and elections to the Board) were reserved to the Governors and required a hefty four-fifths majority vote—giving the United States the only effective veto. In the Executive Board only the members having the five largest quotas had permanent appointed Directors. The rest were elected by, and acted for, groups of member countries. In 1960 the twenty Latin American countries elected three Directors between them but held only 10·2 per cent of the total quota votes. The two African-group Directors were not yet elected. Some European Directors also represented some non-European developing countries. What was perhaps more remarkable was that there was so little open expression of resentment by this relatively powerless majority of members. Compare the fuss at San Francisco over the special powers and privileges taken by the permanent members of the Security Council. Australia, which was in the forefront of that peasants' revolt, sought no such role in the Fund; the unprotesting populist majority stayed on the whole silent and apparently compliant.

Within the oligarchy of rich countries powerful in the Board, the United States was by far the most powerful. No positive step had ever been taken against the wishes of the American Director, and the policies of the Board broadly speaking had tended to reflect the intentions and purposes considered important by the United States.

Thus, if it was not much of a substitute for a world central bank in 1960, the Fund was still a great deal more sophisticated and powerful a piece of international regulatory and mediatory machinery than the world had ever known, both in terms of its legal authority and of the financial resources at its disposal.

With the return of the European currencies to convertibility in 1958 and the prospect that they would shortly accept the obligations of Article VIII and bring the prolonged postwar transition to an end, the Fund in 1960 was in a mood of some optimism, not to say complacency. The lean years were over, during which its rules had been put on ice and its activities restricted. Then the US Congress had looked askance at the administrative deficit of the Fund—a deficit which reflected the low drawing rate in the first ten years—'Why is this body, in which we put two billion dollars, in the red? ' But before the end of the 1950s drawings were in steady demand and quotas had been increased, both marks of confidence in the future of the Fund. External convertibility on currency account, representing for the Fund a large step towards the ideal regime of Article VIII, had been achieved by an important group of countries enhancing the mobility of funds to meet the 12 per cent increase in world trade since the end of 1958; and the first chill of a US recession had passed into a new spring.

The Development of Central Bank Co-operation

A great deal of the international monetary diplomacy of the 1960s took place in the solid Swiss city of Basle, conveniently close both to the French and German frontiers and far from the political clamour of any national capital. This was the scene of the monthly meetings of central bankers, at which so many emergency arrangements were made to make good the deficiencies of international regulatory machinery in the Fund and elsewhere and to supplement the capabilities of national authorities in face of the rapid expansion of international financial dealings.

Ironically, the BIS, at whose headquarters these important meetings took place, was the outgrowth of a kind of ' creditors' club ' or consortium of states, who had first decided, after the 1914–18 war, that they were owed reparations by Germany, and then found they had to discover ways in which the ' debt ' could be scaled down without being altogether written off. Although this was a political rather than a financial debt, the dilemmas of Germany's creditors were not very different from those facing the aid consortia for destitute developing countries today. One major rescheduling of the debt, through the Dawes Plan in 1924, had been completely upset and left in ruins by the general financial collapse after 1929. So long as nothing was put in its place, and the question of German reparations was unsettled, the major monetary powers found it difficult to rebuild the rest of the structure of international finance. The result was the Young Plan of 1930 and the consequent setting-up of the BIS at Basle to manage the issue of bonds for the scaled-down and rescheduled payment of Germany's reparations. The bank formalized an established custom, which had been much encouraged by Norman, of European central bankers getting together, sometimes with their United States colleagues, in quiet, out of the way, spots to compare notes and pass on helpful tips and warnings. As manager of the Young Plan account and depository of the member banks' paid-up capital contributions, the BIS was able to finance its expenses out of its banking profits and therefore was independent of government contributions. Increasingly it was used by central banks for the reinvestment of short-term funds.

This financial independence helped the BIS a great deal to sit out World War II with relative unconcern on neutral territory and under the protection of the Swiss bank laws, and later to resist attempts made by the United States at Bretton Woods to have it closed down.[7] (It is notable, however, that this was one of the few prewar international organizations outside the Western hemisphere to which the United States *did* belong.) A parallel network of inter-central bank contacts, also begun in the 1930s, was that between the Bank of England and the Commonwealth reserve banks in Australia, New Zealand, India, and South Africa.[8]

After the war the central bankers resumed their habitual monthly meetings, part-social and part-business, in the old hotel across the street from Basle's main railway station. In 1950 the bank staff found new occupation by nimbly stepping forward to offer their services as bank managers for the new European Payments Union (EPU). Why the IMF fluffed this opportunity, is something of a mystery. The Fund had, of course, by a decision of the United States, been made inaccessible to recipients of Marshall Aid in 1948, and its interest in European affairs had therefore been temporarily suppressed. It is said that it so happened that the Fund had no one available in Europe at the time the EPU was set up. (Its Paris office, in which Triffin worked, opened a little later.)

The importance of the EPU period, both in laying the foundations of later inter-central bank co-operation and in making possible an orderly and co-ordinated transition from the postwar period to general convertibility of currencies, should not be underestimated. The purpose of the arrangement was to use the bait of American aid to produce a more open and liberal system of payments between the European members of the Organization for European Economic Co-operation (OEEC). The EPU was launched with a working capital of $350m, and was set up by agreement of the OEEC Council in July 1950. Its threefold purpose was to build on the experience of two preceding Inter-European Payments Schemes: to multilateralize the business of settling surpluses or deficits between European countries; to induce the participants to go faster with liberalizing their trade and payments than they might otherwise do by offering them the cushion of an EPU credit line; and to persuade the participants to adopt policies which would avoid extreme positions of surplus or deficit.[9]

This latter objective was the crucial one and the focus of a political conflict in the OEEC at the time. The Americans had wanted to equip the EPU with a strong Managing Board, able to exert pressure on national governments and central banks, to make them carry out their adjustment promises. Britain, supported by the socialist Scandinavians, who shared the Labour government's protective concern for domestic economic planning, opposed this. As a result, the Managing Board, an expert body of seven, plus representatives of the BIS and IMF, was made subject to the OEEC Council. Thus when it was necessary to bring influence to bear on member countries, much more ad hoc methods were used. When the Germans were in chronic deficit in the very early 1950s, the OEEC Council set up a Mediation Group of experts who were instructed to make recommendations to them on their domestic credit controls, raw material restrictions, and fiscal policies. But with other debtor countries, the delicate job of advising was left to the Managing Board. These were mostly small, peripheral countries—Austria, Iceland, Greece, Turkey, Portugal—and the task was often eased by special indulgence towards their protectionist defences and special aid from the United States. But later on, when it came to exerting influence on a more important deficit country, like France, the Managing Board made little impact.

Where the EPU was surely very important in laying the foundations for orderly monetary co-operation in the 1960s was in preparing so well for the co-ordinated approach to convertibility of European currencies. This co-ordination had really begun with the aborted British idea, discussed at the Commonwealth Economic Conferences of November–December 1952, for an inter-Commonwealth system of trade and payments. This had aroused fears, among other members of the OEEC, for the future of the European EPU system. To reassure the Europeans, the British agreed that their approach to convertibility would not risk a fall in intra-European trade and that any move to convertibility would be a collective one. This led, in March 1954, to the setting-up of the Monetary Group under Mr R. A. Butler (the Chancellor of the Exchequer) to examine the problems that would arise if convertibility were achieved. (This Monetary Group can in many ways be seen as the forerunner of Working Party III of the Organization for European Co-operation and Development (OECD),[10] which later became so important.) It was through the technical discussion in various working parties under the Monetary Group that an outline began to emerge of the European Monetary Agreement (EMA), finally approved by the OEEC Council in August 1955.[11]

The essence of this agreement was that the decision of European countries to make their currencies once more convertible into dollars should be taken collectively rather than individually; and that in the meanwhile the change to convertibility should be made gradually rather than—as Britain had tried in 1947—by a sudden, blind plunge.

Thus in 1954, and again in 1955, the amount of gold that had to be used in intra-European monthly settlements was increased, first to 50 per cent of outstanding deficits, and then to 75 per cent. The EMA provided for a European Fund of some $600m, of which $272m was to come out of the old EPU, which it would supersede. It was to be run by a Managing Board, and the fund was to become available when the decision to go ahead to convertibility was taken by EPU members with more than 50 per cent of the then existing quotas. The decision was taken on 29 December 1958. Although in the event little use was made of the European Fund (save for a few small loans to Greece, Turkey, Iceland, and Spain), the EMA had by then already served its most important purpose—to co-ordinate and synchronize national policies to achieve a major change of gear in the international monetary system.

To return to the BIS itself, it was hardly counted in 1960 as an international economic organization of any particular significance, but was seen more as a piece of historical detritus that happened to be of continuing professional and social convenience to central bankers, and which had been fortuitously protected from total decay and desuetude by its financial independence as an operating bank. The rather central role that it would be called upon to play in the ensuing decade as a working mechanism for indispensable inter-bank collaboration and mutual support was generally unforeseen.

Equally unpredictable was the part that was to be played during the 1960s by the OECD. The Convention setting up the OECD, it will be recalled, was signed in 1960, but little was expected of the new organization. It too was widely thought of as a legacy of history—an underemployed successor of the OEEC, a body whose main task of distributing Marshall Aid was completed and whose other commitment—to work for closer European economic integration—had been superseded, so far as the three major European countries were concerned, by the European Economic Community. Indeed, in its final phase since the famous Eccles–Couve de Murville row in December 1958 on the British free trade area proposals,[12] the OEEC had made no progress even in negotiations to liberalize trade; baulked by the United States and by France, it had allowed responsibility to devolve upon the GATT.[13] If the United States now thought its interests could still be served by transforming the Paris organization into the OECD, well and good. But the new body was taking over little more than an empty shell, whence the life and drive had largely departed. There was little sign in 1960 of the OECD's capacity to develop in the course of the decade (and especially through Working Party III) a new kind of early warning system in the management of international economic relations.

Nor, in 1960, was much serious thought given to the likely impact of the EEC on the international monetary system, or even on the monetary relations between the member states. The major thrust was then on tariff reduction and the construction of the common external tariff (CET). The Rome Treaty had been notably and consciously reticent on the precise measure of monetary integration that would be required by the Community and on how soon it would be necessary to go beyond the broad obligations, under Articles 105, 107, and 109, to consult together on exchange rate changes and other monetary matters of mutual concern.

The players in the sub-system

The states mainly involved in international monetary relations in the 1960s form a group I have already labelled for convenience ' the affluent alliance '. This group is smaller than the international society of states familiar to political scientists and international lawyers. What they usually refer to as the international political system comprehends both superpowers, the Soviet Union and the United States; it also includes China, Europe, and the rest of the world. However hostile, no actor in this system can be indifferent to the others. But monetarily speaking, the world is much less truly a unitary system. At least in this period the monetary relations both of China and the Soviet bloc with the rest of the outside world were so limited and tenuous that they can hardly be said to have been participants; their connections with it were only intermittent and tangential. Meanwhile, they were able to operate separate and almost autarkic monetary areas or sub-systems of their own, insulated in very large part from the major monetary system of the world market economy. Thus, two of the most important dramatis personae in the international political system were ' off-stage ' as it were, in the international monetary system. They did not take part, though other players were not uninfluenced by their political coexistence.

Yet the affluent alliance is rather different from the groups which international political scientists often refer to as ' sub-systems ' of international society. Thanks to the largely political and geographical —in a word, strategic—bias of a great deal of international studies and also of international history, a sub-system usually means a regional, or sometimes a cultural, group within the larger group (e.g. ' the Arab states ', ' the Soviet bloc ', ' Francophone Africa '). The affluent alliance, however, is not so much a smaller group within the whole as an oligarchy of the whole, or more precisely, of the larger part of the whole. This larger part, which can also be described as the world market economy, comprises Western Europe and North

America, Latin America, non-communist Asia, Australasia, Africa and the Middle East. It partially includes even such ' socialist ' states and people's democracies as Cuba, Yugoslavia, and the UAR, although its influence on these is less than its influence on other developing countries. And in a more limited way it penetrates and influences in various degrees even those states in the Soviet and Chinese alliance systems which in most of their external economic relations have deliberately cut off their economies from the rest.

The make-up of this oligarchy is peculiar. It was not identical with any other dominant group of states in the international political system, and the states in it acted as if they were in a rather different rank order from any that would be recognizable from the working of other international organizations. It is easier to identify the members of the group than to decide why they are included in it: the United States, Canada, the United Kingdom, France, Germany, Italy, Belgium-Luxembourg, the Netherlands, Japan, Sweden, and Switzerland. The list clearly includes some with only small military capacity— smaller than others excluded (e.g. Australia), which gave signs towards the end of the period of wishing to be included. Some neutral states took part in it, but others (e.g. Austria) were excluded. A high standard of living or per capita income was not apparently the significant criterion of membership; neither South Africa nor New Zealand belonged to it. So far as can be observed, the necessary capability for membership of the group, derived either from a strong reserve position and a record of currency stability, or from a developed involvement in international trade, or foreign investment and international financial transactions. To some extent, it appeared as if a past history of concern with international monetary co-operation was more important than any objective or quantifiable measure of interest in international finance. The group was more or less self-appointed and self-limiting.

Another important difference about this group is that the states in it speak to one another and negotiate with one another through a different class, as it were, of actors. Instead of foreign ministers, UN delegates, and career diplomats, the member states in the group act through officials of national Finance Ministries and of central banks. These are represented at top levels by the Governor of the central bank and the finance minister, but at lower levels by their subordinates. It has been widely believed by the participants and protagonists in international monetary negotiations that this difference in the human media through which nations work together has some significant bearing on the character of their monetary relations, as distinct from their ordinary political and diplomatic relations. But the supporting evidence for this is scanty.[14]

In this exclusive group, the United States in 1960 stood in terms of capability, head and shoulders above the rest. American economic leadership was unquestioned. The country's gross national product by the end of the 1950s topped an estimated $512 billion, compared with a total GNP for all six members of the EEC of $188 billion, and of Britain of $72 billion. Per capita income in the United States was more than twice, at $2,830, the income per head in the EEC ($1,170), or Britain ($1,380).[15] The United States also produced by far the largest share of world manufactures, and although, because of the vast size of the American domestic market, exports were much less important to it than to other countries, it still had the largest percentage single share of world exports of manufactures in 1960:—

US	18	Belgium/Luxembourg	5·1
Germany	16·9	Italy	4·6
UK	14	Netherlands	3·6
France	8·5		

One result of the large size of the US domestic market which was important in international finance was that, assisted by a highly developed capital market, it had helped take the United States farther and faster along the road to economic concentration and the build-up of an industrial and commercial oligopoly of a relatively few large, multi-product corporations. These large corporations were on average much bigger and richer, and more technically advanced, than those of other industrialized countries in the affluent alliance. In any list of 'top companies', the great majority were American, with only a scatter of British, German, Dutch, French, Swiss, etc. In international mergers, therefore, it was usually the US corporation that took over foreign companies and not vice versa. The consequence of this extreme wealth and greater economic, technological and financial development was that the United States exerted a great influence on world trade, accounting for about a sixth of the total turnover. In the second place, it was able to export capital, i.e. to invest overseas and give official aid abroad at an average rate of $8 billion a year or 2 per cent of its GNP. This was a smaller proportion of domestic GNP than the 10 per cent which Britain had invested annually abroad before the first world war, but in absolute terms it was so large that it equalled the capital exports of the rest of the world put together.

From 1940 onwards, this economic pre-eminence had been reinforced, and exaggerated, by political history. World War II had distracted, divided, destroyed, and weakened Europe and Russia but had left the United States stronger and richer than ever and the only country able to offer others both economic aid and military protection. This postwar situation had confirmed and hastened the dollar's new status as the world's top currency, the preferred medium of exchange and—in many cases—store of value of the international economy. The outflow of dollars in official aid and private investment, assisted by the economic recovery of Europe and Japan, produced a situation in which foreigners were able through the 1950s slowly to add to their holdings of dollars and of gold.

As the dollar was a reserve currency, the turning-point came for the United States in 1958 when, for the first time, its gold reserves fell below the level of its foreign liabilities to official holders of assets denominated in dollars. This development in itself went unnoticed, but what did arouse concern was that after some years of comparative economic stagnation the US domestic economy in that year went into recession and produced a large balance-of-payments deficit. It was the resulting outflow of 10 per cent of the US gold stock which drew attention to the deficit.

But realization in the United States of the implications of this situation for American foreign policy was very slow. Only a handful of far-sighted sages, most notably Robert Triffin and Edward M. Bernstein, recognized the significance of these changes. Otherwise, any idea that the American situation in the 1960s might be markedly different from that of the 1950s was strange and bizarre. It was not foreseen that the United States for the first time might feel—and respond to—external pressures on its monetary policy-making. This insouciance is reflected in the literature of the time. An influential American economic historian, Walt Rostow, for instance, in a study called *The United States in the World Arena*, published in 1960, showed complete unawareness of any constraints that the balance of payments might exert on American policy-making; his policy proposals assumed that the international monetary environment would be more or less unchanged. Similarly Henry Aubrey, an American economist more concerned than most at that time with questions of foreign policy and the world outside the United States, wrote optimistically in 1961 about the deficit as a probably temporary and not too important phenomenon. Pointing out the American interest in keeping up a flow of foreign aid and private foreign investment, Aubrey argued, ' since the American reserve position is still basically strong, there is no inclination to subordinate this foreign interest to a concern with a temporary difficulty. The balance-of-payments problem, one hopes, can be reduced to sustainable proportions by policies which do not interfere with the flow of American capital.' [16] Nor, on a more elevated plane, did the famous Kennedy Inaugural of 20 January 1961 make any mention of these difficulties and dilemmas—although in the event the Kennedy administration took more genuine new initiatives in the monetary field than it did in others better publicized.

Various reasons could be found for American complacency. Among them two derived from the strong position of the dollar as the world's top international currency. One was that though the United States had lost gold during the 1950s there was still much left. In 1947 it owned 70 per cent of the world's stock of monetary gold. Ten years later it still owned a comfortable 59 per cent. The prospect of yet more redistribution of this lion's share, therefore, did not seem to many Americans either unreasonable or disastrous. The second reason was the accelerating growth not only of international trade but of international transactions and enterprises of all kinds. The appetite of the international economy for a convenient and acceptable international currency was therefore growing, and it became normal for foreign commercial as well as central banks to hold dollars in ever-increasing amounts. This foreign willingness to hold dollars in increasing quantities amounted to increased foreign lending to the United States and helped, therefore, to finance successive US deficits. Central banks could of course—and did—sometimes present dollar assets for payments in gold, but on the whole they tended to hold rather than to convert the dollars they accumulated. Total official dollar balances, which had totalled $3 billion in 1949 and $10 billion in 1960, had swollen to $51 billion by 1971. The inertia of the international economy helped to sustain the impregnability of the US position.

The instruments available for carrying out American policy and conducting the monetary relations of the United States should also be mentioned. Among the other players the United States was exceptional in several respects. First, there was a statutory basis for the dollar-gold price, fixed in 1934, and much American opinion had come to regard this price as no less sacrosanct than the flag, the Constitution, Thanksgiving and blueberry pie. Other countries habitually held stocks of foreign exchange, chiefly dollars, with which to intervene in the market and stabilize fluctuations in exchange rates. The United States in 1960 did not do this, and had not done so since the 1930s. This meant that other currencies were, in practice, fixed in terms of the dollar, and only the dollar (and the Swiss franc) were fixed in terms of gold. Secondly, most other countries had a single constitutionally established central bank with defined powers. The United States had had since 1913 a Federal Reserve System with the same broad regulatory purposes as other central banks but also some important differences. Not only was the institution not a *central* bank—it was federal in structure but, what was perhaps more important, it shared some of the immunities of the US Supreme Court from short-term political changes. Each of the twelve Governors, representing the twelve Federal Reserve districts, was elected for fourteen years and could not be dismissed. Some divergence of view between the US Treasury and the Governor of the Federal Reserve Board was consequently accepted in Washington as normal. Moreover, instead of having its policy-making body and its executive arm under one roof, as it were, these functions were divided in the United States between Washington and New York. This arrangement made for further conflict and division in US policy-making, for one of the member banks, the FRBNY, was, in two senses, *primus inter pares*. Because of its closeness to the great financial centre of downtown New York City, it was necessarily entrusted with the supervision and regulation of the country's major financial market in New York. And in the formative years of the 1920s, especially under Benjamin Strong, it had then naturally followed that the FRBNY should become, in monetary relations, the voice of America. Thus it had conducted US monetary diplomacy abroad, and had dealt with the Bank of England and with other foreign central banks. It was the FRBNY, and not the Federal Reserve Board in Washington, for instance, that held the US shares in the BIS. This position had been virtually unchallenged until Strong died in 1928. But in 1929 the Board began to assert its authority, notably in changing the composition of the operationally important Open Market Committee, the body charged with the important operational function of managing the market for government securities, so as to subject the Bank to the overriding authority of the Board.[17] During the war, and from 1945 to the mid-1950s, the Bank's potential power as an important international source of short-term credit was again masked, or latent, while the US government undertook direct responsibility for emergency aid to foreign governments under the Marshall Plan and other parallel programmes. With the 1960s and the development of inter-central-bank co-operation, the Bank was to play a much bigger role while, by about the middle of the decade, the Board's decisions on such matters as interest rates and credit requirements were going to have an important impact on monetary conditions outside the United States.

Summing up the role of the United States as lead player in the international monetary system, it could be said that it had been long accustomed to a dominant position. It had confidently expected to continue in it, not foreseeing either domestic side-effects or external difficulties. Since it had first taken up the role at the Bretton Woods Conference, the United States had been the only country able effectively to initiate decisions affecting the system. Even more, it had also been the only country whose assent was so necessary to the others that it was able to veto any move made by other countries, and to arbitrate between opposing points of view when this was necessary. In 1960 it did not contemplate, as yet, any necessity to share this role with others.

A further consequence of the dominant position of the United States in the international monetary system (as in the Western military alliance, with which it partly coincided) meant that both were likely to be substantially affected by any special bilateral relationship developed by the United States as centre country. During the decade, there were five such radial relationships, each of which substantially affected the development of the rest of the system. They were with Britain, France, Canada, Germany, and Japan. In 1960 the significance of each of these was much less apparent than it was at the end of the decade. Of these links, that with Britain was taken for granted as a natural outcome of history, that with Canada as the natural outcome of geography; those with Germany and Japan as the inevitable aftermath of postwar occupation. It was nowhere expected that, far from becoming slowly attenuated as the system returned to full convertibility and financial normalcy, these links would come to be elaborated and intensified. Nor was it anticipated that the relationship with France would so far deteriorate that cool and otherwise rational American economists came to regard General de Gaulle as the incarnation of the devil and Michel Debré as his Mephistopheles.

One of the features of the decade, indeed, was this marked polarization in the character of the radial links established with certain other members of the affluent alliance by the United States. The close, associative links with Britain, Canada, Germany, and Japan became closer; the opposed conflictual ones—primarily that with France but also that with South Africa—became sharper and more disturbing.

Of the five, the links created with Britain developed through the current sterling crises from 1961 to the end of the decade, and the increasing distance separating Washington and Paris will necessarily be two of the main themes running through subsequent chapters of this book. The relationships with Canada, Germany, and Japan were almost as important though they have received little analytical treatment from most monetary economists.[18] With each of these partners— and depending on circumstances which were not exclusively monetary —the United States struck a series of bargains, sometimes making financial or commercial concessions, sometimes bending the rules of international organizations, sometimes asking financial or commercial favours. Each of these arrangements modified in some degree the pressures put during the decade on the dollar and modified, too, the functioning of a system whose rules, in theory at least, applied with equal stringency to all. And although there were other close bilateral relationships within the affluent alliance (between Germany and the Netherlands, between Sweden and the other Scandinavian countries, for example) these were comparatively unimportant.[19]

The closest special relationship of all those cultivated by the United States was with Canada, mainly because Canada's national economy was the most closely dependent on that of the US. It was additionally valued by the United States through the largely accidental inclusion of Canada in the oligarchy of the Group of Ten. For this there were non-monetary historical reasons. Canada had played a leading part in the forging of the NATO alliance, and in the launching of the Marshall Aid programme in Europe. As a result, Canada had been an associate member of the OEEC and was later a full member of the OECD. Thus although Canada's economic ranking, on any statistical basis, was not much higher than that of its fellow Commonwealth country Australia, Canada found itself in the monetary oligarchy of the 1960s while Australia was excluded. And, from the point of view of the United States, Canada had already proved itself by 1960 a useful lieutenant and supporter in international monetary discussions. The close interdependence of the national economies, however, created special problems for the economic management and monetary diplomacy of both governments.

An OECD survey at the start of the decade, for example, pointed out that at the end of 1957 52 per cent of all capital employed in Canadian manufacturing and extractive industries was controlled by the United States.[20]

The United States also bought 60 per cent of Canada's exports, and the capital markets of the two countries were so closely integrated that a 1 per cent change in short-term interest rates in Canada was likely to bring about an 8 per cent change in short-term flows in the United States.[21]

The result of this close interdependence was a particularly acute adjustment problem, one that foreshadowed others in having little to do with the balance of visible trade.

To deal with it, Canada had chosen as early as 1950 to allow the market to decide the exchange rate between its own dollar and that of the United States. In view of the very tough attitude which the IMF, under American influence, adopted at the time on the importance of fixed exchange rates, the indulgence shown to Canada was a fair indication of a special relationship which continued in various ways and by various means to be highly preferential. The year before the Belgians, caught in the wake of the 1949 devaluation of sterling, had floated their franc. The Fund's Executive Board at once passed a resolution hoping that fixed par value would soon be restored—as indeed it was, in two days. The Canadian intention when it was explained to the Board was clearly rather different. Mr Louis Rasminsky, Governor of the Bank of Canada, argued that the heavy inflow of US capital threatened Canada with serious inflation. To staunch the flow with controls was administratively impractical. To do so by revaluation would lose more reserves and accumulate more debt than Canada could afford. Though it was hardly anticipated then that the float would last twelve years, until 1962, it was pretty clear that it was going to last more than a few days. Yet the US Executive Director, Mr Frank Southard, gave Canada a green light by saying that he found Mr Rasminsky's argument ' persuasive '.[22]

And although floating did not solve all Canada's problems—indeed, the economy suffered from persistent high unemployment, high interest rates, and low growth rates—yet these were perhaps the inevitable consequences of dependence on the stronger economy. What the float achieved was a measure of freedom of manoeuvre for Canadian domestic economic management. As *The Economist* noted (24 June 1961), the floating dollar had developed a ' built-in stability of its own. The fact that it had fluctuated within very narrow limits and that a vast volume of funds was always ready to move for exchange or interest arbitrage meant that whenever long-term forces pulled the rate down by a cent, money market operators start thinking about the chance of an exchange appreciation and begin to move in funds, bringing the rate up again.' By the second half of the decade, when the Canadian payments deficit began to rise sharply, the United States once again proved helpful, approving the placing of US defence orders in Canada in 1958 and excluding Canada from the provisions of the Buy American Act and from the restrictions on imports of oil into the United States [23] in 1959. And when President Eisenhower ordered cuts in defence spending overseas on 16 November 1960, Canada was exempt.[24]

All these steps were indulgences which pointed clearly the direction in which the special relationship would develop in the course of the next few years.

The German connection

Whereas the main foundation of Canada's special monetary relationship with the United States was the close integration of the economies of both countries, the main foundation in Germany's case was not economic but military. Germany's perceived need for and dependence on the nuclear protection of the United States and on the presence of American and other NATO forces committed to its conventional defence had two important consequences for the monetary diplomacy of the 1960s.

In the first place, it produced a docility and compliance with American wishes which was the more remarkable as German economic strength continued to grow and to be acknowledged. This strength was never used to defy the Americans outright. Until well into the decade, Germany's representative at the Fund was silent to the point of being self-effacing. And in the IMF Group of Ten [25] Germany could usually be relied on to be particularly helpful. The basis of the alliance obviously was primarily military, but the pay-off was primarily monetary.[26]

The second consequence of the military relationship was that it was itself a source of monetary difficulty, adding very heavily to the adjustment problem between the two countries. Thus, while in a way it made monetary relations easier—because Germany was more susceptible to American pressures than were others—it also made the relations more difficult by increasing the disparity between the external payments accounts of the two countries. It swelled both the US deficit and the German surplus.

As will be seen from the table below, by 1960 Germany had by far the strongest reserve position of any European country. The balance of payments had been consistently in surplus since 1950, with the exception of 1959, but by 1960 the reserves had taken another large jump of $2,200m.

European countries' reserve positions ($m)
(Net reserves plus gross IMF position in 1960)

Austria	782	Norway	397
Belgium/Luxembourg	1,838	Portugal	794
Denmark	393	Spain	713
Finland	345	Sweden	659
France	3,059	Switzerland	2,320
Germany	8,152	Turkey	110
Greece	299	UK	5,669
Italy	3,418		
Netherlands	2,179		

Source: BIS, *Annual Report 1961/2*, p. 133.

The foreign exchange costs of US troops in Germany were a major factor contributing to this surplus. The UN's Economic Commission for Europe (ECE) declared that these expenditures in 1960 'were almost wholly responsible for the present imbalance in West Germany's balance of payments'.[27] They accounted for two-thirds of West Germany's surplus on current account, and had risen fast enough since 1957 to offset the substantial fall in the surplus on the trade account that had set in that year. On the American side, the largest single item of government spending abroad, larger by far than the foreign economic aid programme, was the cost of US forces overseas, most of whom at this time were in Germany.

Generally speaking, a deficit is considered a source of weakness in monetary diplomacy and a surplus one of strength. Yet in the US-German connection, the striking thing was the almost equal anxiety of both Germans and Americans to reduce the disparity in their payments account and to eliminate or minimize the American deficit and the German surplus. This German concern was not wholly to be explained by the parallel military relationship. The continuing surplus, especially when it came from sudden uncontrollable spurts in short-term capital inflows—complicated the tasks of national monetary management and tended to frustrate German governments in pursuit of what seemed to them perfectly sound and reasonable national economic goals. To them, it always seemed that if the payments disparity could be reduced, their political seat would be less hot and more comfortable. For the Americans, the deficit had a much less direct impact on national economic management and they tended perhaps for that reason to pay little heed to the Germans' domestic problems. They were therefore prepared to act and to negotiate within limits largely determined by themselves—to reduce that part of the German surplus which was attributable to the presence of US troops. Thereafter, the Americans left it to the Germans to devise domestic measures which would either cut down the propensity to surplus arising from heavy and erratic capital inflow and from the slow and sluggish recovery of German confidence in overseas investment, or would insulate the domestic economy from the inflationary effects of the surplus.

In the second half of 1960, the alarming outflow of gold drew the indolent Eisenhower administration's attention to the seriousness of the US deficit. ' Action to deal with the German surplus became one of the main objectives of both the Eisenhower administration in its last weeks of office and of the incoming Kennedy team.' [28] Initially, the measures taken were all unilateral. On 6 October 1960 the US Defense Department announced it had given three directives to all US units overseas to ' buy American ' wherever possible. It was hoped that anything from $10m to $30m a year might thereby be saved in foreign exchange. This would help, but not enough. On 16 November the President issued an order limiting the number of dependants who in future would be allowed to accompany men serving overseas and announced quite severe cuts in purchasing abroad. Together, it was hoped these measures would reduce the annual bill by $1,000m.

At the same time the first moves were made to get the Germans to help. At this first approach in October 1960 the Americans failed to get all they wanted—possibly because it was a lame duck administration that was negotiating, possibly because they did not make it sufficiently clear that they meant business.[29] The Germans agreed to make a large repayment of postwar debts, to consider a bigger foreign aid programme, and to take monetary measures to quell short-term capital inflows, all of which would reduce the surplus. They utterly rejected the suggestion from Washington that they should increase their share of the NATO infrastructure budget from 14 to 20 per cent, raising their contribution to support costs to $600m a year.

In January 1961 the Germans sought to make a good impression on the new Kennedy administration by offering to make advance payments for defence purchases and to prepay postwar debts, thus relieving the US deficit to the tune of about $1,000m for the forthcoming year. Kennedy and C. Douglas Dillon, Secretary to the Treasury, rejected this offer. Nor did anything come of a visit to Washington in February by the German Foreign Minister, Herr Heinrich von Brentano. The 6 per cent revaluation of the D-mark in March 1961 exacerbated the problem (by increasing the dollar cost of troops in Germany) for the Americans. But agreement was not reached until November 1961 after the Berlin crisis had underlined the dependence of German economic prosperity on the American nuclear umbrella. Pressed by the United States to reach settlement, Herr Franz-Josef Strauss, the Defence Minister, agreed to buy $700m worth of arms for two years, to pay for the use of US training facilities and to share the costs of American military research and development. These together, it was estimated, would balance the whole foreign exchange cost of keeping US troops in Germany.[30]

To the Americans the offset arrangement seemed the natural and obvious solution to the problem. The fact that it was something of an illusion, inasmuch as some of the American arms sales to Germany would probably have been made anyway, was overlooked. And so was the fact that the military protection provided by the US troops benefited all the other members of NATO and not only the Germans, but the Germans alone had had to put up with the political embarrassment of having to tailor their training and supply policies so that they helped solve the payments problems resulting in part from the presence of US troops in Europe. A logical solution would have been a multilateral one—possibly some sort of Military Payments Union through which military accounts could be settled in special non-convertible currency usable only for defence purposes. But as Fred Hirsch remarked, ' in practice, the United States found it simpler to put the squeeze on Germany direct '.[31]

It is worth remarking that the friction between Washington and Bonn during 1960–1 talks over the offset question did not spill over on to relations between their respective monetary authorities, which continued to develop smoothly and amicably. For example, during the summer of 1961 the market discount on forward dollars in marks rose so high that many German exporters, expecting to be paid in dollars, borrowed dollars forward to exchange for marks spot, at an interesting profit. The borrowed dollars flooded into the Bundesbank, but the latter was relieved by the US Treasury, which brought the premium on marks in the forward market down again by selling dollars freely against marks.

Earlier in 1959, until the revaluation in March 1961, the Germans had tried to use monetary measures to reverse that part of the surplus arising from the capital account—but with very limited success. At first, in January 1959, they tried a cheap money policy, lowering the Bundesbank discount rate to $2\frac{1}{2}$ per cent in an effort to push capital abroad. But on the whole, instead of increasing German foreign investment this started an inflationary building boom at home. In the autumn of 1959 the policy was reversed and the discount rate raised to 3 per cent and then to 4 per cent. Minimum reserve ratios for commercial banks were increased and applied equally to foreign deposits. But the effects once again were perverse. German bankers caught in a liquidity squeeze borrowed abroad, hastily repatriated funds they had lent abroad, and thereby added to the surplus and to the inflation. Bank rate or its equivalent was then only 2 per cent in Switzerland and $3\frac{1}{2}$ per cent in the Netherlands, France, and Italy. But interest rate differentials, in face of increasing anticipation of a change in the exchange rate, were treated as irrelevant. So too was the ban on foreign purchases of German short-term credit instruments and on the payment of interest on foreign deposits. Foreigners still shifted funds to Germany and invested where they could in longer-term assets.[32]

In short, the Germans discovered for the first time the difficulties of protecting themselves from the domestic impact of their strong surplus position. As in Canada, the dilemmas of a vulnerable monetary posture proved to be a fertile source of domestic political and administrative conflict. In Canada the quarrel had been between Mr James Coyne of the Canadian Reserve Bank and the Hon. Donald M. Fleming, the Finance Minister in the Diefenbaker government. In Germany disagreements tended to be between the Bundesbank and the Economics Minister, as the political figure most likely to be blamed either for any rise in unemployment or, more likely, for any overheating, in the German economy arousing fears of inflation. To this threat, history had made Germany especially sensitive. Monetary memories, just as they had made twice-bitten Germans thrice shy of direct foreign investment, also made them more fearful than other Europeans, and certainly more than the Americans, of the social and political dangers of inflation.

On the whole, too, the United States did much less for Germany than it did for Canada to help its partner reconcile the conflicting demands of domestic and external monetary management. Moreover, it was clear even from this first experience that the United States was capable, in blithe ignorance or indifference to the external consequences, of adopting domestic measures that actually exacerbated the difficulties of the Germans. For example, in June 1960 the Federal Reserve Board unquestionably fed speculative inflow into Germany by cutting the US discount rate,[33] and it certainly did not consider restraining US companies from buying up and investing in German subsidiaries until it struck them much later on that this might help correct the US deficit as well as the German surplus. To be fair, however, the Germans also made life difficult for themselves. Their problems might have been less if they had not been so institutionally handicapped and fearful of investing abroad, as did the Americans and the British. And they might have been mitigated if their rather rigid liberal ideology had not for so long inhibited resort to those monetary and exchange controls which they were finally and reluctantly obliged to adopt.

An interesting comparison with the German relationship can be made with Switzerland—a country which shared both Germany's strength, its conservative monetary instincts, and its vulnerability to an influx of foreign funds unsettling the domestic equilibrium—but not its acute awareness of American military protection.

In the 1950s Switzerland had relied on low interest rates and the lack of short-term investment opportunities in Switzerland, to keep down the foreign inflow. But in the summer of 1960 there was a massive flood of hot money, largely due to the withdrawal of Belgian and other investments from the Congo. On 20 August *The Economist* reported an influx of 800m Swiss francs in the preceding six weeks. The Swiss reaction was similar to Germany's. The National Bank made an agreement with the commercial banks—there had been earlier ones in 1937, 1950, and 1955—to ensure that they would pay no interest on new foreign deposits or on any which had entered the country since 1 July 1960. These foreign deposits would be blocked for at least three months, so as to prevent further injections of money into the domestic economy through the purchase of Swiss securities or property. They could be unfrozen, provided they were converted into another currency, or used to buy foreign loans issued by Swiss banks. *The Times*, on 17 August 1960, reported:

Swiss banks are now believed to be working out the average level of customers' balances over the past year or so. If any balance sheet shows a recent sharp increase, he will be given the opportunity of repatriating the funds over and above the average level. If he does not withdraw the money, then it is expected that the balance will be blocked.

The agreement also provided that foreign funds would be subject to a negative interest rate, new inflows would have to pay a commission to Swiss banks of 1 per cent per annum, and could not be withdrawn with less than six months' notice. Lastly, the banks agreed to counteract the inflow by taking up a special issue of bonds, amounting to 400m Swiss francs. These were non-negotiable six-month bonds, yielding only a nominal rate of interest.[34] Swiss banks were also to try and prevent foreigners buying Swiss securities or property. The strategy was to use the authority of the state to make sure that Swiss banks acted as channels for the reinvestment abroad of funds originating abroad. Perhaps because the Swiss had fewer inhibitions about interfering with (or at least setting clear rules for) private finance, the measures on the whole proved rather more effective than those of Germany, though in the spring of 1961 they had to be further reinforced, when the National Bank froze 1,000m Swiss francs in a special account.[35] What was remarkable was that the Swiss, although they seemed comparatively successful in insulating themselves from its worst effects on the scene, yet showed themselves in the 1960s still substantially involved and concerned with the welfare of the international economy as a whole.

The third of the close bilateral relationships operated by the United States within the general system was that with Japan. But in 1960 there was little sign of the importance this relationship would assume by the end of the period and notably in the 1971 crisis. The first reason for this was the much longer time it took Japan, compared with Germany or France, to recover from postwar prostration. While the German tendency to surplus had been apparent well before the end of the 1950s, Japan continued in deficit on current account until 1965,[36] and it was not until the latter part of the decade that the Japanese surplus became a major problem. The second big difference between Japan and the other two partners lay in their much greater ‘ openness ’ to the private market economy, and their consequent difficulty in exercising the power of national economic management. By permission of the United States, Japan was allowed to be eccentric in the affluent alliance, in maintaining throughout the decade a panoply of exchange and investment controls that contrasted very strongly with the wide open invitation extended by West Germany to direct investment by US corporations.

It is true that in June 1960 Japan introduced some major amendments to the original Foreign Investment Law of 1950. This statute had openly sought to discourage direct foreign investment in the Japanese economy, allowing it only when it ‘ contributed to the attainment of self-sufficiency and the healthy development of the Japanese economy, and also to the improvement of Japan’s balance-of-payments situation ’.[37] But the relaxations were not very radical. Foreigners who had been allowed to take a 5 per cent share in Japanese basic industries and 8 per cent in others, were allowed, after June 1960, to increase their maximum share to 10 and 15 per cent respectively.[38]

In return for American indulgence towards this isolationist and enclosed strategy, Japan was to prove exceptionally compliant towards US domination of the system. An ancillary reason why it was easier for the United States to operate this particular special relationship lay in the fact that Japanese economic dependence was more directly on the US government and less—compared, for instance, with Canada's—on the private sector. In 1955 some 70 per cent of Japan's imports had been financed by US aid, and even when in the late 1950s the capital provided by the United States was in the form of loans, these were largely provided by public authorities—mainly the Export-Import bank and later the World Bank—and US commercial banks; not (as in Germany) directly by US corporations.

Britain and France in the system

As to the US-British and the US-French relationships, there was a sense in which one was the counterweight of the other. Both had long and strong historical roots. In the British case, the relationship had been slowly and steadily developing for at least half a century. It was a long-standing and accepted feature of the international monetary scene—and indeed one of the main foundations on which international monetary co-operation between the wider group of developed countries had been built. Although the Americans had rejected the scheme for a key currency system which Britain had put forward at the Genoa Conference in 1922, Strong had agreed on a bilateral arrangement with Montagu Norman; his aim was to try to make easier the international currency role of sterling by allowing British interest rates to stay above those in the United States. And throughout the interwar period, the slow growth of sterling-dollar diplomacy was one of the few directions in which real progress was made in international monetary co-operation. It was around the strengthening New York-London axis that the practice of mutual consultation (and occasional support and co-ordination of national monetary policies) began between the central banks of the developed countries. Stephen Clarke's account of monetary diplomacy in these years [39] brings out how important this was in the diplomacy surrounding the German reparations question for example, and in the precautionary arrangements made for sterling's ill-fated return to convertibility to gold in 1925. It was equally important for the stabilization programmes (referred to above) arranged through the League of Nations for various European currencies in the 1920s. But, as the memoirs of Emile Moreau, the Governor of the Banque de France, [40] showed, the 1920s was a decade in which French suspicions and resentment of this Anglo-Saxon alliance were not always groundless.

Then, after the deluge of 1929–31, with the establishment of the BIS in 1930 and the negotiation in 1936 of the Anglo-French-US Tripartite Agreement not to alter exchange rates without consultation, it seemed as if the axis was being broadened into a more truly multilateral system. Although one purpose of the Tripartite Agreement was to maintain the parity of the newly devalued franc by means of an exchange equalization account, the hub of the arrangement was once again the Anglo-American relationship.

The main object of the agreement [commented Ragnar Nurkse] was, in fact, to regulate the dollar-sterling rate in the common interest of the two leaders and of the currency areas grouped around them. The dollar-sterling rate fluctuated within a moderate range, and it is perhaps significant that after a five per cent depreciation of the pound during 1938, more flexible methods of regulation were abandoned in favour of a rigid stabilization of the rate at 4·68 dollars to the pound from January to August, 1939.[41]

At Bretton Woods all the French suspicions of Anglo-Saxon intentions to run the system on their own terms were naturally confirmed by the restriction of discussion to Maynard Keynes and Harry White and by the scant attention paid by either to alternative proposals put forward by the French or to French opinions on Anglo-American ideas.[42]

During most of the 1950s, as in the 1930s, the special relationship of the United States with Britain was less apparent as it was overlaid by the common dependence of both European countries on the help provided by the Americans through the European Recovery Programme and by their joint collaboration in the EPU. In the aftermath of Suez, however, the old suspicions returned. The standby arrangements made for the United Kingdom in December 1957 and December 1958 (see below, p. 93) had no conditions attached to them by the Fund. But the standby arranged with France in early 1958 had been conditional on important economic commitments, to keep public expenditure below Fr.5,300 billion, and budget deficit below Fr.600 billion. The Banque de France also agreed to avoid further borrowing, and to restrict domestic credit.

Like other central banks, and particularly those in some developing countries, the Banque de France was not unhappy to have the IMF for an ally in a difficult domestic political situation. The Governor, M. Baumgartner, at the 1959 annual meeting of the Fund, gratefully acknowledged the debt due to the Fund for imposing the Fr.600 billion limit on the budgetary deficit, and for the help this gave in imposing upper limits on certain categories of public credit, e.g. for housing. Yet the contribution which the IMF made to the total package borrowed by France in 1958 was a minority one. Out of a total of

$655·25m, $25m came through the EPU, $274m bilaterally from the United States, and only $131·25m from the Fund. This represented one-fourth of France's total quota of $525m, half of which had already been drawn in 1957 in the aftermath of Suez. One-fourth now remained in reserve. By contrast, the United Kingdom in 1956 had drawn $561m from the Fund and had asked for a standby arrangement for $739m. Added together the drawing and the standby represented the whole of Britain's $1,300m quota and increased the Fund's holdings of sterling to 125 per cent of the quota. As for the American and European contributions to the package, *The Economist* (8 February 1958) commented at the time that 'political considerations connected with European solidarity had weighed heavily on the EPU councils and that the desire to give a good start to European integration influenced American generosity as well'.

In 1960 the French had by no means given up their reservations concerning Anglo-American monetary management. But during the years 1958–62 they happened to be deeply absorbed in other matters. In the first place, France was fully engaged in managing its own monetary recovery from the foreign exchange crisis of 1957. There was, at this time, great uncertainty about the likely economic effects of the European common market on the French economy and also on the prospects for the French balance of payments after the devaluation of 1958 and the wholesale demolition of controls. At the outset of the decade, too, France was much preoccupied with establishing a new relationship with her former colonial dependants. Indeed, the contrast of strategies adopted by Britain and France towards their former colonies at the start of our period made a very material difference to the role subsequently played by each metropolitan country in the international monetary system.

Both experienced a major bout of decolonization at this time. Between 1958 and 1964 Britain gave independence to the second wave of colonial dependencies. Beginning with Ghana and Malaya, these were now free to spend their accumulated reserves, held in sterling balances in London, much more freely than they had been able to as colonial territories, and to use these balances if they wished to a greater extent on non-sterling imports. They were also free to hold their national reserves in forms other than sterling.

For a variety of reasons, their independent status stimulated Britain to change its aid policies and to offer government loans to these independent countries on a growing scale. Sometimes, as in some African countries, this was the more necessary because independence had brought about a return flow of capital to Britain. Moreover, not only did the change-over to independence in the Overseas Sterling Area (OSA) increase the potential demands that could be made on Britain's depleted gold and dollar reserves; it also made a significant change to the foreign exchange costs, both apparent and concealed, in British defence spending outside Europe and in particular east of Suez.[43]

Over the period 1958–62 France managed rather adroitly on the whole to separate its ex-colonial territories into the wholly independent—who could henceforward make few monetary claims upon it and whose capacity to burden the French economy was therefore very limited—and the dependent countries of the franc zone, whose freedom was effectively restricted through close association. The first group included not only Algeria but also Morocco and Tunisia. Neither of these followed the franc in the 1958 devaluation, and although they held the bulk of their reserves in francs they became otherwise monetarily independent. The second group of ex-colonial territories consisted of the franc zone countries of West and Central Africa and Madagascar. In 1958 all these were offered a straight choice between federation or total separation and, except for Guinea which overwhelmingly voted 'no'—and was immediately cut off without a sou—these countries accepted membership of the new French Community. However, such was the fever for independence that by 1960 the Community idea had been more or less abandoned; member states asked for and were given their formal sovereignty.

But political independence did not lead to monetary independence. For the most part these African states continued to use the CFA (Communauté Française Africaine) franc and stayed within the monetary unions (one for West Africa and one for Equatorial Africa) established by France in 1955.[44] All these newly independent states signed co-operation agreements with France and from then on all received generous aid. The French Treasury continued to exercise important functions in the franc zone in much the same way as it had since 1945. The CFA franc had a fixed parity with the French franc and was freely convertible into French currency. As a *quid pro quo* France demanded some credit control and each of the countries had to belong to one of the three issuing authorities—effectively central banks—through which all external payments and receipts passed, first being converted into French francs. In theory this system provided unlimited access to foreign exchange but in practice this was limited by French representation on the governing bodies of the central banks, and by a system of import controls effectively imposing a ceiling on total imports from outside the zone.

The preferential tariff and quota system enjoyed by France in the franc zone countries was gradually extended in the early 1960s to trade with France's partners in the EEC. They in return took over some share in the provision of aid to these countries. And for most of the 1960s France continued to support the prices of primary products exported by the states of the zone, and remained their major supplier and customer.

For all its inherently discriminatory character, the system remained unchanged when, in noticeably more leisurely fashion than that of neighbouring anglophone countries, the franc zone states became members of the Fund in 1962 and 1963. Slowly through the 1960s they established themselves as an active group in the Fund, and were largely responsible for the 1967 Rio resolution on commodity price stabilization. But the Fund officials who fretted over Latin American peccadillos regarded unmoved a post-imperial system which, however odd in the context of the rule book, nevertheless showed remarkable financial stability and gave no trouble.

In its monetary relations with France, official circles in the United States were largely unprepared in 1960 for the differences and difficulties that lay ahead. From the first exploratory discussion at the 1961 annual meeting of the Fund, on increasing the Fund's lending capacity, and from the opening conversations in Paris in November 1961, the key role of France when the United States put forward proposals to modify the existing system, and the importance of French influence, was apparent. What the 1950s had not prepared anyone for was the very close correlation between French monetary strength and the new toughness of French monetary bargaining. An official attitude summed up by Giscard d'Estaing in 1965 was 'France has money; therefore she must have an international monetary policy'.[45] The Fifth Republic was much quicker than the Fourth to exploit its diplomatic opportunities and these would be frequent as the need arose for the United States to adapt and extend the network of international monetary co-operation.

The renascent international money markets

No introduction to the international monetary system in 1960 would be complete without some brief mention of international money markets. These were both an important part of the environment within which the governments who were engaged in international monetary diplomacy operated; and they were also the source and cause of a great deal of danger and trouble to these governments, necessitating more and more elaborate international co-operative activity. Many of the case studies that follow will deal with the sudden eddies of turbulence in these markets and with the reaction which these disturbances evoked from central banks and from the governments of leading members in international financial organization.

Between 1958 and 1961 it is no exaggeration to say that there had taken place a major renascence of international financial and money markets. Indeed, the phoenix that rose in those three short years from long-cold ashes was a bigger and improved version of its predecessor, with distinctive new features that made it even faster acting, and more capable of destroying international monetary stability. It has already been explained that the concerted move to convertibility by the European countries in December 1958 had done two things. It had removed the remaining restrictions on traffic between the West European countries; and it had united Western Europe and North America for the first time since the war into a single international market for foreign exchange.

This unification of most of the developed market economies into one economic area was immediately reflected by the rebirth of London as an intercontinental market-place for all kinds of financial dealings. Through the 1950s the first tentative beginnings had been made to reopen the City for business. The commodity markets had begun to start up again in the early years, even under the Labour government. The gold market had reopened in 1954 and the market for foreign exchange and trade finance had been able steadily to increase business as the number of varieties of sterling created by British exchange control of various kinds, over non-residents as well as residents, diminished and the differences between them narrowed. Other financial centres in Europe may have been freer, in the sense that the residents of the country could theoretically buy and sell foreign securities and deal in unlimited quantities of foreign exchange, which British residents could not do. But none was more international in outlook: more than any other centre, London was accessible to foreign banks and its institutions were long accustomed to make a market, to set up a deal, to quote a price on any negotiable asset anywhere in the world. All the different kinds of international activity which had gone on in London before the war—the financing of trade, insurance, shipping, gold, the stock exchange, as well as foreign exchange dealing—could expand rapidly once the great currency barriers had been lifted between the dollar and sterling and between the dollar and other currencies. Moreover, these habits of openness and of versatility surely made it easier for the City to turn, as it increasingly did after 1960, to lend and borrow in dollars instead of in sterling.

An important development for the foreign exchange markets at the start of the period was the evolution of what could be described as customary rules for the maintenance, in open market conditions, of exchange parities between currencies. Once the European currencies had become convertible, the original obligation, under the Bretton Woods Agreement, to maintain each others' exchange rates at their respective support points, not exceeding a spread of 2 per cent, no longer made sense, since it was possible that currency A would be

1 per cent above the dollar parity, while currency B was 1 per cent below, and a reversal of these positions would make the maximum in the AB cross-rate equal to 4 per cent instead of 2 per cent. Consequently, another 'reinterpretation' of Bretton Woods rules by the IMF, in 1959, agreed that the only official support points, at which central banks still had to intervene in the market, were those governing the relation of members' respective currencies to the dollar.[46] As a result of this arrangement, the spread between support points in respect of intra-European exchange rates doubled. In practice, as the customary support points adopted by most central banks, to give themselves a little elbow room, came to be about $\frac{3}{4}$ per cent either side of the dollar parities, the maximum effective spread was about $1\frac{1}{2}$ per cent in relation to the dollar and 3 per cent in relation to other currencies.

Having settled the rules, central banks increasingly found that as foreign exchange markets became more active, they had to intervene more often and more heavily, not only to influence the spot rate but also the forward rate. This was something the leading European central banks, notably the British and French, had sometimes done, briefly, in the inter-war period.[47] Until the return of convertibility and the development of an active foreign exchange market such interventions had not been necessary, except for a brief market operation by the Bank of England in 1957. But from 1961 onwards, beginning with the American and British monetary authorities, intervention in the forward market became increasingly common. And, as Paul Einzig commented,

although the increased extent of intervention compared with the previous period was a matter of degree, the increase was sufficiently extensive to constitute an institutional change ... The presence or absence of official buying or selling and the nature and extent of official operations became a decisive factor in determining the trend of exchange rates. It influenced the attitude of actual and potential private operators to a considerable degree.[48]

By this means, governments themselves became at certain times important players in the market.

If the renascence and unification of the foreign exchange markets at the turn of the decade was one of the important developments influencing monetary events in the turbulent 1960s, the other was undoubtedly the birth of the market in Eurodollars.

What this market is, and why it came into existence, has been explained many times and in many ways. Most of those who operate in it, however, are agreed on one basic point—that it is a response by the market to official obstruction in the international economy. One such operator, Mr K. M. Woodbridge, speaking at a *Financial Times* conference, put it this way:

national regulations are an inhibiting factor and in anything other than a complete and comprehensive form, are not watertight when applied to money flows . . . the stream is the Eurocurrency market and the rocks are the various national regulations. As more rocks go in, the faster the stream flows round them.

The beginnings of the market are usually placed around 1957. The sterling crisis in that year had decided the Macmillan government to restrict the use of sterling for financing foreign trade. British banks tried to get round this restriction on one of their traditional functions of dealing in international short-term credit by using US dollars for the same purpose. They had a further incentive for doing so in the general tightness of credit conditions at the time. This led to the first substantial source of demand for already existing deposits of dollars in Europe and made European financial institutions wake up to the profits to be made out of mobilizing their resources of US dollars, and on-lending them to other banks. A large supply of US dollar deposits was already in existence in Europe, as in Canada, thanks to US aid and trade transactions in Europe, and this supply grew as the US payments deficit increased between 1958 and 1960. Equally important was the reluctance of British and other European banks to repatriate these dollar deposits to their native US money market. This reluctance is explained by American monetary management, which produced in the early 1960s a rather wide interest rate differential between the return that could be earned on bank deposits in Europe and in the United States. This had come about as a result of regulations devised in the 1930s to prevent stock market speculation. In 1933 the US Congress instructed the Federal Reserve Board to make rules to limit the amount of interest payable by member banks in the Federal Reserve System on deposit accounts (time and savings deposits, in American terms). The result was Regulation Q, which allowed only 1 per cent interest to be paid on deposits left for less than three months, and none at all on demand deposits (or current accounts).

'These limitations, when combined with the willingness of European banks to operate on narrower interest margins, allowed the European banks to outbid the US banks in the market for US dollar deposits and to under-cut them in making US dollar loans.'[49] The Eurodollar market, barely nascent in 1960, was destined to have a major impact on the international monetary system and on international monetary relations between states. In the first place, it posed a totally new political problem, one of international management. Most other problems of international monetary relations arose from the maladjustment of national monetary systems to each other. This one lay in the new area of international policy—the political management by one means or another of an international market economy that lay beyond and between the areas covered by national monetary management. For most of the 1960s the problem was side-stepped: everybody's business, as with ocean pollution or the depletion of natural resources, was no one's business. But sooner or later, the choice would have to be faced between accepting the consequences of international economic anarchy; submitting to extraterritorial regulation by one dominant national authority; or co-operating in devising some machinery of international management by which the conflicting interests of national economies and opposed groups and classes would somehow be resolved.

This choice would be the more inescapable because a major effect of the Eurodollar market was to transmit interest rate competition from one country to another and to spread any scramble for liquidity that developed in one country to all the other countries involved in the market.[50] This transmission function was to operate primarily across the Atlantic, from the United States to Europe. Since the ebb and flow of funds was always in response to US policy measures, this served to increase the element of asymmetry in the system which gave the United States a different role in, and a distinctive influence over, the rest of the system.

Lastly, the Eurocurrency markets were to have important consequences for the liquidity problem in the international system. On the whole their main effect, naturally, was to add very substantially to private international liquidity. By 1970 it would have grown from practically nothing to an estimated turnover of inter-bank lending of the order of $50 or $60 billion. Official reserves of gold and foreign exchange, as set out in the table below, grew from $59 billion in 1960 to $89 billion in 1970. It is true that a few governments during the 1960s—notably the Italian—found it convenient to economize their own monetary reserves from time to time, either by drawing directly on the Eurocurrency market or by allowing their commercial banks and other institutions to do so. In this sense it supplemented national reserves and added to official public liquidity. But the main addition was to private liquidity, creating a pool from which funds could be drawn in response to pressures on exchange rates, thus increasing the needs of deficit governments especially to use reserves to intervene in the foreign exchange markets to maintain exchange rates. Governments have needed ever larger reserves in order to cope not only with imbalances in their external trade accounts but even more with the massive shifts of short-term funds across frontiers and in and out of the Eurodollar market.

None of these developments however were even remotely foreseen at the beginning of the 1960s—a blissful state of ignorance which should perhaps give pause to those who seek to be too dogmatic about the problems—let alone the solutions of decades still in the future.

World reserves 1955–71 ($ billion)

	1955	1960	1965	1969	1970	1971 *
Gold	35·4	38·0	41·8	39·1	37·2	36·1
Foreign exchange	18·4	20·3	24·4	29·1	43·9	72·9
IMF reserve positions	1·9	3·6	5·4	6·7	7·7	6·3
SDRs	—	—	—	—	3·1	5·9
Adjusted total	55·7	61·9	71·6	75·4	99·9	121·3
IMF credit tranche	7·9	13·6	12·5	16·8	25·3	27·2
Other unused credits	—	—	3·8	14·5	14·2	11·1

* 1971 figure includes UK official assets ' swapped forward ' with overseas monetary authorities.
Source: IMF, *Annual report,* 1972, table 6.

Notes

[1] Robert Triffin, *Our international monetary system, yesterday, today and tomorrow* (New York, 1968, pp. 178–9. The book was dedicated jointly to Teilhard de Chardin (*The future of man,* 1964) and Jean Charon (*Man in search of himself,* 1967).

[2] For a full account, giving the political as well as the economic background to the Genoa Conference, see S. V. O. Clarke, *The reconstruction of the international monetary system: the attempts of 1922 and 1933* (Princeton, 1973).

[3] In his *Post-war monetary plans* (Oxford, 1949).

[4] Letter to Norman, 14 July 1922 (quoted in S. V. O. Clarke, *Central bank co-operation, 1924–31* (New York, 1967), p. 31).

[5] Ibid., p. 37.

[6] S. V. O. Clarke, *Reconstruction of the international monetary system,* p. 38.

[7] Roger Auboin, *The Bank for International Settlements 1930–55* (Princeton, 1955), pp. 14, 17.

[8] Andrew Boyle, *Montagu Norman* (London, 1967).

[9] Robert Triffin, *Europe and the money muddle* (New Haven, 1957), p. 168.

[10] Its full title, now almost forgotten, was Working Party on the Promotion of Better International Payments Equilibrium.

[11] Michael Palmer & others, *European unity: cooperation and integration* (London, 1968). pp. 96–7.

[12] See vol. 1, Introduction, p. 7.

[13] See vol. 1, pp. 24ff.

[14] Robert Russell conducted an exhaustive research project on this point in 1969–70 (' Transgovernmental interaction in the international monetary system 1960–72 ', *International Organisation,* Autumn 1973) which was directed to discovering whether the behavioural theory of small groups might have influenced those involved in monetary diplomacy. Officials he questioned were agreed that they felt socially sympathetic to their confrères of other nationalities and that relations with them were easier and less formal in consequence. But none seriously claimed that his country's policy or bargaining strategies had been significantly affected.

[15] OECD, *Main economic indicators 1957–66.*

[16] H. G. Aubrey, *Coexistence: economic challenge and response* (Washington, 1961), p. 108.

[17] For a full account of this important piece of background see Milton Friedman & Anna J. Schwartz, *A monetary history of the United States 1867–1960* (Princeton, 1971, paperback), pp. 255–6.

[18] A notable exception to this generalization is William Diebold, jnr., in *The United States in the industrial world* (New York, 1972). Diebold has authoritative and politically sensitive chapters on the special relationship with both Canada and Japan.

[19] The only bilateral relationship which came to have a wider influence on the development of the system was that between France and Germany and this did not become apparent until the later years of the decade (see below, ch. 11).

[20] OECD Economic Surveys, *Canada 1961*, p. 18.

[21] R. E. Caves & G. L. Reuber, *Canadian economic policy and the impact of international capital flows* (Toronto, 1969), p. 75.

[22] IMF, *The International Monetary Fund 1945–65*, i: *Chronicle*, by J. K. Horsefield (Washington, 1970), pp. 273–4. (All three volumes of this history are subsequently referred to as *IMF*. Vols ii, *Analysis* (by M. G. de Vries & others) and iii, *Documents*, were both edited by Horsefield.)

[23] Canad. Inst. of Int. Aff., *Canada in world affairs 1959–61* (Toronto, 1965), pp. 159–60.

[24] Ibid., p. 162.

[25] Or Paris club, created in 1962 originally to supply GAB loans—see ch. 4.

[26] See Roger Morgan, *The United States and West Germany 1945–53* (London, 1964).

[27] *Economic survey of Europe 1960*, ch. 1, p. 39.

[28] Sam Brittan, in RIIA, *Survey of International Affairs 1961*, p. 304.

[29] Only afterwards did the Americans, so it was said at the time, hint that they might have to take some troops away from Europe to protect the dollar (see Council on Foreign Relations, *The United States in world affairs 1960*, p. 57).

[30] *New York Times*, 1 Dec 1961.

[31] *Money international* (London, 1967), p. 322.

[32] See Patrick M. Boarman, *Germany's economic dilemma, inflation and the balance of payments* (New Haven, 1964), p. 281.

[33] There were many historical precedents much more serious than this of US indifference to the international repercussions of domestic monetary policies. The classic case, of course, was the dire effects of the Silver Purchase Act of 1934 on monetary management in countries with a silver-based currency, notably China, and the Latin American countries (see A. S. Everest, *Morgenthau, the New Deal and silver* (New York, 1950)).

[34] See Max Iklé, *Die Schweiz als internationaler Bank und Finanzplatz* (Zurich, 1970). (Cf. the reserve requirements on US banks by the Federal Reserve, and the special deposits demanded by the Bank of England from commercial banks.)

[35] Ibid., p. 121.

[36] The basic balance, including the long-term capital account, was in surplus in 1962, in deficit again in 1963, and thereafter in surplus every years except 1967. The table on p. 277 below gives the details of Japan's balance of payments in the 1960s.

[37] Quoted in J. H. Adler, ed., *Capital movements and economic development* (London, 1967), ch. 3.

[38] *Financial Times* (hereafter *FT*), 29 Mar 1960.

[39] *Central bank co-operation.*

[40] *Souvenirs d'un Gouverneur de la Banque de France* (Paris, 1954).

[41] League of Nations, *International currency experience: lessons of the inter-war period*, by Ragnar Nurkse (Geneva, 1944). For a broader, more political account of the negotiations, see Charles P. Kindleberger, *The world in depression* (London, 1973), ch. 11.

[42] These proposals were made by two French economists, MM. Hervé Alphand and André Istel, but they had been helped by French officials and the proposals

closely followed the 1938 report of M. Paul van Zeeland of Belgium, which had advocated an extension and elaboration of the 1936 Tripartite Agreement (see *IMF*, i. 9 & 37 and iii. 97–102).

[43] For details see S. Strange, *Sterling and British policy* (London, 1971) and Phillip Darby, *British defence policy east of Suez 1947–68* (London, 1973).

[44] Mali left the franc zone in 1962, only to return to it five years later.

[45] Speech to Maison de Droit, Feb 1965 (quoted by E. L. Morse, *Foreign policy and interdependence in Gaullist France* (Princeton, 1973), p. 225).

[46] EB Decision, No. 904 (59/32), 24 July 1959.

[47] A very early instance, cited by Chouraqui, was the intervention by the Banca d'Italia in 1926–7 to support the spot rate by selling lire forward and buying spot. But this had been an expensive game not repeated (see J. C. Chouraqui, *La spéculation et la politique de defense des monnaies* (Paris, 1972), p. 243. This book and Chouraqui's doctoral thesis, 'Les opérations à terme sur devises et l'équilibre monétaire international' (1970), treat the subject very fully.

[48] *The history of foreign exchange*, 2nd ed. (London, 1970), p. 304.

[49] E. Wayne Clendenning, *The Euro-dollar market* (London, 1970), p. 23.

[50] Ibid., p. 167.

3

THE ORGANIZATION OF THE GOLD POOL
AND THE 1961 BASLE AGREEMENT

There were two points at which the international monetary system
agreed and run by governments soon became vulnerable to pressure
from market forces in the international economy—two markets in
which doubts, dissatisfaction and faltering confidence felt by private
operators were apt to be expressed. One was the market for gold; the
other the market for foreign exchange, where official rates set for
individual currencies could, since convertibility, more easily come
under pressure from a market dubious about their permanence.

At the beginning of the 1960s governments were obliged to react to
these pressures with new policy measures and arrangements on the
national level (i.e. in their own domestic monetary management), in
bilateral relations with other states and on the international level with
new forms of multilateral co-operation. Two of these early responses—
the series of agreements for the management of the gold market by
means of a Gold Pool, and the first Basle Agreement for multilateral
action to support a particular currency's exchange rate—had this much
in common: both were examples of what Whitehall calls ' ad hoc-ery '.
Though it can be seen in retrospect that they drew on past experience
and central banking know-how, they seemed at the time to be hasty
improvisations for crisis management. When it came, a little later, to
improving, adapting (and later reforming) existing institutions like the
IMF, the process of discussion, exploratory negotiation and precise
bargaining was necessarily more protracted and the protagonists
seemed warier of safeguarding what they perceived as their national
interests vis-à-vis one another. In the heat of the moment, by contrast,
ad hoc arrangements seemed remarkably free of mutual distrust.

It was the gold market which first gave signs of impending turbulence. Here, although most of the buyers and sellers were private
individuals or corporate bodies, governments were also involved in
varying degrees in market dealing. Some of them wanted to buy gold
in order to hold it in their national reserves, though this preference for
a non-interest-bearing asset was by no means universal or uniform.
Some—the gold-producing states—wished to sell gold in the market.
These governments usually appointed themselves agents for the gold-
mining enterprises in their countries and then were able to choose

whether to sell the gold for foreign exchange or to add it to their reserves. These gold-producing states were peculiar in the gold exchange standard system in that they had this additional means, not available to others, of increasing national reserves.

Not only did governments' involvement in the gold market differ rather widely; activity in the market varied over time and place from almost total quiescence to frantic hyper-activity. For instance, there was—and had been for centuries—a much more active market in gold in Asia than in Latin America or in Africa (except for a time in Tangier). And in certain parts of the world—usually where some element of illegality conferred high rewards for smuggling—the gold traffic was notoriously heavy: into India via the Persian Gulf and in and out of other countries through the Portuguese entrepôt in the Far East, Macao. In the United States and in Britain in recent decades governments had found it possible to enforce laws against the private holding of gold in any significant quantity. But in Switzerland and in France the gold-hoarding habit was deeply rooted. Among the French, in whom history had planted a deep distrust of managed currencies, the habit of private gold-holding oscillated quite markedly with the rise and fall of confidence in the political stability of the national government, and, perhaps less evidently, in the economic stability of the international economy. Such outbursts of private buying and speculation had led the Banque de France to intervene from time to time to quell and sometimes deliberately to punish or frighten the speculators in gold whenever they judged them too unruly or dangerous. But it had learned over the years that this role of market supervision and intermittent intervention could be successful and profitable always provided that the market managers were not over-ambitious and did not seek wholly to control, only occasionally to discipline. Much the same wisdom was to be found in the Bank of England, another central bank with long experience of market supervision and occasional market management.

The involvement of governments—as buyers, sellers, and sometimes as market managers—in a market where most dealing was on private account was inclined, paradoxically, to make it at times rather more mercurial and unstable than it would have been if the private dealers had been left entirely to themselves. For it was a feature of the market that although governments were not often active in it, when they did intervene directly by selling or buying for whatever purpose, their intervention was apt to set off an avalanche of private dealing. Even if their actual intervention was not on a large scale, the market was easily unsettled by their known capacity to intervene on a very large scale. The merest rumour of a government intervention in the gold markets was sometimes enough to set off a speculative movement among the private dealers, multiplying the consequences of the original deal several times over.

Thus it was a market in which governments themselves were capable of exercising a powerful destabilizing influence, even though all of them felt—as the story of the 1960s makes very plain—a common interest in preserving order and stability in it. This interest would undoubtedly have been less direct and general if the Bretton Woods system had not built a place for gold into the network of rules and customs which made up the international monetary system. In particular, the Fund members had tied the interlocking fixed exchange rates between national currencies on which all else hinged to a particular dollar-gold price, that of $35 an ounce.

This price had in fact been set before the war, in 1934, by the decision of the US government, at that time the major influence on both the American domestic and on the world gold market. After coming off gold (i.e. suspending foreign gold payments) in April 1933 the Roosevelt administration started in October deliberately to raise prices, especially commodity prices, in the depressed US economy, by offering first domestic and then foreign gold producers more money. At $35 an ounce, having increased the dollar value of the US gold stock by over $2,800m, the President arbitrarily decided to stop, and the price was pegged at that point by Act of Congress.[1]

In the negotiations setting up the IMF, this US dollar-gold price was accepted as the automatic basis of all other par values. The precedent for this had been set by the exchange rate stabilization policy adopted by the Roosevelt administration which had led to the Tripartite Agreement of 1936 (see above, p. 54). By this agreement the United States had promised to sell gold to the British and French exchange equalization accounts ' at such rates and upon such terms and conditions as the Secretary deemed advantageous to the public interest '.[2] It thus assured the participating countries [3] that they could convert into gold any balances of each others' currencies which they might accumulate through exchange stabilization operations in their own markets. There was a clause safeguarding the United States against loss through sudden exchange rate changes by the other parties. This demanded that they should give 24 hours' notice so that transactions currently in hand between the two countries' central banks could be completed without exchange loss.[4] The effect of the Tripartite Agreement therefore was to link the dollar, alone of the three major participating currencies, to a particular gold price.

Even before the Bretton Woods Conference ended, Britain had unilaterally accepted this US gold price as the basis for the new system of rules. Later, the United States had insisted that countries participating in the new system must agree not to buy gold above par (i.e. above the US gold price) or to sell it below.[5] About the same time the United States had also put it to the British that Congress would not approve any new monetary agreement unless, among other conditions, the British agreed to stick to the $4:£1 exchange rate until after the Fund had begun its operations. The US right of veto over the gold value of the dollar was also accepted. In the final Bretton Woods proposals this veto right was translated into the rule that 85 per cent of the Fund votes were required for any such change. Keynes then persuaded the Americans to change the 85 per cent rule to one (Section 7, Article IV) requiring the approval of all members having 10 per cent or more of the total quotas, thus giving Britain a veto too. Thus a gold-based dollar (or a dollar-priced ounce of gold) became the numéraire of the whole interlocking system of fixed exchange rates.

One last important link tying the international system to gold was the provision in Article III, Section 3b of the IMF Articles of Agreement that each member should deposit with the Fund gold to the value of 25 per cent of its quota or 10 per cent of its net official reserves of gold and US dollars, whichever was the smaller. As membership, quotas, and Fund staff and transactions increased therefore, the Fund itself became a larger and more important holder and handler of gold.

The IMF and gold ($m)

	Holdings	Sales *
1950	1,494	—
1960	2,439	600
1965	1,869	1,750
1970	4,339	3,516·4

* Cumulative totals.
Source: IMF, *International Financial Statistics*.

The underlying difficulty—which became apparent only intermittently—was that this apparently stable gold price, fixed by edict of the US government supported by international agreement, had been superimposed on a private market for gold that was occasionally unruly and sometimes downright anarchic.

It was a situation that prompted two key questions: under what circumstances would this private market represent a serious threat to the international monetary system? And secondly, how should that threat be met and the danger averted?

Both questions had in fact been posed much earlier in the Fund's existence and there had been a flurry of discussion on two issues. One was whether it was permissible for the governments of gold-producing states to subsidize gold mining. The other was whether it was permissible for these governments to sell gold to foreign buyers at a price higher than the fixed price in dollars. Article IV, Section 2 expressly forbade the former but not the latter. It provided that ' the Fund shall prescribe a margin above and below par value for transactions in gold by members and no member shall buy gold at a price above par value plus the prescribed margin, or sell gold at a price below par value minus the prescribed margin '.

After extensive deliberations on the question of mining subsidies, the Fund in effect decided that so long as their effects were domestic, they were innocuous. But it still upheld the letter of the law, ruling out of order all straight subsidies putting a premium price on newly mined gold, but finding permissible various ingenious devices (first worked out by the Canadians and then imitated by other gold-producing states) that dissociated the rate of subsidy from the volume of output. Anxious as the members—and especially the United States —undoubtedly were to preserve the system and its rules, it was clear that the rather active private demand in the gold market in the late 1940s (and again after the outbreak of the Korean war in 1950) might well create a series of black markets in newly mined gold that would cause it to disappear into private hoards, thus limiting its availability for official reserves. A declaration by the Executive Board in December 1947 asserted that the Fund ' has a responsibility to see that the gold policies of its members do not undermine or threaten to undermine exchange stability '. But it only obliged members proposing to introduce new measures to subsidize the production of gold to consult with the Fund on the specific measures to be introduced.[6]

The question of premium sales of gold in the private market was potentially more important to the international system since it involved transnational transactions, whereas the producers' subsidies were internal transactions. Here the Fund, although it had a more doubtful legal position, took a less flexible attitude. On 8 June 1947 the Managing Director wrote on behalf of the Board to all the members declaring that the practice of ' external purchases and sales of gold at prices which directly or indirectly produce exchange transactions at depreciated rates ', if not discouraged, was likely to ' fundamentally disturb the exchange relations among the members of the Fund '. The Fund therefore recommended that all its members ' take effective action to prevent such transactions in gold with other countries or with the nationals of other countries'.

This position was bitterly contested by South Africa, which claimed firstly that the Fund had no legal right to take this line, and that if South Africa had known that this interpretation would be put on Article IV, Section 2, it would never have signed the Articles of Agreement. The question continued to be a source of contention between the Fund and South Africa in the next two years, ending with a direct challenge by South Africa when it announced a plan to sell 100,000 ounces of semi-processed gold to some London bullion brokers at a premium price in sterling, equivalent to $38·20. The premium in this case reflected not only the market's estimate of the market value of gold but also the scarcity of the dollar in international payments (particularly inside the ring of British exchange controls), and the market's consequent estimate of the over-valuation of sterling in terms of dollars. It was conceivable that the South African government hoped by putting through this premium deal to cause the $35 an ounce price, which it never ceased to criticize, to come unstuck.

To sum up, before the end of the 1940s, the Fund had rejected all suggestions that the gold price should be raised and had strongly deprecated premium sales in the international market. It had decided that the private (international) market in gold could be dangerous to the system, especially when governments undertook foreign operations in it. Internal operations (by subsidized purchases for instance) were less dangerous than foreign sales at premium prices. It had rejected the alternative suggestion put forward by the French Executive Director, M. Jean de Largentaye, that the gap between the official and the private (premium) price could be easily eliminated by market intervention, i.e. by sufficient sales of official gold at the official price to bring the premium price down. It had opted instead for a policy of maximum separation dividing—so far as was practical—the private market from official foreign transactions in gold. Tenuous and slender as this division was, it proved adequate through the 1950s. The reasons for this were partly political and partly economic, and can be briefly summarized as follows:—

1. While the private market was active and bullish, most of the governments of the richer developed countries were unable to produce the balance of payments surplus to finance additional purchases of gold for their national reserves. They were thus out of the market.

2. The political stability in Europe established by the European Recovery Programme took the edge off the hoarders' appetite for gold through most of the 1950s.

3. The sterling devaluation of 1949 markedly increased the relative profitability of mining enterprises in the sterling area countries including South Africa, Rhodesia, Australia, Ghana. In South Africa too costs of gold production were rising less fast than in other places. These two factors reduced the urgency of South Africa's complaints against the system.

4. Although the London gold market was reopened in 1954 and international open markets operated in Paris, Geneva, and Zurich, the absence of a freely operating international market for foreign exchange

due to the inconvertibility of European currencies before 1958 put limits on the speculative element in the international market for gold.

However, as soon as there existed in London both a major international market for foreign exchange, free of exchange controls—except for UK residents—and the only truly two-way free market for gold of any size in the world economy, the conditions existed in which a failure of confidence in the par value of one or other of the reserve currencies or in the overall stability of the international economy, was likely to produce a dangerous spurt of activity and speculation in the gold market. This pressure on the London gold market price began to be felt in 1960.

A controversial question here is whether the 1960–1 gold crisis would have been as bad or whether a Gold Pool arrangement would have been necessary if British governments in the 1950s had not put the restoration of the international use of sterling and of London to its former eminence as an international financial centre so high in their order of national policy priorities. This return to what the City regarded as economic normalcy had been begun by the Labour government after the war with the reopening, under Mr Harold Wilson, of the London commodity markets. Two more important steps—the reopening of the London gold market and a major simplification and easing of sterling exchange controls—were taken by the Conservative government on 19 March 1954. The Treasury claimed credit for a deliberate policy of restoring freedom to traders, merchants, and bankers.

An alternative (but not incompatible) explanation is that the British government was forced into both measures by developments in an increasingly active and internationally integrated market—or, to be more precise, in a series of interlocking international markets. These developments were threatening to undermine, perhaps dangerously, the system of exchange controls with which Britain had defensively surrounded the sterling exchange rate, and to rob the City, perhaps permanently, of its cherished function as a world market-place for commodities, gold, and finance. What had happened was that South Africa and other Commonwealth gold producers had been selling gold on other free gold markets, notably in Zurich, either for hard currencies or for transferable sterling. The market operators had discovered how to use commodity shunting and dealing to make an arbitrage profit from the differences between market rates for the different kinds of sterling—differences created in effect by the exchange controls applied differentially by Britain to 'dollar area' sterling, 'resident' (sterling area) sterling, and 'transferable' or non-resident sterling. Other centres, in short, were gaining business at London's expense and the Bank of England was even finding it necessary to intervene to support sterling in Zurich. To persist in the old policies was going to be increasingly expensive as well as increasingly ineffectual. The only feasible alternative—or so it seemed at the time—was to make a bid both to restore confidence and to bring business in all these interrelated markets back to London before it was too late. Moreover, the belief was still unshaken that what was good for the City was good for sterling as a reserve currency—since it tended to be reflected in increased sterling balances; and that what was good for these two was also good for the world monetary system as a whole. Indeed, the Bank of England argued that reopening the London gold market would benefit everybody since it would secure a larger share of new gold for the central banks. And in fact within a mere eighteen months after the reopening of the London gold market, 85 per cent of the new gold coming on the world market was being handled there. The Bank of England was later able to boast that ' London is the largest and most important gold market in the world '.[7]

The British decision had been largely unilateral, even though the Fund appeared to have concurred with it to the extent of altering its rules (Rule F-4) so as to allow a wider margin within which the Bank of England could buy and sell gold and thus intervene—as had always been its habit—to prevent disturbing short-run fluctuations in the market.[8] It may be that the US authorities would have preferred at the time (as they certainly did later) that the London market had remained closed. But the period 1954 to the first half of 1956 was perhaps a high point in British self-assertion—one might almost say insubordination to American wishes. The Suez imbroglio resulted in a sharpened awareness of British dependence on the ' special relationship ', but in 1954 American aid to Britain was waning in importance. And it was largely due to British intransigence that the Eisenhower administration was reluctantly brought in the same year to accept a revision of the stringent Cocom rules applying the strategic embargo policy towards the Soviet bloc.

The great importance of London as a gold market lay in its function as a market for the suppliers as well as the consumers. Other European markets and those elsewhere in the world (e.g. Hong Kong, Macao, Beirut, Bombay, Kuwait, Cairo, Bahrein, Saigon, Bangkok, etc.) were consumers' markets where prices were apt to fluctuate according to largely local conditions. The French market in Paris was the monopoly of the Banque de France, which fed it (at a useful profit, naturally) in times of strong demand.

From the dealers' point of view, Swiss markets (chiefly that in Zurich) were near rivals to London. But the market relationship to government was very different, much less closely involved and therefore a less direct indicator of currency confidence or the lack of it. The

Swiss constitution required the Swiss central bank to maintain a certain level of gold reserves, so that while the economy remained strong, it was itself a buyer more than a market manager like the Bank of England or the Banque de France. Swiss commercial banks themselves normally held part of their assets in gold, while Swiss banking laws, regarding gold holding as a matter of natural prudence, not only allowed Swiss nationals but also foreigners to trade freely and openly in gold and to hold it without fear of disclosure. This freedom encouraged market activity. But there was not then, in Zurich or in any other Swiss centre, the parallel existence of a major international foreign exchange market—even within the same banks and offices— which made London as a gold market so sensitive to currency doubts and fears.

The growth of parallel markets, within and between international financial centres, was to be an important aspect of the rapid advance during the 1960s towards economic interdependence among the developed countries. It was noticed early on by Paul Einzig who wrote the first comprehensive description of the major parallel money markets.[9]

The point about the destabilizing effect on gold markets of proximity to a parallel and active foreign exchange market was well made on a later occasion by Mr Clarence Dansey, himself a London gold dealer. 'Several of us', he explained, 'maintain highly sophisticated exchange trading departments, one of whose functions is arbitraging between the gold and exchange markets. As was noted earlier, gold is bought and sold at the morning " fixing " in sterling. Consequently, if at the time of the " fixing " we have heavy sellers of sterling against dollars, we may be able to work out a better rate of exchange of buying gold against sterling and then finding a buyer of gold against dollars, than by executing the sterling selling order direct in the exchange market . . .'. He added that this was the situation if any one of the major European currencies, no matter whether sterling, French or Swiss francs, or marks, were under pressure. The technicalities would be different, but the end-result similar. 'Exchange markets today are so enlarged in turnover as the result of the growth of world trade and internationalisation of finance that, under present circumstances, they are normally adequate to absorb exchange operations resulting from or connected with gold transactions without undue effect.'[10]

The first shiver in the market came in March 1960, after the Sharpeville riots in South Africa. London dealers feared that more civil disturbances would follow and the supply of South African gold to the market—South Africa was the source of three-quarters of world production excluding the Soviet Union—might be interrupted. A minor price rise, however, was counteracted by some Russian gold sales in

May and the market quietened down again until about August. Then signs began to multiply that trouble was brewing.

The single most important predisposing factor producing this instability in the market was undoubtedly the state of the American economy and its payments deficit, especially in relation to Europe. The year 1960 saw a combination of deepening economic depression at home, of continuing deficit in the US balance of payments, and the political uncertainties of an impending change of President. The unhelpful converse of this picture was the recovering growth of the EEC countries, especially France and Germany, and their continuing payments surpluses fed in part by a strengthening outflow of short-term capital across the Atlantic.

This feature of the payments picture deserves some special attention since it was so big a cause of trouble in 1960–1 and in the years that followed. Between 1959 and 1960 this outflow jumped from $77m to $1,300m, reflecting a disparity between the low interest rates in the United States and the rising ones in Europe. Until August 1960, the US Federal Reserve discount rate was $3\frac{1}{2}$ per cent; afterwards it was brought down to 3 per cent as part of a deliberate effort to combat domestic recession. In Britain, where a deficit on current account was combined with an inflow of foreign funds, bank rate was 6 per cent, and in Germany, where the economy was showing serious signs of overstrain, the Bundesbank had actually raised bank rate to 5 per cent in June although it was reduced again to 4 per cent in October. Both Switzerland and Germany had also imposed penalties on foreign depositors of funds (see pp. 50–2 above). The consequence of this disparity in interest rates set by independent monetary authorities in national markets increasingly interacting with one another was visible in the quarterly figures for the outflow of short-term capital from the United States. The figures are in $m and seasonally adjusted to annual rates:

	Short-term capital	Errors & omissions	Total
1960—I	−400	—	−400
II	−800	−600	−1,400
III	−2,200	−600	−2,800
IV	−2,000	−1,200	−3,200

Some of these funds undoubtedly helped to build up the pressure of demand in the London gold market. Swiss banks, for instance, who were often the first to feel the impact of American outflows, were reported to be buying gold in London on behalf of their clients in July 1960. And after August it seems as if they were joined by agents of European central banks as an alternative to presenting their dollar assets for conversion at the US 'gold window'. When, as a result of this increased demand, the price in London moved above the shipping parity in New York, which was $35·255 an ounce, demand snowballed and private buyers took over from the central banks. The market began to hum with rumours of dollar devaluation or of closure of the gold window in the United States.

The real trouble, in short, started because of fears concerning the key currency in the system—the US dollar. Minor anxieties about market gluts or shortages, or changes in policy by minor players in the international monetary system, might be reflected in momentary uneasiness. But that was nothing to the possibility that there might be a break in the dollar's link to gold or in its exchange-value in terms of other currencies. And undoubtedly, such fears were greatly exacerbated by the political context (see above, pp. 49–50). In all likelihood neither the US deficit nor the interest rate differential, nor any of the minor influences on the gold price would have upset the market if an American presidential election had not been imminent. Eisenhower was retiring and the outcome of the Nixon–Kennedy contest was unpredictable. This introduced a major element of political uncertainty, and there was consequent nervousness about the future of the dollar. Wall Street opinion thought a Democratic victory would be certain to set off rampant inflation and to worsen rather than retrieve the situation. There were even rumours that Kennedy might contemplate raising the official price of gold, although he flatly denied that there was any truth in this rumour.

Earlier, in September 1960, at the IMF annual meeting in Washington, Bank of England representatives apparently urged on the Americans the necessity of countering speculative pressure by replenishing the Bank's stocks of gold, which had clearly been depleted by its attempt to keep the gold price down single-handed. At that time, although Banque de France officials also warned the Americans of the dangers in the market, the US Treasury was deaf to the warnings and was not prepared to support the Bank of England financially in its stabilizing operations. It seems probable, therefore, that when, on 17 October, the market began to move up, the Bank of England deliberately refrained from intervening and allowed the price in London to go as high as $40 an ounce in order to shock the Americans into responding. The price at the morning fixing on Thursday, 20 October, was the equivalent of $36·55 an ounce but sales took place later at over $40. On 21 October, the next day, the US Secretary of the Treasury issued a statement as follows:

The United States will continue its policy of buying gold from and selling gold to foreign governments, central banks and, under certain conditions, international institutions, for the settlement of international balances or for other legitimate monetary purposes at the established rate of $35 per fine troy ounce exclusive of handling charges. Treasury Secretary Anderson has stated many times in the past that it is our firm position to maintain the dollar at its existing gold parity.[11]

The corollary of this declaration was an important Anglo-American agreement, the essence of which was that the United States would provide the funds and the Bank of England would act as agent to intervene in the gold market. The agreement was probably reached at a meeting on 25 October 1960 between Maurice Parsons of the Bank of England and Robert Anderson, Eisenhower's Secretary to the Treasury. Anderson agreed to convert to gold at least part of the dollars which the Bank had accumulated as a result of trying to meet the demands of the market in the past few weeks. Two days later, on 27 October, the US Treasury issued a statement that the interventions in the market by the Bank of England were conducted with the 'full support of the US monetary authorities ',[12] and from then on the Bank of England took command of the market and by making supplies readily available held the price for the rest of the year below $36·50.

The United States was in fact adding some gold of its own to that of the Bank of England, on the understanding that the Bank would continue to act as a buffer-stock manager to hold down prices. It was a bilateral gold pool and in that sense a forerunner to the multilateral Gold Pool that was to follow.[13]

An equally important step was an agreement reached about the same time [14] whereby the European central banks, though they did not then join the bilateral pool, at least agreed not to obstruct it and to restrain their own reserve management policies so as to help it achieve its objective. They promised not to buy from the market whenever the price rose above $35·25. (This was the US dollar selling price plus shipping costs.) [15] Samuel Montagu's annual report stated that central bank buying ' virtually ceased ' in the last quarter of 1960.

What seems to have happened is that this self-denying agreement operated in the last quarter of 1960 but fell into abeyance about February 1961. This occurred when an accidental increase in new supplies to the market brought down the London ' fixing ' price from over $35·50, where it had been in January, to under $35·10 in March, and therefore allowed the central banks to re-enter the market without breaking the agreement. *The Times* City Editor reported of this spring lull as follows:

Since the closing week of February demand on the London gold market has been at such a low level that, with the exception of a few sporadic days, private sales have been adequate to meet its demands. To prevent a still further drift in prices, indeed, the Bank of England quite frequently has even to absorb offerings, for which private buyers were not forthcoming.

These supplies came from a variety of sources including the Soviet Union, for whom gold sales were an important source of foreign exchange.

Gold sales by Soviet Union ($m)

1957	. . 260	1963	. . 550
1958	. . 220	1964	. . 450
1959	. . 250	1965	. . 550
1960	. . 200	1966	. . —
1961	. . 260	1967	. . 15
1962	. . 215	1971	. . 100

It happened that at the same time pressure on sterling in the foreign exchange market caused the Bank of England to sell more gold from its own reserves to support the exchange rate. The combined result was that—without apparently breaking their agreement—the European central banks were able to add $773m and the United States $200m to their respective gold reserves between the end of February and the end of June 1961.

This phase of the market abruptly ended in July–August 1961. The BIS report already quoted noted that although official market management kept the London 'fixing' price below $35·20 for the rest of the year, the 'Vreneli' market price for gold coin in Switzerland jumped from about 16 per cent or 17 per cent over the corresponding gold bar price in June to over 30 per cent above it in July. This was equivalent to a gold bar price of more than $45 an ounce. The supply side of the market tightened: Canada and South Africa fed new gold into their own national reserves instead of the market, and demand strengthened with the general anxiety over Berlin and the reappearance of the US payments deficit at the end of the US fiscal year.

At the annual meeting of the Fund in Vienna in October 1961, Robert Roosa, Under-Secretary at the Treasury, made it clear that the United States was prepared to take stronger action to intervene in the market. Preparations were laid then for the formal proposal at the BIS meeting early in October to set up a multilateral buffer stock for the international management of the gold market. The US contribution to this buffer stock was to be $135m, and it would be exactly matched, collectively, by the Europeans. No actual stock of gold, of course, ever physically existed. And the central banks in practice only made available as much gold to the Bank of England as the latter thought was needed to stabilize the market, and did so in proportion to their respective total commitments. These commitments were as follows:

Germany	$30m
Britain, France, and Italy	$25m each
Belgium, Netherlands, and Switzerland	$10m each

It is noticeable that Sweden was not included in the Gold Pool agreement, nor were Canada or Japan; all were minimal gold holders. Nor was the commitment a formal one. No document, not even an executive agreement, was ever drawn up committing the parties expressly either to the earlier agreement to abstain from buying in the market or to that providing the resources for market management through the Gold Pool arrangements. Later the French contended that they had never understood the commitment to feed the Pool to be more than one for short-term stabilization. They did not feel an agreement had ever been made to fight the forces of the market *à l'outrance* or to suppress a springtide of market pressure. A breakwater, not a sea wall, was their concept of the arrangement. The Banque de France was in fact rather proud of its own record as manager of the national gold market, considered by some to be the outstanding success story of French monetary policy since 1948. By intervening only rarely but always effectively, the French central bank had kept the appearance of control and yet made a profit out of the speculators. In French eyes, the Gold Pool should have had a similar policy.

As well as the multilateral arrangement, the United States had an additional commitment to the Bank of England as agent for the Pool in case of speculation directed against the dollar. In that case, the United States agreed to make special sales to the Pool. Thus, in July 1962, it made a contribution of $35m as well as having to make good half the deficit which the Pool incurred in the previous two months.

The Pool agreement subtly changed the relation of the Bank of England to the London gold market. The Old Lady, formerly in sole charge (as had been the Banque de France in its management of the Paris gold market) was now acting on behalf of seven other national governments each entitled, by implication, to question and to supervise its stewardship.

In November 1961 the Gold Pool went into action, selling gold to the market over a period of a month. The price, which had been at or near $35·20 since mid-August, fell to $35·15 by early December.

The October 1961 agreement, however, was merely one half of a true buffer stock arrangement, in that it provided for the market manager to sell gold to the market but not to buy it. Assuming that price demand would ease sooner or later, it could only have resulted in a loss of gold from official reserves into private hands, and this was no part of the US interest. The deficiency was therefore made good in February 1962, when a parallel agreement was made to cover the buying of gold from the market when demand allowed. As in the case of the selling arrangement, the Bank of England acted for the whole group and distributed the gold rebought in the agreed proportions. By late May 1962 it had bought more than $80m of gold; but this had to be used to stabilize the market during the period of speculation following the fall on Wall Street and the flight from the Canadian dollar (June–July 1962). This was shortly followed by the Cuban crisis in the autumn of 1962, when buying of gold in London probably exceeded the 1960 gold rush; for two days the demand reached $45–$50m, all of which came out of the Pool.

Thus for 1962 the Gold Pool ended up all square. The following year it recorded a surplus (i.e. it was able to buy more gold than it had to sell) amounting to $600m. This trend continued into 1964 until October and the ensuing sterling crisis. The Gold Pool continued to operate through the middle years of the decade until its suspension in March 1968 (see below, chs 10 & 11).

US monetary policies

Before giving an account of the first Basle Agreement for the multilateral support of sterling—a step in international co-operation which, chronologically speaking, overlapped with the Gold Pool arrangement—it is worth noting that the flare-up in the gold market in October 1960 had an important political impact on US monetary authorities and monetary policies. For the first time since the appearance of the US balance-of-payments deficit, it stimulated some fairly radical rethinking of the ends and means of American monetary policy, both at home and abroad. And it marked an important change in international monetary relations in which the United States shifted away from splendid independence towards an acknowledgement of interdependence with other members of the affluent alliance in monetary matters. The United States thus recognized the potency of market forces and the need for collective as well as unilateral and bilateral action to contain them.

Thinking about it afterwards, and speaking in 1964 to a meeting organized by the Federal Reserve Bank of Boston, Mr Charles Coombs, president of the FRBNY, declared that the gold market crisis, more than anything else, had persuaded the US monetary authorities that they would have to develop new ways of defending the dollar. And it did indeed seem that while the warnings of economic pundits and prophets had so far fallen on rather deaf ears, and while the evidence presented by balance-of-payments figures had so far been largely ignored, the insistent forces of the market had finally succeeded in provoking a positive response.

One new way of defending the dollar the United States now discovered was to use its market weight, the monetary capability derived from the vast monetary resources of the government, to influence the market in accordance with its own objectives. By buying and selling heavily in the market, it could—instead of leaving the market to its own devices—intervene to quell and deter (by making less profitable) any tendency to speculative movements detrimental to the dollar. Hitherto, the Open Market Committee of the Federal Reserve System had dealt only in dollar securities as a means of managing public debt in accordance with national monetary objectives. In February 1961, however, the Committee decided that the FRBNY should in future undertake foreign exchange operations on behalf of the Committee, buying or selling foreign currencies in the markets.[16]

The point here was that speculation was potentially more profitable when the gap between the spot and forward markets for a currency was unstable and might become quite wide. As explained by Roosa, the leading architect of this policy change,

Forward trading can provide certainty through a facility open to anyone who wishes to have absolute protection against the risks, not of widely fluctuating spot rates, but of a single change in the official parity. The central bank can, in turn, by varying the extent of its own intervention in the forward market, allow the cost of this speculative hedge to go as high or as low as it wishes within the range of constraint set by the extent that trading pressures work back upon the spot rate from the forward rate.[17]

The main function indeed of the network of swap arrangements with other central banks which the United States initiated in 1961, and which will be described in great detail in a moment, was to underpin these interventions in the forward market for foreign exchange.

While these swaps have, to be sure, been drawn upon to meet various kinds of short-run swings in reserve needs, their usefulness as a backstop to forward transactions has at times been crucial for the fulfilment of operations that successfully thwarted the cumulative development of speculative pressures against the dollar.[18]

Forward intervention was not the only measure which the United States decided it could take unilaterally. One immediate measure taken by the Eisenhower administration on 14 January 1961 was probably more important for its psychological than its economic impact. It put a total ban, from the middle of 1961, on the purchase or holding of gold either by US citizens or US-owned corporations, outside as well as within the country's territorial limits. The latter right had been taken away in March 1933, when the Gold Hoarding Act had authorized the Secretary of the Treasury to call in all gold coin, bullion, or gold certificates and to exchange them for dollars.

A more important response was the change in interest rate policy—
that powerful weapon by which all modern governments seek to exert
influence on the national economy, partly through the market operations by which they manage their own public debt and partly through
the rules which they impose on banks and other private financial
operators in the credit system. Faced by rising unemployment demanding reflationary incentives to investment, and by the outflow of short-
term capital demanding higher rates to keep it at home, the American
monetary authorities began towards the end of 1960 to take steps to
make short-term interest rates in the United States more attractive
to foreign dollar-holders while holding down long-term rates. Reserve
requirements on the banks were eased and the balance of government
debt shifted from short to longer-term securities. These policies, aiming to separate and pursue contrary objectives at opposite ends of the
market, became known as ' operation twist '.

The strategy, however, was not entirely successful: the outflow
continued and other devices aimed at reviving confidence were tried.
President Kennedy declared firmly in his State of the Union message
to Congress on 30 January 1961 that the US dollar would not be
devalued. More effective was the decision to add to the incentives
offered to monetary authorities of other countries to hold dollars
without switching them suddenly and inconveniently either into gold
or other currencies.

The chief means chosen to this particular end was the Roosa bond
—non-marketable bonds normally issued to foreign monetary authorities for two years and denominated not in dollars but in the currency
of the holding country, and thus proof against a dollar devaluation.
A key feature of the Roosa bonds was that the holder could, at his
own option, convert the bonds into ordinary 90-day US Treasury bills
and in turn could convert these bills into cash on demand at two days'
notice. Thus foreign central banks could earn interest while holding
dollars, but their dollar assets could qualify as liquid assets for
purposes of central bank accounting.

Roosa, whose brainchild they were, explained the advantages which
the bonds gave the United States as a reserve currency country. They
increased the borrowing power of the United States without putting
an additional burden on the IMF. And they gave the United States
an added power to provide bilateral credit to one ally or associate
without expense to itself by drawing on the willingness of another to
increase its holdings of Roosa bonds. This facility was exercised,
for example, in 1964 when bonds initially denominated in Italian lire
were retired and, because Italy was then in balance-of-payments
difficulty, were replaced with a corresponding new issue of bonds

denominated in D-marks and held by the Bundesbank (see below, pp. 130–1).

The same objective was pursued by further measures in October 1962. When the Federal Reserve had amended Regulation Q (see above, p. 60) to allow the banks to pay more attractive rates of interest on certain kinds of savings and time deposits, foreign official time deposits were exempted from the regulation altogether.

To sum up, however, two points may be made. First, though US policies were in some measure responsive to the pressures from the balance of payments, it must be stressed that this was not yet by any means the prime objective of the new administration's economic policies. The President's special balance-of-payments message to Congress on 6 February 1961 set out four economic objectives—all domestic. Only a few days later, as a kind of afterthought, did the President add his fifth objective: to restore confidence in the dollar and to cut the US payments deficit.

Secondly, although the new interest-rate policy, the restrictions on gold holding, the resort to forward market intervention, and the invention of Roosa bonds all represented new departures in US monetary policy, and significantly displayed a new concern for the balance of payments, yet apparently no consideration whatever was given to more radical options. There was little disposition in Washington to calculate the results that might be achieved by an attack on the other two items in the deficit: government spending abroad and US investments overseas. As will be seen from the table on p. 83, a breakdown of the US balance of payments in the period 1960–70 shows that military spending abroad in 1960 was $3·1 billion; US private direct investment was $1·7 billion; and US government loans and aid programmes $2·8 billion. By comparison, the item for that year's annual outflow of short-term capital of $1·3 billion was less burdensome. Yet the US administration in 1961 quickly increased government spending on defence, as on space research and public works— mainly because this was a rapidly acting and effective way of bringing down domestic unemployment and reviving economic confidence at home. At this time, there was little recognition in the United States of any compelling need—given the country's great economic strength— to cut the national coat according to its cloth. A series of palliative prescriptions appeared quite adequate to deal with the situation.[19]

The Basle Agreement and the support of sterling

Meanwhile, and as the Kennedy administration settled in and gained the confidence of other governments and of the private operators, the pressures shifted from the dollar to the other reserve currency,

US balance of payments 1960–70 (US$ billion)

	1960	1961	1962	1963	1964	1965	1966	1967	1968	1969	1970
Payments and Receipts											
Goods	4·9	5·5	4·5	5·2	6·8	4·8	3·8	3·8	0·7	0·7	2·1
Services	2·2	3·0	3·6	3·6	4·6	5·1	5·1	5·6	6·3	6·1	6·4
Military	−3·1	−3·0	−3·1	−3·0	−2·9	−3·0	−3·8	−4·5	−4·5	−4·9	−4·8
Goods and services	4·0	5·5	5·0	5·8	8·5	6·9	5·1	4·9	2·5	1·9	3·7
Remittances and pensions	−0·7	−0·7	−0·8	−0·9	−0·9	−1·0	−1·0	−1·3	−1·1	−1·2	−1·4
US govt grants and capital	−2·8	−2·8	−3·1	−3·6	−3·6	−3·4	−3·4	−4·0	−4·0	−3·8	−3·5
US private capital (net)											
Direct investment	−1·7	−1·6	−1·7	−2·0	−2·4	−3·4	−3·5	−3·0	−3·2	−3·1	−4·0
Other long term	−0·9	−1·0	−1·2	−1·7	−2·0	−1·1	−0·3	−1·3	−1·1	−1·6	−0·9
Short term	−1·3	−1·6	−0·5	−0·8	−2·1	0·8	0·4	−1·2	−1·1	−0·6	−1·5
Foreign capital (net) (long term only)	0·4	0·7	1·0	0·7	0·7	0·3	2·5	3·1	6·0	4·0	4·4
Errors and unrecorded transactions	−0·9	−0·9	−1·1	−0·3	−0·3	−0·4	−0·3	−1·1	−0·5	−2·8	−1·3
Balance											
Liquidity basis	−3·9	−2·4	−2·2	−2·7	−2·8	−1·3	−1·4	−3·5	0·2	−7·0	−4·7
Official reserve transaction basis	−3·4	−1·3	−2·7	−2·0	−1·6	−1·3	0·3	−3·4	1·6	2·7	−10·7
'Basic' balance	−1·7	0·1	−0·6	−1·6	0·2	−1·7	−0·7	−1·8	1·8	−3·6	−1·9

Source: Compiled from US Dept of Commerce, Survey of current business.

sterling, and from the gold market to the foreign exchange markets. The turmoil here appeared to have been started off by the revaluation on 5 March 1961 of the D-mark by 5 per cent, which was immediately followed by a nearly equal revaluation of the Dutch guilder. Why this apparently remedial measure should have proved so upsetting can only be explained by the underlying jitteriness of the market in foreign exchange, which could see for itself rather formidable imbalances between the major currencies, as reflected in their payments figures. There was little conviction among those financially concerned that the German-Dutch measures were the end of the story. Had the revaluations been big enough? Or would there have to be a second bite at the cherry? Would they be followed by the French, the Italians, the Swiss—all of whom had also large surpluses? And in particular, would the sterling rate hold steady?

The result of such questions was a rush for cover, a hasty search to secure money by holding it in places in which, at best, it might appreciate and in which at the worst it would be safe from overnight depreciation. On Monday, 6 March 1961 alone, $180m poured into Switzerland; by the following Friday $120m had followed it, and the same week another $200m was believed to have flowed into Germany.[20] Most of these funds came from London. This was mainly because London was a major international financial centre—the place where short-term money, whatever its national origin, could best find a ready and profitable use. But, obviously, if there was any risk of a change in the sterling-dollar rate or even of the sterling-D-mark or sterling-lira rate, the prudent owner or dealer would be wise to make a shift out of sterling. Consequently this was the most chaotic week in the currency market since convertibility—and indeed since the interwar period.

By great good luck, the next Monday was the second in the month, and by BIS tradition the central bankers were due to meet at Basle for their regular monthly weekend.

They emerged with what was apparently the first press statement ever to come from these normally discreet and private happenings. The bankers wished it to be known that they were not contemplating any further change in exchange rates: and furthermore that they were co-operating closely in the exchange markets.

This preliminary rather bald statement was followed a week later by a slightly more informative one which explained that they were acting with a view to discouraging speculation and minimizing the repercussions of 'hot' money movements on countries' reserve positions. Their co-operation was to take the form of holding each others' currencies to a greater extent than previously instead of converting them immediately into gold or into dollars, and of short-term lending of needed currencies: 'These procedures will be temporary, pending the evolution of more permanent techniques for dealing with the problems of international financial disequilibria, particularly short-term capital movement within the framework of, or through reform of, the International Monetary Fund.' [21]

The 1961 Basle Agreement, in short, was neither legally nor formally speaking an agreement at all, but simply a public statement of intentions by central bankers intended to tranquillize and cool an overheated foreign exchange market. The bankers themselves strenuously denied that there had ever been an agreement. 'Il n'y a jamais eu ... de gentlemen's agreement de Basle', said M. Baumgartner afterwards at the Vienna meeting of the Fund in 1961, 'mais il n'y a à Basle que des gentlemen'.[22] And they always insisted on calling it a 'so-called' agreement. Nevertheless its importance as a turning point in international monetary co-operation has been generally agreed. The IMF *Chronicle* in its account emphasized this: 'From this so-called Basle Agreement much has stemmed both as regards closer co-operation between central banks and as regards the supplementation of gold by alternative forms of international liquidity.' [23]

In practical terms, the agreement meant that central banks would undertake two kinds of restorative action. First, they would agree to accumulate foreign currency (e.g. sterling) and to hold it for three or six months on the understanding that the originating monetary authority (e.g. the Bank of England) would reverse the transaction, buying back the sterling and replacing it with dollars or local currency (or, in the Swiss case, gold) at the end of the holding period. *This reversal would take place at the same exchange rates as the original transfer.* With this guarantee, the host central bank could afford to offer a similar exchange rate guarantee to its local commercial banks so that in effect it was often these who held the sterling on behalf of their respective central banks.

The second restorative measure applied mainly to easily identifiable hot money movements. They could be 'recycled', so that the host country to which the funds had fled would neutralize the effect of this movement on the foreign exchange market by immediately depositing a corresponding sum (e.g. a three-month dollar deposit) to the same value to the account of the central bank of the country from which the funds had fled.

The difference between these two arrangements and the 'swaps' later negotiated by the United States and other central banks (see below, pp. 136ff.) is that the swaps were precautionary rather than restorative. A line of credit of fixed amount was agreed which could be automatically activated within the agreed period and up to the agreed amount. It was then reversed, unless (as increasingly happened) it was renewed for a further three–six-month period. During its existence, however, a swap automatically increased the foreign exchange reserves credited to each of the participating central banks. The Basle Agreement caused no such increase but provided the surety that there would be emergency aid of limited duration from the central banks of those countries to whom the hot money flowed for greater security.

There were two politically significant points about the Basle Agreement for mutual support. One was that it introduced, along with Roosa bonds, the principle of an exchange guarantee for a reserve currency, for Britain agreed that sterling acquired by another central bank at (e.g.) a $2·80 rate, would be restored to it at the same rate even if in the meanwhile the official rate were to be altered by devaluation. This was an important departure because the British, by maintaining their intention to restore sterling to its former status as an international currency, had hitherto persistently implied that no such guarantee was needed, and that none could therefore be given.

The other point was that the 1961 Basle Agreement recruited the European central banks as a group to the support of sterling, whereas in previous sterling crises the support had been either automatic, from the IMF under standby arrangements, or bilateral from the United States. The initiative for the recycling of hot money came from Max Iklé, the IMF Governor for Switzerland, but it seems to have been the United States who took the lead in suggesting the publication of the two Basle communiqués.[24]

As noted in the previous chapter, the concept of central bank co-operation was not by any means new; and though it was over twenty years since it had been practised in any significant fashion, there was quite an extensive fund of interwar experience to draw on in dealing with the technical aspects of mutual assistance and support in the management of foreign exchange markets. Perhaps the nearest precedent from that time for the 1961 Basle Agreement was the arrangement that had been made thirty years before, in August 1931, by which the Federal Reserve Bank and the Banque de France each extended credit lines of up to $125m in their respective currencies to the Bank of England to help the latter hold the sterling rate. The failure finally to do so, it could be argued, was less due to the inadequacy of Franco-American support than to the lack of firmness and resolution by the British government, the absence—indeed, the physical collapse—of Montagu Norman, and some ineptitude in the Bank of England's handling of the market. For, at a time when the flight of funds from sterling on the worst day of the crisis—Friday, 18 September 1931—was a mere £18m (compared with the sums ten and twenty times as great that became common in the 1960s and

1970s), a swap credit of $250m adroitly employed, should have sufficed.[25]

The political importance of this new Anglo-American monetary dependence on Europe was to prove evident throughout the 1960s, both in the attempt to expand the lending power of the IMF through the GAB and in the later negotiations for the Fund's reform. It was to have a significant influence on the political and diplomatic relations between European governments and the United States.

Britain was, of course, the sole immediate beneficiary under the agreement, and between March and July 1961 received total support worth $900m under it. Most of this was repaid by the end of September 1961 but only with the help of the $1,500m drawing from the IMF in August and September.

The irony of the Basle story was that the agreement would never have had to be made at all but for the crisis of confidence in sterling. Yet the circumstances in which this failure of confidence threatened the equilibrium of the whole international monetary system could be attributed in large part to the British themselves, and in particular to the obstinate pride of the Bank of England.

In the first place, it was the British government and the officials of the Treasury and the Bank of England who had deliberately encouraged the use of London as an international market place and as a depository for foreign short-term funds. In the previous year, Britain had had a current account deficit larger than in any year since 1951—the post-Korean war crisis. The outflow of long-term capital for direct overseas investment continued unabated and the government had to make large payments to the IMF as well as continuing to bear exceptionally heavy bills for military spending overseas. All of this large deficit, however, had been completely masked by ' other receipts ' of $2·5 billion. The reserves consequently increased by $495m. ' Most of these receipts ', the BIS inferred, ' were due to the level of interest rates in London from June 1960 onwards. The principal items in the $2·5 milliard inflow were unidentified receipts of $1 milliard and additions of the same size to foreign countries' sterling balances.' [26] And the figures show that between June and December 1960 total non-sterling holdings topped their previous 1947 peak at £1,276m. Non-sterling-area official balances increased by $112m and non-sterling-area private balances increased by $224m. (This excludes a freak factor which was the special acquisition of £131m in sterling in 1960 by the Ford Company of Detroit, which intended to purchase shares in its subsidiary, the British Ford Motor Company, and did so the following year. This caused an increase of foreign sterling balances in 1960 and a corresponding decrease by the same amount in 1961.)

In short, the distribution of sterling balances in the period before the Basle Agreement had undergone a substantial change. Between December 1957, which was the last end-year before convertibility, and December 1960, privately held (and therefore more volatile) sterling balances increased from 23 per cent of the total to 33 per cent, while official holdings declined from 77 per cent to 67 per cent. And the proportion of all sterling balances held inside the more 'solid' sterling area declined in the same period from 80 to 66 per cent.

Luring private funds to London—the total inflow in 1960 was put at $600m—with high interest rates, free and open rules, and low costs was part of the story. Providing market facilities for the nascent international business in Eurodollars was another: London already had 77 international banks. In the first half of 1960 US banks increased their deposits in London by £160m and their advances to customers by slightly less. British and other foreign banks did the same. Altogether there was a marked increase in deposits over the whole year by US, British overseas, and other foreign banks and acceptance houses of £424m.

The United States, of course, was also partly responsible for this development in so far as by amending the provisions of Regulation Q it had encouraged a sudden and unexpected ebb-tide of funds from the United States to Europe. This outflow had been deliberately repelled by the Germans and the Swiss and most of it found a home in London. The harvest was reaped the next year when all but 20 per cent of the corresponding outflow of short-term money had to be covered by official British government short-term borrowing under the terms of the Basle Agreement.

There was a second irony in the situation that went back still further into the history of the 1950s. It was that when sterling was in danger of drowning in 1961, it seemed to some continental European eyes at least that it was very largely Britain's own fault that the lifeboats which might have been available were for practical purposes unusable. For this the Bank of England was at least partly responsible. The Bank had rejected American invitations to scale down postwar sterling balances, and had opposed the plan for floating the pound known as Operation Robot. And it was the Bank which had suspected that an EMA might create a rival international mechanism to sterling and thought the job of intermediary between European currencies would be better done—and with greater profit to the City and greater prestige to Britain—by the London foreign exchange market. For it will be remembered that it was as a result of pressure from the Bank of England that the EMA had remained a dead letter. In negotiating the arrangements for it, the Bank therefore had insisted that members could draw dollars from the EMA fund in exchange for accumulated surpluses of European currencies but would have to pay a rate which would always be less favourable than the rate they could get from the foreign exchange market. The only exceptional circumstance when the agreement would provide more attractive conversion rates was when a currency was devalued, the reason for this being that each EMA member enjoyed (as it had under the old EPU) a dollar guarantee of any other European currencies held by its central bank.

The net result had been that the European Fund, which was one part of the EMA, had been used only as an ambulance service for the peripheral weaklings of Europe: Turkey, Greece, Iceland, and Spain. And the multilateral settlement system which was to have been its other part—and could conceivably have been ready to aid Britain in 1961 (when the moment of need arose) was hardly used at all.

Instead, the British had been obliged by circumstances partly beyond their control to look to the United States and to the Fund and not to Europe for support in their hour of need. Thus was established one of the major themes of international monetary relations in the 1960s. This dependence of sterling on backing which only the United States could provide, however, only increased the need of the United States in its turn to seek further measures of multilateral monetary co-operation from European members of the affluent alliance.

Notes

[1] Gold Purchase Act 1935/Gold Reserve Act January 1934, 48 Stat. 337.

[2] The statement of the Secretary of the US Treasury, 13 Oct 1936 (*IMF*, i. 7).

[3] Originally Britain and France with the United States. The facility was later extended to Belgium, the Netherlands, and Switzerland.

[4] See *IMF*, ii. There is a further account in League of Nations, *International currency experience*, p. 147.

[5] Sec. 3, para. 2 of the White Plan, as amended June 1943 (see *IMF*, iii. 88).

[6] EB Decision No. 233–2, 11 Dec 1947 (*IMF*, iii. 225).

[7] *Bank of England Quarterly Bulletin*, Mar 1964.

[8] IMF, *Ann. rep.*, 1955, pp. 97–8.

[9] Paul Einzig, *Parallel money markets*; i. *The new markets in London*; ii. *Overseas markets* (London, 1971–2).

[10] C. M. Dansey, 'Non-official transactions in gold: their effect upon exchange markets', in R. Z. Aliber, ed., *The international market for foreign exchange* (New York, 1969). The book was based on a conference held at Ditchley Park in 1967 which included officials of international financial organizations, national central banks, and market operators.

[11] *New York Times*, 21 Oct 1960. The operative phrase in the statement seems to be 'legitimate monetary purposes'. It was suggested at the time that perhaps the United States had already refused privately to sell gold to some European central banks on the grounds that they might be seeking to buy gold with 'hot dollars' bought in the open market, and that this was not a legitimate monetary purpose. See for example Lombard, *FT*, 25 Oct 1960. The plain implication in any case was that the US gold window was to stay open but it might not invariably be kept so even to official buyers.

[12] *Federal Reserve Bull.*, Mar 1964.

[13] See Lombard, *FT*, 9 Nov 1960.

[14] BIS, *Ann. rep.*, 1962, p. 125.

[15] Dansey emphatically dates this agreement from March 1961. Either he is mistaken or else this later agreement was a reiteration of the earlier one; or perhaps he is referring to a further agreement which included additional central banks.

[16] See *Federal Reserve Bull.*, Sept 1962: Treasury and Federal Reserve Exchange Operations.

[17] Robert V. Roosa, *Monetary reform for the world economy* (New York, 1965), pp. 30–31.

[18] Ibid., p. 32. It will be recalled that the British also adopted this strategy after much heart-searching technical debate in 1962 (see Strange, *Sterling and British policy*, pp. 237ff).

[19] Some part of the blame for this attitude towards the deficit must perhaps be taken by the statistical services. The US balance-of-payments accounts undoubtedly exaggerated the importance of short-term capital outflow in contributing to the overall deficit. They did so by presenting a gross and not a net figure, which would of course have been smaller. That is to say, they included a figure showing US residents' short-term assets abroad, but no corresponding figure showing non-residents' short-term assets in the United States. A full explanation of these peculiarities in the US accounts is given in vol. 1, pt. IV, by George Ray.

[20] Hirsch, *Money international*, p. 242.

[21] BIS press statement, 12 Mar 1961 (quoted in *IMF*, i. 483).

[22] Quoted in Hirsch, *Money international*, p. 243.

[23] *IMF*, i. 483.

[24] *IMF*, i. 483; Max Iklé, in Federal Reserve Bank of Boston, *International central banking symposium*, Oct 1964.

[25] For a full account of the circumstances surrounding the 1931 support for sterling, see Stephen Clarke's scholarly study, *Central bank cooperation*, pp. 182–219. Clarke concluded that ' It is doubtful whether in the circumstances, sterling could have been saved by even the most drastic combination of measures that the authorities of the day could have adopted, but the program that actually was adopted was definitely a second best, even by the standards of mid-1931. While the total amount of credits obtained was considered very substantial, they were not granted in a single impressive package but in two separate arrangements. The first set of credits was unaccompanied by any additional measures to check the pressure on sterling, and the second set . . . was only announced after it was known in the markets that the first credits had been virtually exhausted. The handling of the crisis was a source of frustration and disappointment to the central bankers ' (p. 204).

[26] BIS, *Ann. rep.*, 1960–1, p. 142.

4

THE INTERNATIONAL MONETARY FUND:
NEW RESPONSES

The hypothesis was tentatively suggested in the last chapter that national governments and central banks were apt to react to crisis situations arising in the gold and foreign exchange markets rather promptly and, when it came to the crunch, without too much argument about ends and means, or the sharing out of costs and benefits. The corollary to this, now to be examined, is that the same governments when faced with a perceived need to adapt or modify established international organizations, or to construct new ones, were apt to be much slower in their responses, more suspicious of each other's motives, and more jealously defensive of their perceived national interests—with the result that the consequent negotiations between them tended to be more difficult and extended. If indeed this is so, it should be possible to suggest from the historical evidence why there should have been these two contrasting styles in the way developed countries set about the management of the international monetary system.

Was it because in crisis situations it was the central bankers who had the initiative and they were by nature conscious of a kind of free-masonry in the common defence of monetary order against the forces of anarchy, and at the same time were somewhat indifferent to the political rewards and political penalties of pursuing or of failing to pursue goals dictated by narrow national self-interest? Conversely, was it because in non-crisis situations the responsibility rested with finance ministers who by their nature as politicians could not afford to ignore just such domestic political considerations? Alternatively, was it simply that the necessity to act quickly conveyed to any national representative, whether central banker or finance minister, and to their officials a sense of urgency lacking when there was time to weigh the pros and cons of alternative institutional mechanisms and alternative terms for a written commitment, whether contained in a formal international treaty or in an exchange of letters?

A fourth alternative explanation might be that the decisions taken in crisis situations were actually of less importance, and were seen as less salient to the national interest, than those taken at greater leisure regarding the functioning of permanent international organizations.

The one perhaps involved shorter-term, more easily retracted or more limited financial and policy commitments than the other and could therefore be more nonchalantly assumed.

The evidence to be examined in order to see whether any of these explanations is tenable will include the changes made in the IMF in the late 1950s and early 1960s and the arrangements supplementary to the Fund negotiated in 1962, and subsequently known as the General Arrangements to Borrow.

For although it might seem that the GAB negotiations were a discrete diplomatic event, neatly suitable for case-study treatment, yet they can also and perhaps better be seen as part of a continuing process whose beginnings went back much earlier into the 1950s. By this process the Fund, originally conceived as a rather rigid, almost mechanically automatic mechanism and one with limited resources and restrictively defined functions, began slowly to unbend, to become more flexible, and to expand, both in terms of the resources it could make available to its members and in terms of the circumstances in which it was prepared to assume responsibility to assist them financially. This process of adaptation, the moulding of a written constitution to the exigencies of the real world, was one which greatly accelerated in the course of the 1960s to the point where the Fund underwent very substantial changes in its *modus operandi* and came to occupy a more central role in international relations.

Standby arrangements

A specific development which started before the 1960s but was immensely important for the Fund's role in the 1960s was the invention, and subsequent refinement of, the ' standby ' arrangement by which members could draw more and quicker Fund credit in case they needed it. Complementary to it was the Executive Directors' decision to allow Fund credit to be given to cover deficits occurring on capital as well as on current payments accounts. Both are worth a little consideration. We can consider on the way the related question of the resources which the Fund could make available to its members and the constraints that limited their further expansion within the structure of the Fund itself, thus leading on to the negotiation of a new credit arrangement partly outside the Fund.

Essentially, the standby arrangements were a combination of a declaration by a Fund member of the fiscal and monetary policies which it intended to pursue, and a promise by the IMF to grant drawings to the member up to a fixed amount promptly and without further argument for one year. It was a confirmed line of credit, which enlarged the liquidity of the member, conditionally upon the carrying out of the policies declared in its Letter of Intent and which acted as a confidence-building support for a member's economic policies rather than meeting its immediate balance-of-payments needs.[1] The arrangements were initiated as early as February 1952, when the Fund's Executive Board elaborated the terms on which members could draw on their gold and credit tranches. At the same time, the Managing Director added as a statement of principle, that a member might 'ensure that it would be able to draw if, within a period of 6 to 12 months, the need presented itself '.[2]

The first standby arrangement was granted to Belgium in June 1952, and the following October the Board laid down the general principles governing standby arrangements.[3] While the Fund would apply the same principles to standby arrangements as it applied to ordinary drawings (i.e. they would be subject to a review of a member's payments position and prospects), the standby was only to be given on the understanding that a member would be pursuing particular policies to alleviate specific economic problems within a defined period; in particular, to control inflation, arrest a decline in foreign exchange reserves, prevent any increase in debt service, or lay the foundations for sustained economic growth. While ordinary drawings were supposed to be subject to generally applied conditions, the terms for standbys were more flexible and would vary from case to case.

The rules governing standby arrangements began to develop in 1956–7 and were further refined in 1958–9. Three broad types of arrangement emerged.[4]

In the first category were the sort of arrangements made with South Africa in March 1958 and with Britain in 1957 and 1958. These involved no special conditions. The second group required more definite policy statements by the member making the drawing. For instance, the arrangement made with France in 1958 was made ' in consideration of the policies and intentions of the French government with regard to the stabilization programme '. The third group included arrangements with a much more detailed list of conditions. The countries concerned were mainly in Latin America : the arrangement with Chile, approved in March 1958, included a letter from the Managing Director to the minister of finance setting out Chile's problems and the steps required to deal with them. Chile was required to keep in close touch with the Fund, and accepted the Fund's discretionary right to give notice that it would block the drawing at any time.

Two important decisions at the turn of the decade carried the development of standby arrangements further. In 1958 the arrangement with Peru inaugurated the practice of the Letter of Intent. This set out explicitly the Peruvian government's proposals for corrective action to be carried out as part of its stabilization programme. The

Letter of Intent formally expressed the member's acceptance that standby arrangements were granted on condition that the policies and intentions set out in the letter were followed. It also provided an occasion for the Fund to conduct regular 'consultations' with the member concerned.[5] A feature of earlier standby arrangements was the 'prior notice' clause (as in the Chilean standby). This was included in about thirty arrangements made before 1960, and assured the Fund's right, so long as it gave prior notice, to suspend the member's right to draw further on the standby credit.

For example, in the earlier arrangement with Peru in 1954, the staff pointed out that for members with fluctuating exchange rates and uncertain economic conditions who were embarking on complex stabilization programmes, protective clauses were a necessity. The prior notice right, however, was only exercised once, with Bolivia in 1958. The Bolivian government informed the Board that it was unable to carry out the stabilization programme which the standby had been granted to support, and the staff gave notice that no further drawings should be made until new terms had been agreed upon by the Bolivian government and the Fund.[6] According to Gold, the Board never again invoked this right because the directors considered it would be 'too severe an international reproof to administer to a member'.[7]

The retreat from an open display of toughness by the Fund continued from this point on. When a standby arrangement was made for Paraguay in 1959, the UAR Executive Director, Ahmed Zaki Saad, questioned the propriety of including a prior notice clause. And by February 1961 the Executive Board had come to the conclusion that the clause might be omitted, and could safely be replaced by one which called for 'consultation and agreement' on new terms. Thus the next standby arrangement, with Peru in February 1961, contained the undertaking that Peru would consult the Fund before making a fresh drawing if the government departed from its stabilization programme. This obligation to consult, rather than any visible threat to stop or interrupt drawings, was increasingly adopted by the Fund in its arrangements with Latin American countries. For example, when Guatemala wanted an arrangement in August 1961, the Fund at first stipulated that only $10m of the total $15m standby could be drawn before consultation. But many directors took exception to the implied threat and when the point next arose in 1964, the staff conceded that it was not 'standard practice'.

An alternative technique developed by the Fund to keep its power as creditor without giving overt offence to debtor governments was the declaration of objective performance criteria, concerning, for instance, the limitation of domestic credit to a fixed amount. The first standby arrangement to include such specific commitments was that with Paraguay in 1957; [8] another was with Haiti in 1958. And from 1959 onwards, performance criteria were usually included in standby arrangements; and when drawings were made in the higher tranches, members were asked for specific policy commitments assuring the Fund that stabilization programmes would be pursued. This practice still left room for wide variation in the range and number of these commitments. Sometimes ceilings were imposed on the domestic assets of central banks, or commitments given to maintain specific exchange rates. Sometimes, as in the Letter of Intent attached to the standby arrangement made with Colombia in December 1965, a specific commitment was given linking exchange rate policy to the balance-of-payments results. Or there would be provision for consultations between a government and the Board in the event of a major shift occurring in government policy. The agreements with Australia in April 1961 and with Chile in February 1964 both provided for new consultations (and, if necessary, new understandings between the government and the IMF) if this happened. By 1965 this sort of clause was still being used, but it was gradually being replaced by another which merely called for consultations when any of the objectives of the programme were not achieved.

An illustration of the flexibility which standby arrangements allowed the Fund in dealing with less developed countries can be found in the standby for $100m arranged with India in 1962. At that date the Fund's holdings of rupees were already equivalent to 131 per cent of India's quota, and if the standby were fully drawn upon, the Fund's holdings would rise to 148 per cent of quota. France's Director, M. de Largentaye, noted that the stabilization programme embodied in the arrangement and the Letter of Intent was much less specific than was normally required for drawings in the second credit tranche; there was only one quantitative limitation, on the fiscal deficit. [9] Although this arrangement was approved, subsequent arrangements with India did include more performance criteria.

From even this brief summary it is clear that the customary procedures of the Fund regarding standby credits were largely evolved in the late 1950s and early 1960s through its relations with developing countries, especially with those in Latin America. Inevitably—and perhaps in some degree justifiably—these procedures were criticized for using an international organization to provide a nicely deodorized velvet glove within which the iron fist of the United States could assure American capitalism of the continued economic stability and ' good behaviour ' of the Western hemisphere. The Fund therefore came under attack for putting too much emphasis in its relations with less developed countries on orthodox balance-of-payments policies and for insisting that they put economic stability too far ahead of economic growth in their national priorities.

But these very attacks and the Fund's sensitivity when proud but poor countries objected to the ' strings ' that seemed to be attached to standby credits by prior notice clauses, by performance criteria, and by Letters of Intent resulted in practice in a substantial retreat by the Fund from the more rigid, more overbearingly authoritarian posture it had at first adopted. Not only did it increasingly stand ready to temper the wind to the shorn lamb—in the Indian case, even to be exaggeratedly tender—but it was prepared more and more to rely on a broad commitment on the part of the borrowing country to consult with its staff missions for hard and fast terms regarding economic policies, targets, and exchange rates. And even when performance criteria were laid down and were not achieved, the Fund's accumulating experience suggested that the fault might lie with fallible economic forecasting as much as with the inadequacies of policy. Thus it was that no instance arose of an open dispute between a member and the Fund about failure to observe performance criteria. They were a target, not a condition, of aid. Yet they were not entirely a polite fiction for, as Gold concluded, they

contribute to the adjustment process by encouraging members to pursue programmes that will assist them to overcome their problems, and they assure members of support by the Fund, while at the same time helping to protect the Fund's resources against improper use with a minimum of formality and publicity.[10]

Two results followed from this retreat. One was that the Fund's gradual adoption of both a low profile and a flexible posture in its relations with countries making standby credit arrangements made it much easier for richer and even prouder countries (and notably for Britain) to seek its assistance in balance-of-payments difficulties. For though the overwhelming majority of actual arrangements were with developing countries, these were mostly on a very small scale (see table, p. 98). When a rich country drew—in proportion to its quota —it drew large amounts. Thus Britain drew $1,500m in 1961; $1,000m in 1964; $1,400m in 1965, and the same again in 1968. By comparison, when India drew on the Fund it was never for more than $250m, and most drawings by developing countries were for much less.

Thus, in the light of Fund practice developed in the years between about 1957 and 1962, it did not in the 1960s seem so odd for a British Chancellor of the Exchequer in 1964 and in 1965 to write a Letter of Intent to the Managing Director, detailing the policies which HM government intended to pursue and undertaking, if these policies did not succeed, to take further action in consultation with the Fund (see below, ch. 5). In a way, therefore, it was thanks to the sensibilities of the poor countries and to the inclination of the Fund's Executive Board to humour them during this formative period that the British and the French were later able to make such heavy use of standby credits from the Fund to support and sustain their exchange rates.

The second result of the evolution of standby arrangements was to establish yet more firmly close but private links between the international staff of the Fund and national officials of Finance Ministries and central banks in developed as well as developing countries.

As we have seen, the standby arrangements increasingly rested on the obligation to consult, using this at once as a veil and as a political defusing device. This often added substantially to the clout or influence exercised by the economic policy-makers in national governments. And the increased dependence of standby arrangements on consultation commitments also contributed much to members' acceptance of consultation as normal practice in international monetary relations.

According to the Articles of Agreement, consultation—obligatory under Article XIV on countries whose currencies were not fully convertible—was not required of those that undertook the obligations of Article VIII. But the Executive Board on 1 June 1960 declared that because the IMF could provide technical facilities and advice, ' there was great merit in periodic discussions between the Fund and its members, even though no questions arise involving action under Article XIV '.[11] And in fact consultations were maintained after a large number of currencies became convertible in 1958.

Thus when members in non-dependent situations were regularly consulting the Fund staff, it was not so big a jump for the Fund to insist on consultation as a condition of standby assistance, and again in the event of change in a country's payments position or in the policies adopted to cope with it.

Fund resources for capital deficits

The standby arrangements, however, would have been no use to the developed countries had the original Fund rule stood, under Article VI, that resources were not to be used to finance a ' large or sustained ' outflow of capital. This rule had been confirmed in a formal interpretation, as provided for under Article XVIII, by the Executive Board (Decision no. 71–2). In 1946 this had firmly declared that ' authority to use the resources of the Fund is limited to use in accordance with its purposes to give temporary assistance in financing balance of payments deficits on current account for monetary stabilization operations '.

The general change-over to convertibility of currencies in 1958 and the abandonment of exchange controls on capital flows (and the con-

Drawings on the IMF, 1948–71 (US $m)

	1947–58	1959	1960	1961	1962	1963	1964	1965	1966	1967	1968	1969	1970	1971
Industrial countries	1,910·1	—	—	1,500·0	300·0	—	1,750·0	1,835·0	802·5	—	2,771·0	2,392·3	1,273·0	1,362·0
US	—	—	—	1,500·0	300·0	—	525·0	435·0	680·0	—	200·0	—	150·0	1,362·0
UK	861·5*	—	—	1,500·0*	*	*	1,000·0	1,400·0	122·5*	*	1,400·0*	850·0*	150·0	—
Industrial Europe	799·7	—	—	—	—	—	—	—	—	—	745·0	1,542·0	973·0	—
of which France	518·8	—	—	—	—	—	—	—	—	—	745·0	500·0*	485·0	—
Other developed areas	217·7	50·0	19·3	291·0	15·0	51·5	19·0	112·0	89·5	424·7	92·8	83·7	240·0	111·3
Less developed areas	1,096·7	129·8	260·5	687·5	268·8	281·7	180·0	486·5	556·2	410·0	688·6	395·2	326·3	427·0
Latin America	608·4	114·8	147·0	347·5	95·7	231·5	62·5	147·2	174·0	122·7	273·5	177·2	124·2	173·3
Asia	400·0	8·8	18·8	322·5	85·8	25·6	5·6	278·2	273·8	162·2	197·6	126·8	191·5	143·6
of which India	300·0	—	—	250·0	25·0*	—	—	200·0	225·0	90·0	108·0	36·7	45·8	53·6
Africa	5·6	1·2	—	—	14·2	3·6	37·3	46·1	96·7	75·6	109·5	54·5	65·1	56·5
Middle East	82·7	5·0	94·8	17·5	73·0	21·0	75·4	15·0	11·7	49·5				

* Standby in effect at end of period and not drawn or not fully drawn.

Source: IMF, *International Financial Statistics.*

sequent renascence of foreign exchange markets) created quite a new situation. In 1960 it became apparent that the existing exchange-rate structure could come under heavier pressure from movements of short-term funds than from any changes in a country's balance of payments resulting from trade surpluses or deficits. The most vulnerable currencies were those which were used or held internationally and whose users might, at any time, be afflicted with a sudden failure of confidence in the security of their holdings and the stability of real values.

On 10 February 1961, following the announcement by ten major countries that they accepted Article viii obligations, Per Jacobsson, the IMF Managing Director, drew attention to the dangers of a situation in which, although two-thirds of outstanding US short-term liabilities were in the hands of foreign central banks and governments, a substantial proportion remained with commercial and business firms who were now free to convert them as and when they wanted, into other currencies. The position of sterling was similar. One of the three fields therefore in which Jacobsson considered new decisions would have to be taken, if the Fund were to play a maximum part in international financial arrangements, was the provision of ' adequate measures in official hands to meet the possible impact of international movements of private funds '.[12] By this, he explained, he meant that members who had balance-of-payments difficulties owing to capital flows ought to be able to draw on the Fund.

Most of the Fund's Executive Directors favoured Jacobsson's proposals for widening the use of the Fund's resources. But the French Director, M. de Largentaye, argued that a reinterpretation of Article vi that went beyond the 1946 interpretation was legally impermissible, unless it could be shown that the original interpretation had contained an error of law. Although the other Directors may have suspected that de Largentaye's real objection was that the change would be of most use to the reserve currency countries, the logic of his legal argument was hard to answer. Indeed, the lawyers of the Fund spent several months trying to find a way round it, and the Executive Board met five times in June and July 1961 without reaching a conclusion. Finally, the Executive Director for the UAR blandly and helpfully suggested that the new interpretation should be described as a ' clarification ' of the old. The 1946 declaration was therefore re-worded with the additional statement that the decision did not preclude the use of the Fund's resources for capital transfers. A request from a country facing an outflow of capital would be treated by the Fund in accordance with its accepted principles—that appropriate measures were taken to restore the balance-of-payments equilibrium. By this semantic legerdemain the Gordian knot was cut; an amendment to the Fund's rules that was in fact substantial was disguised as merely procedural.[13]

In marked contrast to this promptitude and flexibility where the reserve currency countries' needs called for change were the delays and hesitations which the Fund displayed in the late 1950s when the developing countries first began to ask the Fund for help with their financial problems.

These were apt to arise when, in poor countries dependent on foreign exchange earned by exporting primary products, commodity prices fell on world markets. The point had been brought home with special force to the developing countries by the publication in 1958 of the Haberler report on trends in world trade,[14] which pointed out the various factors that had contributed since the mid-1950s to a decline in poor countries' terms of trade with industrial countries. Already at the Fund's annual meeting in 1957 the developing countries had expressed anxiety in case a recession in the United States might bring about a further decline in raw material prices—a decline which would adversely tip their balances of payments into deficit. They anticipated making increased demands on the Fund's resources and wished to increase their drawing rights and to ensure that the Fund's liquidity was adequate. The following year in New Delhi, the Governors for both India (Mr Moraji Desai) and Pakistan (Mr Abdul Qadir) pleaded for the provision of short-term assistance specifically for the developing countries. The increase in quotas (see below, p. 102) initiated at this meeting did not entirely meet their point, which was that they were peculiarly susceptible to the instability of world commodity markets and that this required a corresponding effort by the Fund to provide a compensatory financial stabilization. When pressed again, this time from the UN Commission on International Commodity Trade (CICT, a subsidiary established by the Economic and Social Council at the insistence of Third World members), the Fund (after about a year's delay) produced a negative report.[15]

Over the next three years a working party of the CICT continued to chew over the idea of special compensatory finance for shortfalls in export earnings by developing countries. It was also discussed by the conference of the Organization of American States (OAS) at Punta del Este in August 1961. Both were somewhat deterred by the recognition that the Fund would have to change its rules if it was to help. But when asked once again in 1963 to reconsider the question, the Fund staff finally agreed to provide limited assistance. Not only would the Fund receive sympathetically any request from developing countries for a special increase in quotas; it would also meet exceptional requests for drawings if it could be satisfied that (a) the shortfalls were of a short-term character, largely attributable to circumstances beyond the control of the member and (b), that the member would co-operate with the Fund in an effort to find, where required, appropriate solutions for its balance-of-payments difficulties. Furthermore, the Fund would allow special drawings, not normally more than 25 per cent of the member's quota, to offset shortfalls in export proceeds. The Fund also declared that it would be prepared to exercise its power under Article v (iv) in proper cases to waive the rule which limited Fund holdings of such a member's currency to 200 per cent of its quota.

Brazil made the first request for a drawing of this kind in June 1963. Thereafter drawings remained light owing to improved trade conditions up to 1966. Then the Fund softened its policy, first by separating the compensatory facility from the drawing facilities in the sense that the Fund's tranche policies were applied ' as if the Fund's holdings of the member's currency were less than its actual holdings of that currency by the amount of any drawings ' ; [16] and secondly, by allowing ordinary drawings over a certain period to be reclassified as compensatory drawings if the prescribed requirements were met. Even so, the use of the facility has been slight and the total of drawings insignificant in relation to the volume of Fund resources. Under the policy decisions of 1963 and 1966, less than $500m had been drawn up to June 1970. And it is arguable that the facility has added little to the assistance provided by the Fund under the ordinary rules.

(It is worth remarking a somewhat similar pattern of behaviour—a long-drawn-out, dilatory response to an expressed need by the developing countries, eventually followed by the granting of a somewhat empty concession by the rich countries—is to be found on the trade policy side in the granting of a generalized system of preferences for their exports. These were first proposed by Edward Heath at the UNCTAD I conference in 1964 and finally agreed to—with all sorts of limiting qualifications—after six years in October 1970.)

The contrast with the speed with which the Fund reacted when the rich countries wanted to bring about change can be seen not only in the matter of drawings to finance deficits on capital account, already recounted, but also in the revision of quotas in 1958–9 which was a preliminary step to the later negotiation of the GAB.

It is true that the increase in quotas (which of course affected the World Bank's capability in the matter of aid as well as that of the Fund), was partly in response to the needs and demands of the developing countries—but only when these needs were recognized by the United States. This recognition had been lacking when the Third World first began to complain at the Fund's annual meeting in 1957. Treasury Secretary Anderson then replied frostily that he doubted that the shortage of liquidity offered any real threat to the continued growth of world trade. Rather, the recession was caused by the failure of governments, especially those of the less developed countries, to curb inflation and the Fund should reconstitute its resources through the repayment of recent drawings.[17]

The Fund staff, then headed by Edward Bernstein, however, kept the question under review and produced first an interim report in April 1958 followed by a Staff study the next September:[18] ' It is doubtful whether, in the circumstances of the world today, with world trade greatly expanded in volume and value, the Fund's resources are sufficient to enable it fully to perform its duties under the Articles of Agreement '. It recommended that quotas should be increased by 50 per cent.

By this time, the US administration was beginning to change its mind. The reasons were undoubtedly political—the sensitivity of the Eisenhower administration first to its growing unpopularity in the Western hemisphere—it was in May 1958 that Vice-President Nixon, touring Latin America, was pelted with rotten eggs—and equally, to the contrasting rewards currently being reaped by the Soviet Union through a highly selective, and therefore very economical, trade and aid programme.[19] By 1957 the trade turnover between the Soviet bloc and the less developed countries was double what it had been in 1954 and the United States was beginning to be worried by it.[20] Reflecting this anxiety, Senator Monroney (in February 1958) and Douglas Dillon took up the long neglected Third World idea of a UN soft loan agency. Support was also coming from the British, who were by then embarking on the second wave of decolonization and were therefore acutely aware of the financial difficulties lying ahead for their former dependencies. The Canadian Prime Minister, about to play host to the 1958 Commonwealth Trade and Economic Conference in Montreal, took the initiative and proposed a 50 per cent increase in Fund quotas, and President Eisenhower prepared for the forthcoming Fund meeting by setting out, in a public exchange of letters with Secretary Anderson, a three-point plan for a 50 per cent increase in Fund quotas, a doubling of subscriptions to the World Bank, and the establishment under the UN of an International Development Agency (IDA). The President's letter concluded that ' the IMF is uniquely qualified to see that the less developed countries pursue policies which will create stable financial conditions, but its present resources do not appear adequate to the task '.[21]

This American proposal was then put to the Fund meeting in New Delhi. But the European reaction was not entirely enthusiastic. The German Governor, Karl Blessing, considered that an increase in quotas would only be justified if the Fund in future used its means primarily to promote sound internal economic policies. France also hesitated. But the Europeans had neither the power nor the will to stand against an alliance of the United States and Britain when they were supported by the developing countries and by the Fund's staff.

As well as the 50 per cent increase accepted by 35 countries, special increases of more than 50 per cent were accepted by 30 countries, including Canada, Western Germany, Japan, Argentina, and Brazil. China, Cuba, and Panama did not take up the quota increases due to them. The result was to raise the authorized subscriptions of members to just over $14 billion. Of this approximately $2·8 billion was in gold and $11·5 billion in currency.[22] A further result was to reduce the United States voting power, which in 1950 had been 30 per cent (plus Taiwan's dependable vote of over 6 per cent), to under 26 per cent, and the British voting power to 12·36 per cent, giving the Anglo-Saxon alliance, for the first time, less than a 50 per cent combined vote.

When the quota increases became effective in 1959, it was hoped that this would be the last change required for some time. At the 1960 annual meeting, both Jacobsson and the Governors of most member countries could agree that there was no lack of international liquidity and that Fund resources would be adequate 'in any foreseeable conditions'.

It was due primarily to the turbulence of the international financial markets that this optimism lasted rather less than twelve months to the next annual meeting. The very next month, in October 1960, there had been the gold market crisis that had brought about the Anglo-American gold pool and the central bank collaboration that preceded the setting-up of the multilateral Gold Pool in the autumn of 1961. By the spring of 1961, indeed, Jacobsson delivered himself of the statement to the Fund's Executive Board already referred to on p. 99 in which he identified three important fields in which the Fund would have to make progress if it were to continue to play a full part in the international stage. One was to make Fund resources available, as recounted above, for deficits arising on capital as well as current account. Another was to replenish the Fund's resources, even more substantially than by quota increases, by additional borrowing. (This was the process that finally led in 1962 to the GAB and to which we shall come in a moment.) The third way was to extend the selection of currencies used in Fund drawings and repurchases.

This apparently dull and technical question was in fact resolved relatively easily and without much fuss. It caused no great political confrontation and has perhaps been too easily overlooked in most accounts of the evolution of the international monetary system. In fact it was—as Jacobsson rightly perceived—quite important to the continued functioning and effectiveness of the Fund.

Briefly, the situation was that the Fund had operated until the end of the 1950s primarily as a revolving credit system for lending out

US dollars. Its original conception had in any case been rather vague and had unrealistically presumed a kind of bilateralism in international payments that rarely existed. The same problem had plagued the Soviet bloc's attempts to set up a multilateral payments system. The awkward, defeating fact remained that borrowers preferred to borrow the hardest currency, giving themselves maximum freedom of choice in spending, but to repay were inclined to prefer softer currencies that were more easily acquired but less negotiable. In practice, in the Fund's operations until 1960, 87 per cent of drawings had been made in US dollars and 95 per cent in US dollars or sterling. Only 5 per cent had been drawn in other currencies. By 1960, instead of the $14 billion aggregate of members' subscriptions, the Fund's effective resources for drawings upon it were assessed at about $1·8 billion in US dollars, $900m in D-marks, Canadian dollars, and a few other currencies that were likely to be included in drawings. The situation materially altered when the European currencies became convertible and thus acceptable under Fund rules for Fund drawings and for repurchases (repayments of drawings). This, coinciding with the end of the dollar shortage and the mounting US deficit, meant that if drawings on the Fund continued to be made predominantly in dollars, monetary pressure would tend to increase on the United States. Some of the drawn dollars would be used to pay for imports from the surplus countries like France or Germany and would accumulate in those central banks which might in turn present them to the United States for conversion into gold.

The interest of the United States, therefore, and of the Fund (whose resources would otherwise be restricted) was to change Fund practice in such a way that as much of the surplus countries' currency as possible was included in Fund drawings while continuing to allow repurchases to be made in US dollars.[23] Conversely, such a change would necessarily reduce the unspent dollars held by the surplus countries, and ease, if only marginally, the pressure they might put on the United States to exchange them for gold. This sacrifice of leverage even France was prepared to accept in order to enable the mutual aid system to continue to operate—and to do so actually rather more effectively than originally conceived—to the great benefit of international trade and payments. The decision was no doubt made easier by the enhanced status which a multi-currency drawing arrangement would confer on the franc: and by the fact that there were no legal grounds for objecting to the change. All the same, the French restraint seems worth remarking.

What happened was that the Fund's Research Department came up with recommendations which the Executive Board considered in April 1962 and acted on in July 1962. The basic principle was propounded that the Fund should so operate as to increase the flow of currencies from the strong surplus countries to the weaker deficit countries, and that to this end some rough parallel should be kept between changes in a country's reserves and its position in the Fund. This would, the Fund staff suggested, require the Fund to consult with countries affected by drawings. It should also try and convert the currencies drawn into currencies in demand for drawings; to aim at overall balance of currencies in its total operations but not in individual drawings; and to increase the range of currencies drawn as much as possible.

These guidelines, spelt out in greater detail, the Board accepted without demur. Nor was there much objection when between 1964 and 1966 the United States further assisted both the Fund and itself by offering to provide countries repaying the Fund (and who would otherwise have done so in dollars—thus threatening to overload the Fund with them) with a mix of currencies which it would obtain from the Fund by making a drawing on the strength of its own unused quota. To the extent that this would help the Fund function more effectively, the pressures on the United States would be marginally eased. If only because France was sometimes accused of wilful and malicious obstructiveness in the system, it is worth remembering that all of the surplus countries, including France, evidently felt it important that the mutual aid system should continue to operate—and to do so rather more effectively indeed than originally conceived—for the general benefit of world trade and prospects.

The General Arrangement to Borrow

By contrast, the changes required to bring in the GAB in 1962 took much longer and involved tough bargaining and, often, bitter disagreement. For the issues raised by the proposal deliberately and massively to replenish the Fund's depleted resources in lendable currencies other than the dollar and sterling called into question the fundamentals of the international monetary system.

Thanks to the dominance of the dollar in the world market economy of the 1950s, the Bretton Woods code of rules had not worked out nearly as even-handedly between the major currencies as most people had imagined it would. As both the reserve currency countries got into deficit, and as the Fund became more active, it was seen to constitute quite an effective instrument for their support, allowing them to extend their banking role in the system and allowing them an unequal, preferential immunity from the normal pressures of the adjustment process. The basic issues underlying the GAB debate, therefore, were about power and responsibility in the system. The other members of the affluent alliance were being asked to give their consent to a new extension of the asymmetrical privileges of the reserve currency countries. Were they then entitled to ask a political price for their consent? Did the decision-making processes that had come to be accepted in the Fund allow these creditor countries enough opportunity to express their opinions? Did they incorporate enough checks and balances against the power of the heavyweight Anglo-American votes to safeguard their interests? These were essentially political issues and could be settled only by hard political negotiation.

Ironically, however, the first suggestion for something like a General Arrangement to Borrow—an innovation which ended by diminishing the relative status of the Fund in the system—came from its first and greatest Research Director, Edward Bernstein. It can be found in a paper presented to a Harvard seminar in the autumn of 1959, some nine months after Bernstein himself had resigned from the Fund in December 1958. It is possible that if Bernstein and Jacobsson had not disagreed on this issue their incompatible temperaments would have led them to fall out on something else. However that may be, there is little doubt that the resignation of this shrewd, ebullient but very clear-sighted monetary economist was a major loss to international monetary diplomacy in the 1960s. For having once dissented and resigned, it was hard for Bernstein ever to go back. It is a characteristic of international bureaucracies—and applies as much to the UN, to the ILO, and UNESCO as to the Fund and the Bank—that they give great personal power within the organization to their executive heads. Rebels and dissenters are unwelcome. And a return route, consequently, is seldom opened for the recalcitrant or critical subordinate who has challenged the director's judgment—sometimes not even when the boss in question has departed from the scene.

Bernstein's ideas and his Harvard paper had gone significantly farther than the Fund staff's report on the same subject (*International Reserves and Liquidity*) arguing that the quota increase on its own would not be enough and that the increment of reserves should be provided without relying too much on a large gold outflow from the United States. Bernstein therefore urged that:

the larger quotas in the Fund should be supplemented by contingent resources available to the Fund in a period of emergency . . . the Fund does not have to have on hand the exceptional resources it may use on rare occasions in a critical exchange or payments situation . . . the Fund agreement already provides a technique by which the Fund can acquire additional resources in an emergency—that is by borrowing . . . the best way to provide for the emergency resources is to have the Fund arrange to issue three-year debentures bearing interest at the same rate as the US government bonds.[24]

It was six to nine months more before the IMF staff came round in the summer of 1960 to considering this possibility, and it was then decided that the best way of proceeding would be to arrange some sort of comprehensive standby borrowing for the Fund, this time under Article VII, Section II (i). According to the official history, the Managing Director had this in mind when he made his statement to the Board in February 1961.[25]

A staff memorandum in April 1961 concluded that $5½-7 billion would be needed and that the distribution of this sum among the major countries was a matter for negotiation. When the Board discussed these proposals in May 1961, it was clear that the continental European countries, particularly France and the Netherlands, were doubtful about the need to supplement the resources of the Fund. Others were also worried by this time about the weakness of the balance-of-payments position of the United Kingdom, fearing that additional resources for the Fund would only mean that Britain would be allowed to borrow too easily both either for her own good or for that of the system.

Jacobsson, however, continued to push the idea, arguing that it would help protect the Fund against the depletion of gold which would result if it had to buy scarce European currencies; [26] and secondly, that the proposed arrangement was primarily precautionary but would nonetheless help to stem the onslaught of international movements of private capital.[27]

Behind the scenes, and outside the Fund meeting, however, the process of intergovernmental negotiation had already started. The US administration under the leadership of Roosa had started the year in a highly pragmatic mood. The President, after his inaugural address and his economic message to Congress in February 1961, became immersed in foreign affairs and had left international financial questions to be dealt with by the Dillon-Roosa team. Roosa's inclination as he described it, was also pragmatic and experimental: ' the initiation of new working relationships with other central banks, other governments and with the IMF all would be designed initially to meet some significant aspect of immediate need. Most could be established on a temporary or trial basis.' [28] And although the overriding aim in Roosa's mind was to strengthen the international monetary system, he did not visualize that the government should divert the scarce and precious resources of its planning staffs in this formative period to the preparation of an American programme for comprehensive international monetary reform.[29] Others totally disagreed, notably Walter Heller, chairman of the Council of Economic Advisors. Heller, influenced in part by Robert Triffin, was among the able administration economists who were urging the President to take a bold stand in support of proposals looking towards the creation of a new international currency. In the meanwhile, Heller was largely responsible for the strong US commitment to the new OECD and for the elaboration of its consultative machinery—an elaboration that provided an alternative and much more flexible arena for monetary diplomacy between the governments of the affluent alliance than was easily available to them in the Fund, or in any other international body. To a meeting in Paris of the OECD's economic policy committee on 18 and 19 April 1961, Heller took along an especially strong delegation including William McChesney Martin of the Federal Reserve Board, Robert Roosa, and Robert Triffin, who was included as a consultant.[30] At this meeting, Heller proposed the creation of special task forces, which would be sub-committees, and which would meet frequently to discuss detailed programmes and problems of the member countries. There would be groups to consider economic growth (this became Working Party II), short-term capital movements (this was not formed), and the use of monetary policy (this became Working Party III).[31]

Working Party II included all members of the organization. It was decided that Working Party III would include only the larger countries, and would consider their balance-of-payments positions and their relationship to the functioning of the international monetary system. After 'some early strain and embarrassment in selecting a limited group of countries'[32] the membership finally included the United States, the United Kingdom, France, Germany, Italy, Canada, Sweden, the Netherlands, and Switzerland. Belgium, although not formally a member of Working Party III, always had a man there who sat with the Dutch delegation. The first, organizational, meeting of the group took place on 20 April 1961, with Emile van Lennep as chairman, and the first full-scale meeting on 17–19 May. After this, the group met at intervals of three to six weeks, and it is to be presumed (as indeed Roosa suggests) that much discussion of the GAB took place in Working Party III.

Events, meanwhile, were forcing the United States and the Fund to move rather faster than either seemed to have intended at the beginning of the year. After the D-mark revaluation in March, sterling had still been under severe pressure in the foreign exchange markets. In spite of emergency help to the tune of $900m provided between March and July 1961 under the newly-negotiated Basle Agreement, British reserves were still $800m lower than they had been at the beginning of the year. Already in April 1961 the Fund's total resources had consisted of a bare $400m in pounds and dollars and only $1,500m in other convertible currencies. Thus, when the British drew $1,500m from the Fund in August, the United States insisted that less than a third of this drawing should be in dollars, two-thirds in nine other currencies. Not only did this practically exhaust the Fund's lendable resources; it also obliged the Fund to sell $500m of its gold holdings, partly to replenish its own supply of currencies and partly to persuade the nine countries contributing to agree to the transaction.[33] This drawing clearly made an increase in the Fund's resources much more urgent but at the same time seemed to confirm to the opposers of the Jacobsson plan that it was merely a device to bail out the pound.

The difficulties of the British in large part accounted for French doubts and suspicions about the whole scheme. These doubts had been put to Secretary Dillon by M. Baumgartner, Governor of the Banque de France, during a personal visit to Washington in May 1961. Firstly, the French feared that providing the Fund with additional resources with which to support the reserve currencies would only undermine its power and will to impose a desirable degree of monetary discipline on the system. Secondly, they strongly suspected that more powers for the IMF would mean greater economic influence for the United States, and for this reason wanted any increase in Fund resources to be organized on a regional basis, not in the full forum of the Fund where they were still afraid of being outvoted. French suspicions were confirmed by the UK drawing in August 1961 when the IMF hurried to the aid of the British government without imposing as strict conditions as they had done on France in January 1958, neither insisting on specific measures of economic and monetary policy, nor (as they might have done) on a sterling devaluation. Instead the Fund declared itself satisfied with Selwyn Lloyd's measures of 25 July.

The gulf that was emerging between the United States and Britain on one side and the French on the other had an immediate effect on the EEC, challenging the six member countries to try and adopt a united position in response to the proposals which Jacobsson, as he had made very clear, was now going to put forward. But though the meeting of EEC finance ministers at Bad Godesberg early in September 1961 publicly declared that they had reached agreement ' in principle ', some quite wide differences in approach in fact remained.[34] The Germans and Italians were happy to have definite commitments and to leave the decision on the activation of the supplementary credit to the Fund. But the Belgians and the Dutch, supporting France, showed no wish to commit themselves to specific sums and stoutly maintained that creditors should have a right of veto. The Fund and Jacobsson took these objections quite seriously, and in August it was announced that Jacobsson's retirement as Managing Director would be postponed for two and a half years. The reason, so it was suggested, was that he was the only man who could persuade the Continental bankers to abandon the idea of a veto on the plan.[35]

The 1961 Vienna meeting of the Fund

The original plan was to arrange ' firm commitments by the creditor nations to reinforce the IMF as a whole '.[36] But Per Jacobsson's address to the opening session of the Vienna annual meeting in August 1961 already revealed some concessions to the French viewpoint. Although he stressed the need for definite commitments, he also laid emphasis on ' safeguards ' for the lending members, consultation between the Fund and the prospective lender, and rapid repayment if necessary.[37]

Throughout the week taken up by the annual meeting, the French and Dutch continued to exploit their relatively strong bargaining position. Though they were later to diverge on the question of British membership of EEC, at this period they were working closely together in opposition to the Americans. US influence on other Fund members was weakened by its known self-interest in the project. Dillon's speech to the Governors was directed to persuading the Europeans that the United States was seriously determined to combat inflation and to improve its balance of payments. And at this stage, the Americans got little effective help from Britain. Although two Treasury-Bank of England missions under Sir Frank Lee and Prime Minister Harold Macmillan himself had visited Washington earlier in the summer, the British had now drawn so heavily on the Fund and on central bank support that they were unable to take any effective part in the discussions.

Secretary Dillon took the opportunity of the annual meeting to call together the representatives of eight main industrial countries to sound them out on supplementary borrowing by the Fund. Excluding (as yet) Japan, the eight were Britain, France, West Germany, Italy, Canada, Sweden, Belgium, and the Netherlands. This first step, selecting the members of the inner circle of decision-making, obviously much influenced the eventual membership of the Group of Ten. It was taken by the Americans. But it is also evident that the American choice of partners was much influenced in turn by the Fund's need to replenish its holdings of some strong European currencies more than others. Secretary Dillon later the same week reported to the Fund Governors on the outcome of his nine-power meeting. His account stressed that there had been general agreement on four points: that the amount to be borrowed should add decisively to the Fund's resources; that it should be promptly available in case of need; that both consultation and repayment should be assured; and that there would be no weakening of the Fund's policy on drawings.[38] What he did not say was that there was considerable difference of opinion on which of these desiderata were most important; also, on how specific objectives could be secured, and on whether, and how, the potential creditors should keep control over the borrowing facility. This conflict can be deduced from the speeches of the Fund Governors for France, the Netherlands, and Belgium—M. Baumgartner, Dr Marius Holtrop, and Baron Hubert Ansiaux. In Baumgartner's words, ' each country should remain judge of the advisability of the use of its own currency '.[39] He also made it clear that he would much prefer a lending arrangement to be set up *outside* the Fund: ' it is a problem which . . . concerns essentially the currencies of the industrial countries '. Any new resources moreover would be needed only in exceptional cases and France did not intend to commit itself in advance to ' an automatic and rigid solution ' to the problem of capital movements. The creditor countries would need much more specific safeguards than they had with regard to ordinary Fund drawings.[40] Governor Holtrop expressed similar views. He could see only two sorts of emergency in which the proposed new lending should be used. The first case would be a drawing by the United States and the second would be drawings by major countries aimed at counteracting large short-term capital movements. He was more specific than Baumgartner had been about how the lenders would play a part in the activation of the credits: ' It would seem essential that the lending countries, when the Fund shall make a call on them, shall have the opportunity by a collective judgment, to confirm that also in their opinion, the specific emergency, for which the additional resources have been set aside, has indeed arisen '.[41]

If there was to be any sort of compromise, it now seemed clear, the two basic objections of France, Belgium, and Holland would have to be accepted by the rest as a basis for further talks. These, it was agreed, would take place later in the year. Jacobsson's aim was to get an agreement by mid-December. By the end of the Fund meeting the reserve countries had conceded this much: that the lending creditor countries would have a much greater influence than they did in normal Fund operations—even to the extent perhaps of a separate scrutiny of the policies of the prospective borrower. This was what the French and Dutch reservations about consultations had really been aimed at. They held it inconceivable that the Fund would lend their currencies against their wishes, and they wanted to ensure that the creditor countries could get together on their own, outside the Fund, and then inform the Managing Director whether or not it could have the money. Secondly, the United States conceded that the use of the new credits would be limited to helping major countries which were being speculated against or to finance a Fund drawing by the United States.[42]

Before leaving Vienna, Baumgartner held a press conference, at which he reiterated the points which he and those who supported him had made at the annual meeting. He also added that the total of

European currencies being used by the Fund was by now slightly greater than the total of US dollars, which suggested that the voting power in the IMF of the Continental Europeans must be increased. He queried whether the proposed new borrowing arrangements should be discussed in another context, such as the OECD.[43]

In fact, a basis for agreement on the key points was found through bilateral talks between the Americans and the French, on the eve of the OECD meetings in Paris in mid-November. M. Jean Sadrin (the French Alternate Governor), who had been with M. Baumgartner to Washington in the spring, John Leddy for the United States, and Jacobsson met privately in the Hotel Meurice. Notwithstanding Jacobsson's objections, the draft agreement agreed in outline by Leddy and Sadrin was presented on 17 November to a meeting in Paris of the same eight countries that Secretary Dillon had consulted in Vienna, plus a Fund delegation and a representative of Japan. (This last was a notable development since Japan was not at this date a member of OECD.) Jacobsson angrily rejected this first draft, on the grounds that it would impair the Fund's authority. Earlier in the month, Dillon had assured him that the United States would not support proposals that did this. But when it came to the crunch, the Americans were obviously less concerned with the Fund's authority than with the urgency of getting some arrangement agreed. Jacobsson also insisted that the borrowing decision must lie with the Fund though conceding that it was the participating countries who would have to take the lending decision. Slowly, as subsequent drafts were prepared with the help of Fund staff during the next three weeks, this adamant position of the Fund's Managing Director had to be abandoned.

At last, at a convenient meeting of NATO finance ministers in Paris on 13 December, the details of the GAB agreement were made public. It very soon became clear that the substantive decision-making power had passed to the select group that now became known as the Group of Ten (or Paris Club), leaving the Fund only the formal right to call the group together and the formal authority of administering the borrowing arrangement. This point was clear enough to some of the middle-ranking Fund members when the agreement was discussed, and approved, by the Executive Board early in January 1962. Executive Directors for Australia, India, and Brazil were all critical of the ' very exclusive club ' that had been set up, and regretful of the consequent diminution in the Fund's status.

Announcing the decision, M. Baumgartner explained that the new resources—$6,000m in all—would not be purely and simply put at the disposal of the Fund. Their use would be submitted to scrutiny and discussed by the finance ministers of the ten countries which would operate through the OECD's Working Party III. He also explained the rather complex new voting arrangement which would govern activation of the borrowing arrangement. This provided that a loan under the arrangement had to be approved by two-thirds of the participating countries (excluding the borrower) and by a three-fifths majority of their votes. These votes were weighted directly in accordance with their financial participation. Converted into dollars these were as follows:—

The Commitments of the participating countries in the GAB ($m)

USA	2,000	Japan	250
UK	1,000	Canada	200
Germany	1,000	Holland	200
France	550	Belgium	150
Italy	550	Sweden	100
		TOTAL	6,000

Note: For constitutional reasons, the German and the Swedish commitments were made by their respective central banks, not by their finance ministers.

Source: IMF, i. 512.

The voting formula had been carefully devised in order to give the combined voting power of the EEC participants a veto on a borrowing by the two reserve countries, the United States and Britain.[44]

Similarly, a British borrowing would require three-fifths of $5 billion ($6 billion less Britain's own commitment), i.e. $3,000m weighted votes. These also could not be assured from United States, and non-EEC votes (totalling $2,550m); at least one of the three larger EEC countries would still have to vote in favour.

Evidently the neat calculations that gave a united EEC a right of veto were primarily for the record—to establish the right *en principe.* They did not necessarily assume more EEC solidarity than actually existed then or later. In practical terms, Germany's heavy vote of $1,000m would probably assure approval either for Britain or the United States with some minimal support from the Americans' other two close associates, Canada and Japan.

The agreement on the GAB took a novel and dual form. Not only was it embodied in a Decision of the Fund's Executive Board but also in a kind of multilateral executive agreement, a series of identical letters from M. Baumgartner to the US Secretary of the Treasury and to the finance ministers of the other countries involved. The Board Decision was the lengthier and more legalistically drafted of the two documents, and it was to this that governments formally acceded, the minimum requirement for entry into force—seven members with a total commitment of $5½ billion—being reached by October 1962. But all the main points in the GAB were also detailed in the letters to the finance ministers—documents which surely implied some French doubts about the dependability of Executive Board Decisions.

The letters also marked an important stage in the increasing tendency of Finance Ministries to take over prime responsibility for an important issue-area of foreign relations from the Foreign Ministries, to whom they had once been exclusively confided. In the interwar period, for example, though negotiations had often been conducted by central banks, any formal commitment on trade or money matters had usually been handled by Foreign Ministries.

Both forms of the agreement gave first and most attention to the mode of operation of the new credit facility. Requests to draw on or activate the GAB were to go first to the Fund's Managing Director, through established Fund procedures. The Managing Director would then consult the Executive Board and the GAB participants. The latter would then consult each other and tell the Managing Director how much of their respective currencies they were prepared to lend. This was clear from the Baumgartner letters. Otherwise, the different wording of the two forms of the GAB agreement left some obscurity on whether a borrower had to get the agreement of *both* the participants *and* the Executive Board. But it soon became evident that if the former were agreed, the latter (in which the weight of votes gave a veto only to the United States) would not obstruct the borrowing. In short, the crucial decision lay with the participants. The Managing Director might propose a certain distribution of shares in the loan but if the participants did not accept this, they could make alternative proposals. Similarly, it was up to the participants to ask to be repaid early if their own payments position had deteriorated; repayment otherwise conforming with Fund practice of between three and five years. Effectively, participants had the right to withdraw their commitment in whole or in part at the initiation of a borrowing and, on balance-of-payments grounds, at any time after it had been made. Though it was unclear from the original agreement, it was felt later, when an arrangement was first activated on behalf of Britain in 1964, that all the participants should take part in an arrangement, even if only by a token amount, in order to be able to exercise their right to vote on it according to the weighted voting system already described.[45]

That the Fund was the agent of the participants was further emphasized by the provision that it should pass on repayments of any GAB drawings to the creditors, for whom all Fund assets were security.

The initial arrangement was not an indefinite one; it was to hold good for four years only from its entry into force, i.e. until October 1966. In fact it was then renewed for a further four years to 1970 with provision for review in 1968.

But while there were arrangements for extension of the GAB in time there were none in membership. The club was closed to non-members.

Not only could non-participants not use the GAB, but there was no provision whereby they could become participants. The only major country whose currency the United States decided the Group might need to draw on was Switzerland. And Switzerland, as a non-member of the Fund and a reluctant joiner of all but the most neutral or technical of post-League of Nations international organizations, would be content—indeed, would probably prefer—a special ad hoc arrangement. This, at Dillon's invitation, Jacobsson had initiated. As a result, Switzerland—that is, the Swiss Federal Council, not the finance minister—gave an undertaking to the Fund to support any activation of the GAB up to a total in Swiss francs of $200m and to lend directly, not via the Fund, to a borrowing participant in accordance with agreements with it provided that, in the Swiss view, the Swiss balance of payments allowed it to do so.[46]

The restrictiveness of the Group of Ten club was explained and defended (in the Executive Board for instance) on functional grounds—that it was the currencies of the rich industrialized countries that the Fund would need to supplement its own resources and that this special need conferred special rights and obligations on these countries—an argument summed up in the paradox that the GAB was really an SAL—a Selective Arrangement to Lend.

But this functional explanation was in fact a disguise—as the historical case-study above makes quite clear—for a genuine political explanation. As the Indonesian Director (Mr Soetikno Slamet) observed, the reality was that the creditor countries were unwilling to delegate their power to the Fund. And they were also unwilling to dilute their power by adding to the club's membership. The larger this grew the less easy to control decisions made according to the three-fifths weighted voting rule; the less manageable, too, discussion and negotiation of such matters as the creation of a new reserve asset and the solution of the alleged problem of international liquidity (see below, chs 7 and 8).[47]

The price of exclusivity was, as always, heightened resentment among those shut out. More important, perhaps, this smouldering resentment soon burst into a much more inflammatory doctrine that was potentially destructive of the one-world concept that was the ideological foundation for the entire GATT–Bretton Woods–UN system of international economic management set up after World War II. This was, essentially, the Prebisch thesis and variants on it. These denied the supposed equality of states as proclaimed in GATT and the Fund, criticized the system for its unequal distribution of economic welfare, and claimed special rights and dispensations for the poor countries. In a study of decision-making in UNCTAD, Nye finds the roots of the UNCTAD doctrine (and of the militancy in the Group of 77 which was based upon it) in the 1962 Cairo Conference of developing countries, in the discussions in the UN's regional commissions in 1962–4, and in the work of the Preparatory Committee that preceded the first UNCTAD in 1964 [48]—all of which followed closely on the GAB agreement.

In short, while the GAB was undoubtedly effective in reinforcing and upholding the creaking international monetary system of the early 1960s, it also created what was immediately recognized as a rich men's club—and thereby accelerated the opening up of a North-South split in the world's economy, and exacerbated the conscious division of nations into rich and poor, haves and have-nots.

Yet from the beginning it constituted a major addition to the machinery of international monetary co-operation—perhaps the first significant step towards the still far-distant goal of harmonization of domestic monetary management along do-as-you-would-be-done-by guidelines of mutual economic non-aggression. For included in the commitments to the GAB was the important provision that members would consult together and would keep each other informed of developments in their respective balances-of-payments positions ' to insure the stability of the international monetary system'. It was this commitment which undoubtedly put the necessary head of steam behind the discussions in Working Party III, and thus established the continuity of contact between high level Finance Ministry and central bank officials that was the basis of a great deal of monetary collaboration in the middle and later years of the decade.

Lessons about the system

Returning to the hypotheses predicated at the beginning of this chapter, the basic one, it will be recalled, was that there was a contrast in style between the promptness with which central banks reacted under market pressure and the slowness and caution with which Finance Ministries negotiated to adapt or extend international monetary organizations. Various explanations were then suggested to account for the contrast.

The evidence as recounted here for this hypothetical contrast, however, hardly bears it out. Though central banks under market pressure could and did act quickly, they did not always do so (see ch. 6). It was true that most inter-bank commitments were shorter-term and by their nature more easily retracted. But it could also be observed that quite radical changes in the working of international organizations were made quite promptly when, in particular, the United States decided that they were necessary. The distinguishing feature of the GAB, however, was that the United States needed the co-operation—more, an overt financial commitment—from the European states in order to provide the Fund with the extra resources it needed. The controlling power, therefore, lay with their finance ministers. The Fund's staff were inclined to be obstructive. But their efforts were ineffectual and their influence very slight when the Finance Ministries of the main states involved ultimately discovered the basis for a new bargain.

The evidence suggests, therefore, that it is wise to be cautious in making any such generalizations either about the ways specific sectors of national bureaucracies behave, or about the outcome of different types of negotiation—or indeed about the roles played by particular actors such as the United States or the IMF. The latter's perception of where their respective interests lay in a proposed change, and how urgently it was required, was apt to change radically according to changing circumstances, to intellectual fashions and personalities.[49] So, too, was the power enjoyed by other actors either to assist or to obstruct.

All that can be said is that, having once accepted a certain institutional framework and set of rules, most states appeared reluctant to challenge decisions taken within this framework. In general, they were inclined to acquiesce in changes made within it, even when they themselves were opposed to it. Such inhibitions tended to disappear, however, when new initiatives were discussed that required a definite departure in national policy and a significant extension or addition to the machinery of international monetary management.

Notes

[1] See J. Gold, *The stand-by arrangements of the International Monetary Fund* (Washington, 1970) for a detailed analysis. Also F. Machlup, *Remaking the international monetary system: the Rio agreement and beyond* (Baltimore, 1968).

[2] EB Decision No. 102 (52/11), 13 Feb 1952.

[3] These were revised in 1953 (EB Decision No. 270 (53/95), 23 Dec 1953).

[4] *IMF*, i. 432.

[5] For a prototype of a Letter of Intent, see Gold, p. 60.

[6] *IMF*, i. 488.

[7] Gold, p. 166.

[8] *IMF*, ii. 484.

[9] Ibid., i. 570–1.

[10] Gold, p. 153.

[11] EB Decision No. 1034 (60/27).

[12] *IMF*, i. 502.

[13] *Annual Report 1962*.

The two EB Decisions read as follows:

' Interpretation of Articles of Agreement

' The Executive Directors of the International Monetary Fund interpret the Articles of Agreement to mean that authority to use the resources of the Fund is limited to use in accordance with its purposes to give temporary assistance in financing balance of payments deficits on current account for monetary stabilisation operations.

Pursuant to Decision No. 71–2
September 26, 1946 '

' Use of Fund's Resources for Capital Transfers

' After full consideration of all relevant aspects concerning the use of the Fund's resources, the Executive Directors decide by way of clarification that Decision No. 71-2 does not preclude the use of the Fund's resources for capital transfers in accordance with the provisions of the Articles, including Article VI.

Decision No. 1238–(61/43)
July 28, 1961 '

[14] GATT, *Trends in international trade*, report by a panel of experts [Chairman: Gottfried Haberler] (Geneva, 1958).

[15] ' Fund policies and procedures in relation to the compensatory financing of commodity fluctuations ', IMF, *Staff Papers*, viii (1960–1), pp. 1–76.

[16] IMF, *Compensatory financing of export fluctuations* (Washington, Sept 1966).

[17] See *Summary proceedings*, 1957, p. 141.

[18] *International reserves and liquidity: a study by the staff of the IMF* (Washington, 1958).

[19] The credits were worth only an estimated $1,900m, but 95 per cent went to only six poor countries—Egypt, India, Yugoslavia, Afghanistan, Syria, Indonesia.

[20] See the US Dept of State publication, *The Sino-Soviet economic offensive in the less developed countries*, May 1958, with a foreword by Douglas Dillon.

[21] *New York Times*, 27 Aug 1958.

[22] The effective financial resources of the Fund were substantially less than this owing to the uneven nature, as between currencies, of the drawings made on it (see below, p. 109).

[23] So long as Fund holdings of dollars did not exceed 75 per cent of the US quota (in accordance with Art. V, sect. 7 (c) (iii)). This situation was true for the pound sterling for most of the 1960s, when sterling was no longer eligible for use in Fund drawings or in repurchases owing to Britain's heavy drawings on the Fund.

[24] *International monetary reserves for an expanding world economy*, presented to the Seminar in International Economics, Harvard, on 17 Oct 1958 (EMB 58/13), pp. 10–11. Bernstein used virtually the same wording in his study paper to Congress in January 1960 (US Congress, Joint Economic Committee, *Employment, growth and price levels; Hearings*, 86th Cong., 1st sess.)

[25] See *IMF*, i. 507.

[26] See speech in his annual report to the UN Economic and Social Council, *New York Times*, 21 Apr 1961.

[27] Speech to the Centre for Economic and Financial Research, Basle, 12 June 1961 (reprinted in Jacobsson, *International monetary problems*, p. 235).

[28] Roosa, *The dollar and world liquidity* (New York, 1967), p. 9.

[29] Ibid., p. 8.

[30] *FT*, 12 Apr 1961.

[31] Ibid., 18 Apr 1961.

[32] Roosa, p. 27.

[33] See Samuel Brittan, ' International financial diplomacy in 1961 ', RIIA, *Survey of international affairs* 1961, p. 314.

[34] *The Economist*, 9 Sept 1961.

[35] *FT*, 7 Sept 1961.

[36] *The Economist*, 30 Sept 1961.

[37] *Annual meeting, 1961 Summary proceedings*, pp. 28–9.

[38] *IMF*, i. 510–11.

[39] Ibid., p. 510.

[40] IMF *Summary proceedings*, 1961, p. 64.

[41] Ibid., p. 117.

[42] *The Economist*, 23 & 30 Sept 1961; and Sam Brittan in the *Observer*, 24 Sept 1961.

[43] *Le Monde*, 23 Sept 1961.

[44] The arithmetic would work as follows: a US drawing would be the full amount less its own commitment, i.e. $4,000m. Three-fifths of this amount would be $2,400m.

But non-EEC participants (Britain, Canada, Japan, and Sweden) could only muster $1,550m ' votes' between them. However, the EEC veto operated only if there was unity among the three major members of the Six. Approval could be won if the drawing were supported either by Germany (total: $2,250m) or by France and Italy ($2,650m); or by either France *or* Italy supported by the Dutch and Belgians ($2,450m).

[45] See J. Keith Horsefield, ' Charges, repurchases, selection of currencies ', *IMF*, ii. 456.

[46] See exchange of letters dated 11 June 1964 between the Swiss Ambassador to the United States and the Managing Director, reproduced ibid., iii. 254–6.

[47] Eventually the rigidly restrictive character of the membership in the Group of Ten was corrected by the creation of the Committee of Twenty in 1972. But it is arguable that this was over-compensating and that an earlier and more flexible piece-meal expansion would have been less clumsy and more efficient.

[48] J. Nye, ' UNCTAD—poor nations' pressure group ', in R. W. Cox & H. Jacobson, eds, *The anatomy of influence; decision-making in international organizations* (New Haven, 1973), p. 354.

[49] More specifically, Fred Hirsch has argued, according to the phase of ' the cycle of the gold-exchange standard ': ' A consensus among the various functional interests and actors may be attained for internationalist moves in the crisis phase of the cycle of the gold-exchange standard, but will be elusive in calmer or postcrisis periods ' (*An SDR standard : impetus elements and impediments*, Princeton Essay in International Finance, 1973, p. 21).

5

MULTILATERAL SURVEILLANCE

The UK case

If there was one perennial topic which dominated international monetary discussions in the middle years of the 1960s, it was the plight of sterling. For about five years, from mid-1964 to at least the end of 1968, no other national currency attracted so much attention from the monetary authorities of other developed countries, or gave rise to such diplomatic activity and such persistent efforts to restrain and to tame the unruly forces of the foreign exchange markets.

One result, by the latter 1960s, was a very extensive literature of diagnosis, prescription, and prognosis for Britain and its currency. The conclusions drawn varied enormously—and even more so the prescriptions—ranging from those who blamed the weaknesses of British society for infecting and debilitating the economy, and thus the national currency,[1] to those who saw the weakness of the currency in a post-imperial period as having perverted national management of the economy.[2] To this literature the British official contribution had been one of almost studied indifference. But there was much independent debate in and outside the country, and every one of the major international institutions concerned was drawn at one point or another to attempt its own analysis.[3]

It is not proposed here to summarize or even to assess this literature or to rehash old controversies. Nor is it necessary, for the markets were perfectly clear all along why pressure was recurrently put on the pound. They could see that large sterling balances, exceeding by three or four times the total gold and foreign exchange reserves available to the British government, were held by private creditors or by the monetary authorities of countries no longer subject to British political control. Although British residents had never been as free as their European neighbours to earn or acquire foreign assets or to shift their wealth into other currency areas, yet successive British governments had chosen to encourage the establishment of London as an international financial centre, a market-place for commodities, insurance, and banking services and for long, medium, and short-term money. It had become the home of banks and financial institutions operating internationally. The ' overhang ' of balances over reserves and the susceptibility of sterling to large-scale shifts of capital through market operations conducted in London's Square Mile together produced a situation where, if the reserves could not be reinforced, the rate would have to be changed. Hence, quite simply, the crises of the mid-1960s.

What concerns us here is how the international monetary system responded to the sterling crises and what consequences ensued from it for the development of international monetary co-operation and for the primitive machinery of international monetary management. More specifically, did the difficulties in which Britain found itself lead to an elaboration of multilateral surveillance? And how severe and how genuine was this surveillance? Furthermore, was Britain treated more deferentially and preferentially because of its special monetary relationship with the United States and its historical one in the system? It is to these questions that the present chaper will be primarily directed.

It will be recalled from earlier chapters (particularly chs 3 & 4) that the first of the sterling crises of the 1960s, that of 1961, had been very directly responsible for some important extensions of international monetary co-operation. To the facilities available for the stabilization of the operations of national central banks in foreign exchange markets were added a system of mutual aid between central banks, based on the principle of exchange rate guarantees by the debtor central bank and operated through the recycling of hot money by the deposit of a reversing sum (for example, the deposit of Swiss francs for sterling debts) to the credit of the threatened party; and through the extension of short-term holding (i.e. credit) facilities between central banks.

Because of the threatened possibility, due to the substantial and continuing US deficit, that both sterling and the dollar would come under market pressure at once, the GAB had been negotiated in January 1962 with the European countries to provide supplementary medium-term credit. The price was a reduction of the automaticity of credit for stabilization of exchange markets and a dependence of would-be borrowers on the consent of the major creditors.

What had not been decided at the end of 1961 was whether the country asking for a drawing would have to undergo scrutiny of its economic policies by the IMF, which would be acting as the agent for the parties to the GAB. This question had been left open; it had nevertheless been much in the minds of the Finance Ministry and central bank officials who, in 1962 and 1963, had begun the round of multi-hat meetings in Paris, Basle, Washington, and London that were to be so characteristic of the decade. Already over the years central banks had evolved, through the BIS in Basle, facilities for regular and confidential exchange of information and opinions—facilities which had been greatly reinforced and supplemented by the IMF and by OECD's Working Party III. By the time the Group of Ten, following the discussions at the 1963 annual meeting of the IMF, had set up the new committee of deputies, many Continental Europeans were showing signs of anxiety that the British and Americans—though they would not hesitate to make use of the GAB—were not revealing (and seemed stubbornly reluctant to reveal) the full extent of their external difficulties, and were merely concerned to increase the supply of international liquidity in order to avoid the unpleasant domestic adjustment measures needed to put their accounts in order. The Europeans were wondering how they might be made to do so. The French were particularly keen on the multilateral surveillance of bilateral credits and the Germans on assigning to Working Party III the role of encouraging the faster and more effective elimination of imbalances. As at this moment the Americans and the British wanted the Europeans to endorse ' moderate ' quota increases in the IMF (see ch. 9), they had to agree as a *quid pro quo* to a new dependence on bilateral financing and a new stress on co-ordination of national policies through meetings of the OECD and the BIS.[4] A proposal to this end was formulated in the report which the Group of Ten deputies finally produced in the spring of 1964 ' on the outlook for the functioning of the international monetary system and of its probable future needs for liquidity '.[5] The Group of deputies, under the chairmanship of Robert Roosa, had included such people as Dr Otmar Emminger, Emile van Lennep, and Dr Rinaldo Ossola, and had embarked on their task as a result of the discussions at the 1963 IMF meeting. The report did not reach any significant agreement on the liquidity question (see ch. 8), but it observed that the new techniques for providing credit, both multilateral and bilateral, had increased international co-operation and had given national and international monetary managers a better knowledge of the working of the system. However, still more information was needed to reinforce this framework of co-operation and the deputies therefore recommended—and their recommendation was supported by the Governors of the Group of Ten—a system of ' multilateral surveillance ' whereby statistical data on the means used to finance deficits and surpluses on external payments would be given to the BIS and made available also to Working Party III. A ' full exchange of views ' in Working Party III would follow ' with a view to avoiding shortages or excesses in the means of financing existing or anticipated surpluses or deficits . . . and to discussing measures appropriate for each country in accordance with the general economic outlook '.[6]

Thus, well before the onset of the 1964 sterling crisis, an important agreement had been reached in the Group of Ten for an improved system of multilateral surveillance. It was not, therefore, the product of the crisis, nor was it entered into hastily and without careful thought. When the storm broke in November, the creditors, on paper at least, were well prepared to exert some leverage on the embarrassed debtor.

Warning signs for sterling began as early as January 1964 with some unduly high import figures which boded ill for the next autumn when, if the boom continued, they were likely to coincide with the usual seasonal pressures on the reserves from the conversion of overseas sterling area balances into foreign exchange. In his budget speech in April 1963 Maudling had shown his awareness of the rapids ahead of him but had said that he intended to take the strain by drawing on international credits. If it had been only the cyclical boom in stock-building, things might have been easier. But the May trade figures showed a stagnation in British exports that was widely believed abroad to indicate a lack of competitiveness.[7] By the late summer, the trade balance, which always got all the full glare of publicity, was being potently reinforced by a very strong outflow of capital for overseas investment. Taken together, the National Institute of Economic and and Social Research estimated, the basic deficit for the year would be of the order of £500m. Thus the general reaction to the NIESR fore-cast at the time was that it was somewhat alarmist. Yet, when Labour ministers came to power in October 1964, they were greeted with a Treasury memorandum that topped the Institute's estimate, predicting a prospective deficit of £800m. And still, although the market did give some sign of speculative pressure, this did not build up into an exchange crisis until six weeks after the election.

This curious phlegmatism in the market reaction is perhaps worth noting. Fred Hirsch remarked later that the most remarkable aspect of the 1964 crisis was not that it came but that it came so late.[8] So long as the afflicted government and its potential creditors appeared unmoved by the slowly unfolding signs of trouble, the markets shivered but were not deeply shaken. Only when official nerves seemed to be giving way did the market operators—like a horse reacting to a nervous rider—begin to take fright.

By then, the Fund had already acted on its own authority, and, with-out having received an application for a drawing from the United Kingdom, had gone ahead with the activation of the GAB. In July 1963 the United Kingdom had renewed its standby with the IMF. At the time the question had been raised whether the GAB could be activated for a drawing under the standby if the participants in the GAB had not given their consent *before* the standby agreement was concluded. The Fund's General Counsel declared that it could.[9] In the summer of 1964, the standby came up for renewal once more and Britain did seek the consent of the Group of Ten.[10]

They agreed to make available $405m to the Fund for possible future drawings by the United Kingdom. But, informally, it was insisted that Britain in return, should, *not* speed up tariff removal in EFTA (as urged by the Scandinavians) to compensate for the import surcharge which the Labour government had imposed on 26 October and which had been angrily received by its EFTA partners. This condition was especially insisted upon by the French in Working Party III discussions.[11]

In view of the fact that the European commitment to the GAB totalled $2,250m, the sum of $405m was very small (the Fund was reluctant to borrow dollars, as this would have exacerbated the American payments difficulties), and it was suggested that the intention was to ' keep the Fund on a shoestring and the intending borrower in a continuing position of apparent supplication '.[12] The sum was estimated to be about equal to the debts which the United Kingdom had already run up to the Federal Reserve and the European central banks in the preceding few months to cope with the increasing speculation against sterling.[13] Although Pierre-Paul Schweitzer insisted all along that the drawing was never in any doubt and that there was no need for any additional negotiation, the British payments situation and the measures taken so far were subjected to some scrutiny at the Paris meetings. At the Working Party III meeting on 5–6 November and at the Group of Ten meeting on 7 November, there was some criticism of UK policy, and several delegates hinted that deflation was necessary. However, judgment had to be reserved since James Callaghan was due to present his special autumn budget on 11 November 1964.

Much stronger criticism was heard when he had done so, at the OECD annual ministerial meeting in Paris on 2 December 1964. But by this time it was too late for the creditors to use such leverage as they might have had. Now the ministers could not prescribe remedies; they could only hold a post-mortem. Having rejected devaluation, the British government had decided its alternative strategies—the import surcharge in October, the autumn budget, and a 10 per cent increase in bank rate announced on 23 November. This step was interpreted in the market as a panic measure by the government, creating a breach with the Bank of England and a momentary loss of control over the market by the authorities. It was at this point, long after the payments position had worsened, that the market took fright and the question in every mind became not whether the government intended to hold the exchange rate, but whether it could do so.

That it proved able to do so was due to the efficiency of inter-continental telephones and the united determination of central bankers not to allow the market to get altogether out of hand.[14] By these means the oligarchy of central banks, led and organized by the FRBNY, put together a massive $3,000m loan for the support of sterling in less than twenty-four hours.

The post-mortem in Paris in early December focused on the British economic measures, for although no definite terms or strings had been attached by the central banks to the credit package, convention dictated that they would have to be renewed in three months' time.

Fund drawing had already gone ahead but it was also likely that this would have to be extended.

The reaction of the French and Belgians at this meeting was strongly critical. They were convinced that the British measures would not work. The Germans and Italians were obliquely critical.[15] But there was some sympathy for Britain from the EFTA countries and valuable support and encouragement from the United States and Canada. The general line of comment was that no resources had been released for exports and that the net effect of the budget was neutral and could not be counted on to redress the payments situation. All the same, it was still early days to pass judgement on the measures, and satisfaction was general at the British determination to maintain the parity of the pound. If, as many economists came to believe, an important chance had been missed to adjust an over-valued reserve currency, then the finance ministers and central bank Governors of the Group of Ten shared responsibility in some measure with the British government.

The process of collective pressure was continued through mid-December; the Group of Ten and Working Party III met again on 17 December. The expected barrage of criticism from the French seemed to have been deflected by a statement by James Callaghan.[16]

It seems possible that the meetings had one important effect on British policy. On 8 December, after the OECD meeting, monetary policy was tightened. The Governor of the Bank of England wrote to the clearing banks and asked them to limit loans for property development, hire purchase, and personal use, and instead to give priority to export finance and investment by manufacturing industry. So far, however, Britain seemed to have got off very lightly in its encounters with the Group of Ten. Part of the reason for this may be the visits made by Schweitzer, who came to London immediately before the November budget, and it was suggested, at the time that ' his visit may in fact save the UK from the somewhat less welcome probings of individual members of the [Paris] club '.[17] This close contact with the Fund was to become more marked in the series of crises that followed. It may be that the influence of the Fund to some extent protected Britain from fiercer attacks from the Group of Ten, or that the Europeans became less keen to challenge the role of the Fund, at least in the field of surveillance, partly because the Fund was able to do it more effectively.

Precisely where the real power lay or who had the most influence on on the making of British monetary policy at this point is a question which it is still almost impossible to answer with any precision. But, in retrospect, it does seem that the creditors' influence was substantially strengthened by alliance with an internal agency—that is to say, with the Bank of England. The irony of the situation was that it had been a former Labour government which had sought to limit the power of the Bank. Recalling the workers' hardships after the Bank's determined return to gold in 1925, and recalling the apparently hard-nosed attitudes of the Bank and the City to the unemployed in the depths of the depression in the 1930s, Labour had nationalized the Bank of England in 1946. Now it seemed that the Bank was in some sense making a mockery of the nationalization by exercising its independent power, both as monetary manager at home and as monetary diplomat abroad. Fred Hirsch, then *The Economist*'s acute financial editor, certainly believed that the events of the last weekend of November 1964

crucially tilted the balance of effective influence on business finances in the direction of the Bank of England . . . whose authority and calm stood out in comparison with the vacillations of the Government. . . . Abroad, too, the Bank was seen as a rock of stability in London's otherwise shaken authority; and this confidence in the Bank as such necessarily gave the Bank a great leverage with the Government.[18]

Hirsch describes as 'Bank of England medicine' the restrictive measures which the Wilson government undertook in the six months after November 1964. These included the 'request' to the commercial banks to curb their lending, some stiff tax increases in the 1965 budget in April, and the cancellation of the massive TSR-2 aircraft contract.

An alternative, and equally tenable, interpretation of these measures would be that on each measure the advice of Treasury officials for once coincided with that of the Bank of England. Towards the outflow of British capital for foreign investment, however, the Bank would have been permissive; it was the government which insisted on some (not very effective) checks. At the same time, in Hirsch's view the Bank (and in particular Lord Cromer as Governor) was culpable of contributing substantially to the weakness of sterling in the foreign exchange markets by its unconcealed dissociation from the government and from any share of responsibility for the situation. Inevitably, this led to some loss of confidence in the market.

The fact that emergency help had been provided only on a short-term basis gave extra leverage to the creditor countries. In one way or another, Britain would have to seek further help from the IMF. The earlier drawing of $405m had been used up to pay off the debts to the central banks run up during the summer and autumn of 1964. The

$3 billion package put together by the central bankers in November for three months would fall due in February 1965. It was only on the clear understanding that Britain would go to the Fund as soon as possible that central banks agreed to roll over the short-term debt for a further, and final, three months.

Thus, during the early part of 1965, there was some trepidation in case this drawing should meet with stiff opposition and demands for harsh deflation from the Continental creditor countries. The *Financial Times* on 12 February commented that if it were necessary to activate the GAB, 'then the power of the Continental countries to dictate harsh fiscal restraint to Britain will be considerably increased'. But it was also thought that once the British budget was out of the way, it would be more difficult for them to exert pressure. The budget in fact allayed some of the European fears. Taxation was increased by £200m, a capital gains tax was introduced, and stricter exchange controls were imposed.

Also instrumental in soothing the orthodox financiers of Europe, apparently, was Wilson's visit to Paris during April. 'Earlier fears that the continental countries would attempt to put the UK in the dock and demand severe deflationary proofs of good behaviour . . . evaporated.'[19] On 29 April the United Kingdom formally requested a drawing from the IMF of $1,400m. This was the largest drawing for which the Fund had ever been asked and represented 72 per cent of the UK quota.[20]

OECD and Group of Ten meetings which would decide the exact make-up of the drawing were scheduled for the middle of May 1965 and it was at these that the United Kingdom was expected to come under some pressure. But before then the whole issue was settled. During the last week in April the EEC finance ministers meeting in Brussels started their examination of the British economic situation, and continued their discussions in Cannes the following week. Nicely timed to sweeten them were two announcements from the Bank of England. The first, on 29 April, tightened the credit squeeze by calling for special deposits from the clearing banks of 1 per cent (and half of 1 per cent from the Scottish banks) payable in two equal instalments in May and June. These deposits would amount altogether to £93m. Immediately afterwards, on 5 May (i.e. after the Cannes meeting, but before the OECD and Group of Ten meetings), the banks were asked to limit the growth of their advances to an annual rate of not more than 5 per cent.

These tighter credit measures appeared to mollify the EEC finance ministers. They expressed their usual scepticism about the adequacy of British measures, and made their ritual suggestions that British government expenditure was still too high and that more should be done to reduce internal demand. Nevertheless, these tighter credit measures appeared to make them more well disposed in practice, and they agreed not to oppose the British drawing. They also agreed to the renewal of the GAB.[21]

As far as the UK drawing was concerned, the Paris meetings were therefore a formality: ' The European creditor countries had spoken and that was enough '.[22] But the Europeans succeeded in forcing the Fund to increase the proportion of the drawing financed by sales of gold from 25 to 28 per cent, and the lion's share of this went to France and Germany. The Fund was also persuaded to borrow some currency from each of the European members of the Group of Ten, so they would each have a vote on the activation of the GAB.[23]

Some doubt about the efficacy of the multilateral surveillance system seems by this date to have crept in. *The Economist* (8 May 1965) reported that ' some of the wisest heads among the Europeans doubt whether the whole elaborate exercise of additional committees has had much effect in increasing the real influence of the European creditors ' and one of the wise Europeans was said to have asked, rhetorically, ' Suppose Britain had deflated by £260m instead of £600m—would we really have said no? '

The main weakness of the surveillance system appeared to be, in a sense, constitutional. Pressure on the debtor could never be applied continuously, as with a receivership, but only intermittently, when the British needed to extend or renew existing debts. Then tough domestic measures could be judiciously timed to reduce the surveillants' resistance. Later, domestic policies could be reversed or counterbalanced by others and the creditors were powerless to intervene. If they did, they would contravene the principle of sovereignty in domestic economic jurisdiction which each national government was bound, in its own interest, to honour and preserve. Moreover, the officials, whether from central banks of Finance Ministries, who sat on the surveillance committees were busy men with heavy and demanding responsibilities. Their primary professional concern was with the running of their own respective national economies, not with the management of the international economy. That was everybody's job—and nobody's. Their national responsibilities in any case left them very little time to acquire any great familiarity with the financial mechanisms and institutions and the economic conditions and practices of a foreign country.[24]

A growing recognition of this truth may account in part for the subsequent shift of the task of multilateral surveillance from the Group of Ten back to the Fund. Working Party III continued to be an invaluable meeting ground for the exchange of information, for the advance warning of measures capable of creating market turbulence or political outcry, and for the broad discussion of matters of mutual concern. But it was increasingly recognized that for detailed discussion of domestic monetary measures, a professional full-time staff, such as the IMF employed, was more likely to be effective. The British had no objection to this. The Fund had for some time been regarded as a more sympathetic overseer than the Europeans (see above, p. 125). There followed a period in which, although sterling continued as the sick man of the system and surveillance through Working Party III was maintained, no new developments in multilateral surveillance were tried out until the British drawing on the Fund in 1966 led to the first published Letter of Intent from the British government to the IMF.

Before examining it, however, it may be useful and instructive to take note of the experiences of another European country, Italy, which about this time also found itself in acute balance-of-payments difficulties and became the object of an external ' rescue operation '. The points of similarity and of difference with the British experience may throw light on some of the general questions under discussion in this chapter.

The Italian experience

In the first four years after the establishment of the European Community, Italy, although the poorest of the three major member countries in terms of national income, had enjoyed balance-of-payments surpluses. This reflected a fairly balanced capital account plus a surplus on current account. In these years there was still a great deal of rural unemployment, reflected in the relatively slow rise in Italian industrial wages and a modest import bill. The establishment of the EEC gave increased opportunities for migration, and the growth of industrial employment at home increased incomes and imports, especially imports of food and of cars. In 1962 the current account had seriously deteriorated. This continued in 1963 when imports rose in one year from $1,470m to $7,540m.

These difficulties were compounded by large and increasing outflows of capital, generally attributed to the political uncertainties of coalition government and exacerbated by the nationalization of the electric power industry. Investors were further upset by the imposition (in January 1963) of a withholding tax on dividends. The overall result was that the balance of payments shifted from a surplus of $50m in 1962 to a deficit of $1,245m in 1963, of which half was on current and half on capital account. But during the first three-quarters of the year, the reserves fell by only $60m; the deficit was financed almost entirely by commercial bank borrowings, mainly in the Eurodollar market.

Between 1960 and November 1962 these banks had been obliged to maintain a balanced position in foreign currencies vis-à-vis the non-residents. Released from this obligation, their net foreign liabilities increased from $150m in October 1962 to a peak of $1,370m in August 1963. At that point the Banca d'Italia instructed the banks not to increase their borrowings abroad, and to reduce them where possible. From September to December 1963 the net liabilities of Italian banks were reduced by $440m in Eurocurrencies.[25] The pressure of the deficit was thus then transferred to the gold and foreign exchange reserve stocks. These started to drop rapidly, losing $424m in October and November 1963.[26]

At the same time the Banca d'Italia allowed a discount to develop on the forward lira in order the better to defend the spot rate.[27] The change of policy on Eurodollar borrowing was accompanied by some tightening of fiscal and credit policies. Bank credit was squeezed; some indirect taxes on luxuries were increased and some rent controls imposed. But because of the cabinet crisis in the summer of 1963 these measures were lighter and came later than had originally been agreed between the government and the Banca d'Italia. The latter was consequently forced to rely more than it wished on monetary deflation to correct the deficit. The only other step it could take was to instruct the commercial banks, as it did in January 1964, not to let their foreign indebtedness go higher than the level of the previous November or December, whichever was the lower.

Neither this nor the half-hearted fiscal measures, however, halted the outflow of capital or the pressure on the reserves. Only in February 1964, when a new government under Sgr Aldo Moro took office to control inflation, was it possible at last to take the stronger fiscal measures recommended by the Banca d'Italia. These included a special purchase tax on cars, an increase in the petrol tax, and strict hire-purchase controls. There was also a reform of the dividend tax. If shareholders would declare their securities to the tax authorities they could pay a 5 per cent tax instead of the old 15 per cent. Otherwise their tax liability would increase to 30 per cent with no questions asked.[28] Significantly, most chose the latter. There were also to be harsher sanctions for people who evaded tax.

The key role played by the Banca d'Italia in economic policy-making at this critical time was striking, but its power in the country had rather long historical roots. As Andrew Shonfield explained in *Modern Capitalism*, ' the heart of the Italian system of control over lending and investment is the central bank '. Through the Governors' dominant position on the Inter-Ministerial Committee on Credit and through the regulation of *fidi eccedenti* (excess credits, i.e. loans subject to official bank approval) it was the Banca d'Italia that had always had its finger on the controls of demand management in Italy. This was why ' the Banca d'Italia is called upon periodically to carry some of the burdens of workaday government, which in other countries are regarded as the natural responsibility of ministers and their departments '.

This was most noticeable [Shonfield continues] during the balance-of-payments crisis of 1963–4 when the task of formulating a drastic deflationary policy and imposing it on the country—all of which involved a series of highly political decisions—was carried out, in the initial phase at any rate, almost single-handed by the bank.[29]

To continue the story, the February 1964 measures, intended primarily to increase business confidence and lure back the money which had left Italy, did not work. A series of strikes by public and other employees paralysed the country on several occasions in February and March, and a political crisis seemed nearer than ever. On 27 February the Prime Minister, Sgr Aldo Moro, broadcast an appeal ' to save the country from inflation and from depression '.[30] This did nothing to allay anxieties, and in the first days of March there were rumours of devaluation. There was a flurry in the London gold market, and pressure in the foreign-exchange markets grew, especially on the forward rate. The discount on lire bought forward one month rose to nearly 10 per cent.

On 10 March Guido Carli, Governor of the Banca d'Italia, left ' for a routine visit ' to Washington. Five days later, a combined package of international support for the lira, totalling $1,225m, was announced; it was made up as follows:

	$m
a) A drawing (Italy's first) from the IMF	225
b) A standby credit from the US Export-Import Bank	200
c) A 3-year loan from the US Commercial Credit Corporation	250
d) US Treasury credit	350
e) Short-term credit from the Bundesbank	150
f) Short-term credit from the Bank of England	100

Extensive support had meanwhile been given in the foreign exchange market by the US Treasury and the Federal Reserve.

The news of the credits brought an immediate reduction in the speculation and a marked falling-off in the illegal but unsuppressed export of Italian bank notes, usually in suitcases across the Swiss frontier. This loss, in the first half of 1963, was thought by the BIS to have been equivalent to $1,000m.

The striking feature of the Italian rescue operation was that the greater part of the facilities was provided by the Americans and the

IMF, while the Europeans and the EEC appeared at this stage as mere spectators. In Brussels nothing had been known of the rescue operation until the announcement was made from Washington. European central banks, apart from the Bundesbank and the Bank of England, played little or no part in the operation, and Carli had not consulted other central bankers in the Community before approaching the Americans.

This omission brought a ' snooty note ' from Brussels [31] asking the Italians why they had sought help from the Americans rather than from their partners in the EEC. Implying criticism of this unnatural preference, the letter suggested the Italians make restitution by holding discussions with the Commission on their economic situation. The talks were held and produced a Letter of Expectation—a Letter of Intent in reverse, written by the surveillants and advocating a 10 per cent cut in public spending, higher taxes, a tougher credit squeeze, and a wage freeze. The letter was signed by Dr Walter Hallstein, then commissioner for economic and financial affairs, and had reportedly been drafted by M. Robert Marjolin. In fact within two months, by July 1964, most of these measures had been included in the second package of deflationary policies adopted by the Italian government.

In retrospect it looks very much as if the Italian Finance Ministry badly needed an external ally to explain to the voters at home the necessity of acting tough towards the taxpayers and the workers. The Americans showed no inclination for the role—and anyway their backing might have been a political liability. The Germans—whose export surplus to Italy was the key factor in the payments position—were also keen on keeping a low profile. The Commission was an acceptable alternative, lending muscle to national bureaucrats who could use an international organization to legitimize measures on which they were already decided.

Why the Italians had turned to the Americans in the first place is another question, less easy to explain, on which opinions differ to this day on the motivations and purposes of those involved. A veteran financial journalist who listened in the summer of 1964 to many different interpretations, no two quite alike, was reminded of folk stories, recurring with local variations around certain common themes. One such recurrent theme was the essentially practical one, that the situation required substantial help, quickly given, and that the United States—and especially Roosa—was ready and able to provide it while the EEC was not. Other themes were political. One rather extreme one, heard mostly in France, was that the Americans were aiming to undermine (or cut down to size) the Community; possibly, too, to dent the CAP by financing US farm product exports by Export-Import Bank credits. More convincing was the explanation that the Americans were more aware than the Europeans of the strategic risks for the Western alliance arising from an Italian crisis, and therefore were quicker to step in offering aid without strings. A variation was that the Italians had been among the most helpful of Europeans in co-operating with measures to counter US deficit, so they in turn could count on reciprocal help from the United States; or that the Saragat Socialists, occupying a crucial position in the coalition, were strongly pro-American and cool towards the Community. And a final explanation, linking the political with the practical, saw the Americans as the acknowledged guardians and directors of the international monetary system and therefore the first to perceive a threat and the most prompt to avert it. Almost certainly, no single explanation comprehends the whole truth, and, among those involved, different people thought they were doing different things.

At any rate one by-product of the whole affair was some mild activation of EEC thinking about monetary co-operation and consultation. Only a few weeks after the Italian rescue operation, the EEC took the first serious steps towards the co-ordination of members' monetary policies. On 13 April 1964 a committee of the Six central bank Governors was set up and the EEC Monetary Committee was given two new tasks: to ensure that there was consultation, firstly, on all questions of international monetary relations such as seeking outside assistance, and secondly, before the parity of any member's currency was altered.[32] Meanwhile the Monetary Committee, in its annual report, advocated more energetic deflation in Italy, although by now the economy was already going into recession, and added that co-ordination between members should be improved, but this should not be confined merely to measures taken by central bankers. 'It should also embrace the actions of the authorities responsible for financial policy'.[33]

Comparing the British and Italian experiences, it seems that, just as the weakness of sterling in 1964 had strengthened the influence of the Bank of England, so the weakness of the lira still further reinforced the power and influence of the Banca d'Italia. This was about the only point of similarity between the two episodes. The Italian episode had been relatively small in scale and was not perceived to constitute a threat to the system. It had demonstrated the confidence of other members of the Group of Ten in the US sense of responsibility towards the system. It had by chance revealed the weakness and lack of coherence in the EEC. Lastly, it had demonstrated the relative irrelevance to some payments problems of the whole structure of multilateral surveillance through Working Party III. There was never any suggestion that this should be applied to Italy and no great alarm for the possible effects on others of the weakness of the lira. The difference between the roles of the two currencies in the international monetary system also no doubt accounted for the much greater awareness of the dangers of the British situation and for the continuing concern in the United States through 1965, 1966, and 1967 that British policy should effectively end the weakness of sterling. American concern with Italian monetary policy was, by comparison, much more short-lived.

This suggests once more the proposition that during this period the only effective surveillance of the United Kingdom was in fact a unilateral one, by the United States. This interpretation was argued most cogently by a veteran British journalist in Washington, Henry Brandon of the *Sunday Times.*[34]

Brandon strongly argues that US opinion, together with the fear of the market, was the decisive influence on British policy in these years; and that the Wilson government tried hard to imitate Attlee and Macmillan in asserting a ' special relationship ' with the United States but failed to do so. If it was a special relationship, it was only a one-way one. Washington could summon Sir Burke Trend for ' consultations ', and when the United States insisted, it got its way. But at all times the British showed extreme reluctance to tread on American toes. The Americans also were diplomatic but there was no mistaking the iron fist in the velvet glove. ' When they put forward suggestions, these were always presented in question form—whether this or that could be done or would be possible. These discussions were a perfect example of propriety between friends.' [35]

Brandon is referring here to the advocacy by some of the more conservative policy-makers of the Johnson administration of a wage freeze and an incomes policy as solutions to the British troubles. His interpretation was that although Whitehall first strongly resisted and rejected this idea, yet none the less it was American pressure—and more particularly perhaps the belief of Henry Fowler in the effectiveness of the American labour laws, and notably the Taft-Hartley Act—that lay behind the attempt by George Brown to put teeth in the British Labour government's incomes policy and his strenuous efforts to persuade the TUC to accept the ' Declaration of Intent ' to hold wage demands within government guidelines.

According to this interpretation, if it was not always clear that it was US influence on Britain which was decisive, this was because both parties sometimes combined to cast a veil over brutal reality, or because Washington was undecided how to use its power. In the first place American opinion—while naturally resistant to the idea that the weakness of sterling had anything to do with its reserve role—was divided about what other causes the chronic condition could be attributed to. Secondly, Washington was by no means always clear where,

precisely, the US national interests really lay in relation to sterling—
nor how they might best be pursued. For example, the probability
was by now dawning that sterling was over-valued. But to permit or
recommend devaluation would bring difficult secondary problems. To
back too modest a devaluation would only encourage the speculators
without solving the problem. To insist on too large a one would risk
upsetting the whole precarious network of currency rates and even,
perhaps, the fundamental dollar-gold ratio. These were added reasons
for doing nothing to draw attention to the strength of US influence.

By contrast, it is equally evident that the French had no influence
on British policy. In these same years, the French wanted the reserve
role of sterling reduced, if not eliminated; the financial centre role of
the City shared with Paris; the pound's exchange rate abandoned. But
the British made no move to bring any of these objectives any nearer.
When, after the summer of 1967, they were forced to contemplate
them, it was not through the influence of France but through that of
the forces of the market.

The UK 1967 devaluation and IMF package

To resume the story of sterling, the main development in this middle
period concerned the various arrangements devised to allow Britain
to draw on a series of short- and medium-term credit lines. These,
though apparently technical, had important consequences for the system as a whole. In the first place, they served to strengthen and
develop the network of inter-central bank relationships. And in the
second they helped indirectly to restore influence to the Fund.

As already described, Britain had not only drawn the whole
$1,000m of the standby credit arranged with the Fund in November
1964; it had also had to ask the central banks to roll over the $3,000m
short-term credits hurriedly put together in December 1964. It promised thereafter to seek alternative assistance from the Fund, and in
April 1965, asked the Fund to arrange a $1,400m medium-term credit
under the GAB. After the Managing Director had talked with the
Executive Directors from GAB participants (i.e. the Group of Ten)
and after 'prolonged discussion'[36] of the British situation, the
drawing was agreed.

One consequence of these two arrangements with the Fund, in
November 1964 and in May 1965, was to bring the Swiss once more
into closer association with the Group of Ten, so that it was sometimes referred to thereafter as the Group of Eleven. The currencies
drawn from the Fund under the first standby were those of the other
Group of Ten countries plus Austrian schillings and Spanish pesetas.
Concurrently with the Fund negotiations, the Bank of England nego-

tiated a special bilateral agreement with the Swiss National Bank implementing existing arrangements (see above, p. 115) for the co-operation of Switzerland with the GAB on the same reserve ratio as the others. This $80m loan in Swiss francs was followed up in May by a further parallel arrangement for $40m.

The continued weakness of sterling in foreign exchange markets through the summer of 1965 caused Britain to draw the whole of its $750m swap facility with the Federal Reserve plus an additional $140m. The country's debts to the Fund and other central banks now exceeded its owned reserves of gold and foreign reserves by $825m. But more credit was still needed and although Britain had drawn on the Fund credit to repay the winter's central bank borrowing, it looked as though it would have to go back to the Fund yet again.

In September 1965, therefore, the British sought assurance that sufficient short-term credit would again be available to them from the central banks if it were necessary. The suggestion was that it was asked and used not to fill a deficit but in a bear squeeze against market speculators. Since the time was well-chosen, the squeeze was effective but costless. The amount assured was not disclosed but was thought to be about $1,000m.[37] The French this time abstained. And such was the reputation by now established of ' central-bankerly camaraderie . . . not normally found at the less frequent encounters between Finance Ministry officials ' that Weil and Davidson went on to comment,

The abstention of the Banque de France from the September, 1965, package was taken as a shocking repudiation of the central bank free-masonry, not only in Britain but also elsewhere. . . . The unofficial explanation which leaked out was that France considered the British balance of payments to have been in deficit for far too long already, and that a new international support package for the pound would merely encourage the British government to postpone any decisive improvement in its economic policies.[38]

The significant point for our study, however, was that the French gesture of abstention cut no ice. The British got the support they wanted whether the French took part or not.

Nine months later, in June 1966, France once again abstained from multilateral credit arrangements for Britain, while making at the same time a separate bilateral deal. This time it was a temporary-permanent credit arrangement whereby the British were assured that they could rely on up to $1,000m in central bank credit provided the pressure on the pound arose from fluctuations in the overseas sterling balances—i.e. from sterling's reserve currency role rather than from the UK balance of payments.[39]

In marked contrast were the inter-central-bank swap arrangements, which were unconditional and which were now substantially extended.

These swaps, it will be recalled (see above, p. 85), had been devised by the Americans early in 1962. By 1965 they had been built up, through arrangements with eleven countries and the BIS, to a total of $2,800m. In September 1966 this total was increased to $4,500m, adding $600m to the swap lines on which Britain could draw.

The total amount of swap lines arranged by the Federal Reserve now stood as follows:

	$m		$m
Britain	1,350	Switzerland	200
Italy	600	Belgium	150
Canada	500	Netherlands	150
Japan	450	France	100
BIS	400	Austria	100
Germany	400	Sweden	100
			4,500

Note: It would be wrong to regard this as a truly multilateral system of inter-bank credits. Primarily, it was a two-way exchange of credit facilities between the US and Britain, in which Britain was the persistent borrower and the US the persistent creditor, supplemented by mainly one-way credit arrangements from the others to the US, or to the UK. Only very small borrowings under the swap network were made from 1962–6 by Italy and Belgium and by Canada and Japan. The US drew frequently and heavily but repaid quickly, either by exchanging swap credits for longer-term US 'Roosa' bonds on the US government, or by drawing the borrowed currency from the IMF, or more rarely by selling gold for the borrowed currency, e.g. $200m in March 1968.

If there was one year in the entire decade when France's power to influence British monetary policies (because of Britain's application to the Community) should have been at its height, and its power to see that multilateral surveillance of Britain really took some effect, that year was 1967. Sterling's weakness was uncured. The Wilson government had decided that it could no longer afford economic isolation and, overcoming its distrust of the EEC, had set about applying for membership. France, with its power to unlock the door, ought to have had quite exceptional power of leverage.

Yet French influence was still somehow ineffectual. Whether this was because Britain was still more dependent on, and responsive to, the United States than to France, or whether it was because the French overplayed their hand in trying to bend the British to their own way of thinking will be disputed. Certainly, the French made it clear through the spring and summer of 1967 that they held the reserve role of sterling to be incompatible with British membership of EEC. And none of the British—neither the Bank, the Treasury nor Callaghan and Wilson—was ready to accept the unpalatable truth that this role was not necessarily a vital national interest. At any rate, the combined result of French insistence, of British resistance, and of American non-involvement was a diplomatic impasse in which the power of the market was once more enhanced. As Fred Hirsch observed, the weakness of the ' Central Bankers' International ' of the 1960s was that it was able to multiply mutual credit facilities but not to devise and apply an adjustment lever for over- or under-valued currencies.

By being geared to currency defence rather than payments adjustment, it failed by its own test. Invoking central bankers' solidarity in the world exchange structure involves an implicit spreading of the area of commitment; it makes exchange-rates for even middle-sized countries a potential threat to the system as a whole. Thus while the central bankers can deal impressively and very valuably with any speculative assaults on the status quo, they find themselves almost unthinkingly involved in shoring it up. They have no way of coping with a situation in which the speculators are right.[40]

Through the summer of 1967 a series of events, both external and internal, served to confirm the markets' gathering anxiety about the $2·80 sterling exchange rate. In the Middle East there was the June War, reviving doubts about the stability of Arab-held sterling balances. In Britain the dockers' strike against the incomes policy delayed exports and upset the trade figures. But while foreign central bankers were looking for tough, puritanical measures from Labour ministers, the government's backbenchers were getting restive at the high rate of unemployment and were successfully urging on Callaghan the need for reflation. Successive easing of credit policies culminated in August in a major relaxation of hire-purchase rules.

While the Treasury and more particularly the Bank of England were somewhat unhappy about the June and July relaxations, the opposition of these two institutions to the August measures was strong and unmistakable. . . . From then on Treasury policymakers began to see devaluation as a probability rather than a possibility.[41]

Still—and in spite of—some heavy hints dropped to him at the IMF meeting in September, Callaghan hoped to stave off devaluation, if necessary by more borrowing. But the feeling in the market, and thus in most of the key central banks including the French and German ones, was that a sterling devaluation was inevitable and therefore that a loan to Britain without devaluation would be folly in the extreme. If the British had to borrow, they must first devalue. The key questions would be how big a loan, and how big a devaluation.

But while the Germans and Italians who took this view kept quiet, the French seemed (in London, at least) to be deliberately breaking the convention that discussion or criticism of other countries' exchange rates is taboo. While in French eyes, their official attitude was only showing realism, in those of the British it seemed to be set on ' stirring the pot '—on egging on an already edgy market. But the point was that, whether justifiable or reprehensible, the French posture in the autumn of 1967 apparently augmented the power of the market but did not materially extend the influence of France on events.

One of the weapons used by France in this period was the report from the EEC Commission's Economic and Financial Affairs Department on the British application for membership of the Community. The commissioner responsible for this department was M. Raymond Barre, a French official and a Gaullist who held pronounced, and somewhat tart, views on Britain's monetary plight. Completed by the end of September and submitted to discussion in the Council of Ministers in late October, the report was critically dubious about the reserve role of sterling. The United Kingdom's ' delicate balance-of-payments situation ' inhibited measures to stimulate economic growth and there was no visible prospect of radical improvement in the British economy. At the same time, ' the sterling balances might . . . constitute a factor of disequilibrium in the position of the United Kingdom and a source of difficulty for the Community if Britain were to join.' [42] The accession of the United Kingdom, the report concluded, ' would raise economic and financial problems which will have to be examined in depth '. Some financial journalists thought the report ' came as near to recommending devaluation as it is possible to do without actually using the word '.[43]

In line with the Commission's report, the French Foreign Minister, M. Couve de Murville, warned his EEC partners in the Council of Ministers on 23 October that France would not agree to negotiations on the British application until the UK payments were in surplus again and the reserve role of sterling was abandoned. The French measures of liberalization and devaluation in 1958 were once again smugly cited as a model for the British. Although the session was closed, the press were briefed. And at this time *Le Monde*, whether officially inspired (as Whitehall believed) or only sympathetic, certainly backed up the government and fed the uneasiness in the market by some gloomy reporting of Britain's worsening debt liabilities.

By the second weekend in November, when central bankers came to Basle for the BIS monthly meeting, the Bank of England was under mounting pressure and was deeply involved in forward market operations to support sterling. Lord Cromer apparently tried to get a $1,000m loan, to support sterling, but all he succeeded in getting was $250m, arranged through the BIS, and for this he had to give a gold guarantee.

From Basle the centre of attention moved to Paris, where a series of

OECD meetings took place on 14, 15, and 16 November. The British tried to get a loan and discussed with others the size of the devaluation. The central bankers were reluctant to come to the aid of the pound once again, because apparently the earlier June 1966 loan had been granted on condition that Britain retained drawing rights in the IMF to the same amount. If Britain were going to seek renewed aid from the Fund, therefore, the central bankers would prefer not to be involved. And the Banque de France firmly declared that it would only participate in such a loan if Britain's drawing rights at the IMF were frozen.[44] Moreover, the French, alone among the United Kingdom's creditors, refused until the last moment to give any definite idea of whether they would retain their parity, if sterling were devalued, or follow suit. They threatened that if Britain devalued by 15 per cent or more the franc would be devalued by 5 per cent. This threat was the most effective piece of French diplomacy so far. It was directed both at Britain, which was thus persuaded to limit the degree of devaluation, and at the five other members of the EEC, which then had to choose between backing France or risking disruption of the inter-Community exchange rates on which it was believed the whole structure of the common agricultural policy and thus of the Community rested.

Finally, on 18 November, the Bank of England announced the decision to devalue, and that a package of credits was being arranged which totalled $3,000m. Of this, $1,400m would be a standby from the IMF, $500m of which would be borrowed through the GAB. *The Times* (18 November 1967) reported that the members of the Group of Ten had been in touch by telephone for several days, and would be ready to put up the necessary European currency immediately. It also remarked on the change since 1964 in French policy towards the instruments of multilateral surveillance. Now, instead of the Group of Ten, ' France would much prefer the IMF itself to have the main say, on the assumption that it is the Fund which is more to be trusted in making Britain follow a policy of financial discipline than the individual members in the GAB '. But, as noted earlier, this was not a serious issue. Britain, too, preferred the Fund's surveillance, and in consequence it was arranged that the whole negotiation should be left to the Fund. Their staff team arrived in London the day that devaluation was announced, and a Group of Ten meeting was postponed from 22 November until the following week, precisely so that the talks between the Treasury and the Fund could be concluded before the Ten met.[45] These talks were over by 23 November and a Letter of Intent to the Fund's Managing Director, signed by Callaghan for the British cabinet, was sent to Washington on the same day and was published on 30 November (see App. A below).

At the meetings of the Group of Ten and of Working Party III, in spite of an optimistic report on Britain's economic prospects which had just been published by the OECD, doubts were expressed about the dangers of wage inflation and the size of the government's borrowing. It was obviously too late to prevent the loan from going ahead, but in Working Party III it was argued that stricter financial discipline and regular surveillance were required.[46]

This was the first time that a British government had published a Letter of Intent, though Roy Jenkins, who had now succeeded Callaghan as Chancellor of the Exchequer, declared in the House that several had been written privately, by Conservative as well as by Labour governments. The Letter contained two important commitments: first, to hold down the borrowing requirement of the government to £1 billion in the financial year from April 1968; and second, to limit the expansion of bank credit so that the growth of money supply would be less in 1968 than in 1967, ' both absolutely and as a proportion of GNP ' (para. 11). A third object of government policy would be to ' ensure, in co-operation with the TUC and CBI, that the policy for prices and incomes measures up to the requirements of the new situation ' (para. 12). Finally, it was stated in the last sentence (para. 16),

If, in the opinion of the Government of the United Kingdom or the Managing Director of the Fund, the policies are not producing the desired improvement in the balance of payments, the Government of the United Kingdom will consult with the Fund, during the period of the standby arrangement and as long thereafter as Fund holdings of sterling exceed 125 per cent of quota, to find appropriate solutions.

The debate in the House of Commons was a stormy one and the last paragraph of the Letter provoked the gibe that ' the Managing Director is given equal status in making decisions on government policy with the government themselves '. Michael Foot, who had succeeded in forcing a debate under Standing Order No. 9, attacked particularly the paragraph of the Letter which committed the government to maintaining the new parity without resort to any additional restrictions on current payments.[47]

The actual commitments in the Letter, however, were quite vague. The objective of limiting the government's borrowing to less than £1,000m was met and the credit squeeze was tightened in January, March, and again in November of 1968. But the aim of reducing the growth in the money supply was by no means fulfilled. In 1967 the growth had been 9·8 per cent and Domestic Credit Expansion (DCE) was £1,758m. In 1968 DCE rose even further to £1,898m. and, despite the drain on the reserves at the time of the March 1968 gold crisis and the November 1968 D-mark crisis, the money supply was allowed to rise by 6·6 per cent, with an especially rapid increase in the fourth quarter, when the Bank of England completely lost control of the money supply and allowed—indeed encouraged—an increase of £681m, representing an annual rate of 18 per cent.[48] This was pilloried as a Bank ' Blooper ' in *The Economist*. The reduction in the government borrowing requirement had been more than offset by the Bank's management of the National Debt: official purchases of gilt-edged from the public helped to inflate the money supply.[49]

The drawing of $1,400m which Britain had made from the Fund in 1965 was due for restitution in 1968–70, and in the spring of 1969 some $1,000m were still owed on it. A further extension was clearly required. This had been in the air for some time; when it had first been mentioned, in the middle of 1968, the Fund staff had *not* been pressing for harsh conditions to be attached to the loan; but the Bank's mismanagement of the gilt-edged market in the last three months of the year rather naturally tended to harden their attitude. The second Letter of Intent was going to be perceptibly tougher than that signed by Callaghan in 1967.

Mr Jenkins and his Treasury officials were left in no doubt too that a fairly tough budget in April 1969 would be a necessary condition of any renegotiation of the Fund drawing. Tax increases were therefore aimed at reducing demand by £200–250m, and the government's proposed borrowing requirement would involve a massive turn-round in the government accounts. This must have satisfied the Fund, for Britain had reached the point where, with Fund holdings of sterling totalling 173 per cent of quota, it had only a limited amount of its drawing rights left, and where trigger clauses would normally apply.

A Fund team visited London at the end of April to negotiate the standby, and the second Letter of Intent was dated 22 June 1969 (see App. B below). It was much more definite than that written by Callaghan fifteen months earlier, and received an even more stormy reception in the House of Commons. Here the two main objections voiced, notably by Iain Macleod, were that the Letter contained hidden trigger clauses and that British policy was being forced to conform, as on some Procrustean bed, to unproved and abstract theories about the money supply.[50] On the latter point, it was true that the Letter laid particular stress on two important quantities: a DCE of not more than £400m in the year ending March 1970, and a balance-of-payments surplus of £300m for the same period. The Letter also virtually promised not to use import controls as a weapon to bring the balance of payments back into surplus: paragraph 11 stated ' It is the Government's policy to maintain the present degree of trade liberalisation . . .'. Schweitzer apparently felt that the import deposit scheme introduced by the government in 1968 had been a breach of the 1967

Letter, and wished to guard against any more backsliding in British trade policies.[51]

According to an analysis of the difficulties in the undertakings given in the two published Letters made at the time in *The Banker*, these reflected less a change of policy than a shift in the ideas behind policy-making.[52] Despite all the rigorous squeeze policies adopted since 1964, the monetary resources available to the private sector had expanded enormously. The different emphasis between the two Letters, in *The Banker's* analysis, reflected the evolution of economic thinking in London as ' puzzled pundits . . . sought an explanation for this persistent frustration of perfectly orthodox policies '. Callaghan's Letter of Intent had represented ' a dawning understanding that the extent by which a government incurs a borrowing requirement as the natural consequence of deficit spending and fails to finance it by genuine borrowing, the deficit spending simply adds to the monetary resources of potential spenders on personal consumption '. And by May 1969 ' it was clearly established that over this period [i.e. 1965–8] during which ' deflationary ' policies had been stringently applied, no deflation (in any practical sense) had in fact been accomplished '.[53]

Although *The Banker* correctly discerned some change of thinking in Whitehall, it was widely thought that this change was brought about by external pressures and that references to DCE and the money supply indicated a concession on the part of the Treasury to the doctrines of the ' Chicago School ' of monetary economists led by Professor Milton Friedman, of whom Richard Goode, the leader of the Fund missions to London, was said to be a keen disciple.

Possibly more violent, at least in Parliament, was the reaction to what were thought to be disguised trigger clauses in the Letter. *The Economist* (28 June 1969) commented that the most striking thing about the Letter was ' the thinness of the fig-leaf that has been stretched over the trigger clause '. It was widely reported that the Fund had tried to devise a Letter which they thought to be less politically sensitive than the 1967 one. It would have provided for automatic consultation before further drawings whenever net DCE exceeded an agreed figure, probably 2 per cent per annum. ' Expansion of credit would be defined as expansion of money supply less any payments deficit, so that when Britain was in a deficit of over £300m per annum, the permitted increase in the money supply would be nought '.[54] But in the original Fund version, the trigger clause requirements concerning private sector lending were detailed and specific. The Letter, which was eventually signed, replaced these requirements with a simple objective of limiting DCE to less than £400m per annum.

Credit for this dilution goes to Harold Lever, Financial Secretary to the Treasury, who made an 'unannounced but not secret' visit to Washington over the weekend of 12 May 1969. The aim of this trip was alleged to be to remove or redraft the trigger clause in the Letter, which he felt was humiliating and more suitable for a banana republic than the United Kingdom. Lever succeeded, so the story went, in getting the clause disguised, so that Britain did give firm commitments to adhere to certain standards and did agree to regular consultation with the Fund, but the link between the commitments and the Fund's assistance was not so evident or direct as it would be in an ordinary trigger clause. In some quarters this was viewed merely as face-saving, and it was believed that 'the practical force of the agreement will be as stringent as before Mr Lever's visit '.[55] Lever was certainly at pains to deny such press accounts of his visit to Washington: 'The policies agreed upon in Washington are the policies of the British government ', as formulated in the British Treasury, and as finally approved by the British Chancellor.[56] But there were still those who insisted that there was a disguised trigger clause in the Letter. Their arguments were supported by the fact that only $500m of the billion negotiated was immediately available. An alternative explanation less injurious to national pride was that the Fund's rules said emphatically that members cannot normally draw beyond the point where the Fund's holdings of their currency exceed 200 per cent of quota. At the moment when the United Kingdom applied for the drawing, the Fund's holdings of pounds were already £650m below that limit, so that any drawing at all was a concession to British needs.

Several points emerge from this part of the story. The first perhaps is that the fuss over the Letter was, more than anything else, a product of British domestic politics. Mr Jenkins had taken on at the Treasury the hottest seat in the British cabinet. No. 11 Downing Street had been the grave of several promising politicians' reputations since the war— one remembers Selwyn Lloyd and Peter Thorneycroft—and even Hugh Gaitskell and Harold Macmillan had found it hard to wriggle out of responsibility for the consequences of Treasury policies during their time there. By 1967 it was a hotter seat than ever, and Mr Jenkins's first decision, almost after taking it over, was to publish Callaghan's Letter. It was said that when he accepted the job he had not seen the Letter. Certainly, he wanted no responsibility for the terms agreed by Callaghan for Fund help. Nor did he want the odium of any unpleasant measures that might be necessary to fulfil them. But while publication led some to accuse the Fund of being too soft with Britain, others thought it might help to keep the British to their good intentions. Moreover, the Fund had asked for Letters of Intent from Britain before and had never insisted that they be made public and submitted—even post hoc—to parliamentary scrutiny. Jenkins admitted to the House of Commons that it was an unusual step.[57] If Jenkins had kept quiet, it was possible that Parliament would have continued in blissful ignorance of the extent to which its supposed constitutional sovereignty was being slowly eaten away.

The second point is that there was no guarantee that the Letters would prove an effective instrument of multilateral surveillance. As already noted, paragraph 13 of the first Letter said that the government would maintain the new parity ' without resort to any additional restrictions on current payments or intensification of the present restrictions '. Yet the import deposit scheme introduced in 1968 was a breach of this undertaking. Nor were the targets set out in the Letter fulfilled: the 1967 Letter aimed at a surplus on the balance of payments of £200m per annum by the second half of 1968, and at a slowing down in the increase in the money supply. Neither of these was fulfilled, though the government's borrowing requirement was drastically reduced.

Similarly, the policies outlined in the 1969 Letter were based on the April budget, which had been designed with a fresh drawing in mind, and an important accompaniment of it (in American eyes at least) was the Bill to reform the trade unions. Yet in June 1969 the government gave in to the opposition of the trade unions to the White Paper *In Place of Strife*. (This, presented by the Labour minister, Mrs Barbara Castle, proposed new legislation governing trade unions.) *The Economist* (21 June 1969) commented ' everybody is going to remember that this money [i.e. the Fund drawing] has been borrowed from the IMF with a promise to fulfil a Budget strategy of which, in Mr Jenkins's own words at the time, the Castle Bill was an essential part '. This was a mild exaggeration. In fact, everyone soon forgot it—partly because the other targets set in May 1969, unlike those agreed in 1967, were in fact fulfilled. The balance-of-payments surplus was twice the £300m target and the DCE showed a substantial contraction.[58]

The other weapon in the Fund's armoury of surveillance was the consultation procedure. This was more private, more discreet. After the Fund team's first visit the day devaluation was announced, there were further less publicized visits to London in February, July, and November 1968. Whether anything may be deduced from the coincidence of two visits with the moments (in January, March, and November of 1968) when Jenkins tightened the screws of the squeeze is problematical. Each visit was followed by a solemn team report to the Executive Board on the patient's progress but no one was ever clear what would happen if the team had expressed deep dissatisfaction with what the Bank of England was doing. And the judgement of the Fund's General Counsel, Mr Joseph Gold, on the efficacy of the consultation procedure was distinctly cool. He concluded that consultation was not the most important activity with regard to debtors. The consultation clauses ' taken in isolation have probably not made a major contribution to the direction of members' policies '.[59] Gold preferred performance criteria. That, however, might be a lawyer's natural preference for the specific and visible form of influence over the general but intangible. For it might, conversely, be argued that the Fund visits to Threadneedle Street—hitherto an impregnable bastion of elitism in monetary management, well insulated from any external academic influence by non-Bank economists—did in the long run bear fruit in slightly changed attitudes and that nothing else but the enforced consultations would have penetrated so far beneath the carapace of the Bank's complacence and self-satisfaction.

Thus the weight to be attached to particular instruments of Fund surveillance, and even the effectiveness of the surveillance itself, must remain to some extent a matter for subjective judgement. The case that it was influential, as well as the case that it was not, must remain unproven. All that may be said with some confidence is that both parties were a great deal more concerned with appearances than with realities. The British did not want to be made to look ' like a banana republic '. The Fund wished to show the world (and especially the European members) that it was behaving like a tough and vigilant taskmaster. The plain inference would seem to be that everyone—Mr Michael Foot perhaps excepted—was more concerned with the effect of their actions on the confidence of the market than with the effect on the economy.

Another question posed at the start of this chapter was whether the multilateral surveillance devised by the system was severe or not. Were the measures required of Britain as debtor more draconian than those the government would otherwise have applied? Were they more severe than those imposed on other debtor countries?

As to the first question, it would seem that, on the broad strategy of demand management and the use of fiscal regulators, the British government needed no convincing. If the strategy was wrong in whole, or in part, or if its timing was bad—and each of these propositions is arguable—then the prime responsibility was the British government's; the surveillants bear only a minor share of the blame. The only issue on which the surveillants appear to have insisted on a harder line than the British government was at first prepared to take was on the matter of the money supply and the government's demand for borrowed funds. The surveillants did not, however, insist on reduced government spending in any particular direction. On the level of the defence budget, and on investment in large, speculative prestige projects like the RB211 engine, the Fund team, it may be inferred, was silent.

The second question requires comparative evidence for which we have the almost contemporary example of another developed country, Italy, referred to earlier in this chapter. In the next, we shall have that of France, which is also very relevant to the question. In the Italian case, the chief creditor country was the United States and its ' surveillance '—if any—appeared remarkably mild. The EEC sounded as if it would have imposed much more severe deflationary curbs on the Italian economy if it had had the power, but it had not. The Italian government, its hand guided by the central bank, applied the deflationary brakes when it judged the time was right. But the choice was evidently an Italian one and not one imposed from outside, and in making it, domestic political as well as economic considerations played an important part.

It is true that the Italian crisis was less severe and more quickly overcome than the British. But another interpretation might be that the surveillance perceived by the system to be necessary was actually greater the more developed (or monetarily prominent) the debtor country, and not the converse. For the comparative evidence available from the treatment of developing countries falling into acute debt situations in this same period does strongly suggest that the continuum was actually the reverse of that suggested by Mr Lever's incensed remarks about banana republics. Perhaps if Britain *had* been a banana republic, there would have been not more but fewer inquisitorial visitations from the Fund, fewer portentous inquiries into the financing of the British deficit in Working Party III.

This point is perhaps worth a moment's consideration. The three most serious cases of debt among developing countries in the mid-1960s were Indonesia, Ghana, and the UAR. Detailed accounts of these cases will be found in later chapters by Christopher Prout.[60] For present purposes, we need only observe that in all three, the creditors appeared much less anxious to supervise the management of the debtor's economy than they were to make certain it had enough aid to keep it barely solvent financially and precariously stable politically. In this aim the creditors were not always too successful. But negotiations among creditors often seemed more seriously concerned that each creditor should agree to cough up something for the debtor, and that none should bear an unequal burden of emergency aid or postponed repayment from which others might benefit. For instance, the delays over Indonesia's debts, from 1966 when Suharto took over from Sukarno until the final agreement in 1971, were mainly caused by disagreements between the main creditors (who included the Soviet Union as well as Japan) on the rate of interest to be paid and the time-span for rescheduling. In the Ghanaian case—which also dragged on from 1966 to the end of the decade—it was Britain who was the tough creditor and who was opposed—successfully—not only by Nkrumah's successors but also by the Fund and the World Bank. In both cases, the provision of aid was made politically easier because the debt crisis had been brought on and accompanied by a political revolution, giving the creditors a clean new ' reform ' government to deal with.

The one case of the three in which it might be argued that the creditors tried hard to impose severe terms on a poor debtor country was that of the UAR. And by comparison with Ghana and Indonesia, Nasser had been provokingly defiant, towards both the Fund and the United States. But by 1969 the threatened breach had been averted and the defiant debtor was being welcomed back into the fold.

None of these cases would seem to contradict, moreover, the three rather general conclusions which emerge from analysis of the British experience.

The first and most important conclusion was that there was no single principle or code of rules that could be automatically applied to situations of chronic international debt and requiring the imposition of multilateral surveillance on the debtor country. The Fund tried hard to make out that there was such a code. But it was constantly breaking its own rules or making up new ones and the pretence at times wore pretty thin (see below, ch. 9).[61]

The second conclusion, a kind of rider to the first, was that it was always open to a creditor or creditors to opt out, to break step with the rest of the creditors' group and their appointed agents in international organizations. Each creditor was free to offer less help, or more, as its (mainly political) inclinations dictated. (This was where most evidence occurs of interaction between the international political system and the international economic system.) The least flexible creditors in this respect were the international agencies, notably the Fund. In the British case, it was the French who twice broke step and opted out, once in 1965 and again in 1967. In the Ghanaian case, it was Britain; and with Indonesia, it was on occasion, Japan. None of these divergencies, however, much affected the course of events.[62]

The developing countries' experience also bears out the last conclusion to be drawn from the long sad story of sterling, which is that every debt situation is a two-way affair: that the international organizations charged with imposing multilateral surveillance were as likely —possibly more likely—to be affected by the responsibility than was the debtor by their surveillance. Both the Fund and the Bank were very evidently moulded in their structure, attitudes, and mode of operation by the responsibilities they assumed towards developing countries in general and debtor countries in particular.[63]

In the British case, the first international organization to be affected was the OECD, and in particular its Working Party III. When the latter body first began to meet every six or eight weeks in Paris in the spring of 1961, it had had a fairly quiet routine. National representatives— there were usually three or four from each country, including at least one from the Finance Ministry and one from the central bank—would present prepared statements tending usually to explain away or to play down the importance of any recent movement in their external payments positions. It was after 1964, and after the agreement reached at the IMF annual meeting that year in Tokyo, that Working Party III began to grow in stature.[64] Then the British and Americans agreed to bring all bilateral arrangements for temporary credits (including the whole swap network) as well as GAB credits into the multilateral surveillance scheme. Group of Ten members also agreed then to exchange advance information on the ways in which they proposed to finance their balance-of-payments deficits. It was this requirement which led the OECD secretariat to improve on work begun in the IMF to develop a form of presentation of balance-of-payments statistics which would allow national figures to be compared with one another.[65] ' On the basis of these statistics ' Robert Russell, the American monetary historian, concluded, ' the discussions [in Working Party III] became less formal and more frank over the years '.[66] Russell's opinion, however, after some very detailed research and interviewing of those concerned, was not that Working Party III acquired power over member countries—on the contrary, he thought the meetings had ' only a modest influence ' on members' policy decisions—but that Working Party III became by this route an important vehicle for the exchange of information among the group of rich-country governments. These countries used the meetings, he thought, as a valuable occasion on which to explain ' major policy moves *on which they had already decided* '.[67] The only strong indication of influence exerted through Working Party III was that of the United States on British policy, and this is to be seen in the high priority given in Working Party III to the removal or prohibition of trade restrictions, as compared to capital controls which were regarded much more leniently. This was shown in the decision in 1964 to activate the GAB only on condition that Britain should do nothing to make the import surcharge discriminatory.

The other international organization to have its importance inflated —if that is not a pejorative word—by the surveillance of Britain was the BIS. The Tokyo agreement of 1964 led directly to more detailed and systematic exchange of information among the central bankers who went every month to Basle. These special exchanges took place after 1964 at every other BIS meeting and were conducted at a high technical level in great secrecy. Once more, the main consequence was to improve the BIS as a vehicle for mutual information and understanding. This effect lasted beyond the 1967 sterling devaluation and the Basle Agreement of March 1968, which probably marked the end of a period when the BIS was predominantly concerned with the British question. By then, European attention was increasingly absorbed by the US deficit—over which no one was attempting to set up any serious machinery for multilateral surveillance—and the task, after 1967, was increasingly left to the Fund. The impression was widespread that consideration of British policies both in OECD and in the BIS was increasingly perfunctory.[68]

As to the Fund itself, it is evident from the account given earlier that the Fund's close relation with the United Kingdom greatly affected the Fund's own operations and exerted a powerful influence on the interpretation of Fund rules, several of which had to be bent or interpreted anew. At the same time, it was widely thought among the Fund officials that the British example of docile submission to surveillance by the Fund had served in the long run to strengthen the Fund's authority throughout its membership, and notably to make it easier to get the French when their turn came in 1969 to submit to similar treatment. To this we shall come in the next chapter.

The central banks and sterling: the 1968 Basle Agreement

The first Basle Agreement of 1961, it will be recalled, had been no more than a private understanding among the central banks of the affluent alliance that they would, automatically and as a matter of course not requiring special consultation and negotiation, provide short-term support for any currency whose exchange rate was threatened by pressures from the foreign exchange markets. They agreed to do this in two ways. Either they would stand ready to accumulate (e.g.) sterling deposited with them by commercial banks and financial institutions, and to hold it, as it were, so that it made no visible impact on the threatened economy's balance of payments for at least three (and possibly for six) months. They also made arrangements for the 'recycling' of hot money inflows, neutralizing them by the deposit in the central bank of the country of origin of an equivalent sum in the refuge currency. Since, in the short term, neither of these devices upset the co-operating banks accounts, they could be resorted to at minimal cost, but on occasions with great effect.

Although it was proclaimed as a temporary solution to the volatility of foreign exchange markets in a fixed-exchange rate system, ' pending the evolution of more permanent techniques ',[69] the agreement was not rescinded when the GAB had been safely negotiated the following year. On the contrary, it had been precedent and foundation for the rescue of sterling in November 1964. As recounted above, Britain had repaid this credit when a longer-term arrangement was made in 1965 to borrow from the Fund. But as also recounted, in September 1965 the central bankers (excepting the Banque de France) had once more been called on to help the Bank of England with a credit—reportedly around $1 billion in foreign exchange—with which successfully to operate a bear squeeze on the market. Most effectively and dramatically, the recycling technique had been used after the June War of 1967 to counteract the shifting of funds from London to Switzerland by Arab states. Thanks to the Swiss, corresponding funds promptly appeared in London.

Up to the summer of 1966 the system of central bank co-operation, like the swap network which it reinforced, had provided politically unconditional support for sterling. Then, for the first time, the central banks laid down specific terms about the circumstances in which Britain could draw on credit from them. They assured Britain automatic access to a temporary-permanent credit line of up to $1,000m, provided the pressures on the pound arose from fluctuations in the official sterling balances held in London and did not arise from Britain's own balance of payments. This distinction had been suggested, despite some resistance from the Bank of England, by the Dutch, not out of hostility so much as friendship. Of all the Six, the Dutch were most anxious for Britain to be admitted to the European Community. They were also aware of French resistance, on monetary grounds among others, to Britain's entry, and were therefore quick to see the need to meet French objections.

It was this arrangement of June 1966 which foreshadowed the terms of the 1968 Basle Agreement. The latter was even more explicit in the conditions it set for the provision of central bank support for sterling. It not only restricted the credits to pressures on the exchange rate arising from changes in sterling area balances (as had the 1966 credit), but also became operative only when certain arrangements aimed to maintain the stability of the reserve currency system had been negotiated between Britain and its monetary associates. Thus the key decision of the central bank community to take limited liability for the strains on sterling arising from its reserve role—but, by implication, to refuse them on other grounds—really dates not from 1968 but from 1966.

The significance of this development is worth emphasizing, if only because it was one of those turning points at which monetary diplomacy became visibly politicized. A form of international co-operation, hitherto classed as technical and functional, all at once became political as the creditors made a political distinction between domestic and foreign circumstances and by this means subjected the debtor to bargaining processes.

Before mid-1966 ex-colonial monetary systems had, by common tacit consent, been looked at with a blind eye. Like bastards or mistresses, everyone knew about the post-colonial relationships, but they were not to be referred to in polite society.

In the EPU, for instance, although it had been acknowledged behind closed doors that Britain's monthly balance reflected the members' transactions not only with the United Kingdom but with sterling area suppliers of primary products for European industry, yet the fiction of exclusively British membership was most studiously maintained. Special arrangements, in practice, were made for sterling on account of the sterling area, but no sterling area representative was ever seen at meetings of the Managing Board. And in 1951 at the GATT, Australia and New Zealand were given special dispensation (on the insistence of the United States) from the rule which said that when member countries' payments moved from deficit to surplus, they must abandon discriminatory import controls. At that time, Britain was still in deficit and the ruling effectively allowed Britain to have the sterling area treated as a whole, regardless of the fortunes of its component members.

By 1966 this polite lack of interest in the sterling area could be sustained no longer—partly because the British themselves—though not yet in official circles—were beginning to complain that not all their troubles were directly of their own doing but some had been brought upon them by their liabilities towards their associates of the sterling area. For example, William Clark, Financial and Industrial Editor of *The Times*, sought to draw attention to the City's positive contributions to the balance of payments. He also explained clearly how Britain's liabilities to the sterling area were apt to cause uneasiness in the market:

The evidence so far points to a gradual lowering of the sterling content in the official reserves of several sterling area countries. . . And, as the privileges of sterling area membership appear to decline, other countries are likely to follow suit. On the face of it, this may have all the appearances of a currency problem for Britain. It might lead to a run on the central reserves at an inconvenient time. . . . Since total sterling balances (or liabilities) are well in excess of sterling assets and gold, the presentation of all the sterling balances for payment in gold or other currencies at the same time would, undoubtedly, produce a major crisis for Britain.[70]

This was one point—an essentially political one—at which the changed political relationship of Asian and African countries towards Britain made an important difference to the market operators' view of the 'overhang' of sterling balances over British reserves. Political independence might now lead, at any time, to the expression of monetary independence either through the running down or the diversification of these countries' monetary reserves into assets other than sterling. And this risk was a new one which market operators, at any sign of weakness in the sterling exchange rate, could not ignore.

The second point was almost commonplace in Whitehall but perhaps only began to sink in with Europeans as the sterling problem of the mid-60s dragged into its second year, obliging Europeans to pay closer attention to the details of the relation between Britain and its monetary associates. It was simply that a fall in British reserves was at least as apt to result from the deficit position of Australia or Malaysia as it was to stem from a British deficit. The point was rubbed home by several British writers, notably Fred Hirsch who had passionately (but a little too late) argued for a clean devaluation of sterling.[71] It was also rubbed in by Arthur Conan, a former assistant secretary of the Commonwealth Economic Committee who published a scholarly analysis of the current and capital account of the sterling area. Conan's conclusion, looking back over past sterling crises, was characteristically quiet and low-key—but quite definite. ' Post-war crises were very diverse in character and it would be unjustifiable to infer consistently poor performance on the part of the United Kingdom ...'

The contrast between crises in the current balance and crises occasioned by losses of reserves [Conan went on] ... must raise doubts whether any one theory can explain the problem of sterling: more probably different factors create different types of crisis. Secondly, it narrows down to very few cases the crises which can be ascribed to an inefficient economy. For the majority (the reserve crises) the drain on the reserves represented demands by the overseas sterling area or non-sterling countries: in other words, these crises derived from external rather than internal factors.[72]

Between the 1966 central bank credit arrangement for Britain and the second Basle Agreement in 1968, there occurred an important shift of British opinion outside Whitehall and notably in the City. Until the middle of the decade the fear had been commonly felt among British bankers and other financial operators that an attack on any one of the international roles of sterling would jeopardize all, and that foreign interference should therefore be kept to a minimum. About 1966–7 there was a noticeable shift in City opinion; the idea spread that sterling might be more acceptable and stable and the City's job therefore easier if the reserve function were either removed, transferred, or in some way permanently stabilized.

Yet official opinion was much slower to change, probably because the sterling area relationship was one of the few remaining links holding the Commonwealth together and was therefore valued for political and prestige reasons more than for economic ones.[73] At first, until about the winter of 1965–6, Whitehall and the Bank of England

UK external banking & money market liabilities in sterling (£m)

	Total all countries	EEC	Overseas sterling countries [1]								Other countries				
			Total	Australia, NZ, & S. Africa	India, Pakistan, Sri Lanka, & Bangladesh	Caribbean area [2]	East, Central, & West Africa [3]	Middle East [4]	Far East [5]	Other [6]	Total	N. America [7]	Latin America [8]	W. Europe [9]	Other
Central monetary institutions															
1964	1,245		894	389	20	45	124	139	109	68	351	26	16	173	136
1965	1,147		868	191	58	42	110	225	164	78	279	26	29	101	123
1966	1,158		849	211	17	35	97	220	165	104	309	50	7	73	179
1967	1,028		783	162	24	25	61	264	169	78	245	2	5	78	160
1968	854		712	99	78	50	89	197	117	82	142	9	4	42	87
1969	942		842	77	94	40	118	257	148	108	100	5	7	34	54
1970	1,070		968	91	53	47	137	320	184	136	102	3	4	32	63
1971	1,723		1,442	426	58	51	195	306	247	159	281	4	10	64	203
1972															
1st qtr	1,861		1,523	519	60	55	168	329	195	197	338	4	11	77	246
2nd qtr	1,887		1,571	645	108	50	135	279	173	181	316	97	15	76	128
3rd qtr	1,841		1,623	650	145	39	156	302	150	181	218	4	12	53	149
4th qtr	1,905		1,716	615	122	38	179	397	90	275	189	3	11	42	133
1973															
1st qtr	2,082	157	1,751	588	166	41	230	516	96	114	174	3	6	24	141
2nd qtr	2,086	160	1,634	528	145	36	272	473	91	89	292	3	19	28	242

[1] For changes in coverage see notes 3–6.
[2] Includes Bahamas, Bermuda, British Honduras and Guyana.
[3] Gambia, Ghana, Kenya, Malawi, Nigeria, Sierra Leone, Tanzania, Uganda, until Apr 1965 Southern Yemen, and until Dec 1965 Rhodesia.
[4] Jordan, Kuwait, and other Persian Gulf Territories, from Apr 1965 Southern Yemen and until Dec 1971 Libya.
[5] Brunei, Hong Kong, Malaysia, Singapore, and until Dec 1966, Burma.
[6] Cyprus, Iceland, Malta, Gibraltar, and UK dependent territories not elsewhere included, and until Dec 1972 the Irish Republic.
[7] United States and dependencies, and Canada.
[8] Other independent non-sterling countries of the American continent.
[9] Includes the BIS and excludes the EEC from Jan 1973.

Source: Bank of England Quarterly Bulletin.

studiously ignored the question. Or if challenged, official spokesmen and apologists were inclined to point to the relative stability of the sterling balances over the years. This was true enough. British government stocks held by OSA central banks were exactly the same in value in 1966 as they had been in 1962, and although there had been some steady decline in the total of official OSA balances from £1,947m in December 1964 to £1,736m in December 1967, it was not a large one in relation to the total. What the official line ignored, though, was that the stability was achieved by a combination of carrot and stick—the carrot of high interest rates, and the stick of unstoppable devaluation if the market were to observe official holders bolting. But by the summer of 1967 criticism and controversy at home and abroad had at least put official opinion on the defensive. In May Mr Callaghan was disclaiming official concern with the prestige of sterling: ' so far as the rôle of sterling is concerned, whether in its international aspect or as a domestic currency, we are ready for change, subject only to safeguarding the interests of the present holders of sterling '.

' The world rôle of sterling ', he said, was not a ' matter of prestige but a practical matter '.[74] In short, it appeared that Britain had stopped saying ' We will not change ' but was protesting ' We could not change even if we would '.

The sterling devaluation when it came in November 1967 had a perverse effect. Instead of steadying the official holders, it upset them. In the first place it revealed the extent of erosion that had taken place in the structural strength of the sterling area since convertibility. In 1949 all the sterling area countries except Pakistan devalued in step with Britain; and eighteen non-sterling area countries devalued (some by lesser or greater amounts) when sterling did. In 1967 only Israel and Spain among non-sterling countries devalued by the same percentage as Britain: four others (Brazil, Denmark, Nepal, and Macao) devalued by different percentages. Many of the larger sterling area countries (Australia, India, Malaysia, Nigeria, Libya, Kuwait, Pakistan, and South Africa) kept their old dollar rate. Only ten OSA countries who were also members of the IMF devalued by the same amount, and those which followed sterling down were mostly smaller ones like Ceylon, Malawi, Jamaica, and Cyprus.[75] The only large official holders of sterling to devalue with Britain were Ireland and Hong Kong. The devaluing group accounted altogether for only 6½ per cent of British imports and 7½ per cent of British exports.[76]

The consequence for all, whether they devalued or not, was substantial depreciation (in terms of the dollar, the yen, and European currencies) in the value of sterling held as national monetary reserves. For example, the loss for Australia was estimated at some £50m. It was true that this public, or government, loss was balanced by other, mostly private, gains. Australian states, municipalities, and companies which had raised a great deal of sterling over the years for capital investment now had less to repay in terms of Australian dollars. And Australia was one of the more prudent sterling area countries which had been quietly but deliberately reducing the sterling component in its national reserves, adding to the country's official gold holdings, and increasing its dollar assets (and IMF drawing rights denominated in dollars). It had also increased its holdings of high interest rate sterling assets, reducing its more liquid (but less profitable) assets.

But there were others, notably Hong Kong, which had been unable to go in for precautionary diversification and which were badly bitten in November 1967. Hong Kong's losses on official and unofficial sterling balances were something over £50m and those responsible for the colony were twice shy about repeating the experience.

It was indeed Hong Kong that showed the way for the Basle Agreement arrangements. The government, though politically still dependent, had first insisted on its right to revalue against sterling— effectively preferring some stability in its dollar exchange rate to total stability in the sterling rate. The colony's Financial Secretary then started negotiations with London in May 1968 to get a dollar guarantee for its very substantial reserves. Owing to Hong Kong's lack of a central bank, some of these government reserves were deposited with commercial banks. Conceivably these banks could have converted them into assets denominated in other currencies. The British Treasury, either under this tacit threat or out of considerations of justice and equity, agreed that these holdings should be transferred into a special Exchange Fund, where they could *not* be changed into gold or dollars. In return, the Hong Kong government would be offered some special seven-year British government bonds, non-transferable and denominated in Hong Kong dollars. By this means, half Hong Kong's reserves were proof against any further depreciation of sterling in terms of Hong Kong dollars.

An important new factor had meanwhile been added to the situation by the Two-Tier Gold Agreement of March 1968 (see below, pp. 292 ff.). By this the governments formerly associated with the United States in the management of the gold market through the Gold Pool agreed among themselves to leave the private gold market to itself, not to buy or sell in it, and by implication to see that other governments observed the same rule. Sterling area countries which, by this time, might have been contemplating the attractions of larger gold holdings (following the Old Commonwealth example) were now no longer free to acquire gold unless—like South Africa—they produced it themselves. All they could acquire in any significant quantity in place of their sterling assets were dollar assets.[77]

The scramble to do just that began to gather momentum after the middle of March 1968. As recounted later in a British government White Paper:

Diversification of reserves by sterling area countries increased and, in contrast to earlier periods, there was a significant fall in the total of officially held sterling balances as considerable sums were switched into other forms of reserves. This movement was particularly marked in the second quarter of 1968, when holdings of sterling by central monetary institutions of the sterling area were depleted by £230 million.[78]

To save the reserves, Britain was able at first to draw on the credit provided by the central banks in 1966. This had been renewed in February 1968 and was good for a further year until March 1969. But the withdrawals were so heavy that well over half the credit had been used before June and there was no telling how long the scramble would go on. A long-term arrangement for the support of sterling had been proposed in February by Guido Carli, speaking in London to the Overseas Bankers' Club.[79] And after the two-tier meeting in Washington in March, the suggestion was taken up by others, including Sir Eric Roll. Addressing the American Bankers' Association in May, Roll said prophetically that it would be best to get to grips with the sterling balances problem right away, rather than wait for a new crisis to strike.[80]

By the end of May 1968, therefore, a new plan for the pound was very much in the air, and interest was heightened by the government's announcement on 1 June of the terms of the guarantee given to Hong Kong. The new facility for sterling was discussed at the BIS annual meeting in Basle over the weekend 8–9 June, but no final agreement was reached. (A series of OECD–Group of Ten meetings in Paris scheduled for the next few days, at which discussions might have continued, had to be postponed because of the riots and the political situation there.)

At this point the British government realized that it would have to act quickly but apparently felt that it would disrupt Commonwealth relations if sterling area countries were not treated roughly alike or if the terms of the guarantee given for their sterling holdings were to vary too much. At the same time, it would be very dangerous if any major governments were to refuse outright to stop getting out of sterling. A high-level interdepartmental troika was therefore set up to direct from London the negotiation of a reasonably standard set of agreements with each of the countries thought of as belonging to the sterling area—and to do so with the utmost speed. The troika consisted of Samuel Goldman from the Treasury, Kenneth Christofas from the Foreign and Commonwealth Office, and Christopher McMahon from the Bank of England. Senior officials were sent off in all directions with instructions to give as few concessions as possible to official sterling holders but to generalize the terms they agreed to all other holders. It was something like a GATT negotiation by telex. One of the toughest assignments, given to Frank Figgures, was to negotiate with the Australians. Much easier, since the earlier deal had pioneered the way, was Arthur Snelling's in Hong Kong.

In the two months of simultaneous negotiation, from mid-July through August and September, three main issues arose between the United Kingdom and the OSA countries.[81] The first was the question of gold guarantee. This was demanded by several countries, notably Singapore, on at least part of the official reserves in London. The British argued that a dollar guarantee would be enough to protect holders against abnormal exchange risk. A gold guarantee was not given on dollar holdings and was therefore said to be unnecessary. In fact, Kuwait had on several occasions asked for a gold guarantee and had repeatedly been refused. It was true that Britain had agreed, with others (in the Bretton Woods Agreement on Fund drawings, quotas, and subscriptions, in the EMA, and with other central banks involved in the network of swap facilities), to underwrite the gold value of British commitments in international arrangements. But this was considered a quite different matter from underwriting individual sterling balances with a gold guarantee.

An added reason for British reluctance to give a gold guarantee was that no one knew whether the recently agreed two-tier gold price arrangement was going to last. There were a good many observers who thought it might soon break down and that the end-result would be a substantial increase in the official dollar-gold price. If this were to happen, obviously Britain—had it given a gold guarantee to sterling holders—would be over-compensating them since the guarantee would increase their purchasing power in terms of dollar and all other currencies as well as in terms of sterling. On this point, therefore the British negotiators were adamant.

The second point at issue—assuming that a dollar but not a gold guarantee was given—was how much of a country's sterling holdings should the guarantee cover, and on what terms? Would it be for three years, with provision for renewal in 1971, or for five? And would it be a 100 per cent guarantee, or something less? And what measure of stability in the holdings would be exacted as the price of the guarantee? This was where the British negotiating team allowed themselves just a little room for manoeuvre. In all else, the m.f.n. principle reigned supreme. But by means of the concept of the Minimum Sterling Proportion (MSP) it was possible to vary from client to client both the proportion of the balance stabilized and the proportion guaranteed.

The deal was that the official holders of sterling would exchange for the guarantee a promise to maintain a fixed ratio between their sterling holdings and their total monetary reserves. If the total fell, they could not just get rid of the sterling and hang on to the gold and dollars. The sterling component was to be reduced only in fixed proportion to the total reduction. But the level of the MSP agreed by each government could vary from that agreed by others, without the difference being disclosed.[82] Some countries had already run it down quite low; others were still lumbered with a high proportion of sterling in their reserves. Of these some were more anxious than others to diversify. Once the level of the MSP had been negotiated, however, the rest of the terms of the guarantee were standardized. It would apply not to the whole of the official holdings, but only to 90 per cent. It would not apply at all to private unofficial sterling balances, even though the Treasury had acted via the forward exchange market from about 1964 until the 1967 devaluation to provide cheap forward cover to unofficial sterling holders. But if individual sterling area governments wished to pass on the cover to private holders of sterling, that was up to them.[83]

The net result was to manage a crisis by effecting a standstill, to stop the scramble out of sterling and to petrify the reserve ratios of dollars to sterling in which the sterling area countries found themselves in the summer of 1968. Politically, this served to preserve the system against any additional destabilizing movement, and Britain from another sterling crisis. The arrangement took the ultimate responsibility for the sterling area away from Britain and left it with the BIS and its members.

The third question, simply put, was what next? What was the longer-term objective, once the crisis had passed? Was it to phase sterling out as a reserve currency, as Roy Jenkins was said to have told Labour MPs he intended to do?[84] Or was it to preserve it? The answer was ambiguous. The British White Paper admitted that the role of sterling as a reserve currency had not expanded, and had recently contracted, but emphatically asserted that 'it will continue in the future as a major part of the international monetary system'.[85]

One test would be whether Britain continued to offer the inducement of high interest rate to sterling holders. It was arguable that with a guarantee against depreciation, this was no longer necessary. Indeed, if the intention was to manage an orderly diversification of reserves instead of a disorderly and destabilizing scramble, it would not have been inconsistent to make the holding of sterling at least no more attractive than other reserve assets and possibly slightly less attractive, so that when the arrangement was renegotiated a series of graduated reductions in the MSP could be anticipated. The OSA central banks wanted to have *both* the guarantee *and* the high interest rates, and they naturally resisted any suggestion that one could take the place of the other. In the event, Britain concurred and continued to offer a high rate of return as well as a guarantee. And nothing explicit was said in the agreement about long-term intentions.

Nor did the central bank creditors write any such commitment into the terms of their enlarged arrangement for the support of sterling. The communiqué which they issued after their September meeting merely said that the BIS, backed by the twelve central banks, would make available $2,000m to the Bank of England, and that the 1966 arrangements would be progressively liquidated.[86] The facility would initially be available for three years, and could then be renewed for a further two years. Repayment would be from 1974–8, i.e. from the sixth to tenth year.

The financing of the facility (i.e. the BIS side of it) was to take three forms:[87] first, the OSA countries were to be invited to deposit their non-sterling reserves with the BIS, where they would earn interest, and from which they could be withdrawn at any time. These would then be passed on to the Bank of England to help finance the run-down of the sterling balances. Thus, ' by this neat banking arrangement, the foreign currencies required to cushion the effect on British reserves of the running down of sterling balances, will, in part at least, have been provided by the OSA countries themselves '.[88] This was the first part of the financing operation; if it was insufficient, the BIS would borrow in international capital markets; the currency it borrowed would be swapped for dollars to lend to the Bank of England. If these two sources together failed to yield enough funds, then the central banks would come into the picture,[89] but whatever the BIS managed to raise in world markets would be offset against the $2,000m credit offered by the central banks. The total money available to finance the rundown of the sterling balances was therefore $2,000m *plus* whatever the OSA countries decided to deposit with the BIS in Basle.[90]

In a real sense, therefore, the additional commitments undertaken by Britain and by its central bank backers were not immediate but only contingent liabilities—and thanks to the MSP, the contingency was minimized. It was limited to fluctuations in sterling balances resulting from the holders' own balance of payments. To the extent that sterling area countries would need foreign exchange to finance a deficit, this could be found, thanks to the facility, without depleting Britain's own gold and dollar reserves, even though it might result in increasing Britain's debt liabilities. Britain's liability was transformed from an obligation to provide foreign exchange for sterling held in London into an obligation to write up the value of guaranteed balances in case sterling should be devalued or the dollar revalued to the extent needed to maintain their value in terms of dollars.

Alternative opportunities for change or reform had been rejected. The chance was missed of arranging terms for the funding of the sterling balances in whole or in part, as many critics of British policy had often proposed. This could have been done by allowing each sterling area country to decide what proportion of their holdings they were willing to leave permanently on deposit in London and what proportion they would like to move away or would like to feel free to move away. The sum of the latter ' movable ' balances could then have been matched by a long-term loan in dollars or mixed currencies to Britain.

For this to have been done, three conditions had to be fulfilled. The British had to be genuinely prepared to see the managed decline of sterling as a reserve currency, to accept all the political implications that this entailed, and to assume the necessary long-term debt necessary for its achievement. Second, the Americans had to be ready to take over the role of banker to all those sterling area countries who might prefer dollars to sterling as reserve assets. And thirdly, the central banks had to be prepared to offer large enough and long enough credit to make the funding credible in foreign exchange markets.[91]

The unacceptability of the first condition was almost certainly the main reason why the 1968 Basle Agreement stopped short of phasing sterling out. Neither the Bank of England nor the Foreign Office and Treasury thought it necessary or desirable. Only in the summer of 1972, as part of the entrance fee for unobstructed British entry into the Community, did Georges Pompidou extract from Edward Heath a vague declaration of intent to do so—a declaration still not implemented and conveniently forgotten three years later.

The second condition was much less of an obstacle. Although it could be argued that the dollar would only be weakened if new depositors increased the overhang of liabilities to reserves, yet much American opinion had by now come round to accepting the role of world banker as a desirable one. The centre-country view prevailed that it not only conferred power and prestige but was also profitable.

About the third condition there is some doubt. Some British comment suggested that the $2 billion provided by the BIS bankers, because it fell about $1,800m short of the total of official OSA sterling balances, was not large enough to finance their orderly rundown of the reserve role *in toto* and that therefore the petrifying guarantee had to be given.[92] However, this sounds suspiciously like an excuse. And it seems on the whole improbable that the necessary finance would have been refused if Britain at any time had come up with a well thought out programme for an orderly rundown. Though such a plan might have been too much to expect in the crisis atmosphere of August 1968, it could have been attempted in 1970, anticipating the agreement's renewal in 1971.[93] By that time the sterling area countries had gained experience of using the BIS to hold (and invest) their dollar balances, and this device could have been employed more extensively to economize on the amount of new credit that had to be mobilized for the operation. But the option was not considered.

The facility did *not* lead to any general rundown in official holdings of sterling by OSA countries. On the contrary, the total turned round after the agreement was announced and from the fourth quarter of 1968 until the first quarter of 1973 never ceased, quarter by quarter, to increase.

But along with this remarkable overall increase in the propensity to hold sterling went several important defections. Libya, for example, thanks to the exploitation of its oilfields in the 60s, had become, by 1970, one of the five heavyweight holders of official sterling. When the time for renewal drew near in 1971, Libya announced its decision—primarily for political reasons—not to renew its agreement. Kuwait, another, though less militant, oil-rich heavyweight, also opted out of the general renegotiation, coming to a separate (and secret) understanding with the Bank of England. The third and last of the heavyweights to leave (at the time of writing) was Malaysia which, having asked and failed to get a gold guarantee in May 1971, withdrew altogether from the Basle arrangements in October 1972, letting its sterling reserves fall below the hitherto agreed 36 per cent. (This largely accounted for the drop in total official holdings in 1972–3.)

At no time, apparently, before or after the 1968 agreement did the sterling area countries concert their bargaining tactics in dealing with Britain. Individually, some tried (like Malaysia, Australia, Hong Kong, or Kuwait) to get themselves a better deal, with more or less success according to the leverage respectively available to them. The bilateral habits of a long-established system of radial relationships with London as its centre appeared to persist, even when the Arab states or the developing countries as a group were behaving in the Fund, the UN, or elsewhere as a collective pressure group. And in each relationship, monetary compliance or awkwardness did not necessarily have much correlation with political attitudes. Eire, for example, remained throughout the least difficult heavyweight holder of sterling. Hong Kong, having started the demand for a dollar guarantee, continued, in spite of its dependent status and miniscule size, to assert its need for special treatment. By 1973 Hong Kong was the largest single holder of official sterling; but its MSP was still as high as 89 per cent. And it was asking, as yet in vain, for a guarantee in terms of its own currency.

When this was refused, the British official who was Financial Secretary to the Colonial government was outspokenly critical of Britain. This paradoxical nonconformity was explained partly by Hong Kong's position as a financial as well as commercial entrepôt, and partly by its acute economic dependence, even for fresh water, on mainland China. Earlier in the 1960s China had announced its intention of shifting its holding of foreign exchange for commercial transactions out of sterling into other currencies, including Swiss francs and Japanese yen. As sterling and dollar exchange values depreciated, therefore, Hong Kong's unrequited imports from China became dearer.

In general, however, the significance of the MSP undertaking was that it allowed any one of the OSA countries to opt out of the arrangement—even to do so suddenly and provocatively—without risk of causing a panic in the markets. It was a kind of insulating mechanism, permitting the orderly separation of the contented sheep from the unwilling, restless goats. Henceforward the market only took fright from the reserve role of sterling when, as in September 1973, Britain itself showed indecision and there was general uncertainty over the renewal of the Basle Agreements.

But it is worth reiterating that the MSP undertaking was not, in the event, the means of getting Britain to chase away all sterling holders, sheep and goats. It may have been intended as such by some, or even by most, of the European central bankers who had agreed to provide the supporting credit. Carli, for example, had consistently argued that Britain would be better relieved of the responsibilities of running a reserve currency. The French, although not party to the facility, were in doubt about it and had influenced official opinion both in Belgium and in Germany. In getting Britain to use the facility to phase out the reserve role, however, the central bankers were under one particular and very powerful political constraint. In each country, their own status and position rested heavily on their power to advise governments on the rate of interest as a major weapon of public policy for the management of the national economy. If they lost control of that, they lost everything that made a central bank an important seat of power in the state. By common consent therefore, central bankers tacitly agreed that the choice of interest rates was a matter of strictly domestic concern, sacrosanct from foreign comment and counsel. There was thus never any suggestion from BIS meetings at Basle that Britain should bring interest rates down in order to deter OSA central banks from holding sterling reserves.[94]

But as the time drew near in 1971 when the three-year agreements came up for optional renewal, it looked as though the central bankers were going to lean on Britain to move in this direction by the alternative disincentive—that of reducing the guarantee. In April 1971 there was reportedly talk of a plan to encourage OSA countries to accept lower MSPs and therefore less extensive dollar guarantees. This was just before the most crucial phase of the negotiations for British entry into the EEC began in Brussels. In the course of these, Geoffrey Rippon gave the Six, and in particular France, an assurance that Britain would see to an orderly rundown of the sterling balances. The French somewhat surprisingly accepted this rather imprecise undertaking. What emerged in September 1971 was an all-round cut of 10 per cent in everyone's MSP. The news first came out with individual announcements by New Zealand (15 September) that the MSP would be lowered from 70 to 63 per cent; and two days later, by Australia that the cut there would be from 40 to 36 per cent. Britain then announced that (with the exception of Libya and Kuwait) all MSPs would be extended for another two years, but would be cut by 10 per cent. It was a decision clearly reflecting the overall shift of influence over British policy away from the United States and towards the EEC and especially to France.

By this time, of course, the world was in the throes of the international monetary confrontation started off by the US economic measures of 15 August 1971 (see below, p. 338). Dollar convertibility was suspended, with far-reaching effects on the relative desirability of holding dollars and sterling as reserve assets. Both were now inconvertible into gold, and the dollar overhang had greatly increased. Sterling assets paid better interest and holders might reasonably prefer them to dollars. Even if Britain *had* really intended to run the balances down, the changed circumstances gave it the ideal excuse that this was difficult to do against the wishes of official holders of sterling.[95] Some ambiguity in official British statements was evident and was probably the result of some indecision at the top, and of some internal dissension and inter-bureaucratic conflict below—both unduly prolonged, no doubt, by the concentration of official minds at this time on the short-term problems of crisis management.

Possibly, too, the latest shift in American thinking about the role of the dollar in the international monetary system, and the possible attractions of an SDR-based system added to the advantages as seen from London of following Mr Asquith's dictum, ' Wait and see '. The solution of funding the sterling balances had hitherto been rejected on the ground that it would substitute an inescapable burden of debt repayments to the funding creditors for the liabilities of a banker towards depositors which, with luck, might never have to be liquidated. Britain had debts enough without adding to them. If the United States was now thinking in terms of transforming old dollar balances into

Fund accounts denominated in SDRs, perhaps sterling's salvation lay in the same direction. Any offer to dollar holders could hardly be refused to sterling holders and the debt to the IMF might then be permanent, immutable but, most important, non-repayable.

When the agreements came up for renewal a second time in 1973, Britain therefore prevaricated. While there was still such uncertainty about developments in the international monetary affairs, a Treasury statement [96] said, it would not be sensible to work out substantive agreements for a long time ahead. The guarantee was to be extended for six months only and would be implemented if daily rates over that period fell below $2·4213. This declaration by the Treasury was not the first time that Britain had appeared to act unilaterally towards the other parties to the agreements. Four months after Britain had floated sterling, the Treasury announced that it would hold itself bound by the Basle guarantee when the middle sterling-dollar market rate stayed below $2·3760 for more than thirty days. At the end of November 1972 these conditions had been met, and an estimated £60m was added to the sterling value of official holdings under the Basle Agreement in order to maintain their dollar value. Recalling 1968, it seemed that the end of dollar convertibility had noticeably weakened the bargaining position of the old sterling area countries,[97] allowing Britain to act in much more cavalier fashion with respect to their reserve holdings.

For the rest, the agreement had succeeded in achieving what all the affluent alliance and all the sterling area countries wanted most of all: security from anarchy and disorder in the markets. It did not achieve what some wanted and others either did not want or were lukewarm about, that is, the rundown of the sterling balances and the end of the reserve role of sterling. Once again, it proved easier in monetary diplomacy to procrastinate than to take a positive decisive choice, easier to choose a moderate middle-of-the-road solution and, because of inhibitions and disagreements of a basically political nature, to avoid the more radical one.

The Basle Agreements were also, in retrospect, a rather important stage in the developing use by governments of monetary guarantees for mutual protection against the risks attendant on exchange rate instability. There had been a time when countries like the United States or Britain had scorned to offer anyone guarantees on their currency holdings. For any country with the status of international banker to stoop to reassuring particular holders as to the value of their holding in terms of some other monetary asset once seemed *infra dig*. The process by which this high-and-mighty attitude was dropped began in a small way early in the decade with the issue to other governments by the US Treasury of 'Roosa bonds', which were denominated (and therefore repayable) not in dollars but in foreign currencies. The same principle was taken a great deal further for sterling with the 1968 agreements. By 1973 it had gone so far that central banks, including the Federal Reserve, were prepared to exchange guarantees that currencies borrowed from each other for the purpose of intervening in the market to stabilize unwanted movements in the rates would be repaid at the higher rate—if the borrowed currency had meanwhile appreciated.

The device of currency guarantees had by then developed into quite a sophisticated adaptive measure, by which developed countries substituted for the single reliable international monetary medium that all would have liked to enjoy, some limited measure of security against the costs of an imperfect and unpredictable adjustment process between national currencies.

Appendix A: Letter of Intent from the British Chancellor of the Exchequer to the Managing Director of the IMF, 23 November 1967 [98]

My Dear Mr Schweitzer,

I am setting out in this letter a statement of the policies and intentions of the Government of the United Kingdom.

2. The United Kingdom Government reached their decision to seek the International Monetary Fund's agreement to a reduction in the parity of the pound sterling in the light of their latest periodic review of the position and prospects of the United Kingdom economy, including the outlook for the balance of payments, to the end of 1968.

3. The Government's main objectives of policy remain the achievement and maintenance of a strong balance of payments, together with a high rate of economic growth which will make for full employment.

4. So far as the balance of payments is concerned, the Government's aim, at the new rate of exchange which has been concurred in by the Fund, is an improvement of at least £500 million a year. On present prospects for world trade this should mean a surplus in the second half of 1968 at an annual rate of at least £200 million. Beyond that there should be a further substantial rise in the surplus as the full benefits of the change in the United Kingdom's competitive position are felt.

5. At the same time as they took their decision on the rate of exchange, the Government decided that measures should be taken as and when required to free resources from domestic use on the scale necessary to secure the improvement referred to in paragraph 4 above.

6. As the Fund Board will be aware, calculations of the effect of a change in the parity of a currency, and still more of the timing of such effects, are necessarily extremely speculative. This makes it difficult to decide precisely, in the initial stages, on the scale and timing of the

measures that are required to make sure that the improvement in the competitive position is not lost through insufficient capacity at home being available to meet the expected increase in demand as it builds up over time.

7. The Government is satisfied that the measures announced on 18th November, 1967 will bring about a sufficient shift in resources in the coming months to go a very long way towards achieving the improvement needed to achieve their balance of payments objective. These measures—details of which are annexed to this letter—will, together with the effect on purchasing power at home of the devaluation itself, lead to a reduction of home demand by about £750 million to £800 million below what would otherwise have been the case.

8. The Government is fully aware of the possibility that further measures will be needed to maintain the momentum towards the balance of payments improvement referred to in paragraph 4 above. They intend to take further action once it becomes apparent that such action is required to secure the necessary balance of payments surplus.

9. The next review of the position and prospects of the United Kingdom economy and balance of payments will, in the normal course of business, be carried out in February, 1968. At this time it should be possible to assess more accurately than can be done at present the effects of the decisions announced on 18th November, 1967. In the light of the review, the Government will make a decision on the precise nature of any further action required. They will be happy to consult with the Managing Director on the results of this review, and again after the further reviews which are planned for July and November, 1968.

10. Fiscal policy will continue to play the most important rôle in making room for the needed improvement in the balance of payments. It is the Government's intention to ensure that the Exchequer's borrowing requirement for the financial year beginning 1st April, 1968, is kept under firm control. So far as can be seen at present, this entails holding down the borrowing requirement to not more than £1 billion—the appropriateness of which estimate and the measures necessary to ensure that it is achieved will be reviewed with the Managing Director in accordance with the timetable specified in paragraph 9.

11. The steps that have already been taken and will continue to be taken give rise to the expectation at present that bank credit expansion will be sufficiently limited to ensure that the growth of money supply will be less in 1968 than the present estimate for 1967, both absolutely and as a proportion of GNP, despite the expected substantial recovery of reserves. It continues to be the Government's policy to meet its own needs for finance as far as possible by the sale of debt to the non-bank public and interest rate policy will be used to this end. In the consultations mentioned in paragraph 9, the actual course of bank credit in relation to the expected course will be taken into account in determining appropriate policy actions.

Prices and incomes policy

12. The Government's object will be to ensure, in co-operation with the TUC and CBI, that the policy for prices and incomes measures up to the requirements of the new situation. It will be the Government's intention to maintain the policy set out in the White Paper, Prices and Incomes Policy after 30 June, 1967 (Cmnd 3235), under which there is no entitlement to a ' norm ' or standard increase in pay, and increases in pay and prices have to be justified against criteria of the national interest which are equally relevant to the new situation. There is no criterion for pay increases related to changes in the cost of living. To support the application of the policy, the vetting arrangements will be strengthened in order to ensure that the rise in wages and salaries does not exceed what the economy can afford over the next twelve months.

The Government has already started talks with Managements and Unions on alternative ways of achieving this objective.

Exchange control

13. The Government is determined to maintain the new parity without resort to any additional restrictions on current payments or intensification of the present restrictions. The Government, moreover intends to abolish all remaining restrictions on current transfers and payments as soon as the balance of payments allows. Similarly, as the balance of payments strengthens, the Government will consider what relaxations can be made in the present restrictions on capital transfers.

Request for a standby

14. The Government are convinced that the above measures will lead to a strong balance of payments. It is important, however, for the stability of the international monetary system to establish confidence in the new parity from the start. The Government therefore require a standby of $1·4 billion from the Fund to pay out its economic aims, both domestic and external, which it believes are fully in conformity with the aims of the Fund.

15. Before making purchases under this requested standby arrangement with the International Monetary Fund, the Government of the United Kingdom will consult with the Managing Director on the particular currencies to be purchased from the Fund.

16. The Government believe that the policies here outlined are adequate to achieve the economic goals described in this letter. If, however, present policies should turn out to be inadequate, the Government is firmly determined to take such further measures as may be necessary to achieve these goals. If, in the opinion of the Government of the United Kingdom or the Managing Director of the Fund, the policies are not producing the desired improvement in the balance of payments, the Government of the United Kingdom will consult with the Fund, during the

period of the standby arrangement and as long thereafter as Fund holdings of sterling exceed 125 per cent of quota, to find appropriate solutions.

Yours sincerely,

J. CALLAGHAN

Measures Announced on 18th November, 1967

1. Fiscal Policy

(a) As announced in the supplementary statement on Defence Policy of July, 1967 (Cmnd 3357), defence expenditure was planned to stay below £2,000 million a year at 1964 prices and to be down to £1,900 million by 1970–71. It has now been decided to achieve this reduction by 1968–69, so reducing the cost of the planned defence programme in that year by over £100 million (exclusive of terminal costs and expenditure arising from the change in parity).

(b) Civil public expenditure as a whole (i.e. including nationalised industry investment and local authority expenditure) is planned to rise over the next few years. Reductions will be made in 1968–69 to reduce the total planned for that year by £100 million.

(c) The premium (seven shillings and sixpence a week for men) paid to manufacturers under the Selective Employment Payments Act will be withdrawn—except in Development Areas. This will reduce payments by over £100 million in a full year.

(d) Payment of the export rebate will terminate on 31 March, 1968. Exports up to that date will qualify, exports thereafter will not. This will save just under £100 million in a full year, of which approximately two-thirds will be realised in 1968–69. Abolition of the rebate requires legislation which is now being prepared.

(e) The rate of Corporation Tax will be increased in the 1968 Budget from 40 per cent to 42½ per cent. The new rate will apply to profits for the year to 31 March, 1968. Allowing for side-effects, the additional yield is estimated at about £95 million in 1969–70 and approaching two-thirds of that figure in 1968–69.

2. Monetary policy and hire-purchase restrictions

The Bank Rate has been increased to 8 per cent from its previous level of 6½ per cent. This high rate has been chosen in order to reinforce the impact on confidence of the Government's measures by the offer of an exceptionally high rate of return on funds invested in London. By raising the cost of credit Bank Rate at this level will also reinforce the impact of the credit restrictions on demand.

Severe but selective restrictions are being placed on bank lending to the private sector. New ceilings have been imposed which will prevent aggregate advances rising above their level at 15th November in the case of the London clearing and Scottish banks, and end-October in the case of other banks.

Identified lending for exports, and under the schemes providing guaranteed finance for exports, and shipbuilding, will be excluded from the ceilings. Within these ceilings the priority categories for lending have been more narrowly defined than hitherto, leaving a wider area of non-priority borrowers whose demands can be compressed in order to accommodate priority lending.

Hire-purchase restrictions are also being tightened. The minimum deposit on cars will be raised from 25 per cent to 33 and one third per cent, and the maximum repayment period will be reduced from thirty-six months to twenty-seven months. In addition a ceiling is being placed on lending by finance houses restricting their lending to the level at end-October. These measures are likely to reduce net borrowing by some £100 million in 1968.

Appendix B : Letter of Intent from the British Chancellor of the Exchequer to the Managing Director of the IMF, 22 June 1969 [99]

Dear Mr Schweitzer,

The Government of the United Kingdom hereby requests of the International Monetary Fund a stand-by arrangement under which for a period of one year the United Kingdom will have the right to purchase from the Fund currencies of other members in exchange for sterling in an amount equivalent in total to $1,000 million. The Government intends to make an immediate drawing of the equivalent of $500 million. Before making a request for a further purchase under the standby arrangement, the Government will consult with the Fund and reach understanding regarding the circumstances in which such purchases may be made. Before making purchases under the requested stand-by arrangement, the Government will consult with the Managing Director on the particular currencies to be purchased from the Fund.

2. The purpose of this stand-by is to support the Government's economic objectives and policies. It will facilitate the repayments of external debt now falling due, including the scheduled repurchases of sterling from the Fund in respect of the 1965 drawing by the United Kingdom, and will assist in maintaining stability in the international monetary system.

3. In accordance with the normal practice of the Fund in regard to applications for standby facilities, I summarise in this letter the Government's main economic objectives and policies, as set forth in my Budget speech on 15th April, 1969 and other recent statements of policy.

4. As I said in my Budget speech, it is the Government's policy to do everything necessary to put the United Kingdom balance of payments on a secure and healthy basis, as an essential means to sustained growth and prosperity. The Budget was designed to continue and strengthen the balance of payments strategy which the Government has been pursuing. The objective is to obtain a substantial and continuing balance of payments surplus.

5. Strong action has been taken, and the balance of payments has already improved considerably. Progress has not been as large or rapid as the Government wished but the Government intends it to continue and strengthen. The Government is taking and will continue to take the action necessary to this end. The growth of public expenditure and private consumption is being limited so that there is room for the desired substantial and continuing balance of payments surplus to develop. The intention is to make sure that the turn-round in the structure of the United Kingdom economy gains full momentum. Substantial further progress is intended and expected during the next year. In the financial year ending in March, 1970 the objective is to obtain a surplus of at least £300 million on the current and long-term capital account of the balance of payments.

6. Public expenditure for both 1968-69 and 1969-70 is running within the totals announced by the Government in January, 1968 (Cmnd 3515). In 1968-69 aggregate expenditure is estimated to have increased in real terms over the previous year by 4·1 per cent. This was within the announced limit of 4·75 per cent. For 1969-70 public expenditure will again be held within the totals announced in January, 1968 which allowed for an increase of 1 per cent in real terms over the planned level for 1968-69; the increase over the actual outturn for 1968-69 will be larger.

7. The full year yield of the increases in direct and indirect taxation made in the 1968 Budget, in November, 1968 and in the 1969 Budget, is in total some £1,500 million. The Central Government borrowed £1,331 million net in 1967-68. In 1968-69 the Central Government borrowing requirement (excluding receipts from import deposits) was about £70 million. In 1969-70 the Central Government's accounts (again excluding import deposits) are intended to be in surplus by at least £850 million, and the current estimate is of a surplus approaching £1,000 million, an improvement of more than £1,000 million over the previous financial year.

8. As was also stated in the Budget speech, the Government attaches the greatest importance to monetary policy, which provides an essential support to fiscal policy. The rise in money supply in 1968 of £986 million was broadly in line with the growth of GNP; but the increase in credit in the economy was too high, and the Government intends not to permit credit to be supplied to the economy on anything like this scale in 1969-70.

9. The Government will therefore watch closely the development of domestic credit expansion during the year. The Government's objectives and policies imply a domestic credit expansion for the private and public sectors in the year ending 31st March, 1970 of not more than £400 million, compared with some £1,225 million in 1968-69. It is the Government's policy to ensure that the course quarter by quarter of domestic credit expansion as a whole, and of the Central Government borrowing requirement within it, is consistent with the intended result for the year as a whole, and to take action as appropriate to this end.

10. The statutory powers relating to prices and incomes policy introduced in the exceptional circumstances following devaluation continue in
effect until the end of 1969. Thereafter the powers of Part II of the 1966
Prices and Incomes Act will be activated, and will be used to defer, in
appropriate cases, the implementation of a pay settlement or price
increases for three to four months in the context of a reference to the
Prices and Incomes Board. Further guidance to negotiators will be issued
in a new White Paper later in the year.

11. The Government is confident that its present policies will
strengthen sterling as an integral part of the international monetary
system. Freedom of international trade and current payments continues
to be an aim of policy to which the Government attaches great importance. It is the Government's policy to maintain the present degree of
trade liberalization, and to abolish as soon as the balance of payments
allows the restrictions which it currently maintains on travel expenditure
and small cash gifts, and also the import deposit scheme.

12. The Government believes that the policies set forth in this letter
are adequate to achieve the objectives of its programme, but will take
any further measures that may become appropriate for this purpose.

13. The Government will consult with the Fund from time to time, in
accordance with the regular policies of the Fund on such consultation,
about the course of the United Kingdom economy and any further
measures affecting the balance of payments that may be appropriate.

Yours sincerely,

ROY JENKINS

Notes

[1] Most notably the Brookings report, *Britain's economic prospects*, by Richard E.
Caves & associates (Washington, 1968).

[2] This was the argument of my *Sterling and British policy* (London, 1971). The
book owed a great deal to the earlier works of Judd Polk, *Sterling; its meaning in
world finance* (London, 1956); Andrew Shonfield, *British economic policy since the
war* (London, 1959); Fred Hirsch, *The pound sterling: a polemic* (London, 1965);
Sam Brittan, *Steering the economy; the role of the Treasury* (London, 1969); John
Cooper, *A suitable case for treatment: what to do about the balance of payments*
(Harmondsworth, 1968), and A. R. Conan, *The problem of sterling* (London, 1966).

[3] OECD, *United Kingdom* (Paris, 1967); EEC Commission, *Opinion on the application for membership received from the United Kingdom, Ireland, Denmark and
Norway* (Brussels, Sept 1967).

[4] See N. I. Momtchiloff, 'The IMF and the Ten: surveillance instead of reform',
World Today, Nov 1964, pp. 497ff.

[5] *Statement by the ministers of the Group of Ten and Annexe prepared by their
deputies* (London, 1964). See also ch. 9.

[6] Ibid., deputies' Annexe, para. 37.

[7] Indeed there were grounds for thinking this to be so, although British inflation
rates in the early 1960s had been less than those of France, Italy, and Japan and
wage-costs had increased more slowly than in every industrial country except the
United States, yet the increase in British export prices from 1961 to 1964 had been
6 per cent a year against a drop of 5 per cent in Japanese prices, no change in
American prices and an increase of only 1 per cent in German prices (see Hirsch,
Money international, p. 36).

[8] Hirsch, *The pound sterling*, p. 123.
[9] *IMF*, i. 5f. & 8.
[10] *FT*, 5 Nov 1964.
[11] *Observer*, 8 Nov 1964.
[12] *The Economist*, 14 Nov 1964, p. 749.
[13] Ibid.
[14] *New Yorker*, Mar 1968.
[15] *The Times*, 3 Dec 1964.
[16] Ibid. & *FT*, 16 Dec 1964.
[17] *FT*, 5 Nov 1964.
[18] *The pound sterling*, p. 131.
[19] *FT*, 22 Apr 1965.
[20] *IMF*, i. 403 & 569.
[21] *Le Monde*, 5 & 6 May 1965.
[22] *The Economist*, 8 May 1965.
[23] *IMF*, i. 569.
[24] On this point see Hirsch, *The pound sterling*, p. 104.
[25] See BIS, *Ann. Rep.*, 1964–5, p. 139.
[26] As disclosed later (see *The Times*, 15 Feb 1964).
[27] M. de Cecco ('The Italian payments crisis of 1963–4', in R. A. Mundell & A. K. Swoboda, eds, *Monetary problems of the international economy*, Chicago, 1969, pp. 387–8) explains that this strategy was effective in the short term, for about six months from September 1963 to March 1964. Then the disparity in the two markets obliged the Banca d'Italia to intervene, 'pledging large funds to offset sales of forward lire'.
[28] *The Economist*, 29 Feb 1964, p. 890.
[29] *Modern capitalism* (London, 1965), pp. 180–2.
[30] *FT*, 28 Feb 1964.
[31] Sam Brittan, *Observer*, 29 Mar 1964; see also Agence Presse Europe, no. 1789, 19 Mar 1964.
[32] EEC Monetary Committee, *6th ann. rep.*, Apr 1964.
[33] Ibid., p. 11.
[34] Henry Brandon, *In the red, the struggle for sterling, 1964–6* (Harmondsworth, 1966), p. 94.
[35] Ibid., p. 94.
[36] *IMF*, i. 569.
[37] Gordon L. Weil & Ian Davidson, *The gold war* (London, 1970), p. 112.
[38] Ibid., p. 113.
[39] This was proposed by the Dutch and carried, despite some British resistance. Once again, Austria and the BIS itself were included. It was an important turning point, and a forerunner of the 1968 Basle arrangements when the central bank community more openly and formally took limited liability for strains on Britain arising from the reserve role, while refusing them on other balance-of-payments grounds, thus by implication specifying more clearly than hitherto the conditions of their assistance.
[40] *Money international*, pp. 255–6.
[41] Brittan, *Steering the economy*, p. 353.
[42] EEC Commission, *Opinion on the applications for membership received from the UK.* . . .
[43] Weil & Davidson, p. 120.
[44] *The Economist*, 25 Nov 1966, p. 873.
[45] *Guardian*, 23 Nov 1967.
[46] *The Times, FT*, 30 Nov & *Observer*, 1 Dec 1967.
[47] 755 HC Deb., 1145, 5 Dec 1967.
[48] *The Economist*, 15 Mar 1969.
[49] Brittan, *Steering the economy*, p. 388.
[50] 785 HC Deb., 1521–1635, 25 June 1969.
[51] *The Economist*, 28 June 1969, p. 13.

[52] On this point, see *The Banker* editorial comment, Sept 1969.

[53] 'Monetary management—the confidence factor', ibid., pp. 875ff.

[54] *The Economist*, 17 May 1969.

[55] Ibid.

[56] 785 HC Deb., 1634, 25 June 1969.

[57] 755 HC Deb., 644, 30 Nov 1967.

[58] BIS, *Ann. rep.*, 1969–70.

[59] *Stand-by arrangements of the IMF*, p. 67.

[60] See below, p. 390 n. 11.

[61] This rather important hypothesis is one that might be borne in mind and tested against by the French experience in 1969.

[62] With the UAR, and indeed with Cuba, it may be argued that the United States when it diverged from the rest did have an exceptional power to skew the system. This is a hypothesis which is important enough to require more extensive research and analysis.

[63] See the author's contribution on the Fund and the editors' conclusions on this point in Cox & Jacobson, *The anatomy of influence*; and Ed. Bernstein's contribution to R. N. Gardner & M. F. Millikan, eds, *The global partnership* (New York, 1968). See also above, p. 96.

[64] Interpreted at the time as an 'open challenge' to the Fund's central role and authority (see Momtchiloff, *World Today*, Nov 1964).

[65] See George Ray's contribution to vol. I of this Survey.

[66] R. W. Russell, in *International Organization*, Autumn 1973.

[67] Ibid.

[68] The *Guardian* even suggested that it was actually subversive of Fund authority. It commented on 25 Mar 1969 that swap credits had 'proved much more permissive than the long-term credit available for the IMF . . . as a result the central bankers have gained influence over their own governments but have done much to undermine the disciplinary power of the IMF'.

[69] BIS communiqué (quoted in *IMF*, i. 483).

[70] W. M. Clarke, *The city in the world economy* (London, 1965), p. 161.

[71] In *The pound sterling*.

[72] A. R. Conan, *The problem of sterling*, p. 105.

[73] See Strange, *Sterling and British policy*.

[74] 746 HC Deb., 1322, 9 May 1967.

[75] The full list was: Cyprus, Gambia, Gibraltar, Guyana, Ireland, Jamaica, Malawi, Malta, Mauritius, Southern Yemen, Sierra Leone, Trinidad and Tobago, and other ex-British West Indies except the Bahamas. These all devalued by 14·3 per cent with Britain. New Zealand devalued by 19·45 per cent; Ceylon by 20 per cent; Iceland by 24·6 per cent; Fiji by 8·95 per cent; and Hong Kong (after revaluation) by 5·7 per cent.

[76] Benjamin Cohen, *The future of sterling as an international currency* (London, 1971), p. 195.

[77] See Strange, *Sterling and British policy*, chart, p. 76.

[78] *The Basle facility and the sterling area*, Cmnd 3787 (1968), pp. 3–4. See table, p. 154.

[79] *FT*, 12 Feb 1968.

[80] Ibid., 29 May 1968.

[81] *The Times*, 30 Aug 1968.

[82] The White Paper only revealed that Australia's MSP was to be 40 per cent. Later, as will be seen, most of the other MSPs became known.

[83] *The Times*, 30 Aug 1968.

[84] Ibid., 20 May, 1968.

[85] Cmnd 3787.

[86] *FT*, 10 Sept 1968.

[87] *Sunday Telegraph*, 15 Sept 1968.

[88] Paul Bareau, 'Sterling after Basle', *The Banker*, Oct 1968.

[89] Contributions were roughly as follows: USA $600m; Germany $400m; Italy $220m; Holland $100m; Belgium $80m; Switzerland $200m; and a total of $400m from the following combined: Canada, Sweden, Denmark, Japan, and Norway (*FT*, 10 Sept, *Le Monde* 12 Sept 1968).

[90] *Sunday Telegraph*, 15 Sept 1968.

[91] It was arguable that it would be more costly than the stability achieved by the Basle Agreement (see on this point Stephen Cohen, *International monetary reform, 1964–9* (New York, 1970)).

[92] *FT*, 23 Sept 1968.

[93] Cmnds 3834 & 3835 (1968), *Exchange of notes and letters concerning the guarantee by the United Kingdom and the maintenance of the minimum sterling proportion by certain overseas sterling area governments and Exchange of despatches and letters.*

[94] There were 33 three-year agreements, 31 five-year ones.

[95] Indeed, after the decision to float sterling, in April 1972, the sterling holder stood to gain if sterling appreciated against the dollar, but would not lose if the rate moved the other way.

[96] *The Times*, 7 Sept 1973.

[97] One of the last distinguishing features of the sterling area—its preferential treatment under British exchange controls on investment of British capital overseas —disappeared at the same time as the float, when the same restrictions were applied to the old sterling area as to the rest of the world.

[98] 755 HC Deb., 648–52.

[99] 787 HC Deb., 1008–10.

6

THE EUROCURRENCY MARKET

One of the most important monetary innovations of the 1960s was, without question, the international market in Eurocurrencies. No history of this kind would be complete that did not give some account of its growth and development; some explanation of its impact on the monetary policies of states both in managing their national economies and credit structures and in maintaining stability and order in their external monetary relations; and some broader assessment, too, of its impact on the international political economy.

Before 1960 this whole structure of international credit, now generally taken for granted, barely existed. By 1970, without any individual or institution planning or intending it, the total pool of Eurodollar deposits had become substantially greater than the total gold reserves held by governments ($39 billion) or the total dollar reserves held by governments ($37 billion), let alone the total of SDRs ($3 billion). Its capacity for growth—which in the mid-60s was still a matter of controversy and doubt—had been fully established and its management had become a matter for increasing concern. Before the end of our period, two of the most important eminent living authorities on international monetary economics, Guido Carli and Fritz Machlup, had pointed warningly to its self-sustaining and expanding capacities (see below, p. 193).

Like other technical innovations, the Eurodollar came to be recognised as a good servant but a bad master. It had admirably met the need of a variety of borrowers and lenders and their intermediaries for an internationally acceptable and easily negotiable instrument of short-term credit, available in large quantities and largely free from administrative control. It had added to everyone's convenience and made financial life easier—and for some very much more profitable. But equally it stood accused of hindering and obstructing the efforts of those who had to manage and supervise the monetary welfare of states. By transmitting external influences to domestic money markets, it had added to their difficulties, breaking down the insulating wall within which authorities tried to maintain a desired money supply and level of interest rates. It allowed operators to frustrate the intentions of national managers by letting them escape national jurisdiction by resorting to the growing international credit market. Furthermore, it had provided a pool of footloose funds which could rapidly be shifted in and out of national currencies. Thanks to the Eurocurrency markets, the velocity of movements in foreign exchange markets markedly increased, making it much more difficult at certain times for national authorities to maintain fixed and stable exchange rates.

This international market for Eurocurrencies was one of several ingenious devices made necessary by the much faster rate of change in the international economic and social systems than in the international political system. It enabled operators and enterprises in the rapidly growing international economy to treat wealth, in the form of a monetary medium of exchange and credit, as if the world really were a single economic system and one currency area, as if national frontiers and restrictive statutes did not exist. It could be called a gearing or meshing device by which private agents operating in a relatively static political order took advantage of the greater opportunities offered by an increasing dynamic international or transnational market economy.

James Rosenau, one of the most fertile and perceptive writers on contemporary international society, has aptly characterized a good deal of international economic co-operation as ' adaptive politics '.[1] The study of international monetary relations suggests that this idea of Rosenau's can be taken a step further, with the hypothesis that adaptive policies and devices in the public sector are often made necessary only by the spontaneous development of adaptive devices in the private sector. The latter, indeed, is (and always has been, at least since the invention of the telegraph and the railway) a fertile bed for all sorts of adaptive devices. In the 1960s the Eurodollar was only one of many. At least as important was the expansion in the operations of international business—the so-called ' multinational company ' that planned its production, finance, management, research and development, and the distribution of its products as a single global enterprise. The multinationals' successful expansion (especially that of US-based corporations in Europe) in turn encouraged the development of international banking and of multinational consortia banks; and these in their turn actively fostered dealing in Eurocurrencies and in other financial instruments, such as Eurobonds, convertible bonds, internationally transferable certificates of deposit, bonds denominated in more than one currency, and assets incorporating the ingenious notion of flexible interest rates. While the international banks perfected these financial inventions, the multinationals elaborated, among other things, the tax-avoiding international holding company. As any top executive engaged in international management or finance is well aware, all these adaptive devices, in each of the main fields of international economic enterprise, were so closely interconnected that it is impossible to speak of one without reference to the others.

All of them, too, owed a very great deal to technological advance, especially in transport, communications, and mechanized accounting. None would have worked so easily or developed so fast without the availability of frequent and rapid air transport; without a 24-hour telephone network; without computer systems allowing rapid and accurate calculation to improve the speed of both record-keeping and of decision-making. More specifically, all three also owed much to the development of direct inter-office communication by means of telex machines. These had first been used by press agencies and newspapers, who discovered that where it was necessary to keep certain channels of communications more or less permanently open, the telex was both cheaper and more reliable than telegraph or telephone. It was also secret and was less subject than either telephone or telegram communication to official interruption or human incompetence—as western journalists reporting the Czech invasion of 1968 quickly discovered.

In this chapter we are concerned with only one adaptive device, one of the financial meshing mechanisms of the 1960s, the Eurocurrency market. Not because it was more important but because it did have a very direct impact, via foreign exchange markets, on the adjustment mechanism between national currencies. And it did (however marginally and perhaps inadequately) prompt some adaptive response from governments in international monetary co-operation. It may be helpful to ask more specifically what it was about the Eurodollar market that aroused the attention of states and how they responded. Equally, when and why in face of an important new factor in the international monetary system, they remained passive and supine.

Definitions

A short (and therefore over-simplified) description of the Eurocurrency market is that it was in the 1960s the most important international market dealing with short-term credit, most of which was then denominated in US dollars. A Eurodollar loan therefore is just a large wad of expatriate dollars which may be borrowed from a bank at rather high interest rates for short or medium terms. A more authoritative definition, given by the BIS in 1964, stated that the Eurodollar was 'a dollar that has been acquired by a bank outside the United States and used directly or after conversion into another currency, for lending to a non-bank customer, perhaps after one or more redeposits from one bank to another '.[2]

Another formulation by Fred H. Klopstock of the FRBNY reads:

By generally accepted definition, Eurodollars come into existence when a domestic or foreign holder of dollar demand deposits in the United

States places them on deposit in a bank outside the United States, but the term also applies to the dollars that banks abroad acquire with their own or foreign currency and then employ for placement in the market or for loans to customers.[3]

The point Klopstock is making is an important one for analytical purposes, because it emphasizes the twin functions of the Eurodollar market. It is both a mechanism for the creation of credit by which deposits made by savers are passed on to investors—a function performed in national credit structures by, e.g. building societies and savings banks, as well as joint stock banks—and it is a mechanism providing liquidity to the banking system by means of which banks are able to borrow and lend large sums among themselves.

Neither of the authoritative definitions make any mention of Europe or explains the prefix 'Euro'. It just happens that the market for the expatriate dollars grew up in Europe and that most of the dealing in Eurodollars was done by banks in London or in other European financial centres. Moreover, the only reliable statistics for many years on the volume of the Eurodollar market came from the BIS in Basle, which based its figures on dollar deposit liabilities of banks in ten reporting countries, of which eight were European.[4] Thus the term Eurodollar has often been loosely applied to deposits in Toronto, Rio de Janeiro, or indeed Hong Kong, Singapore, or Kuala Lumpur. The latter market in 'Asian dollars' is really only an offshoot of the Eurodollar market, dealing in dollars (and other leading currencies) deposited in local banks and re-lent to Asian borrowers. Pioneered by the Bank of America in Singapore in 1968, it has since grown rapidly, thanks largely to deliberate relaxation of banking regulations and reserve requirements by the governments of Singapore and Malaysia. Sometimes, too, the term is stretched even more elastically so that it is used—improperly—in place of the generic term 'Eurocurrencies', i.e. to include Euromarks, Eurosterling, Eurofrancs, EuroSwissfrancs, Euroguilders, etc. By the end of 1970 the market in Euromarks especially was beginning to become increasingly important, but through most of the 1960s the Eurodollar market was still very much larger than all the other Eurocurrency markets put together (see table p. 184, below).

Because, therefore, most Eurodollar activity took place in Europe and most took place actually in US dollars, these semantic imprecisions need not be taken too seriously.

Rise and growth of Eurocurrency markets

Although it was the private sector that conceived and developed the Euromarket as an adaptive device, some responsibility for it lay with the British and American governments whose decisions, between them, provided both the incentive and the opportunity.

There was, of course, nothing especially new about extraterritorial bank deposits. Since the Middle Ages, and certainly for the past two or three hundred years, bankers had often accepted deposits in currencies other than their own local one, and all through the twentieth century most big banks had taken in quite large sums of foreign exchange, including dollars, from their customers. Hitherto, however, the normal practice was to return sterling deposits to London and dollar deposits to the US money market through the banks' agents in New York. What was new in 1957–8 was the non-repatriation and the subsequent extraterritorial use of dollar deposits as a credit instrument in international financial transactions. This use might well have remained on an insignificant scale but for three special circumstances. These were an unsatisfied demand for short-term credit; a large and regular supply of the wherewithal to fill it; and an interesting rate of profit for those prepared to bring willing lenders in touch with willing borrowers.

On the demand side, an influential governmental decision was that of the British government in 1957, when it put a stop to the traditional practice whereby London banks provided sterling credit instruments for the finance of foreign third-party trade. That was the year in which Britain lost a quarter of its gold reserves in two months and the inclination to limit operations that carried a risk for sterling was natural enough. Thus frustrated—but unwilling to lose good customers —the resourceful London banks began to use dollar deposits. Instead of returning dollars to the US money market, as had customarily been done through the London banks' agents in New York, these dollar deposits were developed as an extraterritorial credit instrument.

On the supply side, the key measures were those of the United States—not just the payments deficit which was the fount and source of foreign-held dollar balances, but more specifically certain restrictions on banking imposed by the US government. It was these which gave the operators such a strong incentive to develop this unsupervised, extraterritorial market. In the first place, the financial chaos of the years 1929–33 had induced the Congress to endow the Federal Reserve Board with additional powers over the activities of banks. One consequence was the edict known as Regulation Q which, in effect, applied an interventionist price control on the rates which US banks could offer on short and medium term deposits. These maximum rates of interest ruled unchanged between 1935 and 1957; and although the permitted maximum was raised to 3 per cent for the longer-time deposits on 1 January 1957, and between 1962 and 1966 crept up to $5\frac{1}{2}$ per cent, the differential persisted between deposit rates in Europe and the United States. This differential allowed banks in Europe to take deposits for a little bit more than the US rate and to relend them at a little less than the US lending rate—in other words to undercut banks in the United States by taking a narrower margin of profit. (The banks in Europe included London branches of US banks as well as British and European and even Australian and other non-European banks.) Thus one could say it was not Regulation Q itself which was the precondition for Eurodollar business but the fat-cat rigidities in US banking habits that it had fostered. As a British authority on Eurodollars, Clendenning, has commented, 'The unwillingness of US commercial banks to accept lower operating margins was just as important as the limitations imposed by Regulation Q in the formation of the Eurodollar market '.[5]

Had it not been for Regulation Q and the rules governing banking in the United States, the international market for short-term finance denominated in dollars would have been indistinguishable from the domestic market. Thus it would have been much more closely comparable (save, of course, in the volume of supply and demand) to the international market for sterling bills that existed before World War I.

Subsequently the imposition of the Interest Equalization Tax (see below, p. 213) on foreign borrowing in US money markets powerfully encouraged the practice, among the US multinationals and others, of borrowing untaxed dollars outside the United States from the Eurocurrency market.

There were other important factors of a primarily political character. In the early years, an important source of supply of Eurodollars came from Soviet and East European banks who for trading purposes sometimes held quite substantial dollar balances. Recalling perhaps the way in which the US government in the late 1940s had arbitrarily sequestered Yugoslav gold holdings deposited in New York, the Soviet bloc banks were unwilling to let their dollar holdings out of Europe—but also were not slow to appreciate this novel opportunity to put them to profitable use.

More important in the long run were the two major politico-economic circumstances attending the birth of the Eurocurrency market: the return to currency convertibility and the general toleration accorded the US payment deficit. Relaxation of exchange control (where it occurred) meant that European banks and their customers could legitimately hold dollars instead of being obliged to sell them immediately to national monetary authorities—who at that time would merely have added them to foreign exchange reserve accounts. The growing deficit on the US balance of payments increased supply; at the same time, the demand for new sources of credit sharpened as the result of tight money policies being pursued in Europe. Clendenning deduced from the Bank of England's statistical series showing the non-resident business (deposits and advances) of the British overseas banks and accepting houses in London (which is the only statistical series spanning the nascence of the Eurodollar market) that it grew steadily from the beginning of 1958, i.e. *before* the change to convertibility.

In the next fifteen years the Eurocurrency market grew without interruption and at an accelerating, if uneven, pace. Starting from scratch, its estimated size had grown to around $9 billion in 1964; to $16 billion in 1966; to $44 billion in 1969; to $57 billion by the end of 1970; and by 1972 to over $80 billion. The annual rate of increase then went as high as 30 per cent, against a rise of 24 per cent in 1971 and 29 per cent in 1970. The word ' estimated ' is used advisedly; another of its characteristics, besides size, is that it is (and always has been) less well measured and less completely understood than national credit markets. Since the mid-60s the BIS has made informed annual guesses about the size of the market but has always stressed that they are only approximate, that some double-counting is probable, and that the limits of the market—since Eurodollars can so easily be converted into local currencies and vice versa—were uncertain at any given moment. As the BIS explained in its Annual Report for 1970–1 (p. 157):

There is no fixed supply of funds available to the market which moves from country to country according to shifts in the geographical demand for credit, but rather the market is able to expand its own resources by attracting funds from various national markets to meet demand from whatever borrowers are prepared to pay the necessary prices.

Thanks to the BIS, the broad outlines of the market's development from 1963 to the end of the decade can be discerned, although some lacunae remain. These are mostly due to the unevenness and incompleteness of banking statistics produced in different countries which sometimes make the flows of funds through and in-and-out of the market a matter of guesswork and presumption. A notable attempt to put together the available data given by the US, UK, and other monetary authorities was that by Klaus Friedrich.[6] This study showed that before 1970 the main participants and beneficiaries were the developed countries—the United States, Canada, Japan, and the leading industrial countries of Western Europe. Through the 1960s the developing countries of the Third World were persistent net creditors —that is to say their assets regularly increased more than their liabilities, and on balance funds came into the Eurodollar market from Latin America, from the Middle East, and from other Asian and African countries. Other persistent net sources of creditors, according to Friedrich, were Canada and the European group, although the figures for the European group include funds deposited by US corporations established in Europe and Third World funds deposited with Swiss banks. More recently, according to the London journal *Euromoney* (January 1973), there was a significant growth in medium-term Eurocurrency loans to developing countries.

Up to about 1963 the main participants in the market were thought to be central banks; thereafter the market was used much more by commercial banks and by their non-bank customers.

The major dealers or operators have been British and Swiss banks—or to be more precise, London and Swiss banks. For though the initial development was by the British overseas banks in London, these met increasing competition during the decade from American, European, and other foreign banks already or newly established in London. US banks abroad, for instance, which handled about a third of the total Eurodollar business in 1964, were handling about two-thirds by 1969, according to Friedrich. In the earlier years the major demand came from European and Japanese industry, though an influential factor in the demand side in the middle years was the borrowing habits of the British local authorities. As noted by the BIS, their borrowing drew on the Eurodollar pool: 'whenever their rates for short-term money have exceeded the corresponding Eurodollar deposit rates on a covered basis, it has been profitable for banks to take dollars on deposit and switch them into sterling for lending to local authorities '.[7]

The major influence on supply throughout, however, has come from monetary trends in, and the monetary policies of, the United States, especially monetary policy measures affecting US capital flows. Indeed, the four major turning points in market trends all coincide with steps taken by the US monetary authorities to control capital movements: the proposal for the Interest Equalization Tax in 1963; the voluntary guidelines programme for 1965 (which so boosted the demand for short-term finance in Eurodollars that Friedrichs concluded that it 'marked the beginning of American demand as a dominating aspect of the Eurodollar market'); the Johnson foreign investment controls of 1968 (see ch. 9); and the reversal of US domestic policies at the end of 1970 (see ch. 14).

And it was the US payments deficit, with the associated expansion of direct foreign investment by American corporations and the associated use of the dollar as an international currency, which was the most important necessary condition for the continued functioning and growth of the market. These phenomena were in a chicken-and-egg relationship, but together they made sure of a continuing supply of expatriate dollars. On the demand side, the necessary condition has been the continued growth and expansion of the developed country economies and the consequent persistent demand for credit. If at any

time this growth had been arrested or reversed, there is little doubt
that the Eurodollar market would have been in serious trouble.

Although it is true that in the last two or three years of our period
the volume of Euromarks traded became much more important, the
dollar still remained dominant in the market.

External liabilities of European banks in Eurocurrencies ($m at end-year)

	Dollars	D-marks	Swiss fr.	Sterling	Guilders	Total non-$
1968	26·9	3·0	2·3	0·8	0·3	6·9
1969	46·2	4·6	4·0	0·8	0·4	8·6
1970	58·7	8·1	5·7	0·9	0·6	15·6
1971	70·8	14·9	7·8	2·1	0·9	27·2

Source: BIS, *Annual Report, 1971–2*, p. 151.

The effects of the market's growth

As one might expect, the extent of the changes brought about as a
result of the growth of the Eurodollar market were seldom appreciated
by those involved until some years after. The major effect was probably on the structure and character of international banking—that
is the private sector of the international economy. But there were also
discernible changes brought to national banking operations and
national financial institutions. As already noted, the market affected
national governments and their monetary authorities in various ways
and in different degrees; and it affected what might be described as
the international public sector, that area in which national monetary
management was evidently ineffective and in which control or regulation or supervision (if it was to be exercised) had to be done
collectively through international agreement or organization. Diagram-
matically this political economy approach, focusing on each of the
four sectors in turn and analysing both the political and economic
effects could be expressed by a simple matrix, as below:

	International	National
Private sector		
Public sector		

Thus, taking first the international private sector, the question is
how the Eurocurrency market has affected the functioning of banks
and other institutions making international financial transactions. Perhaps the whole answer is not yet apparent, but part of it is. Clearly the
growth, and of course the profitability, of Eurocurrency credit has
helped immensely to bring about a rapid development of what
Alexander Swoboda has called an international banking system.[8]

One indication of this is the extent to which large banks in the leading developed countries depend for their business on the international side of their operations. This is true whether one looks at the US banks which have taken part in a remarkable piece of colonization of what Londoners call the Square Mile, at the British overseas banks, or at the leading French, German, Swiss, Japanese or Italian banks. US banking corporations, licensed under the Edge Act (1919) to engage in foreign banking, numbered 2 in the late 1930s; 8 by 1955; 35 by 1965; and 70 by 1970.[9] Another indication is the extraordinary growth in a rather short space of time of international banking consortia. Although it used to be customary for large banks to have arrangements for mutual aid with a series of foreign ' correspondents ' in different financial centres round the world, this has proved inadequate to the demands of the Eurocurrency age. Now banks find it advisable—possibly because of the greater risks involved in international business—to team up with a group of others of different base nationality in a variety of joint-venture arrangements. These not only spread risks but also add greatly to individual lending (and borrowing) potential and to the range of activities open to each of them. There are now at least eighty of these consortia in existence and probably many more.[10] It seems unlikely the process will stop here. And it appears that the development of one adaptive device in the private sector is apt to foster and facilitate the development of others.

In Swoboda's estimation, the four features of the Eurocurrency market which have helped to bring about the internationalization of the banking systems of the developed countries are: first, its size; second, its extent, reaching into all corners of the world without discrimination; third, its ' product similarity ', leading to an increased responsiveness in national markets to external interest rates and charges; and fourth, the mainly dollar denomination of Eurocurrency credit.

The responsiveness to external interest rate movements which he mentions is, of course, part of the wider process of permeation of national societies and economies by transnational influences which has been noted and described by a number of writers.[11]

In the national private sector there are few domestic capital and money markets that have been unaffected, although the attention given to this by the economists has so far been patchy and disjointed. One consequence has probably been the breakdown observed in a number of countries of cartel-like arrangements in the private banking system. Hirsch observes that Eurocurrency lending rates ' had a considerable effect in Germany and Italy in particular in improving the terms at which large firms, no longer dependent on the domestic banks alone, could borrow.' [12]

Of all places, London has most felt the impact of the Eurodollar business. British overseas banks which might have declined along with the use of sterling and the dismemberment of the imperial banking system which nourished them, have not faded away or, like the Suez Canal Company or Booker Brothers, gone into enterprises quite foreign to their original purpose. On the contrary, they have had a new lease of life. While they have had to compete with a flood of US and foreign banks—now numbering nearly 250—they have yet managed to hold on to an ever-growing volume of business for themselves. London has therefore remained a major international financial centre, though one dealing in dollars (and now increasingly D-marks) and not sterling. Zurich, Brussels, and Frankfurt, more than Paris or Amsterdam, have also increased their importance as financial centres.

In the national public sectors—that is, the field of state governments and central banks—the growth of Eurocurrency business has probably had, on balance, an adverse effect, at least in most European countries. It has on the whole made it more difficult for the authorities to discharge their responsibilities, both as supervisors of the credit structure and therefore of the supply, and hence the value, of money within the state, and as guardians of particular parities for the national currency, i.e. of stable terms on which the national currency can be exchanged for those of other national economies. National monetary management has been made more difficult mainly because of the increased opportunities (and profitability) opened up by Eurodollar dealing for arbitrage operations. In this way it has increased the internal constraint on the use of monetary policy as a weapon for internal economic stabilization and indeed has caused monetary authorities to look for new methods of domestic monetary management either in increased exchange controls, or in more active forward market intervention, or in swap arrangements with commercial banks, none of which have proved wholly satisfactory or free of new and unforeseen complications. It is only fair to add that it may sometimes have acted as a stimulus to reform, for instance, William Clark has suggested that in France the growth of the international market ' heightened the authorities' awareness of the relative backwardness of the Paris money market and was therefore probably behind the plans made by M. Debré in 1966–7 to reform and liberate French banking and exchange controls and more recently the further reforms of M. Wormser '.[13]

As noted above, the active Eurodollar business served to transmit interest rate competition from one country to another and to spread any scramble for liquidity which developed in one country to the other countries involved in the market. To the extent that the defence of a national parity was a national as well as an international problem, the

Eurodollar market made it more difficult to insulate the national economy from short-term outflows or influxes and has made less effective the market management techniques developed to this end in the 1930s (see below, ch. 14).

Moreover, the vulnerability to destabilizing forces liberated by Eurodollar business is very uneven. All the European countries have at times discovered themselves almost defenceless against trends in the market set off by changes in US policy. The United States, on the other hand, was not only less affected: it was undoubtedly preserved in its dominant position in part through the popularity of the Eurodollar. It was largely this that persuaded a great many central banks, commercial banks, and non-banks (the three classes of participants in the market) to hold dollars at rates which the US Treasury was not then prepared to offer them. If they had not done so, the other central banks of the developed world would have had to choose much earlier whether to increase their dollar holdings or to present their dollars for exchange into gold from Fort Knox. To the extent that the boom in Eurodollars increased the time during which the United States was able to run a payments deficit and to finance the conduct of foreign wars and the acquisition of foreign enterprises with IOUs held by foreigners, it must be counted as of benefit to the United States.

In the international public sector, some of the effects simply reflect in an international dimension the effects in the national context and the problems thereby created for national monetary management. For example, the difficulties created for national governments in maintaining particular exchange rates while pursuing concurrently certain domestic economic objectives meant that new strains were simultaneously felt on the whole Bretton Woods system of semi-fixed exchange rates, and especially so at moments of uncertainty and failing confidence in the foreign exchange markets.

The adjustment process in the international system was similarly affected to the extent that the addition of the Eurodollar element to other short-term monetary movements and capital flows made the trade balance between countries—and incidentally a great deal of conventional economic theory based on international trade as the main factor in the adjustment process—increasingly irrelevant. This led to a realization that, against such a background of increasingly volatile and 'hidden' transnational shifts of funds, the search for an objective standard by which to measure and recognize national deficits and surpluses—a problem the IMF thought it had solved years before—was probably futile. So much depended on the arbitrarily chosen method of calculating the totals on either side of the balance of payments.

Thirdly, the Eurodollar expansion made a major addition to the volume of *private* liquidity in the international monetary system. This not only eased, or made less acute—as pointed out above—the adjustment problems of the United States; it also required a corresponding increase in public international liquidity, i.e. in official monetary reserves available for the settlement of temporary imbalances and for market intervention and management. It was not, as had so often been argued in the long liquidity debate of the 1960s, the increase in international *trade* that made agreement on SDRs so desirable in 1968 but rather the increase in all the things affecting the *non-trade* balance—in international production, for instance, and in the volume of business done across national exchange-control frontiers in the foreign exchange and the Eurodollar markets.

These effects related to the continuing problem of finding a workable system by means of which national currencies could be related to one another in a stable yet flexible international monetary system. Or to put it another way, changes in the money markets (of which the Eurodollar business was one of the most important) were making increasingly obsolete the public sector adaptive policies so carefully devised at Bretton Woods and later revised and amended. The other effect the Eurodollar business had even more materially worked to produce was of a different order and related not so much to the relation between the nationally-divided political system and the internationally-united economic system, as to the growth and development of the latter.

As this accelerating international economy demanded a convenient and acceptable international monetary medium which it could use, and as it discovered new forms which this could take (internationally negotiable certificates of deposit, international bonds denominated in multiple-currency units of account, to name just two besides the Eurodollar); and as truly international money markets developed and grew, a new international monetary problem emerged—that of international monetary management—the job which within national economies had originally caused central banks to be set up as necessary instruments of economic protection for a political structure. The international banking system, in other words, raised the question of how soon it would be necessary to think about a new departure in international action, the creation of some mechanism or arrangement that would undertake the functions of a world central bank. Judging by the history of national monetary management there are four such functions or tasks that the market cannot do for itself, and that some politically legitimate, recognized authority—be it a central bank, government department, semi-private body, or some combination of the three between them, sooner or later has to undertake for the safety and security of the monetary system.

One, the most basic, is the regulation of the monetary medium in which the market deals. Without some stable medium of exchange, transactions are inhibited. In national systems, the central bank has to oversee the money supply and, through interest rates and other regulators, the proliferation of credit instruments, so that the monetary medium does not depreciate in relation either to goods or to other forms of money (currencies). With the Eurocurrency market, confidence rested on the supervisory functions of the United States (and the West German) monetary authorities. But when, as Machlup, Carli, and others began to point out in the early 1970s, the Eurodollar market began to indulge in a new 'magic of credit creation', the question arose whether the magicians—or perhaps Machlup should have called them the sorcerer's apprentices—would need to devise some international machinery to restrict its power to create credit and to assure greater stability for this international monetary medium.

A second function is to regulate the operators—to decide who may operate in the various financial markets, and on what terms; what balance to strike between open competition, reducing costs but perhaps increasing risks, and restricted entry, which may be safer but can also inhibit innovation and growth. In national systems, such rules concerning reserve and liquidity ratios for banks and other financial institutions are laid down (and sometimes changed) to safeguard both the banks' depositors and shareholders and the market as a whole.

Sometimes a national authority, with the same regulatory purpose, may impose a queuing system on would-be borrowers, preventing too many new issues being offered at once. Here, the financial self-interest of a national government may conflict with the general interest which as market authority it is supposed to ensure. Indeed, kings and governments from the earliest times have always been tempted to exploit markets, instead of impartially regulating them. In modern conditions, the result may be an excessive dependence of government on short- or long-term debt and a skewing of the market or a depreciation of values. Internationally, it is now possible—and especially since the 1974 energy crisis deficits—to imagine that one day a scramble among governments or other borrowers to raise funds simultaneously on the Eurocurrency market will bring a threat of disorder, so that either agreement will have to be reached or some neutral regulatory authority established.

Complementary to the regulatory function is the supportive function, to provide a safety net of some kind protecting other operators in the market against the spread of panic and a general collapse of financial confidence. This is necessarily a discretionary function. It cannot be laid down in advance whether it will be in the general interest to allow an Overend Gurney, a Baring Brothers, a Penn Central or a Kreditanstalt to go bust, upsetting equilibrium and destroying confidence, or whether it should be propped up and sorted out. At present the Eurocurrency markets have few built-in safeguards against the risk of one operator being burdened with an unlucky combination of defaulting borrowers. This is perhaps one reason why the banks, in prudent self-protection, have tended to join up in consortia groups, like the Orion group, for mutual support. But if the market continues to grow at the same rate as it has in recent years, it is probable that sometime a ' lender of last resort ' will be needed, as in national money markets. It was indeed possibly significant that the Managing Director of the BIS himself flew at once to Beirut in 1966, when the imminent collapse of the Lebanese Intra Bank first became known.

On the whole, however, it is clear that the problems just listed remained, for most of the 1960s, potential and theoretical; and that the monetary managers of the affluent countries showed little inclination to exercise any of these functions in the Eurocurrency markets. The record of the 1960s was marked by a general complaisance—even indifference—to these long-term questions of international monetary order and management. The Eurocurrency market was still regarded as subsidiary to national money markets—a novel adjunct that must not be allowed to frustrate national monetary policies—but not, as yet, an international policy problem in its own right.

The first seven or eight years of the market's existence, indeed, passed without any intervention at all by the major central banks. Then in 1965 the BIS made use of dollar balances deposited with it to bring down the market-rate of interest on Eurodollar loans. This not only earned a useful yield for the BIS; it also assisted the British whose high interest policies, designed to attract short-term funds to London, were feeling the competitive impact of the Eurodollar market. Coincidentally, and apparently fortuitously, the Banca d'Italia also fed the market by swapping its own dollar reserves with Italian commercial banks. This killed two birds with one stone, reducing Italian banks' borrowing from the Eurodollar market and improving the situation on the market. As Clendenning observes, ' fortunately, both these objectives were desirable at the appropriate time '.[14] The result at any rate was that Italy, a large net borrower in the market in 1964, had become a net lender by the middle of 1965 and pressure on the market was eased.

The first conscious attempt to concert central bank actions for the purpose of stabilizing the Eurodollar market came in 1966. By that time, the first major expansion of the network of American banks beyond the territorial United States had taken place, while the capacity of US monetary controls remained limited to the continental United States. US banks developed the habit of repatriating dollar funds to rebuild their year-end position. In 1966 this caused a sudden dearth of Eurodollars and a jump in one day of nearly 1 per cent in the rate at which they could be borrowed. The US, British, and Swiss central banks, with the BIS Banking Department, concerted spot and forward market intervention strategies to bring the rate down again. The German and Italian central banks assisted by preventing their own banks' year-end window-dressing from exacerbating the situation created by the American banks.

In 1967 the Eurodollar market appeared to act as what Karl Kaiser, evaluating some of the political implications of an interdependent world economy, aptly called a 'transmission mechanism',[15] allowing the Middle East governments involved in the June War easily to shift funds out of sterling accounts in London to the European mainland. The intention was to put pressure on the British balance of payments. But the response of the BIS was to extend its swap line with the Federal Reserve Board from $400 to $550m and later to $1 billion, thus increasing its capability as market stabilizer.

Equally important were the co-ordinated forward market operations decided on by a group of seven central banks (those of the United States, Britain, Italy, Germany, Switzerland, Belgium, and the Netherlands) in the wake of the 1967 sterling devaluation. Total funds mobilized were some $1,400m and the operation used the forward markets for foreign exchange to induce the return of hot money (from Germany especially) back into the Eurodollar market. The underlying purpose was not so much to stabilize the Eurodollar market itself as to prevent, or rather to counteract, its use as a channel for currency hedging, destabilizing the foreign exchange markets and thus threatening the whole fixed parity system.

Thus by 1968 this inner group of central banks had developed an informal practice of acting in European markets to counterbalance any disturbance likely to menace stability in the gold or foreign exchange markets. 'Without the stabilizing intervention', wrote Clendenning, 'it is doubtful that the Eurodollar market could have come through the currency crises of 1967 and 1968 completely unscathed.'[16] But in fact no one ever pretended that the intervention had been primarily intended with this intention in mind. Rather it was a by-product of central bank co-operation in defence of dollar parities.

The last year of the decade was chiefly notable in the Eurocurrency markets for the gigantic pull of dollar funds back across the Atlantic to the United States. And just as the situation had been created by the monetary management of the US authorities, so it was only they who were able to exert much remedial influence upon it. When they did so, in fact, it was *primarily in defence of their own domestic power base*, i.e. to repair their own capacity to control US banks. As Charles Coombs's official accounts relate,

First, the Board amended Regulation D (which governs reserves of member banks) so as to eliminate a technical loophole which had led banks to increase their use of overnight borrowing of Eurodollars. Subsequently, the Board amended Regulation D and Regulation M (which governs foreign activities of member banks) by placing a marginal reserve requirement of ten per cent on Eurodollar takings by member banks and on United States assets acquired by foreign branches from their home offices.

Only later, in the early 70s, did the United States begin to act in the interests, primarily, of the international financial community and by implication of the international economy. When in November 1970, for instance, as a result of the changes in the US economy, the tide of Eurodollars was setting in the opposite direction, the Federal Reserve did deliberately intervene with some warning changes in reserve requirements to moderate the ebb. It did so

by raising from ten per cent to twenty per cent the reserves required to be held against Eurodollar borrowings in excess of the reserve-free base level, and at the same time, amended the regulations regarding the computation of the bases. The changes did not require any banks to put up reserves immediately, but they served to signal the Board's concern over the rapidity of repayments.

Later, in 1971, it took further action to divert some of the funds:

On January 15, the Export-Import Bank announced that it would offer $1 billion of three-month securities at six per cent to the foreign branches of United States banks, and at the same time, the Federal Reserve Board amended Regulation M to permit United States banks to count holdings of these securities toward maintenance of their reserve-free Eurodollar bases.[17]

This immobilized $1 billion which might otherwise have accrued to foreign central banks.

For most of this time, however, the central banks had been busy undoing with their left hands what little good they had achieved with their right hands. Apparently in blissful innocence, they had been busy reinvesting their own dollar deposits, often via the BIS, so as to create additional Eurodollars and incidentally accelerate the growth of their own money supply by adding to the lending capacity of their commercial banks. From 1966 onwards the practice began to produce a rapidly widening discrepancy between the sum of central bank foreign exchange reserves (dollars mainly) reported to the IMF and the total of sterling and dollar liquid liabilities to official holders (dollar and sterling balances) as reported by the Bank of England and the Federal Reserve. From $1 billion, this discrepancy grew to $4½ billion by the end of 1968 and to over $8 billion nine months later. This process was graphically described by Fritz Machlup as the magicians multiplying their rabbits.[18] Governor Guido Carli, equally perturbed, wrote of the dangerous 'magic of credit creation' through the Eurodollar market.[19] By June 1971 the central banks at last took the major self-denying step of agreeing to suspend their reinvestment of dollar deposits in the market. But a good many rabbits had by then got loose and it was still not clear how many had been recaptured— that is, to what extent the central bankers had disinvested funds already placed in the market.

On the longer-term question of regulation of the Eurocurrency market, opinion at the end of the period was still undecided. Even the Europeans who had been most inconvenienced (to put it mildly) were far from agreed on the desirability or otherwise of further controls. Most notably, the British (particularly the Bank of England) thought them unnecessary. But Dr Herman Abs, chairman of the Deutsche-bank, argued strongly for a licensing system, to regulate access to the market and for controls over the volume of funds in the market, including action by the United States to offer preferential interest rates to official dollar holders. Dr Rinaldo Ossola, Professor Carli's deputy at the Banca d'Italia, went further, arguing that it had repeatedly been through the intermediation of the Euromarkets that official parities had in recent years been exposed to speculative pressure for revaluations that were often not economically justified. 'In reality, in a system in which a market mechanism is capable of engendering to an almost unlimited extent means of payment denominated in dollars, this money will abound on the market and the other currencies will find themselves implicitly appreciated.' Consequently, Ossola argued, controls must be imposed on the Eurodollar market in its own interest and in the interest of the whole parity system.[20]

Such controls would presumably include rules governing the recourse of central banks to the Eurocurrency markets; rules governing the acceptance by central banks of commercial banks' dollar deposits; the imposition of reserve requirements on dollar balances held by all Eurobanks and the effective practice of international open-market operations, such as the United States did briefly essay first with the Export-Import Bank and then through the Treasury in 1970–1. Clearly, the active collaboration of the United States would be a *sine qua non*, but of this there was, by the end of 1971, little sign.

We can see from the history of the Eurocurrency markets that it is the original response of governments to perceived dangers in the national financial markets that produces national banking regulations.

These then give added incentive to operators in an increasingly international economy to escape from the national regulations—just as excise duties increase the incentive for smuggling or high taxes increase the incentive for tax evasion. Adaptive devices are thus discovered by the operators to extend and develop a parallel international market, free of political rules and restrictions. National authorities—governments and central banks—then find it necessary either to submit to erosion of their capacity to supervise and regulate the national markets and the national economy or to devise new (and sometimes restrictive) policies to compensate for their loss of power in other directions. In the international system as a whole, the erosion of power is very uneven. The dominant economy with the dominant international currency is least affected; the most open, unprotected, most liberal economies are most vulnerable—compare Germany in this respect with Japan. More than that, as the asymmetry in the system is actually increased, the susceptibility of the rest to the effect of economic developments in the dominant economy is actually increased, as is the power of destabilizing market forces at work throughout the system.

Notes

[1] James N. Rosenau, 'Adaptive politics in an interdependent world', *Orbis*, Spring 1972.

[2] BIS, *Ann. rep.*, 1963–4, p. 127.

[3] *FRBNY Monthly Review*, July 1968.

[4] The other two were Canada and Japan.

[5] *The Eurodollar market*, p. 25.

[6] *A quantitative framework for the Euro-dollar system* (Princeton, 1970).

[7] BIS, *Ann. rep.*, 1964–5.

[8] A. K. Swoboda, 'Multinational banking, the Eurodollar market and economic policy', *Journal of World Trade Law*, Apr 1971.

[9] Irving Auerbach, *FRBNY Monthly Review*, May 1971.

[10] N. Harwich, 'International consortium banking', London Univ. doctoral thesis, 1974.

[11] Notably R. N. Cooper, in *The economics of interdependence*; Ed. Morse, 'The modernization of national societies' and 'The transformation of foreign policy', *World Politics*, Apr 1969; R. O. Keohane & J. S. Nye, jr, eds, *Transnational relations and world politics* (Cambridge, Mass., 1972).

[12] *Money international*, p. 170.

[13] *Money markets of the world: what the future may bring* (London, Laurie, Millbank and Co. for private circulation, 1971).

[14] *The Euro-dollar market*, p. 174.

[15] 'Transnational relations as a threat to the democratic process', in Keohane & Nye.

[16] *The Euro-dollar market*, p. 175.

[17] 'Treasury and Federal Reserve foreign exchange operations', *FRBNY Monthly Review*, Sept 1969.

[18] 'The magicians and their rabbits', *Morgan Guaranty Survey*, May 1971.

[19] 'Eurodollars: a paper pyramid', *B. Naz. del Lavoro*, June 1971.

[20] Statements by Abs and Ossola on Eurodollar market regulation made at a seminar at International University, Luxembourg, in Nov 1972 (see *The Banker*, Dec 1972, pp. 1560–2).

7

THE LIQUIDITY DEBATE 1960–5

Most observers of international economic relations would probably agree with Sir Eric Roll that next to the problem of the developing countries, the problem of international liquidity was the most fully and frequently debated issue of the 1960s.[1] The decade that had begun with the publication of Triffin's diagnosis and prescription[2] ended in apparent triumph with the Group of Ten's decision to put the agreed scheme for SDRs into operation with the first issue of $3½ billion in 1970. Tentative as this was, there were many then who fervently hoped that from this first acorn of internationally-created reserve assets would grow a spreading oak of international monetary management.

The progress—although the word prejudges the question—from one event to the other was uneven and often seemed seriously in doubt. And where the background noise for some episodes in the history of international monetary relations in the 1960s seems to have been the grumblings and rumblings of the market, and for others to have been the clashes and confrontations of foreign policy and diplomacy, in this case it seems to have been the more subdued sounds of academic debate and of private, even esoteric, intellectual dispute among professional economists.

An important question to keep in mind, therefore, with this part of the story is how big an effect the unofficial liquidity debate in the economics profession actually had on the attitudes and actions of governments. There had been other times, after all, in international affairs when private discussion had preceded, inspired, and influenced official policy and planning. For instance, there had been the debate on international organization that had taken place largely among private or semi-public groups especially in the United States during the latter part of World War II; in the nineteenth century there had been the anti-slavery debates in Britain and later in America. More recently, the Bretton Woods Agreement and the Havana Charter for an International Trade Organization had been prefaced by much private as well as by official discussions.

A rather curious aspect of the liquidity debate was the suddenness of its appearance on the intellectual scene. Search the economic literature of the 1930s and 1940s and there is no mention of it. The word 'liquid' had originally been used to describe the attribute of an asset. It referred to cash and other easily negotiable assets as contrasted with securities, loans, and other assets not so easily used as direct means of payment. Then, by association, it was applied to persons. Someone, or some enterprise, was in a liquid position who owned a high ratio of liquid (i.e. disposable, negotiable) funds in proportion to the calls likely to be made upon him or it. Liquidity meant simply the capacity to pay promptly.

(' Liquidity preference ', it is true, had figured quite largely in Keynesian analysis of economic processes in the general theory; and Keynes's diagnosis of a depression model explained the inadequacy of investment in part by the undue preference of owners of wealth as a group for holding their capital in the form of cashable savings rather than investing it in risk enterprise.)

The concept of aggregate liquidity, however, seems to have been of quite recent invention and seems to have emerged largely from discussions within the IMF. Partly as a result of the sudden calls made on it after Suez, the Fund's holdings of US dollars fell in the last three months of 1956 by nearly a third, leaving only $1,142m to cover commitments under standby arrangements to various members totalling $1,117m. If everyone then entitled to draw on the Fund had done so at once, it would have found itself in a highly illiquid position. An emergency solution was first found early in 1957 by selling $600m of Fund gold to the US Treasury. But the problem of the Fund's liquidity remained. An increase in quotas was one obvious remedy and the possibility was raised at the annual meeting in September 1957. The Governor for Pakistan, Abdul Qadir, spoke for many developing countries when he suggested that Fund quotas were apparently too small for the increased volume of world trade. But it was a Frenchman, the distinguished M. Baumgartner, then still the Alternate Governor, who by an easy but logically indefensible progression from one idea to another, voiced the fear—often to be repeated in the next few years—that the world economy might soon suffer from ' a lack of liquidity '.

We shall come in a moment to examine this comparatively new idea more closely. Here the question may be asked: why did it make so abrupt an appearance? The answer must surely be not so much that finance ministers and Governors of central banks were afraid that the Fund would be obliged for lack of liquidity to close its doors or to suspend operations, as that they dreaded the onset of a general economic depression. This fear was the product of prolonged familiarity with the condition of dollar shortage and the consequent fear that in the absence of large continued injections of this apparently essential element in world prosperity, the international economy would relapse into its old and dreaded state of depression, unemployment, and needless poverty.

As to the imprecision of the term in the sense in which it was used by M. Baumgartner, this arose from a confusion of the concept of liquidity for a specific institution, the Fund, with the concept of aggregate liquidity throughout the world economy—as if, like some overheated combustion engine, it was in danger of seizing up for lack of oil. It is not difficult to see that this idea of aggregate liquidity was either so imprecise as to be practically meaningless or else it was self-contradictory. Except in a case where commitments to pay were all to one third party, the insufficiently liquid units would be paying each other, and one participant's liabilities would therefore be another participant's assets. It was thus impossible simply by aggregating particular liabilities to assess the degree of general liquidity in the system.

The multiplicity of possible meanings of liquidity used in an aggregate sense—and therefore its consequent imprecision—was admirably demonstrated by Fritz Machlup in one of his brilliant essays in semantic dissection:

Whereas it is quite reasonable to include both the borrowing capacity and asset-liquidating capacity of any one central bank as part of its liquidity, the inclusion of such facilities in an ocean of an 'aggregate liquidity' of the international system as a whole cannot pass an examination where proper standards of logic are maintained. As one bank can borrow only what another bank lends and can dispose only of as many assets as are bought by others, the increase in liquidity of the borrowers and sellers involves a reduction in the liquidity of the lenders and buyers.[3]

Machlup's conclusion, in short, was that the term was concise only at the expense of precision.

This imprecision had several consequences. It meant that argument was always possible about 'how much was too little'. No objective, non-political criterion could ever be found therefore to discover whether, at any given moment, trade was being starved of 'liquidity' or not. Machlup in fact dismissed the whole idea as 'trendy new economists' lingo', a new disguise for the old complaint against the gold standard system that it provided an 'all too narrow gold cover' and that it was this which accounted for the inadequacy of the money supply and for stagnation and slow growth in the world economy. Yet there was more to it than that. For since the old gold standard days, the relation of the domestic money supply to the amount of gold in the national reserves held by central banks had long ceased to be either direct or uniform. A decline in national reserves—national liquidity—no longer automatically led, as many examples in the 1950s clearly showed, to domestic deflation. Moreover, the pyramid of private credit was continuing to grow apace and perhaps to an accelerating degree to do so independently of the state of inter-central bank credit. This was shown, for instance, by the difficulties of holding the line on export credit terms between the various members of the affluent alliance. In other words, it was not impossible for there to be a shortage of aggregate official liquidity (assuming for the moment that such a concept had any meaning) at the same time as a sufficiency or even an excess of aggregate private liquidity. Thus the imprecision of the term when it was used primarily to refer to aggregate inter-central bank liquidity may also have served to obscure the equally important question of aggregate private liquidity. For, given that the secular problem was inflation and instability and not—as was believed at the time—deflation and depression, the failure of the system to control private liquidity was perhaps just as significant as its growing concern over public or official liquidity.

The fourth and last curious feature of the liquidity debate in the 1960s was the difficulty experienced by some of the chief members of the affluent alliance in perceiving and assessing their national interests. It was one of those questions where official opinions were capable both of indecision and of rather sudden change of mind as to what the vital interests of the state were and how they could best be served. The economists have on the whole been more concerned with the search for a means of ascertaining the international need for liquidity on some objective criterion or combination of criteria.[4] They therefore saw the question all along as a mainly technical one, and they sometimes found it strange that governments did not apparently know their own minds or were capable of suddenly reversing the whole direction of their policies. Consequently they tended to ignore this rather striking feature of the liquidity debate. But it is perhaps worth recalling that similar reversals of state policy, resulting from a reassessment of national interests, are not such uncommon occurrences in international history, especially in political history. France, aided by Talleyrand, revised its opinion of French interests in the fate of Belgium in 1830. More recently, when the fate of the ex-Italian colonies was discussed in 1946, both the Russians *and* the Americans changed their minds as to what best suited their interests.

In this instance, it will be recalled, the question first arose in 1945 at the Potsdam Conference. Stalin put in a Russian claim for some of the territory of the defeated states and suggested the Soviet Union might be named as trustee under the UN for one of the Italian ex-colonies. At that point the United States put forward a counter-proposal for a collective trusteeship, a sort of UN administration of all three colonies—Libya, Eritrea, and Somaliland. The apparently insoluble problem was finally turned over by a totally divided Council of Foreign Ministers to the UN General Assembly in 1949. But before this abdication of responsibility took place, the Russians rather astonishingly had adopted the original American position, favouring UN administration and collective trusteeship. Yet by then the last thing the United States wanted to encourage was a Soviet presence in the Mediterranean. The Americans therefore opposed the solution they themselves had originally suggested, leaving it in effect to Sforza and Bevin to sort out between them some acceptable division of responsibility among the Western allies.

In the liquidity debate, a strikingly similar exchange of diplomatic roles took place in 1965 with the French, who had originally bewailed the lack of liquidity and proposed the Composite Reserve Unit (CRU) scheme (see below, p. 218), now reversing gear into opposition [5] and the Americans going from reverse into forward gear with Secretary Fowler's speech to the Virginia Bar Association (see below, p. 225) and thus opening the door for the first time to a consideration of reserve asset creation.

The present chapter will trace the developments of the debate as far as this point, leaving the actual period of negotiations over the creation of international reserve assets between 1965 and 1968 to the following chapter. Here it will be seen that the preliminary and apparently unproductive period was itself divided into two phases. The first phase was one primarily of unofficial debate and discussion and of governmental unconcern and lack of interest in the various plans for radical change. In the second phase, beginning about the winter of 1962–3, a growing number of governments were becoming aware of their political interest in the issues and a growing number of influential central bankers were giving it serious consideration. The next two to two and a half years were a period of what the strategists would call contingency planning, in which the pace accelerated and the discussion came down, off the general and rather idealist plane on which it had started, to a more mundane level of what was politically practicable and might be acceptable to the national governments chiefly concerned.

Before turning to developments on the diplomatic side, an explanatory note or two may usefully be interjected on the main issues under discussion in the unofficial debate. This necessarily involves summary treatment of a large and varied literature, selecting only the main points in order to identify those which later had some bearing on the diplomatic exchanges between the governments of the Group of Ten. [6]

In the first place, this unofficial debate was not one but several, overlapping and interrelated, debates. There were three main issues as well as a number of subsidiary ones. The first was how to deal with a US payments deficit which was increasingly recognized as a permanent and not a temporary feature of the international monetary system. It was Triffin who, by pointing out that if the first problem were solved—i.e. if the deficit were eliminated—then the cure might be a more serious threat to the system than the condition it remedied, because by drying up the most important source of international liquidity it would throw the world into a deflationary spiral. The second problem therefore—assuming that the system was as basically unsound as the reformers said—was how to reform it. This was a much more complex debate since there was wide disagreement both about the nature of the unsoundness in the system and its causes. Consequently, remedies were apt not only to be various (as with the first problem) but also sometimes mutually exclusive and conflicting.

The third and last issue concerned not so much the instability or inherent unsoundness of the system as its inherent injustice. The complaint was less against its susceptibility to breakdown than against its misdirection in terms of the political and social welfare of an international community which included more poor countries than rich ones. The issue was simply how to reform the system so as to direct more of its wealth towards the developing countries. It so happened that many of the reformers, like Triffin himself, Bernstein and Maxwell Stamp, had themselves either been international civil servants or had worked closely with international organizations and were sensitive to this criticism of the system and wished to do something about it. The developing countries themselves were just at this time beginning to complain vociferously—had indeed been the first to complain—of a lack of liquidity, meaning that their need for funds to cover current deficits and capital investments outran their resources in foreign exchange.

Thus it happened that the perception of the three problems more or less coincided in the space of two or three years. The early 1960s, it will be recalled, were the years when the inadequacy of the increase in World Bank quotas agreed in 1959 came under sharper criticism than ever. At the end of 1961 the UN General Assembly, embarking on its self-styled Development Decade, set a goal of at least 5 per cent annual increase in the GNP of every less developed country by the end of the 1960s and a similar annual rate of 6 per cent for the 1970s.[7] The same year saw the newly established Development Assistance Committee (DAC) of OECD start its work, thus showing at least some token concern for the problems of developing countries. This was also the year in which the United States launched the Alliance for Progress in the Western hemisphere, in which the IDA began operations and its associated World Bank affiliate, the International Finance Corporation, eased its rules on equity-financing in order to become more effective. The economists who were considering how to reform the monetary system were not immune to the general mood. But the issue of who was to benefit from the system was really quite separate and distinct from whether the system—regardless of who benefited—was in danger and needed reform in order to keep going at all.

This was Triffin's basic contention and his was the first and indeed by general acknowledgement the most widely discussed and influential of the various plans for radical reform. The earliest of his two articles published by the Banca Nazionale del Lavoro in 1959 consisted of diagnosis; the second of prescription. Recalling the short-lived return to convertibility between 1926 and 1931, Triffin found the inherent stability of the system to be rather less in 1958 than it had been then. He argued that the necessary liquidity in the system, to keep pace with the expansion of world trade and payments, had been provided through the willingness of most (although not all) countries to accumulate a substantial portion of their monetary reserves in the form of sterling and dollars.

The trouble with this solution—known as the ' gold exchange standard '— is that it is bound to undermine, more and more dangerously as time goes on, the international liquidity position of the currencies used as reserves by other countries and, by way of consequence, to impart an increasing vulnerability to the world monetary superstructure built upon the so-called ' key currencies '. Indeed, the additions to international liquidity made possible by the system are entirely dependent upon the willingness of the key currency countries to allow their own net reserve position to deteriorate, by letting their short-term liabilities to foreigners grow persistently and indefinitely at a faster pace than their own gold assets.

I recall . . . how this led in 1931 to the devaluation of the pound sterling, to the collapse of the international gold exchange standard, and to the consequent aggravation of the world depression.[8]

On almost every page, Triffin's argument harks back to the experience of the 1930s, drawing a parallel between the position of the United States in the 1960s and of Britain in the interwar period. Both sterling in the past and the dollar in the present, Triffin believed, were subject to impossible dilemmas, especially in the management of interest rates, between the conflicting demands of domestic growth and stability, and of international growth and stability. And although the argument was flawlessly logical and rational, Triffin's main weapon was emotional—the sharply perceived fear, still extremely potent well into the 1960s, of a recurrence of world depression. ' Those who do not remember the past ', he quoted from Santayana in his *Gold and the Dollar Crisis,* ' will be condemned to repeat it.' By thus evoking this haunting spectre from the bad old days, public attention that might have been unmoved by other arguments was successfully aroused. It was like the fear of German rearmament felt in the British Labour movement in the 1950s in that its power to swing opinion derived far more from a kind of evocative folk-memory than from reason.

The only way out, Triffin preached, was the internationalization of the foreign exchange component of world monetary reserves. The ultimate goal for Triffin was quite explicitly the creation of a world central bank, the substitution of adequate international control for inadequate national control of the economic environment. To achieve this, he was prepared to play on collective fears and phobias and to turn every temporary crisis and problem into an argument for radical political reform disguised as technical innovation. Throughout the 1960s he was ever ready to devise what were in effect a series of variations on his original plan, conceding details but never altering in any important respect his ultimate intention. He was by no means unaware of how radical his ideas were nor so unworldly that he did not see the political resistance they would encounter. But he believed that, as impious men in acute danger may be brought to pray, so states in economic desperation might be brought to abdicate. Another of his books, *Our International Monetary System*, declared by implication his belief in man's capacity to evolve an increasing degree of control over his economic destiny and environment. Triffin was also convinced that as a prophet and diagnostician, he had more often been right than his critics. He had been right, he thought, over the EPU which he had vainly urged on the Fund when he was head of their new Paris branch office in 1947. He had been right again to discount the danger of dollar shortage during the US recession of 1953–4. And he claimed in the long run to have been right too over the incipience of a dollar glut foretold earlier in *Europe and the Money Muddle* (1957). What was nevertheless misleading was the implied analogy in all of Triffin's writing between monetary management on the national and on the international scale. The political problem of imposing a central bank's authority over rival private banks of issue financially responsible to their shareholders is obviously of a very different order from the political problem of imposing an international monetary authority over central banks whose prime responsibility is political—to national governments perhaps less jealous of their sovereignty than fearful of the displeasure and dissatisfaction of national electorates. This essential difference Triffin, as an economist, was inclined to gloss over. His proposal for the addition of ' paper gold ' to the lending resources already controlled by the IMF seemed deceptively simple. In brief, the plan proposed that every member should agree to hold at least 20 per cent of its official reserves in the new reserve asset, and to convert into it all the national reserves previously held in the form of foreign exchange—i.e. in dollars or in sterling. These assets would then become the new medium of international official transactions and of Fund lending. The ' inflationary bias ' for which Keynes's original Bancor scheme had been criticized, Triffin suggested, could be checked by arranging a presumptive ceiling that would limit the increase on the Fund's loans and investments (plus the increase in monetary gold) to between 3 and 5 per cent in any one year. Only by a qualified majority vote of the Fund's member governments, he went on to suggest, would it be possible for this ceiling to be breached. Yet it cannot be emphasized too strongly that the addition of paper gold to the members' reserves was not the key point. It was the substitution of internationally created reserve assets for nationally controlled reserve assets like sterling or dollars that was the revolutionary principle. The sugar coating was the promise that, by this painless means, world economic recession would be avoided. The bitter almond inside was the implicit introduction of international monetary government.

Curiously little of the unofficial debate focused on this point—perhaps because most of the participants in it were economists and were more interested in the diagnosis of the state of the economic system than in the essentially political question ' Whose finger on the trigger? ' One notable and important exception was Robert Roosa, the New York banker who became Under-Secretary for Monetary Affairs at the Treasury and was probably the most influential figure in US monetary policy in the period 1961–4. On several occasions, Roosa attacked Triffin's proposals on the ground that the very idea of a world central bank was fruitless and impractical. Such a man-made ' superbank ', Roosa argued, would be weak and unstable unless—which was clearly preposterous—it had a supergovernment to back its claims, support its authority, and guarantee its debts. Otherwise, it would have less real monetary power than the US government, which had the richest national economy in the world to tax or borrow from. If the US government had been subject to loss of confidence in its capability as world banker, how much more likely that confidence would falter in an international financial bureaucracy with no national economy to support it.

Simply to establish the superbank would require all countries of the world to give up their present reserves and accept instead the fiat issue of a superauthority existing without a superstate. But assuming that could be done, what would happen when differences of view began to exercise conflicting pulls upon the central organisation?
. . . Those differences will prevent the systematic direction of the superbank on uniform and consistent lines. The outcome, if it is not utter

chaos . . . is likely instead to be a drifting back towards systems of reliance upon clusters of currencies, and dependence on the strength given them by the economies which underlie them.[9]

Among the economists, there were several eminent voices which dissented from Triffin's basic diagnosis, though on a wide variety of grounds, and who proposed alternative ways of reforming the system. James Meade, for example, the quiet, retiring Cambridge professor regarded by many as a leading authority on the financial analysis of international trade and payments, asserted that it was not the inadequacy of liquidity that was the chief problem so much as the inflexibility of exchange rates which gave rise to the need for larger reserves. This was an opinion which was to gain steadily in professional support through the decade. It was notably shared by Milton Friedman, the doyen of the Chicago school of monetarist economists, but Friedman was more dogmatic about the ability of the market rather than the clumsy and heavy hand of government to solve the problem, and less internationalist in his concern than Meade.[10] Another distinguished dissenter was Harvard's veteran economist, Gottfried Haberler, who found Triffin's prediction ' a great exaggeration ' and thought the same ingenuity lavishly and prematurely spent on the liquidity problem ' could be profitably applied to the more basic and neglected problem of how to improve the adjustment mechanism '.[11]

One supporting voice—or at least partially so, which must have embarrassed Triffin, for he seldom publicly acknowledged their agreement [12]—was that of Jacques Rueff, the veteran French economist, whose appearance on the international monetary scene had begun as financial attaché in London under Poincaré and had been marked about the same time by his editing of the Moreau diaries,[13] which had made no bones about the political character of French monetary policies and attitudes in the 1920s. In June 1961 Rueff, having voiced his alarm in official circles without apparently getting much response, published identical articles in *Le Monde*, the *Neue Zürcher Zeitung*, the *Corriere della Sera*, the London *Times*, and *Fortune*.[14] Rueff also drew comparisons between the current situation and the ' house of cards ' which collapsed in 1929, and the susceptibility of the dollar to the effects of large movements of funds. Rueff's remedy for the situation, however, both then and later, was a deliberate increase in the price of gold in dollars and the repayment in gold of dollar balances accumulated by central banks in their reserves. In spite of its wide dissemination, Rueff's idea was never much discussed by the other economists. It was believed to be primarily nationalist in motivation; historically regressive in prescription; and—what was perhaps most damning—politically unacceptable because of the benefits it would confer on South Africa and on the Soviet Union. Significantly, perhaps, it found no support at all among economists in North America, although in Western Europe it was advocated both by Michael Heilperin of Geneva and Roy Harrod, Keynes's disciple and biographer, at Oxford.

The Bernstein proposals, first published just before the Rueff articles, were taken much more seriously, not only because Bernstein's reputation with the Fund staff was still high but also because the proposed reforms appeared more gradualist and practical, seeking to improve the system rather than to transform it. The most important suggestion was for a Reserve Settlement Account attached to the Fund, which would provide the Fund with a supplementary mixed bag of currencies, all carrying a gold guarantee and bearing interest, which it could distribute to members in proportion to their contributions and then lend to countries subjected to short-term capital outflows. The connection in the Bernstein Plan between the new multiple-currency asset and gold, and the implicit substitution of multilateral control over its management for unilateral US Treasury control over the dollar as a reserve asset soon appealed to the French.

Their elaboration, or modification, of the Bernstein proposals took the form of the CRU proposals. But in these the French soon began to suggest the *total* substitution of dollars and sterling reserve assets by CRUs, finding in Bernstein's ideas an unintended stick with which to beat the Americans.

Still more concerned than Bernstein not to attempt too radical a change and to build for preference on established practices of international monetary co-operation and organization, were the other reformist proposals. Among them, that of Xenophon Zolotas, the Greek central banker, for example, suggested the mutual holding of larger working balances (compensating reserve deposits) by the reserve countries—an extension of the swap principle; the gold guarantee of such working balances; and the separate tax and interest-rate treatment of official as distinct from commercial balances in reserve currencies. At this almost cosmetic, face-lifting level such system-preserving proposals were of more interest to the technicians (and to those primarily aiming at preserving the system) than they were to the radical reformers. What they tended to do was to seek solutions for immediate problems such as capital movements, while the radical reformers concentrated on the long-run reserve problem.

Of the latter the first and best-known of the plans which were mainly intended to deal with the problems of poor countries, was that proposed by Maxwell Stamp, a British banker, once a Fund Director but no longer with any official status or axe to grind. This plan, though it had roots in the long UN aid debate, could properly be said to have been the most important single source of the argument that later

came to be known as ' the link '. It deliberately combined an answer
to the liquidity problem with an answer to the development problem.
It proposed an IMF issue of gold certificates which members would
agree to accept in international payments transactions and which
would be allocated by an international aid agency to developing
countries.[15]

Needless to say, the idea had little appeal to policy-makers, British
no less than American, whose resistance to UN appeals for more and
better aid had been as consistently unrelenting in practice as they had
been sympathetic in tone. Roosa, once more, spoke not only for the
United States but for most of the governments represented on the
DAC:

It would be quixotic to hope . . . that the new arrangements [among the
developed countries] will solve the liquidity needs of the underdeveloped
countries; for in a full sense, nothing can. So long as these countries are
energetically pursuing development programs, any international reserves
not actually required as current balances will be consumed in the purchase of more imports. Mere increases in reserves, therefore, will largely
disappear.[16]

Recalling the question posed at the start of this chapter—whether
the unofficial liquidity debate had any significant impact on official
policies—the answer, judging from the pronouncements of American
officials and political leaders, would seem to be an emphatic ' no '.
(To feel called upon to refute the propositions put by the reformers,
and to give the reasons for doing so hardly counts as having a significant impact.) Certainly, judging by their words, the US policy-
makers rejected two out of the three issues in the whole debate,
denying that the gold exchange standard system needed reform in order
to avoid throwing the world into a trade recession, and denying that
the system needed to be changed to give it a special bias to assist the
developing countries. The only real issue they were prepared to deal
with was the US deficit. The only real questions in their view were what
to do about it. And even this had been denied and ignored until
President Kennedy entered the White House in 1961. It seems a
reasonable hypothesis that he was then less impressed by academic
argument than by the flurries in money markets and especially in the
gold market at an important moment in his election campaign in
September–October 1960; and by the consequent anxiety expressed
by his own advisers about the effects—both domestic and external—
of the mounting deficit.

It is interesting that in this initial phase of the debate the Fund staff
on the whole gave support to the negative US attitude towards all
plans for radical reform. The Staff Report produced under Bernstein
in 1958 had examined the case for a cause or connection between the

amount of liquidity and the tendency in the international economy towards trade depression.

The conclusion that can be drawn from a comparison with the past is [therefore] . . . that the contribution of reserves to the achievement of full employment, to the increase of world trade, and to the genesis of both inflation and deflation is not a dominant one. Major world trends of production and trade are not determined solely by liquidity. The developments of the last forty years or so have been dominated not by changing liquidity ratios but rather by two major wars, several minor wars, vast expenditures preparing for wars, and large expenditures to repair the damages of wars.[17]

Thus it side-stepped the argument that the inherent instability of the system could cause a sudden crisis that would be reflected by a shortage of liquidity and also by a failure of financial confidence. This was really the nub of Triffin's case, but the Fund staff chose to treat the liquidity question on a more superficial level. The debate in the Fund, therefore, between 1958 and 1961 was focused on the question of whether the organization needed to have *its* liquidity increased—a rather different question (see above, pp. 200–1): 'It is doubtful whether, in the circumstances of the world today, with world trade greatly expanded in volume and value, the Fund's resources are sufficient to enable it fully to perform its duties under the Articles of Agreement.'[18]

The official response

The new administration that came in after the 1960 elections did mark a significant turning point in official attitudes to the liquidity debate but one that some of the reformers misinterpreted. The chief change was that this administration was ready to take the deficit seriously and intended to do something about it, not that it was converted to a belief in radical or even moderate change in the system. That came—inasmuch as it ever did—much later. For the next two years the whole emphasis was on unilateral action and bilateral co-operation, and it was not until the end of 1963 that the American government would support a study of the liquidity problem and another eighteen months before they were ready for serious negotiations.

President Kennedy's programme for dealing with the deficit had been outlined first in a campaign speech in Philadelphia on 31 October 1960. It had pointedly *not* included any American support or initiative looking to major reform of the system. Such was the nervous state of the international financial markets that a mere hint of support for radical change it was felt could have destroyed confidence in the existing payments arrangements and jeopardised any prospects for orderly progress towards eventual major reforms.[19] In the month following the election, President Kennedy prepared to take decisive and determined action. C. Douglas Dillon, the Secretary-elect of the Treasury, his deputy Henry Fowler, and Robert Roosa, as Under-Secretary for Monetary Affairs, were set to work out in greater detail a policy to restore the balance of payments. And before the year ended the President had directed a special group of economic advisers to report to him at high speed on the economic situation and the balance of payments, using the outline prepared by the Treasury team. Kennedy made it clear that

he wanted a domestic economic program that was consistent with the restoration of balance in our international accounts, that he wanted to postpone consideration of overall monetary reform on an international scale until the position of the dollar itself had been reasonably secured, and that he wanted us to develop harmonious relations with the Federal Reserve as it then existed, with no suggestion of any structural change. He did, though, want us to begin immediately to enlarge our working contacts for financial collaboration with the governments and central banks of other countries.[20]

The three advisers were Alan Sproul, a former president of the Federal Reserve Bank of New York, Roy Blough, professor of economics at Columbia, and Paul McCracken, professor of economics at Michigan. Blough had been a member of Truman's Council of Economic Advisors and McCracken of Eisenhower's. They reported on 18 January 1961, two days before the President's inauguration, strongly supporting the fixed gold price of $35 and advocating an empirical, piecemeal set of solutions to the balance-of-payments problem. This section of the report ended:

There will still be unresolved of course the questions of whether, under present monetary arrangements, the need for international liquidity will increase and whether this will require the further piling up of foreign short-term dollar balances in excessive amounts. That is a problem which must be confronted eventually, but our immediate task is to remedy the current imbalance in our international accounts, so that the confrontation will not take place in an atmosphere of crisis and dollar weakness.[21]

This special report in its turn was the guideline for the President's special message on gold and the US balance-of-payments deficit which was sent to Congress on 6 February 1961. This was a fraction more forthcoming in its consideration of the question of international monetary reserves:

We must now, in cooperation with other leading countries, begin to consider ways in which international monetary institutions—especially the International Monetary Fund—can be strengthened and more effectively utilised, both in furnishing needed increases in reserves and in providing the flexibility required to support a healthy and growing world economy.[22]

The message categorically affirmed the administration's confidence that the measures it proposed would cure the 'basic long-term deficit' in the balance of payments and check the outflow of gold. As confidence grew in the new executive, apparently, its leaders felt it was safer to refer to the problem. But none of them changed his mind on the main point. Dillon, according to Roosa, 'felt certain that no basis existed for ready agreement on the tender issues of national interest that would necessarily be raised by any complex plan for a sweeping monetary change affecting all countries '.[23]

It is true that there were others, also close to the President, who were urging more decisive action on the international monetary front. Among these were the chairman of the Council of Economic Advisors, Walter Heller, and a group of presidential brainstrusters that included Professors Galbraith, Walt Rostow, and others. During 1961 Dillon and Roosa had the upper hand in this conflict of advisers. Kennedy soon set up a special Cabinet Committee on the Balance of Payments chaired by the Secretary of the Treasury. This group established a sub-committee of deputies chaired by the Assistant Secretary of the Treasury for International Affairs which kept the details of the US balance-of-payments developments under continuing review and analysis and maintained close watch over the fulfilment of a so-called gold budget, which was intended to be an important tool for scheduling and limiting the flow of spending 'across the exchanges' by any sections of the Federal government.[24] And as the President became increasingly absorbed in foreign affairs, international finance was left to this committee and to the Treasury team.[25] Roosa thought that the consequent confrontations within the administration, assisted by the forthright discussions in Working Party III which took place in the spring of 1961, helped to impress on everyone the seriousness of the balance-of-payments question. 'The views, apprehensions and problems of representative officials from so many of the other leading countries, . . . chastened somewhat further any remaining hopes by some members of the Administration for more sweeping or decisive action.'[26] But by this, he did not mean reforms as radical as those of Triffin or the Stamp Plan but rather more drastic action by the United States acting unilaterally or through bilateral negotiations to achieve balance-of-payments equilibrium, including steps such as giving official dollar balance holders a gold guarantee, or redeeming some of them by paying out 'several billion dollars in gold or by consolidating foreign liabilities into a large long-term loan'. The Treasury team were not prepared to go as far as this, although by the early summer of 1961 Dillon, Roosa, and William McChesney Martin, chairman of the Federal Reserve Board, began to think about the possibility of persuading other countries to make larger funds available to the

United States through the IMF on some sort of contingent basis.[27] By August, the Congressional Joint Economic Committee's Subcommittee on International Exchange and Payments was saying in no uncertain terms that the progress of the twelve previous years was threatened by the inadequacy of the monetary system. And it was recommending long-term borrowing by the IMF from the principal industrial countries. It advised the elimination of the 25 per cent gold backing for the domestic currency, a measure eventually taken in March 1968. It also advocated the study of future reserve needs and the adequacy of international liquidity—a measure of preparedness that the Administration was not yet ready to take. By this time the negotiations on the GAB had started. And by the time the arrangement was eventually agreed in December, the creditor countries succeeded in gaining some control of the proposed borrowing operation (see above, pp. 113ff.).

Throughout 1961 and in the early part of 1962, the declared hope of the Kennedy administration was to have corrected the deficit by the end of 1963. A steep increase in the outflow of short-term capital in the last quarter of 1961 did not extinguish this hope, but it did prompt further essays in the bilateral financing of the deficit. Having started operations in D-marks and Swiss francs in the aftermath of the D-mark revaluation of March 1961, the Federal Reserve from March 1962 onwards built up a network of swap credits with the central banks of the Group of Ten, with the BIS itself, and with Australia and Switzerland (see above, p. 136).

The Americans placed much reliance on this device, both to keep the deficit manageable and to prevent speculative raids on the dollar. Speaking at the annual conference of the American Bankers' Association in May 1962, Roosa showed just how much he hoped for from the scheme: he said that the idea was to build up American foreign exchange holdings so that they might be able to handle 'a considerable part of the normal swings in payments patterns, leaving the gold reserves available to cover more fundamental and lasting adjustments'. Providing for any large increases in long-run liquidity requirements might best be done by these means.

Explorations along these lines are far preferable, it seems to me, to the often proposed types of action (involving still more difficult decisions and negotiations) that basically involve an oath of allegiance by all governments and central banks to a synthetic currency device, created by an extra-national authority bearing neither the responsibilities nor the disciplines of sovereignty.[28]

Roosa reiterated the same convictions in yet another article which appeared immediately before the IMF 1962 annual meeting in Washington a few months later.[29] This article was, he later confessed, intended to provide 'an inconspicuous but public sketch of our own views'. It dismissed the idea of dollar devaluation; heaped scorn on the idea of guarantees for dollar holdings and thought a 'superbank' impracticable. The most promising and reliable pattern for new developments would, he suggested yet again, be an extension of co-operation through the mutual holding of foreign currencies and of co-operation through existing organizations—the OECD, the BIS, and the IMF.

By such means, clearly, Roosa was indirectly engaging in the liquidity debate. This from about 1962 was no longer confined to the reformers and academics—the amateurs, so to speak—but was increasingly joined by the professionals—ministers of governments and the leading central bankers. Recalling the privacy and the some-times inscrutable silences of Montagu Norman and his colleagues in the interwar years, the openness of discussion of this question was surely something of an innovation in the system.

Roosa's article just referred to indeed was neatly timed to appear just before the Fund meeting and neatly timed, too, to spoil a British initiative by the Chancellor of the Exchequer, Reginald Maudling, for a mutual currency account under the IMF. In the light of subsequent developments, it now seems as if the Maudling Plan was not very revolutionary or even incompatible with Roosa's empiricism. All it suggested—building clearly on Britain's recognition of the value to sterling of the 1961 Basle Agreement (see above, ch. 3)—was that the Fund should provide a cushion of rather longer duration than the BIS could give to countries in deficit, by holding their currencies in a mutual currency account, giving them a gold guarantee, and paying a modest rate of interest to the creditors. The underlying presumption was that the deficit would only be a temporary aberration and that the creditors would be able to use up the currency deposited with the Fund as soon as the balance righted itself. Only much later, did Mr Maudling envisage the possibility that arrangements would have to be made for repayment of outstanding deposits on the lines of the EPU but over 'an indefinite period'.[30] Unlike the EPU, however, the credits would not be transferable.

As a diplomatic manoeuvre, the Maudling proposal was a failure. It had not been 'cleared' with the Americans either at the Treasury or the Federal Reserve Board before it was put forward. The result was that Maudling was publicly snubbed by Roosa and the general reception at the Fund meeting was consequently cool. The implication was that when the United States was ready to take the initiative in the reform debate, it would prefer to take it on its own and not leave it to the British. Sterling's precarious position and the solicitude of other members of the affluent alliance were clearly making the British over-presumptuous. In American eyes, Maudling risked upsetting the

European central banks, whose confidence it was a top requirement of US monetary diplomacy to retain.

At the Fund meeting many of these central bankers were still harping on the importance of monetary discipline for the reserve currency countries. 'Internal liquidity should be sufficient', said Dr Karl Blessing, 'to provide adequate time to remove imbalances, but it should also be scarce enough to enforce monetary discipline.' Governor Holtrop for the Netherlands echoed these sentiments. 'Radical reform would actually result in relieving monetary authorities for an indeterminate period of time from the discipline of the balance of payments.'[31] President Kennedy's speech to the meeting included the assertion that the United States would always be receptive to suggestions for expansion and improvement of the international monetary system. But he managed not to mention either the pound or any other currency apart from the dollar and 'seemed to be saying that what was good for the United States was good for the world'.[32]

In retrospect, however, Roosa was prepared to concede that the Maudling Plan had proved to be 'a most valuable catalyst'. It had kept the debate going at a time when it was flagging through widespread complacency and it had provoked a number of amendments and counter proposals, some of which later proved fruitful of new initiatives. For example, Fred Hirsch points out that the essential of the proposal was in fact put into practice by Italy in August 1966 when $250m in lire were deposited with the Fund, outside the GAB, in exchange for dollars which the Fund did not want. The lire deposit was gold-guaranteed and interest-bearing.[33]

The beginning of a gradual change of direction in American policy came at the very end of 1962. In rather sharp contrast with an optimistic statement which Roosa had made to Congress on 13 December, McChesney Martin, in a speech at Pittsburg on 28 December, was much more pessimistic about the outlook for the balance of payments. He threw doubt on the Roosa policy of accumulating reserves of foreign exchange while the deficit lasted. The calm in the market, he said, must not blind international monetary managers to the inadequacies of the system.[34] *The Economist*, for one, saw this speech as a possible watershed in US financial policy. It was clear by this time that the balance-of-payments deficit, which it had been hoped would be eliminated by the end of the year, was not responding to treatment as quickly as had been hoped. The 1962 improvement (on the liquidity basis) had been much less than the estimate. By March 1963 Secretary Dillon had confirmed that the Treasury had had to abandon the hope of balance by the end of the year.[35] A vaguer target of balance some time in 1964 or 1965 was imperceptibly substituted. And the conviction was growing that the problem would be more difficult to solve than the Kennedy administration had at first foreseen.

Then an unexpected and substantial increase in the deficit in the second quarter of 1963 to an annual rate of more than $5 billion made new measures essential and provoked two important shifts in US policy. At home, the Federal Reserve Board raised interest rates by putting up its discount rate from 3 to $3\frac{1}{2}$ per cent—the first change since 1960 and the first of a series of increases. Regulation Q was also changed to allow a higher maximum rate of 4 per cent on three-month time-deposits. Since mid-1960 average short-term rates in the United States had stayed below 3 per cent: by the end of 1963, they were up to $3\frac{1}{2}$ per cent. For foreigners, borrowed money was to be made dearer still. A few days after the Federal Reserve action, on 18 July 1963, a second special presidential message was sent to Congress on the balance of payments. It recognized that the hard core of the deficit was the outflow of short-term capital and that this would have to be dealt with by direct unilateral action. The chief measure chosen was the Interest Equalization Tax, which would add an extra 1 per cent on the cost of foreign borrowing in US money markets and on foreign stocks and shares bought by US residents (see above, p. 181).

On the longer-range perspective, the President's message contained two important items. First, the United States had arranged a standby for $500m with the IMF. This was the first time that the Americans had made such an arrangement and it marked a basic change in their attitude: ' In place of aloofness, there is now full commitment to the idea that the IMF is for use by all who justify their need.' [36] The new balance-of-payments measures aimed to improve the balance by $3–$3\frac{1}{2}$ billion a year. The implications of this for American external financial policy were brought out in the final part of the message. Kennedy reaffirmed that the effort to strengthen the dollar's defences would continue and also that the United States would ' continue to study and discuss with other countries measures which might be taken for a further strengthening of the international monetary system over the longer run '. The President went on to mention American concern for ' the growth of international liquidity to finance expanding world trade '. The closing of the deficit would ' cut down our provision of dollars to the rest of the world '. Then came the cautious announcement of American readiness to consider reform:

As yet, this Government is not prepared to recommend any specific prescription for long-term improvement of the international monetary system. But we are studying the matter closely; we shall be discussing possible improvements with our friends abroad; and our minds will be open to their initiatives.[37]

This statement clearly indicated a substantial change in American policy, for which the main credit must surely go to the obduracy of the payments figures. Roosa suggests that he himself began to change his mind during an enforced retreat, caused by illness, from official business in the autumn of 1962, and that, following private discussions with Dillon, Fowler, Martin, and his deputy, J. Dewey Daane, he embarked, early in 1963, on a series of 'special journeys' coinciding with the meetings of Working Party III in Paris. These, significantly, were taken to central bank headquarters—Rome, Frankfurt, London, Stockholm, Brussels, and Amsterdam. And they aimed ' to explore interest in launching joint new studies for additional steps to assure the adequacy of international liquidity over the long run '.[38]

A supplementary influence on official opinion in Washington came from the prestigious research centre, the Brookings Institution, from whom the government had commissioned a special long-term study of the US balance-of-payments situation. This report,[39] published in July 1963, foresaw a continuation of the US deficit until about 1968. The authors of the report concluded that this would lead to a liquidity shortage and world deflation unless prompt action was taken. It accordingly recommended that the Kennedy administration should immediately press for new international credit machinery, preferably linked with the IMF. It even hazarded the thought that transferring part of the reserve function to an international organization, as a means of obtaining agreement on an international liquidity system, should not be unwelcome to the United States.

The two key points on which therefore Dillon and Roosa now changed their opinion were, first, that the end of the American deficit might indeed (as the reformers had always argued) herald a serious liquidity shortage. And the second, that deficits could be structural and would not be susceptible (as they had at first believed) to a quick cure. Instead, there would have to be adequate credit available to deal with them. Experience had also borne in on them that there was a limit to European tolerance of American ' ad hoc-ery '. The central bankers had shown that they had a limited willingness to hold dollars in their reserves. Nor had they been too keen to purchase Roosa bonds.

Just how far Roosa's ideas had altered since the previous year was indicated in an article ('Reforming the international monetary system ') in the September 1963 issue of *Foreign Affairs*. Once again timed to precede the Fund's annual meeting, this article put forward quite a different view from the 1962 one. Roosa argued that the point had now been reached where governments might fruitfully address themselves to the question of the adequacy of international liquidity, though as he presciently pointed out: ' No consensus can be expected without a long period of exploratory discussion followed by extended negotiation '. He saw four possible avenues of inquiry. The first would enlarge co-operative credit arrangements under the existing system. The second would enlarge Fund resources and increase flexibility. The third would do all these and create further reserve currencies. Fourthly, some or all of these measures could be combined with a Fund empowered to create and allocate credit. Without endorsing any particular sort of reform, Roosa recommended a joint review of the system, which would lead to a 'definitive appraisal' by the governments themselves. The scene was therefore set for such a study to be initiated. Certain other changes, meanwhile, had occurred elsewhere than in the Fund and in the US administration. Following the death of Per Jacobsson in May, Pierre-Paul Schweitzer had taken over as Managing Director. While by no means a reformist, he was less optimistic than his predecessor had been about the adequacy of liquidity, and supported the idea of a study of the question, both within the Fund and outside it.

As for the Europeans, dismayed by the prospect of a continued outflow of dollars from the United States, they were becoming keener on a better balanced, more effectively managed system.[40] They were thus ' finally ready to admit the need for a radical review of the operation of the present international monetary system, even if only to avoid the long-term implications of continued, haphazard and precarious bilateral financing of the key currency countries' deficits '.[41]

The Roosa group

The United States had indicated to its Group of Ten partners in May, before the July 1963 policy package, its new-found readiness to explore the question of international monetary reform. The August break gave time for the July measures to show results so that, before the Fund's annual meeting at the end of September, the United States could initiate a collective study of the liquidity question from a position of apparent strength.[42]

Preparations were therefore made in advance of the Washington meeting for study to proceed both within the Fund and in the Group of Ten. Schweitzer obviously knew the Group of Ten's intentions when on 23 September he told the Executive Board that the Group of Ten would take the opportunity of the Fund meeting to discuss the liquidity question and that he would attend some of their discussions. He also said that he thought parallel inquiries should be welcomed, and not resisted, by the Fund: the Fund would be found to be the instrument through which the bulk of any required expansion of international liquidity could most suitably be carried out. He proposed to say as much in presenting his annual report.[43]

The day after he had done so, on 2 October, the Group of Ten's decision was made public in a press statement issued on their behalf by Treasury Secretary Douglas Dillon. This stated that although ' the present national reserves of member countries . . . seemed fully adequate in present circumstances to cope with possible threats to the stability of the international payments system ', the ministers and Governors thought it would be useful ' to undertake a thorough examination of the outlook for the functioning of the international monetary system and of its probable future needs for liquidity ', and had therefore ' instructed their Deputies to examine these questions and to report to them on the progress of their studies and discussions over the course of the coming year '.[44]

In the Fund, these studies were to absorb ' much of the effort of the staff ' over the next two years,[45] reflecting the organization's final recognition both of its own self-interest in the outcome of the debate and of its enforced subservience to what the deputies could agree amongst themselves.[46] Schweitzer went to some pains to see that the deputies were supplied with the Staff Papers and that the Fund was represented at meetings both of the ministers and their deputies.

It was at this point, before the negotiating stage was actually reached, that the leading governments made it clear that though they would work with and through the Fund, they did not propose to engage unofficial academic experts in their discussions, however general and theoretical these might be at times. It was perhaps understandable that the academics, having in a sense initiated the whole debate, should feel a trifle piqued at this rebuff. The suggestion at the end of the 1963 Fund meeting that perhaps the Roosa group might hold hearings in the manner of a Congressional committee had been briskly rejected. One central banker was reported by Professor Fritz Machlup as explaining that though ' the economists had for years been busy spawning plans and proposals, they had not come up with any new and practical ideas, and their views were so much in disagreement with one another that their advice was practically useless to those in charge of decision-making '.[47]

This rejection by the Group of Ten was all the more wounding because the Bank and the Fund had from the beginning—and rather exceptionally among international agencies—made a practice of inviting distinguished economists to attend their annual meetings as guests. The snub stung some of them, led by Professor Fritz Machlup of Princeton University, to embark on a joint study that would identify the sources of disagreement both in the judgement of facts and in the importance attached to various objectives of the international monetary system. ' Perhaps ', they suggested, ' some of the differences in judgments of fact can be resolved by further study, and some of the differences in judgments of value may be reduced by a non-emotive analysis of their places in a common hierarchy of higher goals.'[48]

There have not been many occasions in recent international history when so many top-rankers in a profession have addressed themselves in this way to a major policy-making issue. A possible parallel might be found in the Pugwash conferences of scientists begun in the late 1950s, and it may be worth noting that this pattern of influence by unofficial groups which can later be seen (for example, in the 1972 Stockholm conference on problems of the international environment) was first set in the two areas—nuclear physics and monetary economics—where the threat to international stability was felt to be most acute.

The original list of the 'Bellagio Group', as they were sometimes called, numbered forty. But Paul Samuelson, Milton Friedman, James Meade, Ed. Bernstein, and four others could not attend. The 32 remaining participants included almost all the other respected names in the profession in North America, Europe, and Japan, among them Jacques Rueff, Robert Triffin, Roy Harrod, Harry Johnson, Peter Kenen, Charles Kindleberger, Arthur Bloomfield, Bertil Ohlin, Kyoshi Kojima, Walter Salant, Gottfried Haberler, and one financial journalist, Fred Hirsch. Though about half were of European origin, most by sympathy and/or adoption were American.

After a preliminary meeting of the American economists at Princeton, a mixed group of eighteen met at the Rockefeller Institute's Villa Serbelloni, above Bellagio on Lake Como, in January 1964 and again in March. But their conclusions, as will be seen later, had little visible influence on the work of the officials, except perhaps to offer them a conveniently wide choice of possible solutions to technical difficulties.

The deputies, meanwhile, started their work in November 1963 and met monthly through the ensuing winter. Their terms of reference were very wide—'the outlook for the functioning of the international monetary system and of its probable future needs for liquidity'[49]— and the membership, though limited to government appointees, was distinguished. It included Dr Otmar Emminger, Dr Rinaldo Ossola, and M. Emile van Lennep. Robert Roosa took the chair. Yet after only two meetings it was clear to Roosa and others that about the only thing on which the Group could agree was that if any new initiative were ever to be taken, it would be theirs and not that of the Executive Board of the Fund. Roosa stated publicly that the appointment of the Group had 'raised unrealistic hopes for an easy solution'.[50]

The chief points of disagreement were two: whether liquidity should be increased or not and who should exercise control over it. Roosa, while still favouring the gradual evolutionary approach, stated more firmly than before that a greater use of credit facilities would probably be necessary in the future and stressed the potential of the IMF in this area. The Europeans resisted the idea of a US-dominated Fund with the power to create and allocate a new reserve asset, and were inclined to favour instead some new system of rules that could be operated automatically. This tied in with their strict adherence to the Fund rule book in the concurrent debate over a possible increase in quotas (see below, p. 221).

It also explained the attention paid by the deputies in their winter meetings to the CRU reform scheme. This, it will be recalled, had originally been suggested by Bernstein as a multilateral substitute for the reserve currency roles of sterling and the dollar. CRUs, created by the deposit with the Fund of the main national currencies used in the international commercial and financial system, would be issued to countries to hold in their reserves. The French suggested that one CRU should be allotted for every nine units of gold in existing national reserves and that the allocation should be in strict proportion to the existing national gold stocks, on the principle of ' to him that hath, much shall be given '. International payments accounts would then be settled in gold and CRUs in a fixed proportion so that the United States, unless it corrected its deficit, would suffer an immediate gold loss. A further result would have been to increase the *de facto* value (and perhaps in the course of time the *de jure* price) of gold, once more rewarding the gold holders and penalizing, relatively speaking, the holders of dollars and sterling.

These proposals were the most provocative expression yet of feelings widespread throughout Europe about how the international monetary system ought to work. Essentially, these derived from the philosophical principles of the French (and American) revolutions and of the Enlightenment, asserting the fundamental equality of rights and duties of states in the international system as of individuals within the state. No one had a divine right to a deficit any more than monarchs had a divine right to override the popular will. It also tied in with the neo-classical approach to economics that discounted the inequalities of power between producers and consumers, buyers and sellers, creditors and debtors in the real world and based theoretical analysis on a broad assumption of equality of actors engaged in economic processes. Similarly, in international economics, neo-classical theory assumed that prices paid in transactions, e.g. for sugar exchanged for railway engines, were decided primarily by the operation of the law of comparative costs, with each party negotiating from a position of equal market strength.

The antithesis to this view, expressed in many different ways and many apparently different issues, has been called ' the centre country ' view.[51] This asserted that the country with the dominant national economy in the system could not be treated in the same way as the other countries. Because of its possession of the top, or key, currency, the welfare of its national economy was central to the welfare of the international economy. And although its role as international banker conferred privileged rights (e.g. to avoid devaluation or to pursue heavy foreign investment), it also had special responsibilities in the system for the maintenance of order and stability—responsibilities which it dared not ignore. In international theory, this might be called an elitist view not too different from the high Tory traditions of many European conservatives and empire builders, both British and French. It was most often expressed, naturally enough, in the Anglo-Saxon countries, and perhaps until the 1967 devaluation of sterling was most articulately expressed by the British. Before about 1965 the American version was much less apparent or explicit; and at the 1963 Fund meeting, the Americans were still a long way from openly adopting the centre country posture. Indeed, they could be said not to have done so fully before August 1971. The 1963 July measures still seemed to acknowledge America's earnest intention to restore equilibrium to the recalcitrant balance of payments and therefore to behave in the system with a responsibility equal to that of its other members. Dillon's speech at the Fund meeting plainly acknowledged that the prospect of international monetary reform would not relieve the United States of the 'compelling and immediate task of reducing its own payments deficit'.[52] The habits of neo-classical thinking still exerted a powerful influence on many American minds and were to continue to do so for several years to come.

It was at this meeting that the new French Finance Minister, M. Valéry Giscard d'Estaing, frontally attacked the existing system for its lack of corrective mechanisms and for the built-in asymmetry which gave the reserve currency countries unequal rights to run deficits and accumulate debts. These criticisms clearly revealed the reasons for the French Government attachment to the CRU idea. But since the Americans had no scheme of their own in mind—and since the British Maudling Plan had died for lack of support—the CRU was the only reform scheme to receive any detailed consideration in the deputies' discussions.[53]

However, they could not recommend it since it got no support from the Americans. By the spring of 1964 the grounds of American objection to the plan had become clear; first, that CRUs would gradually supplant dollars in other countries' reserves; and secondly, that the link between gold and CRUs would limit the necessary increase in international liquidity and might, on the contrary, even reduce it. Predictably, therefore, the Group of Ten deputies' report, published in August 1964, was a compromise document which did not disguise the clash of opinions; it proposed no immediate changes and backed no reform scheme. While agreeing that liquidity might not always be adequate for world needs, the Group failed to reach a consensus on the question of the creation of reserve assets. It discussed the possibility of agreement between Group of Ten countries on the introduction of a new asset and the possibility of gaining acceptance for the idea that claims on the Fund, perhaps related to members' gold tranches, could be used as reserve assets. But it came to no collective conclusion except that ' all such proposals raise complex questions '.[54] In other words, there was serious disagreement on such issues as who should belong to the decision-taking group, how control of created reserve assets should be exercised and by whom, whether account should be taken of the reserve needs of individual countries (especially the reserve currency countries) or whether some estimate could be made of the system's need for increased liquidity. The only recommendation which the deputies felt themselves able to make was for the appointment of a further group to study the problem. To these continued discussions we shall return. But some account must meanwhile be given of the parallel and closely related discussions of the manner and methods by which liquidity could meanwhile be increased through the existing mechanisms of the Fund.

The increase in Fund quotas

On the whole, the tenor of the IMF report on liquidity,[55] published concurrently with the deputies' report in August 1964, uninhibited by disagreement among the authors, showed greater readiness to explore the possibilities for adaptation within the existing system, and especially of how changes in the practice of the Fund might be devised to make credit easier and less costly. It acknowledged that as international trade expanded, disequilibria would not diminish, and that gold and the dollar would make progressively smaller contributions to liquidity in the system. It therefore considered that a ' broad exploration ' of possible ways to meet future inadequacies of liquidity would be desirable.[56] While conceding the usefulness of bilateral swaps and similar arrangements, it pointed out that these were usually only made available for short periods and then only to a few countries. By the use of multilateral machinery, and especially through the Fund itself, both the scope and the duration of credit could be extended. The first and most obvious possibility here was a substantial increase in Fund quotas. This might be more readily acceptable if members were allowed to deposit gold certificates instead of gold with the Fund. Another was to make access to members' credit tranches easier and more automatic. A third was to allow countries to increase their drawing rights on the Fund in return for the deposit of bonds or other special long-term assets with the Fund—i.e. investment of Fund resources in member countries. These three possibilities had been outlined earlier by Schweitzer in a speech in May 1964 to the New York Chamber of Commerce.

The first of these possibilities had by then already been submitted informally to the Fund's Executive Directors. A Staff Paper, written in March, 1964 and part of the wider study already referred to but dealing specifically with the question of increasing quotas, had suggested that there should be a 50 per cent all-round increase in Fund quotas—these were due for quinquennial review in any case in 1965—and that this should be preceded by selective increases designed to reduce disparities between members' quotas and their respective economic strength.

In view of American interest in using the Fund to help ease the immediate problems of the dollar and of the Fund's own interest in expanding its international role, it was predictable that there would be some follow-up to these suggestions. The discussions that ensued were interesting both for the points of substance that divided Fund members and for the forward light they shed on the attitudes of European members of the Group of Ten before the actual start of negotiations on SDRs.

Schweitzer took the initiative all along. In June 1964 he put before the Executive Board two chapters in his draft Annual Report stating that the Fund should proceed to ' an early examination of quotas ' as ' the normal way to make it possible to expand the operations of the Fund and to enable it to play a greater role in the provision of international liquidity of a more or less conditional kind '.[57]

This submission stung the five EEC Fund Directors to an early and rare show of unity—a memorandum declaring such a recommendation premature and urging its excision from the Annual Report. The five Directors, however, were overruled in the Board, and the redrafted Annual Report actually went further and stated categorically that ' there is a case for an increase in Fund quotas '.

Thereafter the French, taking (as before in the Fund) the extreme opposition position, were supported sometimes by one, sometimes by another of their EEC partners. The Belgian Executive Director later stood by France in holding that there should be no increase at all, while the Dutch, Germans, and Italians went half-way to meet the British and Canadians and opted for the compromise figure of a 25 per cent increase.

On the Fund secretariat's proposals for mitigating the gold subscription rules laid down by the Articles of Agreement, the French also adamantly opposed any modification. Article III, section 4 (a) read as follows:

Each member which consents to an increase in its quota shall, within thirty days after the date of its consent, pay to the Fund twenty-five percent of the increase in gold and the balance in its own currency. If, however, on the date when the member consents to an increase, its monetary reserves are less than its new quota, the Fund may reduce the proportion of the increase to be paid in gold.

The Fund studies had suggested that this final sentence could be used and perhaps developed further to make it easier for developing countries and for the United States to enjoy the increase in quotas without paying out the full proportion of gold.

It is not difficult to see why the French were opposed to this. The United States had already, by their £500m drawing of foreign currencies from the Fund, found one way to shift foreign-held balances from European central banks to the Fund. If Fund members were now allowed to 'pay' for their increased quotas not in gold but in dollars or gold certificates, this would have the same effect and take some of the heat off the dollar.

By December 1964 the Executive Board was deadlocked on this point, although by now there was tacit agreement that the quotas should go up by 25 per cent. M. René Larre for France totally opposed any general use of the second sentence of Article III, section 4 (a) and was broadly supported by the German and Dutch Directors, Herr Ulrich Beelitz and Dr Pieter Lieftinck. However, their opposition was undermined by a parallel decision by the ministers of the Group of Ten that the impact of the quota increase on the reserve currencies would have to be mitigated by one means or another. The Fund staff had originally proposed among other devices a kind of recycling of the gold paid in to the Fund as a consequence of increased quotas. To avoid depleting US and British gold stocks, as countries cashed their dollar or sterling balances to pay gold into the Fund, the Fund would make 'general deposits' of gold with the United States and the United Kingdom, as with a bank. Thus, although the Fund would not physically hold as much gold, its accounts would be unaffected, while the gold stocks actually in Fort Knox and the Bank of England would remain undiminished.

When the US Director assured the Board that the United States would invite the Fund to take back its gold deposits as soon as the balance of payments improved sufficiently, and M. Schweitzer insisted that there was no other way round the difficulty, German support for M. Larre melted away and only Dr Lieftinck supported him.

In the subsequent negotiations over details, the French won only one small victory on the special increases in individual quotas needed to take account of the improvement in the economic and financial position of certain countries—notably Canada, France, Germany, and Japan. Since no member could be forced to accept an increased quota, the French refusal to accept any special increase made it difficult for Germany to take the full increase of quota warranted by its improved financial position. With the support of Germany and Belgium, France also made it a condition of accepting the other proposed special increases that their overall effect would not be to raise total quotas by much more than the agreed 25 per cent.

When, in February 1965, the quota plan came to one of the Board's rare decisions-by-vote, Germany abstained and only France voted against the mitigating arrangements devised for the protection of the dollar. These were passed by 175,595 votes to 8,125 votes. Approval by the Governors casting the necessary 80 per cent of Fund votes was thus assured and was given in April 1965.

On balance, therefore, the United States had got its own way in the matter of increasing quotas. But it had not got all it wanted, and had had to fight hard against the opposition. The latter, led by the French, had been supported more readily in the earlier than the later stages of a clash by the Germans, the Dutch, and sometimes by the Belgians. It had also been aided a little by the concern of the Fund staff to preserve the legitimacy of their authority and not to bend or ' reinterpret ' the rules too blatantly to suit the Americans. The Italians had been conspicuous by their absence in this European front line and had noticeably changed their position since the lira crisis of 1963–4 and the American rescue in March 1964. Where before they had been inclined to discount the need for reform of the system, they now favoured it, and agreed that control should rest with the Fund.[58]

The Ossola Report

This somewhat reluctant agreement by the Europeans on the increase in Fund quotas did not signify any concurrent rapprochement of opinions on the reserve creation issue. At the 1964 Fund meeting in Tokyo—as at so many other meetings—the fundamental argument was over control of any new asset. Karl Blessing of the German Bundesbank, in addition to his usual strictures on the need for discipline rather than liquidity, firmly stated that the Fund should stick to its current lending policies. It was not the system which needed improvement, he argued, but countries' adjustment policies, and in financing deficits we ' should pay more attention to price stability than to expansion and growth '.[59] The remarks of Dr Holtrop of the Netherlands were in the same vein, though slightly less opposed to changes in the system. The control of a new asset would be as important as its creation, he asserted. He much preferred a restricted group to a Fund-based reform.[60] Giscard d'Estaing, the French Finance Minister, from whom fireworks had been expected, appeared in his speech to be readier than most observers had thought to reach some compromise. The possible future creation of additional liquidity, he insisted, should be in the form of owned reserves governed by an automatic formula and 'objective rules'. 'The responsibility and burden' for these operations would be in the hands of a restricted group of countries, who would co-operate closely with the Fund.[61] Although advocating the end of the gold exchange standard, he conceded that central banks would for some time continue to hold dollars and pounds in their reserves.[62]

The British Chancellor of the Exchequer spoke in favour of more liquidity, under Fund control. Maudling viewed with dislike the French and Dutch preference for owned reserves. 'While we cannot all be in deficit at once, we tend in practice to manage our reserves as if we could.'[63] Douglas Dillon, in his speech to the meeting, was less strongly in favour of Fund control than Maudling appeared to be, but at a subsequent press conference he came out firmly against the French view, criticizing it as restrictive, reaffirming the US desire to build on the existing system, rejecting the European argument that the Anglo-Saxon deficits caused inflation and stating that the Fund should be at the centre of any reforms.[64]

The divergence of views was clearly still very wide—too wide to permit of any agreement save within the framework of constitutional rules laid down for Fund decisions. Why, then, was the question not dropped? Why did the finance ministers and central bankers endorse the continuation of the liquidity studies with varying amounts of enthusiasm? The answer must be, first, that all of them were concerned with the preservation of the system from shock and disorder and the continuation of study was a very cheap price to pay for maintaining the appearance of international goodwill.

Secondly, the consideration of reform in general terms gave the Europeans an excuse to go on nagging the Americans about their deficit. The United States also had nothing to lose by it, since the proposed study was to be purely factual. Its terms of reference were 'to provide a description and analysis of each proposal' for the creation of reserve assets, taking into account the implications for the functioning of the system as a whole, in preparation for an evaluation of the various plans by the Group of Ten. A committee was therefore set up under the chairmanship of Dr Rinaldo Ossola, an appointment which emphasized the technical rather than the political character of the study and avoided putting an exponent of either extreme position in a position of influence.

The Ossola Committee met while the Fund's Executive Board was still arguing over the terms of the quota increase. It finished its work in May 1965, though the report was not made public before August. By this time it had been completely overtaken by domestic developments within the two main protagonist countries, developments which materially changed their respective debating postures.

Although the more important and significant change was undoubtedly that in the United States, chronologically the first to take place was in France. General de Gaulle's famous press conference (see below, p. 285) extolling the merits of gold was given on 4 February 1965. From this it was clear to everyone that the General had been finally won over to the ideas consistently put forward by Jacques Rueff. However, as the General made no change at the Finance Ministry until he put M. Michel Debré in place of M. Giscard d'Estaing in January 1966, it was not immediately clear—even perhaps to Giscard himself—whether France would go on supporting the CRU reform plan. By May, when the Ossola Committee finished work, the French were known to have lost interest in its discussions.[65] They had by then firmly rejected the idea of reform in the Fund and had proposed that the BIS, not the Fund, should manage the issue of CRUs. In June Giscard d'Estaing was still arguing against an increase in the gold price and maintaining that the CRU was part of the French plan for monetary reform.[66] For a while, the new French attitude was not altogether clear. Lack of interest in the whole idea of reform was implicit in the nostalgic homage paid to gold as the disciplinary numéraire of a smoothly, safely, and equitably working system; but it was not made explicit until M. Debré took over as Finance Minister. Debré, almost unknown among international financial diplomats, was a hardline Gaullist. The implication of his appointment was underlined by the concurrent removal of the chief French official responsible for international monetary negotiations, M. André de Lattre, from the Finance Ministry to the Banque de France.

The changes in the United States also coincided with changes of leadership at the top. Roosa left the administration at the end of 1964, Dillon in March 1965. President Johnson appointed as his successor Henry Fowler, with Frederick Deming as his deputy at the Treasury.

After only three months in office, Fowler took the opportunity of an engagement to address the Virginia Bar Association on 10 July 1965 to announce a major change in US policy on monetary reform. He said that the United States now stood ready to ' attend and participate in an international monetary conference that would consider what steps we might jointly take to secure substantial improvements in international monetary arrangements '.[67] This would have to be preceded by careful preparation and international consultation, and Fowler suggested that this preparation should be undertaken by a committee whose terms of reference could be decided on at the forthcoming Fund meeting in September.

The decision to make this announcement was apparently a personal one.[68] Though it had presidential approval, this speech had not been preceded by any consultation with Congressional leaders or with finance ministers of the other Group of Ten countries, though Fowler was said to have had talks on this subject with Mr James Callaghan, Chancellor of the Exchequer in Britain's new Labour government.[69] The announcement came only a few days after President Johnson had appointed a group, whose membership included Dillon, Roosa, and Bernstein, to advise the Treasury Secretary on the liquidity question.

Besides the change of leadership, two other factors may have influenced the American decision. In February the administration had made some major changes designed to alleviate the balance of payments, including voluntary controls on investment abroad and an extension of the Interest Equalization Tax (see below, p. 264). These had sharply improved the payments situation, which now once more allowed the United States to play its hand from an improved position. Secondly, a growing body of opinion in the press, and more particularly in Congress, was beginning to favour the deliberate creation of additional liquidity, regarding it not as a threat but as a support to the position of the dollar. The conclusion of the Ossola Report and the imminence of another gathering of finance ministers and central bank Governors made the moment opportune for announcing the change. What had now been made abundantly clear was that US interest in the possibilities of more radical reform than could be negotiated within the Fund was a necessary though not also a sufficient condition for progress. It was at this point that the liquidity debate passed out of the stage of study and debate into that of negotiation.

Notes

[1] Sir Eric Roll, *The world after Keynes* (London, 1968), p. 153.

[2] First published in two articles in the journal, *Banca Nazionale del Lavoro Quarterly Review*, Mar & June 1959; later reproduced with minor changes in *Gold and the dollar crisis*, published at Yale in the autumn of 1960. This also contained the text of Triffin's statement to the Joint Economic Committee of Congress made on 28 Oct 1959.

[3] 'The fuzzy concepts of liquidity, international and domestic'. This was first published as 'Liquidité, international et national' in Banque National de Belgique, *Bull. d'Information et de Documentation*, Feb 1962, and was reprinted in English in Machlup's *International payments, debts and gold: collected essays* (New York, 1964), p. 255.

[4] See, for example, 'The need for reserves: an explanatory paper', prepared by the IMF Staff in January 1966 and reprinted in IMF, *International reserves, needs and availability* (1971), pp. 369ff.

[5] This certainly is how it looked—though the French still argue that their prime objection all through was to the method of liquidity-creation, by swelling dollar balances, and that for them the question of more or less liquidity was a subsidiary one. And the Americans argue that their concern all through was to maintain the smooth functioning of a system which at different times, under changing pressures, presented different needs.

[6] A good many of the contributions to the debate were made in the form of articles in academic journals. A useful collection of these from a score of distinguished economists can be found in Herbert T. Grubel, ed., *World monetary reform : plans and issues* (Stanford, 1964).

[7] See UN General Assembly resolution 1710 (XVI), 19 Dec 1961.

[8] *Gold and the dollar crisis* (Yale, 1961, paperback), pp. 8–9.

[9] *The dollar and world liquidity*, pp. 102–3.

[10] See Friedman's statement to the Joint Economic Committee's Sub-committee on International Exchange and Payments (the Reuss committee), 89th Congress, 1966, reprinted in Lawrence H. Willett & Thomas D. Officer, eds, *The international monetary system; problems and proposals* (Englewood Cliffs, 1969).

[11] *Money in the international economy* (London, 1965), p. 61 of the rev. ed., 1969.

[12] One rare exception was in a transcribed discussion with Rueff, published in the *Sunday Times*, 3 July 1966.

[13] *Souvenirs d'un Gouverneur de la Banque de France.*

[14] An English translation of the text of Rueff's 1961 article can be found in Grubel, *World monetary reform*; the original French is reprinted in Rueff's *Le péché monétaire de l'Occident* (Paris, 1971), p. 20.

[15] First published in the *Manchester Guardian* in autumn 1960; and in greater detail in autumn 1962 in *Moorgate & Wall Street*, a finance-house review jointly issued by Philip Hill, Higginson, Erlanger Ltd and Harrison, Ripley & Co.

[16] *The dollar and world liquidity*, p. 105.

[17] *International reserves and liquidity.*

[18] *IMF*, iii. 410.

[19] Roosa, *The dollar and world liquidity*, p. 6.

[20] Ibid., p. 13.

[21] Roosa reprints the report in full, ibid., p. 292.

[22] Also reprinted in Roosa, pp. 302–15, and *American foreign policy: current documents 1961*, p. 1224.

[23] Roosa, p. 8.

[24] Ibid., p. 28.

[25] See also Sam Brittan, in *RIIA Survey of international affairs*, 1961, p. 311.

[26] Roosa, pp. 27–8.

[27] Ibid., p. 31.

[28] This part of the speech was not reprinted in Roosa's *The dollar and world liquidity*, but was reproduced in *The Economist*, 26 May 1962.

[29] In the *Business Review* of the Federal Reserve Bank of Philadephia, Sept 1962, reprinted as ch. 5 of *The dollar and world liquidity*.

[30] This possibility was sketched at a conference of the Federal Trust for Education and Research in May 1965.

[31] IMF, *Annual meeting 1962, Summary proceedings.*

[32] *The Times*, 21 Sept 1962.

[33] *Money international*, p. 371.

[34] *The Economist*, 5 Jan 1963 and *The Times, FT & New York Times*, 29 & 31 Dec 1962.

[35] *New York Herald Tribune*, 8 Mar, *The Economist*, 16 Mar 1963.

[36] *The Economist*, 20 July 1963.

[37] *American foreign policy: current documents 1963*, p. 1100.

[38] Roosa, p. 35.

[39] Walter Salant & Associates, *The US balance of payments in 1968* (Washington, 1963).

[40] *New York Times,* 19 Sept 1963.

[41] Triffin, *The world money maze,* p. 290.

[42] Stephen Cohen (*International monetary reform,* p. 48) suggests that this was a deliberate tactic.

[43] *IMF,* i. 543.

[44] Ibid., pp. 543–4.

[45] Ibid., p. 587.

[46] *The Economist,* 21 Sept 1963.

[47] *International monetary arrangements: the problem of choice; report on the deliberations of an international study group of 32 economists* (Princeton, 1964), p. 6.

[48] Ibid., p. 6.

[49] Group of Ten Statement, 2 Oct 1963 (*IMF,* i. 543).

[50] *Guardian,* 31 Dec 1963.

[51] Notably by S. V. O. Clarke in an unpublished paper written in May 1971 for the Council on Foreign Relations, 'A view of international monetary negotiations 1966–70', to which I am greatly indebted. Clarke rightly observes that the clash between these two opposed attitudes was never solely on national lines. Throughout the decade of the 1960s, monetary authorities in the United States and in other Group of Ten countries often held ambivalent positions straddling the two.

[52] IMF, *Summary proceedings,* 1963, p. 42.

[53] See *The Economist,* 2 May 1964; *New York Times,* 26 Apr 1964.

[54] *Statement by ministers of the Group of Ten and Annex prepared by their deputies,* p. 12.

[55] Reproduced as chs 3 & 4 of the Fund's *Annual report,* 1964.

[56] Ibid., p. 32.

[57] Ibid., p. 35.

[58] *The Economist,* 12 Sept 1964.

[59] IMF, *Summary proceedings,* 1964, p. 52.

[60] Ibid., p. 68.

[61] Ibid., p. 207.

[62] *The Times,* 10 Sept 1964.

[63] IMF, *Summary proceedings,* 1964, p. 168.

[64] *New York Times,* 12 Sept 1964.

[65] *FT,* 6 May 1965.

[66] Speech to the Institute of Banking and Financial Studies, Paris (see *The Economist,* 19 June 1965).

[67] *American foreign policy: current documents 1965,* pp. 231ff.

[68] *The Economist,* 17 July 1965.

[69] Ibid., 3 July 1965.

8

THE LIQUIDITY NEGOTIATIONS 1965–9

Having taken the decision to change US policy on reserve creation, Secretary Fowler soon set to work to see that his seizure of the initiative brought results. He arranged a series of visits to European capitals for early September 1965, starting in Paris and proceeding to Rome, Bonn, Stockholm, Brussels, The Hague, and London. These visits would give him the opportunity of meeting personally the finance ministers and Governors of central banks (or their deputies) who would be coming to Washington later in the month and of exploring with them in advance some of the issues that were likely to arise.

The Europeans, however, did not wait for Fowler to arrive. Meetings of the EEC's Monetary Committee in Brussels and of the Group of Ten in Paris in July made it plain that the Europeans for their part did not think much of the idea of calling another Bretton Woods. The general view was that it would be better to explore first how much agreement could be found among the ' major powers '. The Group of Ten deputies briefed their new chairman, Dr Otmar Emminger, to go to Washington and tell Fowler this. The result was an agreement in advance of the Fund meeting to proceed with caution. It was expressed in a request (formally made by the Group of Ten Ministers and Governors to their deputies but actually drafted by the deputies) to explore once again what basis of agreement could be found for the future creation of reserve assets.

The change in the chairmanship of the deputies from Roosa to Emminger proved timely. Emminger had been Germany's Executive Director at the Fund from 1953 and was on the Governing Board of the Bundesbank. He also sat on the EEC's Monetary Committee. He already had proven adept at the time of the GAB negotiations in finding compromises. Moreover Germany's strong need to maintain close and harmonious relations, both with the United States, on whose military protection it depended, and with France, whose partnership in the European Community was indispensable, meant that a German would be the best possible broker between the opposed French and American positions.

A further recommendation was that Germany's posture in the monetary negotiations had appeared to the Americans to show more disinterested concern than some other European countries for the

welfare of the system. It may be that sometimes they were running
with the hare and hunting with the hounds, but Stephen Cohen quotes
a German official as saying that what was important in determining
liquidity needs was the world-wide need, not the needs of any one
country or any single group of countries.[1] In the Atlantic community,
the Germans strongly favoured contingency planning against monetary
—as well as against military—disaster and therefore drew a sharp
distinction between agreement on what ought to be done in case the
need arose for additional liquidity, and the subsequent agreement that
the need had actually arisen and that the prepared plans should be
put into effect. As Karl Blessing made clear at the 1965 Fund meeting,
German opinion did not feel that the need necessarily arose when the
poor countries ran short of the aid they considered necessary for
economic development, nor when the reserve currency countries—and
especially Britain—ran aground in monetary squalls. ' Such grounded
ships must be refloated by making them lighter '.[2] Blessing argued that
the need might not even arise when the US deficit disappeared since
no one knew for sure whether newly mined gold or sales of Soviet
gold would appear to fill the gap.

Reflecting the country's traumatic experience of inflation and other
forms of monetary instability, Germany all along joined with the
other Europeans in extolling the virtues of discipline in running the
international system. ' I cannot help thinking ', Blessing said on
the same occasion, ' that too perfect a machinery for financing balance
of payments deficits weakens monetary discipline and contributes to
creeping inflation '.[3] The Germans implied that the United States had
some obligation to do as she would be done by. If exchange rates were
fixed, even countries with sound monetary policies could not always
avoid importing inflation. Therefore, as Blessing had argued the year
before, however good the system of financing deficits, there could be
no substitute for domestic adjustment by the centre country and ' in
financing deficits we should in the future pay more attention to price
stability than to expansion and growth '.[4]

Between German and French points of view, the key difference, as
Cohen remarks, was that ' the Germans, unlike the French, wished to
build on the gold-exchange standard, not dismantle it. They wanted
to control the international role of the dollar, not destroy it.'[5] The
Governor of the German Bundesbank, backed by the German government, believed that Europe's regained financial power could best be
used to improve the workings of the gold exchange standard and to
curb the excesses of reserve currency countries, and that this would
be much safer than any French plan to make over the system so
radically as to oust the dollar from its position altogether.

All these attitudes found close echoes in the other four EEC countries. Holtrop, Governor of the Netherlands Central Bank, for example, backed up Germany in drawing a sharp distinction between the making and the activation of contingency plans. And by and large, the five EEC partners differed only on fairly minor points. For example, the Dutch wanted to attach any newly created asset to gold, not as closely as with the CRU scheme but so as to make use of its disciplinary power by ruling that it should be transferred in a fixed ratio with gold transfers. The Italians, showing anxiety to discourage the French and others from making further embarrassing conversions of dollar reserves for gold from US stocks, advocated the ' harmonization ' principle by which big gold holders would settle their deficits mainly in gold but accept reserve currencies when in surplus. Thus payments imbalances would be settled in such a way as to redistribute gold reserves more equitably, taking from those that had them and giving to those that had not. This was ingenious and reflected the sophistication of Italy's high-powered team of monetary diplomats, notably Dr Guido Carli, Sgr Emilio Colombo, and Dr Rinaldo Ossola. Though they were a fertile source of compromise solutions, they sometimes tended to overestimate what was politically acceptable. If the Germans occupied the natural role of broker between France and the United States in the Atlantic community, Italy and the Netherlands sometimes played the same role between Germany and France in the EEC. The Italians, exercising much more independence at home than other monetary diplomats, were also more often aware that the issues to be settled were fundamentally political and not technical.

The Belgians, more than most perhaps, hoped that it might be possible to continue to work through the Fund. The first IMF Executive Director, Camille Gutt, had been a Belgian, and Belgium had established a customary right to nominate Elected Directors (first Hubert Ansiaux, later André van Campenhout), who sat for a curious little group which included Austria and Turkey as well as Luxembourg and at various times had also included Iceland, Denmark, Finland, and South Korea. A consistently held Belgian view was that the liquidity problem could be materially eased if countries had the right to draw automatically on their gold and super-gold tranches in the Fund and if they got into the way of regarding these drawing rights as part of their reserves and just as good as gold.

The British role in the whole affair was that of anxious—and obviously not uninterested—but silent bystander. A British finance minister had been the first to put forward a formal proposal for reform with the Maudling Plan in 1962. The next year Maudling urged speed and decried the apathy of others. The major requirement, as the British saw only too clearly, was not the discovery of a technically ideal solution but the negotiation of an acceptable intergovernmental agreement. But it was just here that Britain's weakness robbed it of the power to influence or the freedom to propose. The British, whether Conservative or Labour, were ready to consider with open minds any proposal that others might make—especially if it added to the security of sterling and thus lessened the constraints at home and abroad which the currency's weakened position imposed on British policy-makers. Once Britain had applied for the second time to join the EEC, until the French veto of December 1967, Britain's silent embarrassment at the disagreements within the EEC and between the Commission and the United States was if anything increased.

The reasons for the relatively passive roles played by Japan, Canada, Switzerland, Sweden, and the other Scandinavian countries were different. In the first two cases, both countries were concerned that the failure of the others to agree would damage the prospects for world prosperity but were powerless, because of their close dependence on the United States both as a source of capital and as a source of their major reserve asset, to exert influence on American policy. The Canadian role of broker, exercised so dramatically at times past in NATO and the UN, was virtually abandoned in the SDR debate. Japan's political power to ease or obstruct the attainment of American objectives was as yet neither realized nor exercised. The Swiss attitude was at first one of non-involvement. In spite of Switzerland's part in the OECD, the Gold Pool, and the BIS, as well as in the ad hoc management of many crises, there had been no Swiss among the Roosa or Ossola groups. As a large gold holder, and a small dollar holder, it could be argued that Switzerland was not directly concerned with the problems of the gold exchange system. Yet the dependence of the Swiss economy on income from foreign investment, tourism, and trade implied a dependence on the continued welfare and stability of the international system of which the Swiss were well aware. When the Emminger group assembled in November 1965, the chairman welcomed the two representatives, Dr Max Iklé and M. Lademann, from the Swiss National Bank. Taking no very active part, they still held a watching brief and were sometimes able discreetly to add their weight to that of the other Europeans.

Scandinavian apathy was more complex. Cohen's explanation, that there was ' a lack of the power-politics instinct ',[6] is not wholly convincing. More likely, although concerned that the system should not be damaged, the negotiating strength even of Sweden was limited by deliberate Scandinavian lack of interest in the acquisition of large quantities of gold and the relative unimportance of their accumulated reserves of dollars. Moreover, in dealing with the United States or with the EEC group the Scandinavians had often looked for support to Britain, but Britain in this issue was impotent. At one point the chairman of the Bank of Norway,[7] complaining that decisions were being taken by too restricted a group of countries, urged his fellow Scandinavians to make common cause together. But even had they done so, it is doubtful if they had the necessary monetary-diplomatic muscle to influence others.

The question of reserve asset creation had now been under discussion in unofficial circles for six or seven years and had been argued among officials for two years. A substantial body of written reports, articles, and books had been built up and the topic was no longer a novel one. This had brought some clarification of the chief underlying issues and had given the developed countries time to make some assessment of their respective national interests.

The report, published in June 1964, of the Bellagio Group of thirty-two economists (see above, p. 217), for example, fairly reflected majority opinion among academic economists. This had distinguished three main strands in the broad debate about the state of the international monetary system and whether and how it needed reforming. Though often, admittedly, intertwined, these were: the problem of adjustment in general and of exchange rates in particular; the problem of confidence in the two main reserve currencies which threatened to bring disruptive switches in reserve holdings between national currencies and from currencies into gold; and the growth of international liquidity, which depended partly on the make-up of reserves and partly on the efficiency of adjustment between currencies. A fourth issue, which some members of the group would have liked to add, was that of the distribution of liquidity within the system between rich and poor, north and south, and what came later to be known as the ' link ' between the creation in reserve assets and aid to developing countries. In practice, however, this fourth issue was quietly forgotten as introducing too many difficult and highly political considerations.

But, as Fred Hirsch points out,[8] there were good reasons why it was the third strand which attracted the lion's share of official attention. The role of gold, and changes in exchange rates and the reserve currency role of sterling and the dollar, were tender and sometimes therefore taboo topics for the Americans no less than for the British. Thus although the Bellagio Group were right in seeing the liquidity issue as only one of the three main conceptual questions about the functioning, or malfunctioning of the system, and in perceiving its intimate connection with the other two, the questions for monetary diplomacy had perforce to be seen much more narrowly. The fact, remarked on by Hirsch, that the Bellagio conceptualization was later accepted in the 1966 Emminger Report did not prove that it had any marked influence on the course of monetary diplomacy, except possibly to present the official discussions to world opinion, and particularly, of course, to opinion in the economics profession, as more technical and less political than they really were.

(Few economists even today are prepared to admit the extent to which their own liberal internationalism during these years served in a very real way to sugar the pill of defending US national interests to the rest of the world. The addition of an international reserve asset apparently controlled by the authority of a multilateral organization, staffed by international civil servants and under the control of no one national state, seemed an end wholly to be desired by men of goodwill. It was easy to imply that anyone who was against SDRs must be some sort of narrow and reactionary nationalist. It was easy to lose sight of the fact that the solution of the problem was prejudged in some degree by the predefinition of its nature in a way favoured by one (US) perception of the international interest which was not necessarily shared by others.)

To begin with, the Americans, supported by the British, did not want to discuss the exchange rate between the dollar and gold and between the dollar and sterling and other currencies. They also totally rejected discussion of means by which the confidence in the future value and acceptability of the reserve currencies might be increased. In so far as it was raised at all, they preferred the adjustment process and the question of exchange rates to be discussed in OECD Working Party III. These issues were therefore effectively sterilized.

The issues for official negotiation, as distinct from independent unofficial analysis, therefore related to the terms on which additional liquidity, supporting but not supplanting the dollar as a reserve asset, could and should be injected into the system.

For the negotiating teams there were five inescapable questions on which agreement had to be reached before any action could be taken on reserve asset creation. These were recognized in the Emminger Report, which finally emerged in July 1966.

The first concerned the form that the new reserve asset should take. Should it be a drawing right or a new, owned-reserve asset? Secondly, what should be its relation to gold? Should there be a fixed ratio in national reserves between gold holdings and holdings of the reserve asset, or should the reserve asset be transferred between countries in a fixed ratio with transfers of gold? Or should it merely have a fixed value in terms of gold? Thirdly, when should the new asset be created? Under what circumstances and for what purposes? Should it wait until after the US deficit had been corrected or could it be created before this point had been reached? Fourthly, how was the asset to be created and by whom? Should it be by agreement of all the members of the Fund? By all or only by most of the countries in the Group of Ten? Who should have a veto power and on what issues? Fifthly and lastly, there were the organizational arrangements for the introduction and then for the management of a reform scheme. Through whom—the Fund, the BIS, or some new body—should the assets be distributed and on what basis should the distribution be made? What rules should later govern the holding and transfer of these assets?

The story so far has surely made it clear that the paradigms of agreement on all these points would have to be fixed by a bargaining process in which the key protagonists were the United States, France, and Germany. The United States had a clear veto power. Nothing it rejected could be included in the negotiated agreement. If it rejected the idea of a CRU created out of deposits of a group of currencies and linked in its use to gold holdings, then this was a non-starter. If it rejected the gold link except for a guarantee of value for the asset, then no asset linked to gold could be created. What was less clear—but which emerged as the negotiations proceeded (and from quota talks in the IMF)—was that the EEC when it acted as a group also had a veto power. That is to say that any substantial point which threatened to divide the EEC would be unacceptable to Germany and Italy. It was not yet clear, however, what these substantial issues were likely to be or to what extent France, standing alone, would be able to block a proposal generally acceptable to the other Europeans. It was difficult in September 1965 to be very optimistic about the prospects of reaching agreement between France and the other five members of the EEC. In June 1965 French representatives had walked out of the Brussels Council of Ministers and progress of any kind in the Community had been brought to a standstill. Considering the depth of their disagreement with the United States and their alienation from their EEC partners, it was rather remarkable that the French, though they maintained an almost unbroken silence at meetings of the deputies through the winter of 1965-6, continued to take any part in them at all.

The group under the chairmanship of Dr Emminger had begun work in November 1965 and by January the chairman had produced a compromise proposal that sought to bridge the main gaps. This had first been worked out in the EEC's Monetary Committee. The ' Emminger compromise ', as it was inevitably called, tackled four of the main issues: —

1. The asset would be distributed only to members of the Group of Ten.

2. It would be handled by the IMF in a separate account from its ordinary transactions.

3. The unanimity rule would apply to the original terms and conditions of issue but weighted majority voting would be used for subsequent executive decisions on (e.g.) annual issues.

4. Issues would be made independent of gold holdings and no rules on the ratio of gold to new units in national reserve holdings would be made. But there might be a one-for-one rule on the settlement of international claims. (That is, there would be a gold link for current transactions in the new asset but not for holdings.)

How far the United States was prepared to accept these proposals was indicated almost at once in the President's Economic Report to Congress, published in January 1966. This made it clear that the United States did not deny that the key decisions would have to be taken by the affluent alliance and seemed to be agreed that the distribution of the new reserve asset would have to be restricted to industrialized countries. Where it differed was in recognizing that some concurrent increase in automatic drawing rights through the Fund would have to be made for the semi-developed middle powers such as Australia, Brazil, Argentina, and to the many poor developing countries.

This conclusion represented an important shift in American assessment of the national interest. In Roosa's days at the Treasury, the United States had seen the aid problem as sharply separate from the liquidity problem and from the improved management of the monetary system. Roosa was the original opponent of the 'link', and though he later shifted his opinion in some respect, he continued as late as 1965 to argue the case against mixing the two issues.

Countries which had not already met the self-qualifying test of the market place by providing currencies that could be effectively used by other countries—that is countries who had not in previous years been able or prepared to see flows of their own currencies for monetary purposes result in added claims on their real resources by other countries—would not automatically obtain any of the new reserve asset.

Instead, he believed, these countries would receive their shares of the newly created asset after its initial distribution by earning them through trade or by qualifying for them through meeting the credit standards or the age requirements judged appropriate by the creditor countries themselves. This would effectively reinforce the essential reliance upon the principles of national sovereignty, and upon the principles of balance of payments discipline,

There is no monetary escape route from the elements of economic discipline—neither within or among countries. Any innovations in the international monetary system, if they are to be successful and sustainable, will have to reinforce the discipline of the market place within each individual country while they also reach out to enlarge, or to redistribute, the supply of international liquidity.[9]

Henry Fowler, however, was much more conscious than Roosa of the weakness of US relations with the developing countries. The first UNCTAD Conference in 1964 had shown the depth of resentment felt against the rich countries and the frustrations with the system felt by the poor countries. Usually for strategic reasons there were some of these whose goodwill the Americans valued quite highly. Moreover, if the United States was going to have difficulty in reaching agreement with the Europeans, it would need not only goodwill but actual support where it could get it, even from the ' tail ' of little small-vote countries in the Fund. The United States and Britain shared with the developing countries an immediate shortage of national reserves and an interest—as Blessing had put it—in ' raising the tide level higher ', an interest which gave a bias towards growth and expansion even at the risk of inflation. It was an inevitable alliance of debtors against the hard-nosed creditors. Nor were the Europeans under any illusion that their power would be impaired if the circle of decision-making were to be widened. In the climate of the 1960s, so long as everyone subscribed in some measure to UN humbug of one state, one vote, it was difficult to defend the unrepresentative exclusiveness of the Group of Ten. And the longer the Ten talked, the less easy it was to keep the ninety waiting outside the door. Indeed, in February 1966, thirty-one of the leading developing countries had set up a special propaganda group to campaign for a share in the creation of any new liquidity, knowing that they could probably count on some support from the staff of the Fund, if not the OECD, and that this would be useful since it was clear by now that the Group of Ten would need the co-operation of the Fund staff as the administrators of any practical scheme. As Cohen commented:

Although the Fund was the logical choice to administer a new international asset, any approach to its Managing Director that it set up a special affiliate to manage a new reserve asset for only a limited number of its members would have evoked strong overtones of prejudice and privilege. Therefore it would probably have been rejected by the Fund.[10]

Besides that, the Group of Ten, even if augmented by such countries as Austria, Denmark, and Australia, would not have the voting power necessary to amend the Fund's Articles of Agreement to establish a new Fund operation. And of all the developed countries, France, with its clientele of closely-linked franc zone African dependants, least shared the American concern that the Group of Ten should try to avoid looking like an affluent oligarchy refixing the rules of the international monetary system to suit themselves.

Pushed by the Americans, therefore, the finance ministers and central bank Governors of the Group of Ten in July 1966 agreed ' that deliberately created reserve assets, as and when needed ' (a point left unresolved) ' should be distributed to all members of the Fund on the basis of IMF quotas or of similar objective criteria '. And to this end they proposed that the deputies should start a series of joint meetings with the Executive Board of the Fund. This was a smart move. The weight of influence would still lie with the rich countries who would be twice represented—by their Fund Directors and by their two deputies—yet there would be other Fund Directors, some of seniority and standing, to represent the other ninety or so Fund members. Moreover, to make plain the limits of the concession granted by the Group of Ten, the communiqué of the Hague ministerial meeting on 25–26 July 1966 acknowledged that any reform plans would have to give due recognition in its arrangements for majorities and voting procedures to ' the particular responsibility of a limited group of major countries with a key vote in the functioning of the international monetary system and which in fact must provide a substantial part of the financial strength behind any new asset '.[11] Thus the Europeans' concern that their negotiating power should not be diluted by any expansion of the decision-making group was satisfied.

The United States in its turn had to agree to the majority opinion that ' attainment of a better balance of payments equilibrium '—not as the United States had hoped to say just a ' substantial reduction '—in the US deficit was a necessary precondition for the creation of new reserve assets. Equally the majority rejected the French demand that the United States should first have been ' in external balance for a lengthy period of time '.

The Emminger Report

This meeting of the Group of Ten at The Hague probably represented the high point of French isolation. The deputies' report presented at the meeting (along with the Working Party III report on the balance-of-payments adjustment process—see above, p. 122) made much, on each of the main issues, of the degree of unanimity among the nine and gave a good deal of attention to the relatively unimportant technical questions such as the rules governing the holding and transfer of the new assets once created.[12] In fact, the French member had taken no part in these discussions on the grounds that France totally rejected all need for contingency planning—and indeed believed it to be ill advised because it ' would give rise to an irresistible temptation to activate the agreement prematurely ' and that this remedy was ill-chosen because the real source of trouble in the system was the persistent deficits of the reserve currencies. The French position was now closely reflecting the views of Jacques Rueff. These were the more influential, especially with the General, because Rueff, unlike other retired or superseded French officials, had remained aloof and independent, seeking place neither with the state or its various dependent agencies nor in banking or business. During the summer of 1966 Rueff became more and more convinced—so he explained later [13]—that the progressive deterioration of the situation was leading inevitably to a grave monetary accident likely to bring disastrous consequences and to inflict profound suffering. He thought that the time had come to demonstrate that his position was constructive as well as critical. In July he allowed the *Sunday Times* to publish the transcript of a discussion between himself and Triffin in which he was at pains to emphasize their concurrence in diagnosis of the situation. Later, on 26 and 27 September, respectively, he published an article, in French in *Le Monde* and in English in *The Times*, setting out his fears and his proposals. Briefly, these were that there should be general agreement to double the price of gold. Armed with the increased value of its reserves in Fort Knox, the United States would then repay in gold the dollar balances accumulated by foreign central banks. Because of the larger overhang of sterling balances compared with British gold stocks, the same solution would still leave five-sixths of the sterling balances outstanding. Rueff suggested that the other gold-holding countries should agree to make a long-term loan of gold to enable the British government to repay sterling holders. Although Rueff claimed that his solution would be of great profit to the United States and would generally benefit the system, the net effect would have been to double European gold holdings while leaving those of the United States, after repayment of dollar balances, the same. In the article, Rueff also sharply criticized the ban on discussion of the rise in the price of gold by the Group of Ten's experts.[14]

Meanwhile, in the Emminger Report, French opposition was only recorded where necessary. The conclusions (paras. 90–103) summarized the bases for agreement rather than the points of disagreement. They were followed by an outline of five schemes, which the majority of nine considered the main ones.

Scheme A was based on the Emminger compromise presented at the beginning of the winter and was broadly supported by Germany, Italy, Belgium, and the Netherlands. The new asset would be open to all countries with convertible currencies accepting the obligations of multilateral surveillance and would not only be gold guaranteed but when transferred would have to be matched with an equivalent transfer of gold unless this requirement was varied by the creditor country.

Scheme B was an American plan for a two-tier solution, creating reserve units with a gold guarantee for the Group of Ten and SDRs for the other IMF members.

Scheme C originated with the British and also contemplated reserve units with a gold guarantee which 'operating members' only would be obliged to hold between a lower and upper limit. 'Any accumulation of units by an operating member above his upper holding limit would at the member's option be convertible into gold by other operating members who were below their upper-holding limits.' The distinguishing feature of the scheme clearly was that, though it would be administered by the Fund and limited to GAB countries plus Switzerland, it allowed for one or more countries—it was not clear how many—to opt out or to limit their participation. This was evidently a dodge to prevent French non-co-operation from blocking progress.

The last two schemes were derived from the IMF proposal made earlier and also had the same aim in mind. Scheme D for the creation of SDRs would allow members having two-thirds (instead of 80 per cent) of total quotas and 'including a majority of certain specified members' to agree to grant Fund credits in their own currency. Scheme E suggested the creation of a Fund affiliate, the International Reserve Fund (IRF), for the exchange of claims expressed in IRF units of gold weight—an institutionalization of the existing swap network extended to other countries and presumably offering credit on somewhat longer terms.

The flaw in these last three plans was not technical but political. The EEC Four (Five, including Luxembourg) were not prepared, it was now going to be made clear, to agree to the United States going ahead without them and they were not prepared to go ahead without making very strong efforts at least to reach some agreement with the French. Therefore any scheme which envisaged the exclusion of France and which publicly proclaimed the disunity in the Community was not to be contemplated. It was embarrassing enough to have had the disunity of their monetary diplomacy advertised at this very moment by the exclusion of France from the major extension of the swap network from a total of $2·8 billion to $4·5 billion—a larger increase than had ever been arranged.

This Community attitude proved to be a major determinant of the outcome of the entire negotiating process. It was made clear in a communiqué issued after an informal meeting of finance ministers of the EEC in Luxembourg on 12 September, and was implicit not so much in the text as in the tone. This pointedly abstracted from the Hague communiqué the four points on which the EEC *could* agree: an end to the US deficit; no previous implementation of liquidity plans; the 'special responsibility' of the Group of Ten; and the exclusion of the aid question. The French in their turn were prepared to give up the 'empty chair' tactics, to attend, even if in silence, the continued deputies' sessions proposed by the Emminger Report, and to seek to devise some common external policy with their Community partners. The Five would do no more than reiterate their intention to hold up activating the reserve creation until the United States mended its ways.

The first joint IMF–Group of Ten meeting

Who had the best of this bargain it is hard to say. In the EEC context, for Germany, Italy, and the Benelux partners the accord was a move in the right direction. But the French government may already have decided that opposition *in absentia* was seldom effective in international organization and that the French voice would put backbone in the opinions which all the Europeans shared about the Americans but which the Germans and Italians were too soft and gentlemanly to state bluntly or to press home. This conviction certainly seemed to lie behind the French outburst at the first of the joint meetings of the Fund's Executive Board and the Group of Ten's deputies, held in Washington in November 1966. It was an occasion where the general atmosphere, by all accounts, was one of unexpected sweetness and light. The differences supposedly dividing the monetary diplomats who sat as members of the exclusive rich man's club of the Group of Ten, and those who sat as members of the Bank and Fund—both UN agencies with many poor members and a lively concern with poverty and development—were shown to be largely caricature. They were, after all, all serious monetary diplomats, even those from the developing countries, and there were real enough differences dividing them without looking for artificial ones.

The agenda of the first meeting was set by Schweitzer and seemed well calculated to offend the French. Each of the five items related to created reserves—the objectives, the nature, the distribution and use, and the circumstances of activation. Even some newspapers noticed that it 'reflected the view that the only topics to be discussed were ways and means of creating " paper gold " '.[15] The French deputy, M. Maurice Pérouse, Director of the Treasury, publicized his objection that the price of gold had not been put on the agenda. Come to that, he suggested, if multilateral surveillance was thought by the OECD group to be such a good idea, should it not be applied equally to continued US deficits and to the rate of interest by which the United States was persuading its creditors to hold dollar assets in lieu of gold? Both suggestions were totally rejected by Schweitzer, who replied via a press conference that the problem of gold would not be put on the agenda and would not be discussed at the next meeting either. At the time, Dr Emminger concurred, but he may have privately thought this a very undiplomatic response and perhaps pointed this out to Secretary Fowler. For on 3 December there were press reports in *The Times* and *Le Monde* that the Group of Ten would, after all, appoint a working party to examine the position of gold in the international monetary system and that the subject would be discussed at the second joint Fund-Deputies' meeting on 26–27 January 1967 under the broad item of 'improvement in the international monetary system'.

(This working party did in fact meet at least twice—in January in Amsterdam, when Dr Kessler of the Netherlands Central Bank took the chair, and in March in London. The United States and its allies in the Fund had tried hard to curb France's 'obsession with gold' with gag and a tight rein. Neither had worked. The alternative tactic of a looser rein and a readier ear to its complaints worked much better. The disagreements among the Six made sure that nothing concrete resulted from the committee's work. But equally the French could not complain that they were being denied a hearing.)

Meanwhile, there was a clear need for some quiet diplomacy. The second joint meeting was to be held in London and by protocol the chairman would be British—James Callaghan. On 14 December 1966, therefore, Callaghan went to lunch in Paris with Michel Debré to see what could be sorted out. The next day Debré talked with Secretary Fowler, who had also come to Paris to see him. An editorial in *Le Monde* a fortnight later shrewdly discerned a 'gentleman's agreement' between the French and the Americans in which no doubt the British, anxious to appease France on the question of British entry into the EEC, had played some part. The deal was that the French would drop their insistence on a higher gold price and the Americans would drop their preference for a new reserve asset with no gold links. The editorial—wrongly as it turned out—over-interpreted this as a resuscitation of the old CRU scheme pursued by Giscard d'Estaing.

The French change tactics

Signs of a change in French policy came with the new year, at the second meeting of EEC finance ministers and central bank Governors at The Hague on 16–17 January 1967. In return for abandoning their extreme position on gold—which, if *Le Monde* was right, they had already decided to do—the French obtained some important concessions from their EEC partners. These did not, however, involve abandoning any important policy objectives. It was rather that the French succeeded in getting their Community partners to help them pursue a strategy which at the worst would delay agreement in the joint Fund-deputies' meetings and at best would strengthen the power of Europe in the decision-making process. The communiqué [16] spoke only of an agreement ' to study forthwith in the EEC Monetary Committee the improvement of the machinery of international credit '. What this meant in effect was that they would reopen the whole argument about additional drawing rights in the IMF as an alternative to the newly created assets. Now the French were stealing the clothes worn by the Americans when they set out in 1964 to get a 50 per cent increase in Fund quotas, only to meet then with bitter French opposition. At the second joint meeting held in London on 25–6 January, therefore, there was no progress with negotiation but a good deal more exploration. Equally, there was no further mention in the discussions of an increase in the gold price.

What is clearer in retrospect than it was at the time is that, at some point between the end of November 1966 and the middle of January 1967, an important change took place in French policy, a change which had begun rather tentatively in Luxembourg in September and which was finally made fully evident only in April 1967 at the Munich meeting of the Six. At Luxembourg it had been clear that a change of some sort was in the wind and that the French were ready to abandon the strategy of splendid isolation. It was not clear until the spring of 1967 whether they would choose to obstruct from within, adopting the same sort of tactics that the Soviet Union had used in the cold war period at the UN, or whether they would seriously seek—without of course tipping their cards—to negotiate a deal.

During this transitional period around the year's end no one quite knew what French policy was, not even all those who spoke for France. Michel Debré, in an interview with *Le Monde* on 8–9 January 1967, was still banging the same old drum for an increase in the price of gold and the imposition of discipline on the United States.

But it was a period when the diversity of French opinion became more open and articulate. Several books and articles published at this point helped to widen the discussion. One, *La réforme de la système monétaire internationale*, edited by Emile Roche (President of the French Economic and Social Council), consisted of a discussion between Albin Chalandon (a member of the Economic and Social Council and president of the Banque Commerciale de Paris), Rueff, and de Largentaye. Rueff's views were already well known; Chalandon favoured a new reserve asset with its use partly linked to gold; and de Largentaye favoured the reform of the Fund so as to increase French and European influence in it. Another book, by Professor Robert Mossé, author of the most authoritative work in French on the Bretton Woods Agreement, now argued that the Bretton Woods arrangements had failed only by being overly modest. Mossé also criticized both the French and Anglo-American official attitudes: ' Souhaitons que se développe en Europe dans les années à venir un plus large débat, affranchi du fétichisme de l'or et de la nation, affranchi aussi de certaines conformismes anglo-américaines '.[17]

About this time, too, a series of influential articles appeared in *Le Figaro* by France's most distinguished writer on international relations, Professor Raymond Aron,[18] and one of the few in the field with a sound grasp of both the politics and the economics of the issues. Aron bluntly criticized official policy. It was, he said, playing with fire: ' Selon la coutume on commence par prophétiser, et on finit par aider le destin à réaliser la catastrophe baptisée inévitable.' True, the United States was abusing the gold exchange standard system and taking an unjust profit from it by its power to invest in European industry at rates of 5 per cent or more, while borrowing official dollar balances at 4 per cent or less. But in this situation, what Aron called the technico-psychological guerrilla warfare pursued by France was accomplishing nothing. Perhaps it was time to look for constructive solutions to real problems—such as a code of rules for US investments in Europe. Even *Le Monde's* well-informed financial correspondent, Paul Fabra, now suggested that perhaps a voting system based on a combination of Fund quotas with GAB commitments would meet the European dissatisfaction.[19]

At the Hague meeting of EEC finance ministers and central bank Governors on 16–17 January 1967 M. Debré had proposed that the Commission's Monetary Committee should be asked to study, and report back on, means whereby international credit facilities available through the IMF could be improved. For France actually to propose a positive act was something new and confirmed the impression that a shift of some kind in French policy was in the wind. That it committed no one was less important than that it had been made at all. In the long liquidity debate, as financial journalists had noticed by now, negotiations were often ' officially called studies lest they come to nothing '.[20] This tactic also gave a breathing space while the French government's energies and attention were engaged in conducting the elections of March 1967. As it turned out, the results of those elections showed less wholehearted support for the General than he had hoped. And in the meanwhile other developments helped to bring home the point that if the French were to get European backing to bargain with the United States, they could not afford to take too long about it.

Two sets of figures produced at the IMF–Group of Ten London talks in January 1967 had helped to moderate the European determination that the United States should be made to correct its deficit *before* a reform scheme was activated. One set showed that official gold reserves over recent years had remained remarkably stable and that new supplies of gold had gone almost entirely into private hands. The result was that the rate of total gold reserves to world trade measured by total imports, and even of all reserves to imports, was steadily declining. Moreover, the substantial gold loss by the United States had been accompanied by only a very small rise in the gold reserves of other countries. The possibility had to be considered afresh, some economists concluded, that a managed increase in liquidity would be needed before the US deficit was corrected.

The United States meanwhile was showing signs of growing impatience. It would soon be two years since Secretary Fowler had decided that something should be done and the negotiators still had nothing concrete to show for their efforts. In November an internal departmental memorandum had been circulated in the Treasury Department raising the then still heretical question whether the United States could not suspend gold conversion for official dollar holdings. This was an early indication of a general change in American opinion, rejecting the penitent, defensive posture hitherto assumed and favouring a much tougher US policy line. In March 1967, at the annual American Bankers' Association conference at Pebble Beach, California, which was attended by quite a few foreign bankers, Secretary Fowler emphatically ruled out any increase in the dollar gold price, but hinted broadly that the US might be forced into 'unilateral action . . . or withdrawing from commitments' if it did not get the necessary co-operation from other countries in coping with its balance-of-payments difficulties.[21] In Paris early in April, the US Vice-President, Mr Hubert Humphrey, as good as said that time was getting short in the liquidity debate. Professional and congressional opinion was also moving towards a harder line. The active and knowledgeable Congressman Henry Reuss (a Republican from Wisconsin and a member of the Joint Economic Committee) had called for tariff barriers and even tourist bans against France, and there had been talk of excluding countries asking for gold from US capital markets. In line with the general centre-country view of the dollar's role in world affairs, Professor Charles Kindleberger of the Massachusetts Institute of Technology, backed by a group of other economists, was pressing vocally for the demonetization of gold. Even the bankers were joining in. The heads of the two largest US banks, Chase Manhattan and the Bank of America, both urged early in April 1967 that the United States should 'go off gold'. And France's most important ally, Germany, was already under direct pressure from the United States to conclude with it a new offset agreement on defence costs and to agree explicitly not to present any German dollar balances for conversion into gold (see below, ch. 9).

The French, chastened by all these developments, took the point.

Top level talks between M. Debré and the German Economics Minister, Professor Karl Schiller and the Finance Minister, Herr Strauss, laid down a working paper for a common EEC negotiating position.[22] From now on, although the press often discerned a hopeless impasse in the negotiations over monetary reform, the cliff-hanger was an artifact of bargaining. The hagglers might shrug their shoulders and walk away but it would only be tactical, never final.

Attempting a popular explanation of the eventual compromise, Professor Fritz Machlup subsequently demonstrated once again his brilliance as a semantic analyst. ' Disagreements on political matters ', he argued, ' national or international, can be resolved only if excessively clear language is avoided, so that each negotiating party can put its own interpretation on the provisions proposed and may claim victory in having its own point of view prevail in the final agreement.'[23] Thus, he argued, just as at Bretton Woods the British and the Americans had been able to resolve their difference by the use of ambiguous wording, so in the negotiations leading to the 1967 Rio Agreement on SDRs, the seemingly irreconcilable French and Anglo-Saxon positions had been brought together by the omission of those words which drew attention both to the American preference for a reserve asset and the contradictory French willingness only to create a new credit facility.

What the omission of the controversial words accomplished was acceptability, not only of the future special drawing rights, but also of the plan to create them. It enabled each of the representatives of the parties to the agreement to go home and tell their heads of government that they had won.[24]

But although *in the end* this was the manner in which the remaining differences were overcome, it was not the means. (And, as Machlup himself went on to explain, the distinction between credit and money in any system where credit instruments are habitually used as a medium of exchange has always been an unreal one.) It was therefore incorrect to say that the decision to agree was made possible by the semantic solution. This interpretation unduly underrated the political background. The contingency plan for SDRs proclaimed at Rio was reached by means of a preliminary reassessment on both sides of respective national interests. This came first, and was reflected in an increased flexibility thereafter in diplomatic manoeuvre and a consequent search for compromise wording that would save face. The attitudes of the two main parties were changed first by developments in the international economy and then by reassessments of where their best interests lay. The Americans recognized the value of having French agreement even to a second-best solution: and the French recognized the need to make the most of what bargaining power they had rather than be left in impotent isolation. It was only then that it was possible to look for and to find the necessary semantic means to an agreement which would avoid undue loss of face by either side.

Thus the necessary basis for the Rio Agreement can be fairly clearly discerned in the points made in the communiqué [25] issued by the EEC finance ministers after their meeting in Munich in April 1967. The first and most important was that ' reflections on measures to be adopted should there be future needs of additional reserves ' were not ruled out by the present sufficiency of liquidity. The second laid down strict conditions under which any measure to create additional reserves or alternative solutions would be activated, i.e. general agreement that a shortage existed, a better operation of the adjustment process, and a better balance in financial transactions. The third was that the Six should increase their influence in the IMF and its voting procedures. And fourthly, when these conditions had been met, ' it will in the future be possible to envisage the creation, within the IMF, of conditional and unconditional drawing rights '. This meant, in effect, that there would be no more meaningful discussion of reserve units. The argument would now turn on how much of the new credit units would be available, to whom, and on what terms. More particularly, the key questions would be how soon they should be allocated, and how much of the credit drawn upon would be repayable—the so-called ' reconstitution question '. The Europeans declared their conviction in the fifth point of the Munich communiqué, that debtors who had exhausted their drawing rights or used them constantly and for a long time should be obliged to ' reconstitute ' their position (i.e. to make repayment), though it was left undecided how stringent this requirement would be. Also undecided was the European position on the rules regarding transfer of drawing rights and the obligation of other countries to accept drawing rights from persistent debtors. This, the communiqué said, would have to be considered further in detail. Furthermore, it was clear that the Six were not agreed yet on how the drawing rights would be managed in the Fund (i.e. in a separate account or not) or on the acceptable magnitudes of new credit.

This Munich agreement was essentially a Franco-German one. ' In return for the French promise to support further contingency planning and the concept of unconditional drawing rights, the Germans agreed to shift their support from the creation of reserve units to a new drawing right facility within the Fund.' [26] Neither the Italians nor the Dutch were too pleased about the outcome, both of them having been on record as favouring the creation of new reserve units of some kind. Sgr Colombo, notably, made no secret of his resentment that this resort to bilateral dealing had broken the Community code of open diplomacy among all six members. The Belgians, however, stayed studiously neutral, being only too glad that the inter-Community strife had been overcome.

Just as important as the substance of the agreement outlined in the communiqué was the resolve of the finance ministers—as M. Debré explained to the press afterwards—to act in concert at the forthcoming Group of Ten and joint Group of Ten–IMF meetings. If any differences arose, they would immediately be referred either to the experts or to the finance ministers of the Six. The same technique had recently been tried and proven workable when M. Jean Rey, the President of the EEC Commission, had negotiated with the United States on behalf of the European Community in the latter stages of the Kennedy Round.[27] It was worth seeing what the same appearance of solidarity could accomplish in monetary diplomacy.

Dr Emminger also explained [28] that the monetary agreement had won important concessions from the French and had not, as the Anglo-Saxon press was implying, been a total sell-out by the Germans. At this point the text of the report on reforming the IMF which the Monetary Committee had been asked in January to prepare for the Munich meeting was not made public. It was, however, important because, although the Six were still unclear about how they would resolve their other differences, this was one issue on which they could agree. The Monetary Committee suggested simply that since the Bretton Woods rules were that decisions on quota increases in the Fund and amendments of the Articles of Agreement required 80 per cent of the total votes, and since the US after the last increase in 1965 could count on 22·29 per cent of the votes and the EEC on only 16·84 per cent, the rules should be changed raising the required minimum vote to 85 per cent of the total.

The Fund as broker

The Americans were at first inclined to underrate the solidarity of the Six and reluctant to abandon hope that the French could be isolated and enough progress made at the third joint Fund–Deputies' meeting due to take place in Washington on 24–26 April for a plan to be ready for the Fund's annual meeting at Rio in September. But official optimism reflected by M. Schweitzer was not shared by the better informed commentators, who saw at the end of the Washington meeting that the ' progress ' was mainly technical and that ' the crucial matters of substance were not tackled this week though they were discussed '.[29] It was about this time that the Fund, recognizing its dependence on the outcome of direct bargaining between the main protagonists, began to show a new flexibility. Instead of offering its own ideas and proposals in the hope that its authority would give them influence in the discussions, the Fund staff changed, so to speak, from a table d'hôte to a more cafeteria style of bureaucratic support, offering the parties a choice of plans, and later a whole range of alternative solutions, on disputed points. At this meeting, the staff produced two 'illustrative schemes', one showing how reserve units could be operated by a Fund affiliate, and the other showing how new facilities could be created as an extension of existing Fund arrangements. At this point, too, the vain search for acceptable 'qualitative and quantitative criteria for assessing the need for international liquidity' was finally abandoned. It had predictably proved as hopeless as the League's long search for a definition of 'aggression' or the UN's discussions of what constituted a 'threat to the peace'. As in those analogous cases, the only way out of an impasse reached through states' unwillingness to commit themselves to a formula was agreement that it would be so when it was agreed to be so; liquidity would be inadequate when it was collectively judged to be inadequate. In national polities, authority made such formulas superfluous. Courts could be left to interpret even so vague a phrase as 'the public interest'. In international society the lack of any agreed authority repeatedly makes even the most carefully drafted formula suspect and unacceptable.

The other sense in which April 1967 was a bit of a turning point was that it was at Washington that M. Debré donned the pose of optimist. It was a clever gambit, for it implied that if the talks now failed or made slow progress it would be through American, not French, obduracy. From Munich on through the summer, even into the August holidays, France made no objection to the increased tempo of meetings, which were sometimes arranged to follow so closely on one another that there was barely time to unpack.[30]

The large Fund–Deputies' meetings—in Washington in April and in London on 18–21 June—consisted of about 100 people and were obviously too unwieldy for the actual bargaining process which, it was now clear, would be the necessary prerequisite of agreement. Their function, rather, was more to keep everyone informed—of any concessions or compromises that stood some chance of being accepted—not only the delegations of countries not directly engaged in the bargaining but also the Fund staff who would be the ultimate draftsmen; and secondly, to legitimize as truly collective whatever solutions might be found by a much smaller caucus of decision-makers.

These were reached at no great horse-trading session as in tariff-bargaining, but bit by bit over quite an extended period of almost two and a half years, from the spring of 1967 to the autumn of 1969. Few of the really important decisions were reached either at Rio or later at Stockholm. As with other kinds of diplomacy, the large initiating conferences were very largely stage-managed and the public fanfares recorded only pre-arranged agreements.

A necessary condition was always agreement in the European Community. For instance, at the EEC finance ministers' meeting in Brussels on 4 July 1967 the Germans and Dutch, who had started by favouring reserve creation, agreed that some requirement for repayment or reconstruction on the users of drawing rights should be made. This agreement, supplemented by bilateral exchanges which took place in July and August between the Germans and the Americans, allowed the Italians to come forward at the London meeting of Group of Ten finance ministers and central bank Governors on 18–19 July with a suggestion based on the old notion of ' harmonization ', which was at least accepted as a possible basis for compromise on which the deputies could work. This idea was simply that, although there would be no obligation to repay as with a credit, there would be an obligation after a certain lapse of time to restore the original ratio in a country's reserves between special reserve drawing rights and other reserve assets.[31]

The other necessary condition was some concession or even appearance of concession on the American side. Thus the US position was at first opposed to any change in the Fund voting rules. Then, by mid-July, Secretary Fowler was conceding that they might be changed if (as the Americans wanted) more than $1 billion drawing rights—perhaps $2 billion—were distributed annually over a five-year period, but that otherwise they should remain unaltered. Later, in early August, the Americans began to drop the idea of a $2 billion annual issue and yet to accept the European demand for veto rights in the Fund. The sticking point was that there should not be a bloc EEC vote which would allow France to maximize its power to obstruct decisions in the Fund. The EEC's veto, in short, would be conditional on European agreement.

On the reconstitution or repayment issue the final compromise was not reached until the end of August, at the Group of Ten ministerial meeting in London on 26 August 1967. Between the French demand that only 50 per cent of a country's drawing rights would be used on average over a four-year period without any obligation to repay (i.e. that over 50 per cent use carried a reconstitution requirement), and the American reluctance to impose any but the most token repayment rule, Dr Emminger proposed the compromise figure of 75 per cent (i.e. reconstitution only required for the final quarter of a country's total drawing rights). This the Americans would have accepted, but not the French. Finally, with the Germans and Italians backing the Americans, France indicated readiness to accept a figure of 70 per cent averaged over five years and this, proposed by Canada, was accepted unanimously.

The Rio meeting

This bargain still left undecided the key questions of when and how much? Also unsettled were what arrangements if any (other than total withdrawal from the Fund) could be made to allow what even the French, stuck for a translation, called 'l'opting-out' by dissident Fund members; the details of constitutional change in the Fund; and the gold guarantee of SDRs against dollar devaluation. What the finance ministers of the Group of Ten had achieved was the outline of a contingency plan to present for general acceptance when all the 107 Fund members assembled at Rio in September. They further agreed that 'decisions on the basic period for, timing of and the amount and rate of allocation of the new drawing rights should be taken by the Board of Governors of the Fund by a majority of 85 per cent of the total voting power.' The 70 per cent deal was not mentioned in the communiqué. It was stated only that use of drawing rights would carry the obligation on members 'to reconstitute their position in accordance with principles which will take account of the amount and duration of the use'. The details agreed in London were left to the Fund to announce after approval by the Executive Board on 11 September 1967. One important point which then emerged was the agreement on a limited obligation to accept SDRs. Beyond a figure equal to three times a country's original allocation, a country could refuse to accept more (i.e. twice the original allocation if it had itself used none, three times if it had used its own allocation in payments to other countries). Drawing rights would have a gold guarantee and carry a small interest rate. They would be issued to all members accepting the associated obligations in proportion to existing Fund quotas but would be kept by the Fund in a separate account from general Fund drawings. They would be issued for a base period of five years and could be used either to acquire currencies for use in settlement or as intervention to maintain exchange rates, or could be directly transferred to the accounts of SDR creditor countries. SDRs could also be used to repossess balances of a country's own currency held by others, provided the latter agreed. This would enable the United States to negotiate for the exchange of SDRs for dollar balances which otherwise could be converted for gold from US gold reserves.[32]

The one substantial point settled at Rio was that the constitutional changes in the Fund should be part of the contingency plan deal and not, as the Americans tried unsuccessfully to insist against a united EEC, a separate issue to be treated and voted on its merits. Once again, the Six found it relatively easy to unite in defence of any measure that would improve their power to influence Fund operations and decisions. The results were finally worked out first by the EEC's Monetary Committee in the closing months of 1967 and translated into the appropriate constitutional amendments by the Fund staff in time for the Stockholm meeting in March 1968. They were not insignificant. The 15 per cent veto rule was to apply henceforth not only to quota increases and SDR issues, but also to 'uniform proportionate changes in par values' (i.e. the gold price) and to consequent waiver of the maintenance of value of Fund assets (i.e. whether, if the gold price changed, Fund assets and accounts should keep their gold value or be devalued with the dollar). The Community countries also got legal confirmation of the point that members' rights to use their gold tranche should in future be fully automatic and that the Fund would pay interest on the so-called 'super-gold tranche'—the extra credit with the Fund acquired by any member whose currency was so extensively drawn from the Fund that it was in effect giving a one-way increase in its quota commitment to the other members.

More significant than these changes in the voting rules in changing the balance of power within the Fund was the creation of a new body to which appeal could be made when the Executive Board 'interpreted' Fund rules, old and new. This had always been a source of resentment among the French and with some other European directors. On more than one occasion the reinterpretations (which could be passed in the Board by simple majority of the weighted votes) had turned the original rule on its head and had therefore amounted to extensive new rule-making power.[33]

Now, in case of disagreement, there was to be a standing committee of the Board of Governors to whom interpretations by the Executive Board could be appealed and whose decision would be final unless the Board of Governors as a whole decided otherwise by an 85 per cent majority. On this standing committee each member would have one individual vote. It would not in practice be much used, but its very existence would ensure that in future more strenuous efforts would be made to reach a US-EEC consensus in interpreting the rules.

Given the scope for liquidity creation inherent in the SDR facility, and particularly the potentiality for using SDRs to provide help for the United States and the United Kingdom, it was understandable that the Common Market should have sought a voice in interpretations greater than they had under the existing Fund articles.[34]

The Stockholm meeting

The opting-out issue was settled at the ministerial meeting at Stockholm on 29–30 March 1968. On this, also, the Five now supported

France, and the Americans reluctantly had to give way. France insisted on a continuing, instead of a once-for-all, right to opt out. That is, that a country accepting the activation of the SDR plan could still at a later date dissociate itself from a subsequent allocation and renounce its obligations to accept SDRs as a substitute for convertible currencies—retaining nevertheless the equal right, having once opted out, later to opt in again. As with the GAB, France wanted the principle of consent to be applied continuously and not, as with most international agreements (including the Bretton Woods Agreement) only at the outset. This important concession Richard Gardner judged to have been 'the *quid pro quo* for the substantial extent to which the SDR compromise favours a liberal solution to the liquidity problem', putting SDRs well over on the ' money' side of the ' money' versus ' credit' spectrum.[35]

Where the other Community members jibbed, however, was in holding up agreement on the contingency plan any longer. At Stockholm, Debré, reflecting French frustration and irritation at the ease with which the United States had just obtained the agreement of its Gold Pool associates to the two-tier gold price arrangement (see below, ch. 9), demanded wider discussion of the gold price and the whole international monetary system. When this met general resistance, France refused to endorse the reform plan, abstained on the vote, and reserved its position until publication of the full text of the SDR amendments. By this move, of course, nothing was lost, and time, in which to see how confidence in the dollar survived the two-tier agreement and how readily the SDR scheme won approval of governments, was gained. As with the old 1965 debate on quota increases, the French knew that their absence would not hold anything up but it might marginally increase French bargaining power if this were to be reinforced by developments in the system.

As it turned out, however, it was not developments in the system so much as developments in France itself that altered the whole bargaining situation. The student demonstrations of May 1968 and the fatal weakening of the General's domestic political base had a direct effect on the market valuation of the franc and thus on French reserves. The two together finally undermined French opposition to the SDR plan and deprived French negotiators of the will to extract the last ounce of concession from every bargaining situation.

Although the French display of pique and peevishness at Stockholm had not held up acceptance by the other nine finance ministers, there was still some way to go before the paper gold plan could be put into operation. Since it involved amendment of the Bretton Woods Agreement, it had to be ratified by sixty-five countries having 80 per cent of Fund votes, and, according to Article XVII, it also had to have the written acceptance, in accordance with their national constitutions, of members casting 75 per cent of the votes. Once legalized, it could only subsequently be activated in agreed amounts over the first base period by the affirmative vote in the Fund of members casting 85 per cent of Fund votes.

This necessarily somewhat lengthy ratification procedure was completed by 28 July 1969 and the minimum number of written acceptances was deposited with the Fund ten days later. By then the deputies were confidently anticipating the event and were already involved in a new series of bargaining sessions to decide the remaining issues of how much and when. Yet again the outcome was decided by the time-honoured procedures of haggling and slow approximation towards the point of compromise. This was once more ultimately determined by no objective criterion but by the relative determination of each side to shift as little as possible from its initial position.

What, however, had changed since the summer of 1967 was the perception of threat to the system and the perception of possible national and international need for additional liquidity. The Fund staff, resuming their more assured ex cathedra tone of voice, reported the range of estimates of annual liquidity needs for the next three to five years to lie between $3\frac{1}{2}$ and $6 billion a year. Their estimate, supporting that of the US Treasury, lay between $4 and $5 billion. If, as they thought likely, gold and dollar and other foreign exchange holdings increased by $1–1\frac{1}{2}$ billion annually, this would still leave a gap of $2\frac{1}{2}–4$ billion to be filled by SDRs. More to the point, the European Community deputies raised their 1967 bid of $1 billion annually to a bid of $2 billion. Mr Paul Volcker, the new Under-Secretary for Monetary Affairs at the US Treasury, proposed $4–5 billion. Preliminary agreement on a short three-year initial period and on 'front-loading' with a substantial first-year allocation made it easier for the Europeans (now once more including the French) to rise to $2\frac{1}{2}$ billion and the US to drop to $4 billion. The difference was more or less split at $3\frac{1}{2}$ billion for the first year, which would be 1970, and $3 billion for each of two subsequent years. In effect, without fuss, the contingency plan was to be activated without further delay, all demands for a prerequisite end to the US deficit being quietly buried. M. Schweitzer was to propose formal approval by the Fund Governors at their annual meeting in Washington, which he duly did on 3 October 1969.

Conclusions

It was by then just over four years since Henry Fowler had made his tour of European capitals to assess the issues to be negotiated and the differences to be resolved. Final agreement had been a long time coming. Indeed, it is hard to think of many other international negotiations that had been quite so long drawn out. Why was this so?

Several different answers have been given to this question and they tend broadly to correspond to the different assessments that have been made about the significance and importance, political and economic, of the end result.

One explanation, commonly encountered in the American literature, is that the long delays were simply due to the cussedness of the French and in particular to the obstinacy and perverse nationalism of General de Gaulle. But there was more to it than that. Even the drastically abbreviated account given above of the sequence of events in the long negotiations suggests that France alone could not have obstructed faster progress. French obstinacy was only influential because, on certain key points, France was supported by other Europeans, including some, like the Swiss, who were not even members of the European Community or specially concerned for its survival. About the end of 1966, it will be recalled, the General rightly discerned that there was quite a lot of common ground amongst the Europeans and concluded that it could be used to elicit support for French opposition to American wishes on certain questions provided compromises were sought on others. Had this not been so, there would have been no advantage to France in abandoning the posture of embattled isolation —a posture which (as the fight over quotas in the Fund had shown) did not materially delay decisions. In the SDR negotiations therefore it was not so much French obstruction as the difficulty of first finding common ground between France and other Europeans, especially Germany, that took the time, and then of finding out by the Americans how far the European front was in fact as solid as it pretended to be.

The second explanation, commonly implied in much of the economic literature, points to the complexity and technicality of the SDR Agreement. But though it was true that there were many questions of technical detail to be settled, this was not a prime reason for the delay. Whenever technical difficulties had been encountered during the negotiations, there had never been any lack of ingenious solutions on offer, either from the IMF staff, from US Treasury officials, or from the European Community's Commission in Brussels, and all of these could readily draw on the extensive unofficial literature.

Technicality, indeed, has commonly been much less important than other factors in protracting international diplomacy. Agreements on customs classification,[36] on pharmaceutical descriptions or on telecommunication rights—all of which can be highly technical—have seldom, in themselves, caused lengthy bargaining. And the reason why

disarmament talks—which possibly take the prize for long duration—
went on so long was not that they were sometimes technical but that,
although the opposing parties' demands seemed impossible to reconcile, yet neither wanted the odium of bringing the talks to an end. Thus
in both the interwar and the post-cold-war periods, disarmament talks
dragged on basically because both sides wanted to demonstrate their
inexhaustible desire for peace and détente and neither side wanted the
embarrassment of ending them.

There is more similarity between the liquidity negotiations and such
protracted tariff bargaining sessions as the Kennedy Round. In both
cases a multiplicity of perceived interests had to be accommodated in
one bargain package. In both cases, too, the outcome had to be
defined in precise rather than in general terms. This took time. In
1947–8 the negotiations for the International Trade Organization took
longer than those establishing other UN specialized agencies. But the
reason why the Havana Charter took so long to draft and was so
wordy was not that it was technical but that it laid down rules, and
these rules had to accommodate policy objectives that were sometimes
mutually contradictory.

Inasmuch as the SDR Agreement was a kind of collective legislative
instrument setting up an operating mechanism, it might best be compared to the UN Charter. This too had emerged from a long bargaining process, beginning at Dumbarton Oaks and continuing at the San
Francisco UN Conference on International Organization (UNCIO).
In both cases, the resulting agreement was likely in some marginal yet
undetermined way to alter the environment within which national
governments operated. In the UN, too, the oligarchy of big powers
had been anxious to safeguard their exclusive rights and freedom of
action and to decide the main structure before involving the multitude
of middle and small powers and giving them the appearance of a share
in the international decision-making. In neither case was the mechanism going to bring about any basic change in the nature of the
system. But a new, palliative dimension was to be given to it. It was
the realization that no state engaged in international trade or in international finance, whether as borrower, investor, or dealer, would be
unaffected by the introduction of SDRs that made the agreement one
that was politically important as well as technically complex.

Of the two views which broadly accept the political importance of
the agreement, one is approving and hopeful, the other disapproving
and dubious.

Those who are disapproving tend to stand at either extreme of the
political spectrum. At one end are the monetary purists, conservatives
in the sense that their chief concern is to conserve and secure the
system. Apart from the French, Swiss, and Belgians, one could note

as Anglophone examples, the late Dr Paul Einzig and Eric Chalmers, author of *The International Interest Rate War* (1972). Einzig regarded the initials SDR as standing for ' Speedier Doom Results ', and argued that the indirect assistance which the new arrangements afforded to the United States merely relieved the Americans in some measure of the need for self-discipline and monetary restraint, opening the door to indefinite monetary expansion. Chalmers also thought it encouraged ' the resumption of a relaxed US attitude toward external payments deficit ' (p. 240).

At the other end of the spectrum are the critics of American imperialism who have suggested that the United States, by its monetary diplomacy in the late 1960s, was managing for the first time in history to get the rest of the world indirectly to finance its penetration of other national societies and economies and its growing ownership of foreign business enterprise. In this process, the US victory in the liquidity negotiations reflected its power over the other nations in the imperialist network (*sic*).

Their interests are aligned with the United States to the extent that US military and economic power is used to secure the imperialist system and push back, if possible, the borders of the non-imperialist world. At the same time, they are worried about their own skin and the competitive threat of US business and finance. Hence the jockeying for power that does take place within the limits of the present international monetary arrangements.[37]

In Magdoff's view therefore, the SDR negotiation was only important to the extent that it affected the central issue, which was the future role of the dollar.

Similarly, in a book seeking to give a left-wing interpretation of American foreign economic policy in aid, trade, and money, Michael Hudson [38] described SDRs as

akin to a tax levied upon payments surplus nations by the United States to pay for the exchange costs of American departures from an economic drive toward world empire to a drive toward classical military imperialism. It was a tax because it represented a transfer of goods and resources from the civilians and government sectors of the payments-surplus nations to payments deficit countries—a transfer for which no tangible quid pro quo was to be received by the nations not embarked on the extravagance of war.

On the other hand, many of those economists in the United States and elsewhere who proclaimed the agreement as a ' historic achievement ' and ' a major benchmark in the evolution of the international monetary system ' [39] did so in hope and approval. It was the first trailblazing step in the deliberate collective management of the international economic system—a system that had hitherto been at the mercy of arbitrary variations in the supply of precious metals and of the unbridled decisions of those countries whom fortune and history had endowed with currencies which others were prepared to use and to hold in their reserves. Even if, as was evident at the very moment of issue, the invention of ' paper gold ' was not going to solve the problems of the international monetary system, and even if the asymmetries produced by the American deficit were not in any significant degree going to be diminished nor the risk of world depression for ever banished, yet the hope lingered among many expert observers that what had been achieved once, in small measure and with difficulty, could be done again, bigger and faster. Now that the ice of national monetary sovereignty had been broken, perhaps longer, stronger steps could follow small ones.

This was, of course, an illusion. It was not a case of ' ce n'est que le premier pas qui coûte '. The agreement was a compromise which left the major problems of the role of the dollar and of gold, the functioning of the adjustment process and the balance to be achieved in international monetary management between stability and liquidity, expansion and security, still undecided. It made no easier or harder the decision to substitute international for national monetary management. For this, the three main forms of national monetary reserves—gold, dollars, and SDRs—would have to be permanently consolidated into a single international credit money, either by agreeing on a fixed relation between the three (for example, by putting them in a central reserve settlement account) or by eliminating first gold and later, dollars, altogether. But as Professor Harry Johnson observed,

The logical end of this line of reasoning would be the equivalent of the establishment of a world central bank, a central bank of central banks, which would provide for the growth of the international money supply in the same way as a national central bank provides for the growth of the national money supply. The problem with this solution is that it goes very far beyond the degree of international collaboration that national monetary authorities have so far been able to achieve in the operation of the international monetary system. The issues that would have to be resolved—especially the balancing of the objectives of high employment and price stability against each other—are precisely those on which nations have been most divided in the recent past.[40]

Similarly, Sir Eric Roll, who himself had played an important part in many of the discussions of the 1960s, saw that both the provision of adequate liquidity and the introduction of greater flexibility in exchange rates, though they appeared to ease the process by which national currencies coexist and adjust to one another over time, also raised considerable problems of a political character.

The question is whether this can be achieved under the kind of international political structure we have developed so far. Despite the relatively high degree of co-operation between sovereign governments that has been achieved and appears likely to continue, it is doubtful whether our institutions (in the complete sense, including organization, mechanism, procedure and attitude) are yet adequate to the task without further restriction of national sovereignty.[41]

In fact it is rather remarkable that there is hardly an economist of international reputation who has not pointed out the political obstacles lying in the path of further international agreement. Some accept them. Some deplore them. But they all concede the power behind them and the subordination of economics to politics. Indeed, in recent times there has been no clearer test of the functionalist theory of international organization than the SDR negotiations—nor one which has more conclusively refuted it. It is not true, to judge by this experience, that technical co-operation is less political than other kinds of co-operation, nor that there is any sort of progression from one act of co-operation to the next.

To sum up all these factors—French obduracy, the technicality of the subject matter and the perceived political importance of the whole project to all concerned—have contributed something at some point to the delay. But none were sufficient conditions; there were other factors too. Two in particular may be noted.

One was the changing background to the negotiations. Had this been static, it would not have been as necessary as it was for the protagonists repeatedly to revise their perception of national interest in the outcome of the talks.

The strong influence of the political and economic environment within which decisions are made in and by international organizations was well brought out in a recent study edited by Robert Cox and Harold Jacobson. This treated comparatively eight organizations as 'systems that are not fully autonomous but rather are subject to environmental forces that become major constraints upon and determinants of decisions'.[42] The study's concluding chapter observed that the environment of the world market economy required certain minimum regulation—as in GATT and the IMF—but that changes in the system since the 1940s had chiefly accounted for the adaptation and in the monetary field the proliferation of institutions, an adaptation, however, which left untouched the oligarchic structure of influence which predominated in them.[43]

The changes affecting the SDR negotiations took place both in the political dimension (with, for example, decreasing European dependence on US military protection and changing relationships between the members of the European Community), and in the economic dimension, with decreasing apprehension of the dangers of continuing US deficits and increased need for collective defence against an expanding and unregulated foreign exchange market.

In a sense, the market for foreign exchange, like that for Euro-currencies and for gold, was itself an actor in the diplomatic game. For in all three cases the game was not the old diplomatic one of inter-state relations but the much more complicated new one of international politics, of negotiated collective action against a hyperactive international economy.

The other factor which made the negotiations difficult and tended to protract them, especially in the latter stages, is more easily understood by political scientists than by economists. It was that it involved a major revision of an important international organization. The low reputation in which international agencies generally are held makes this difficult for some people to believe. But the fact is that few international organizations have ever undergone major *statutory* revision or amendment. Academic discussion—whether relating to the League, the UN, the GATT, or the EEC—has been plentiful. But the resistances in the real world usually proved too great; the inclination of states, once having created international organizations, seems to be to leave them alone. Even if organizations become obsolete and useless— like WEU or CENTO or the Council of Europe—they are seldom repaired nor yet wound up and done away with. Rather they are abandoned, like derelict hulks on a deserted foreshore, or superseded sputniks orbiting unregarded in space.

In the case of the IMF, it was possible to make the revision only because the state which had used its superior bargaining strength in 1943-4 to cut down the Fund's power to supply liquidity to the system had changed its mind and was now arguing for the more liberal approach that Lord Keynes had unsuccessfully urged at Bretton Woods. Such reversals of policy towards international organization happen very rarely. When they do, amendment and the revision of inter-state agreements become feasible but the process cannot help but be somewhat lengthy and complex.

Moreover, notwithstanding the tremendous concentration of expertise on the negotiations, the solutions finally chosen were seldom those which the experts would have judged to be objectively most efficient and satisfactory. The distribution of SDRs on the basis of existing IMF quotas was a case in point. As Kindleberger shrewdly observed, ' it is a practice in bargaining to pick on some previously agreed or obvious solution rather than undergo the pain of reaching a new unique solution. . . . The IMF quotas provided a political solution to an unresolved economic question.' [44]

As regards the effects on the relative status of international organizations, the SDR Agreement appeared to restore to the Fund the authority filched from it by the Group of Ten in the middle 1960s. Yet, as the process of negotiation itself had shown, this authority rested on very slender foundations and was easily usurped. At any point when the main protagonists were disagreed, or when they reached conclusions amongst themselves different from that reached by the Fund's staff, the latter was completely ignored or bypassed. At the same time the Group of Ten had not been unduly keen on innovation. All proposals for new organizations or even for new affiliates of existing ones had been abandoned and the new arrangement was superimposed on the Fund structure, taking full advantage of its authority and respectability as a fully multilateral organization.

A careful distinction also needs to be made between the revision of constitutional arrangements within the Fund and the reality of political power in managing the international monetary system. It was not correct to interpret the SDR Agreement as a sharing of power by the United States with Western Europeans except on those very limited issues that could be settled within that organization. The power of the United States to create both public and private liquidity through the expansion of official and unofficial dollar holdings abroad was in no way qualified—as was clearly shown by the experience of the early 1970s.

Finally, the impotence of financial experts, even up to the level of ministers and Governors' deputies, in international monetary diplomacy was clearly demonstrated. The experts had had their uses but in the last resort the key decisions had always been taken, if not by heads of state then by finance ministers. It was the finance ministers, not the foreign ministers, who had been, all along, the ultimate negotiators. Moreover, in each of the leading members of the Group of Ten—in the United States, France, Germany, and Britain—the shift (already apparent) in the domestic political system of power from foreign ministries to finance ministries was carried a significant step further. It did not follow, however, that private financial institutions, such as banks, had had much increase in power in the international system. They had had ample opportunity for profit, and for comparatively unrestricted expansion and growth. They had had little visible influence on the course of international monetary diplomacy.

Notes

[1] *International monetary reform*, p. 66.
[2] IMF, *Summary proceedings, 20th ann. meeting*, 1965 (cited ibid., p. 66).
[3] Ibid.
[4] IMF, *Summary proceedings, 19th ann. meeting*, 1964.
[5] *International monetary reform*, p. 68.
[6] Ibid., p. 74.
[7] Royal Norwegian Information Service Press Bull., no. 9, 1 Mar 1967.

[8] *Money international*, p. 281.

[9] Roosa, *Monetary reform for the world economy*, pp. 120, 129. The book was based on the Elihu Root Lectures given by Roosa in May 1965.

[10] *International monetary reform*, p. 104.

[11] Group of Ten, *Communiqué of Ministers and Governors and report of deputies* [The Emminger Report], July 1966.

[12] See Section B of the report, pp. 11–17.

[13] In *Le péché monétaire de l'Occident*. See chs. 6 & 7.

[14] Ibid., p. 142.

[15] Bernard Nossiter, *New York Herald Tribune*, 30 Nov 1966. *Le Monde* described the subsequent tiff with Schweitzer under the caption ' Scabreuses Byzantineries '.

[16] *Bull. of the EEC*, 1967, no. 3, p. 35.

[17] *Les problèmes monétaires internationaux* (Paris, 1967), p. 381 in 3rd ed. (1970).

[18] Author of *Peace and war* (1966) and many other books.

[19] *Le Monde*, Jan 1967.

[20] Richard Mooney, Paris correspondent, *New York Times*, 22 Jan 1967.

[21] *American foreign policy, current documents 1967*, pp. 164ff.

[22] Ibid., 18 Apr 1967.

[23] *Remaking the international monetary system*, p. 7.

[24] Ibid., p. 10.

[25] Agence Internationale pour la Presse, *Europe*, Daily Bull. 2664, 18 Apr 1967 (see also Cohen, p. 124).

[26] Cohen, *International monetary reform*, p. 125.

[27] See Ernest Preeg, *Traders and diplomats* (Washington, 1970), ch. 11.

[28] In the *New York Times*, 21 Apr 1967.

[29] Ed Dale, ibid., 27 Apr 1967.

[30] See chronology in vol. I, p. 437.

[31] It was about this time, incidentally, that this emollient euphemism came increasingly into general use. As Machlup had pointed out, it judiciously avoided conflict-generating words like ' credit ' or ' asset ' and thus aided compromise (*Remaking the international monetary system*).

[32] For full details see Outline of a Facility based on Special Drawing Rights in the Fund, 11 Sept 1967 (attachment to Resolution 22–8 of Annual Meeting 1967, *Summary proceedings*, p. 272). See also Cohen, app.

[33] See S. Strange, ' Monetary managers ', in Cox & Jacobson's *Anatomy of influence*, pp. 277–84.

[34] ' Politics of liquidity ', in Robert Cox, ed., *International organization*, p. 283.

[35] Ibid., pp. 280, 282.

[36] See vol. I, pp. 412ff.

[37] Harry Magdoff, *The age of imperialism; the economics of US foreign economic policy* (New York, 1969), p. 109.

[38] *Super imperialism: the economic strategy of American empire* (New York, 1972), pp. 239–40.

[39] Martin Barrett & Margaret Greene, ' Special Drawing Rights: a major step in the evolution of the world's monetary system ', *FRBNY Monthly Review*, Jan 1968, p. 10.

[40] Harry G. Johnson, ' The international monetary crisis, 1969 ' in his *Further essays in monetary economics* (London, 1972), pp. 304–5.

[41] *The world after Keynes*, p. 177.

[42] *The anatomy of influence*, p. 25.

[43] Ibid., pp. 431–2.

[44] Charles P. Kindleberger, *Power and money* (New York, 1970), p. 221.

9

BOLSTERING THE DOLLAR 1965-9

Parallel with the liquidity negotiations just recounted, went a variety of other measures to bolster the weakening position of the dollar in the international monetary system. Some of these were measures taken unilaterally by the United States; some were the result of bilateral understandings reached between the United States and other closely associated countries; and one, the two-tier gold price arrangement, required the multilateral co-operation of a number of other countries.

None of these supportive efforts can properly be considered in isolation from the others. Although superficially the unilateral policy changes made by the United States were matters of domestic management and jurisdiction and do not appear to belong in a history of international monetary relations, it is clear on closer analysis that they are an integral part of the story. For the final breakdown of the Gold Pool arrangement in March 1968 and the extreme market pressure on the dollar that preceded it must be counted in large part as the result of the failure of the other measures, unilateral and bilateral, adequately to improve the balance of payments of the United States, and of the reluctance of the US government to contemplate any of the alternative options open to it—either to accept stringent deflation at home; to curb military spending or corporate investment abroad; to devalue; or to run down the gold reserves.

Unilateral measures

The first package of unilateral monetary measures devised by the United States to protect the dollar was, it will be recalled, put together early in the Kennedy administration by the Roosa-Dillon team in 1961 (see above p. 81). The next important step adopted was the Interest Equalization Tax (IET), of 1 per cent on domestic purchases of foreign securities. This had been proposed in July 1963 and had finally emerged from the Congress in August 1964, more than a year later.

The following year, in February 1965, the Johnson administration asked US corporations voluntarily to accept restraining ' guidelines ' on their foreign investment programmes, and US banks to accept similar restraints on eight- to ten-year foreign loans. Corporate investments were not to increase more than 5 per cent above the amounts outstanding at the end of 1964. Five hundred large US-based multi-national corporations were singled out and expressly asked to expand their exports and to cut down capital transfers to their foreign subsidiaries. The IET was extended for two years and was widened to cover bank loans of longer than one year.[1] At the same time the United States, by now well aware of the existence and continuing expansion in the Eurocurrency market, nevertheless adopted a hands-off attitude towards it, seeking neither to control the operations of US banks and their clients in it nor initiating any inter-central bank measures to supervise or regulate it. The result, undoubtedly, was to create an engine for the more rapid transmission of speculative movements both between currencies and in and out of gold.

In its domestic credit management, the United States had long been accustomed to devising its interest rate policies entirely according to the requirements of the domestic economy. There had, it is true, been a brief period in the 1920s when Benjamin Strong, after consultation with Montagu Norman, had sought where possible and without injury to domestic interests to manage US interest rates so as to ease the management tasks of the Bank of England.[2] But by the 1960s this was almost forgotten and it seemed quite a new departure to use interest rate measures to trim the balance of payments as well as to regulate the domestic economy and credit structure.

From 1960, for the first four years of the decade, the United States had allowed some rise to take place in short-term interest rates but at the same time had skilfully managed to prevent this from affecting long-term interest rates. These had been kept stable and by most European—especially German—standards relatively low. But by the middle of the decade the lid on long-term rates began to give way. In late 1964 there was a sharp rise in short-term rates and this, after easing back a little in the spring of 1965, was resumed in July 1965. This time there was a spill-over effect on long-term rates. One contributory factor was certainly the increased US government demand for credit to finance the Vietnam war. Another was an increase in industrial borrowing to supplement restricted bank loans and the capital resources (hitherto plentiful) that could be generated from the cash flow of large companies. In the absence of fiscal restraints which might have checked the inflationary tendency—but which were politically unacceptable with Congressional elections looming in November 1966 —the result was a rise in US interest rates by the autumn of 1966 to peaks that had not been reached for forty years, since the 1920s. In September 1966 the US Treasury bill rate was raised to $5\frac{1}{2}$ per cent and interest rates for Eurodollar credits went to new heights. US government bonds paid what then seemed a very high return of $4\frac{3}{4}$ per cent and new corporate issues paid $5\frac{3}{4}$ per cent. A side-effect was a slump in housebuilding, checked by the high cost of mortgages, and a marked slowing-down in the growth of the US economy in the first half of 1967 without any noticeable check to the rate of inflation. And though the appeal of the British Chancellor of the Exchequer, James Callaghan, to the finance ministers of the United States, France, West Germany, and Italy at the Chequers weekend conference in January 1967 to bring interest rates down did not seem to evoke much substantial response, in fact most of the major countries, including the United States, did bring their rates down in the following six months. By mid-1967 the US Treasury bill rate was down again to $3\frac{1}{2}$ per cent and the Federal Reserve had eased reserve requirements on bank holdings of small savings and time deposits. What was significant was that this had little effect on long-term rates which stayed high. And in June 1967 the war in the Middle East started another upturn in short-term interest rates taking US Treasury bill rates higher and higher, until in late 1969 they reached $8\frac{1}{2}$ per cent.

The net effect, in short, of US interest rate management was at first to encourage foreign holding of dollars and a great expansion in the market for extraterritorial dollar deposits. It could be argued that without these measures there would have been embarrassingly acute pressure on US reserves of gold much sooner than 1970–1. On the other hand there was a point beyond which higher short-term interest rates, far from reassuring foreign dollar holders, gave them the jitters; the effect on the balance of payments was so slight as to undermine rather than bolster market confidence in the future value of the dollar. The tighter money policy of 1966 mildly improved the US trade account but this was more than offset by further increases in military spending and indirect foreign investment abroad and by further outflows of short-term capital. These went up $800m in 1967 over 1966, more than offsetting the cut of $500m achieved in long-term capital outflow for direct investment.

Politically and psychologically, moreover, this must be counted to have been a costly policy—costly both to the Western alliance and the security of Europe that it was supposed to be defending, and costly to the affluent alliance and the world market economy with whose security and stability the United States was entrusted. American official pronouncements, American economic literature, and most of the discussion in international economic organizations have all played down both the character and the consequences of American interest rate policies in the period 1966–71. But the incontrovertible facts are that it was a policy of chopping and changing, of blowing hot one minute and cold the next; and that the rather dubious benefits were reaped by the US economy and US politicians while the not inconsiderable costs were borne by the Europeans, whose economies were much more profoundly shaken by the suck and flood of the Euro-dollar slop back and forth across the Atlantic—more particularly because the flows tended to concentrate on one or two national economies and were not evenly spread over the European as they were over the North American continent. It was a policy to prompt this sort of sour comment: ' America not only provided more of the raw material for international hot money, but herself attracted or repelled it entirely at her own convenience, with scant regard for the disruptive effect this had on other countries' external payments balance and domestic liquidity.' [3]

If the United States had not shown, in the fifteen or more years after 1945, such extremely tender concern for Europe's economic problems, Washington's frigid unconcern over the difficulties of monetary management experienced in 1969–71 by Germany, France, Britain, and other European countries would have been less resented. Being hotly wooed and then coldly jilted is always more painful than never being wooed at all. The result was that many Europeans, instead of blaming each other, began (not without justification) to blame the United States for the inflation that was slowly defeating them. They felt much less inclined consequently to listen sympathetically to American complaints about European protectionism and the need to improve the contribution of trade to the US balance of payments.

Bilateral support—Canada, Germany, and Japan

But this is to run ahead of the story. In the short run, the relatively slight contribution of unilateral monetary policy measures to the US balance of payments made it all the more necessary for the United States to seek special support for the dollar from Canada and Germany, and all the more willing to keep Japan quiet by keeping the door to Japanese exports in the American market wide open.

In fact, negotiations with Canada had been more or less unavoidable from the very first moment that the United States started to use monetary discrimination to improve its balance of payments. For each of the unilateral policy measures taken by the United States, from the IET on, were of immediate and major concern to Canadians. In the early 1960s before IET was even suggested, as much as 40 per cent of foreign issues in US markets had been made on behalf of Canadian borrowers. In 1963, when the Province of Quebec borrowed $300m in order to nationalize the power companies, this figure rose to 60 per cent. Thus, it was important to Canada to gain exemption from the IET, both to safeguard industrial investment and to defend the balance of payments; with the return to a fixed exchange rate in 1962

Canadian reserves would be lost if the habitual trade deficit were not offset by a large continued capital inflow from across the border. Moreover, many of the provincial governments and cities as well as Canadian companies would have had serious budgetary problems if they had not been able to continue rolling over short-term debts in the US markets at US interest rates.

Under Diefenbaker in 1957–8 Canada had tried, and failed, to find in Britain an escape from financial dependence on the United States and an alternative source of capital for development. On the other hand, for the Americans an exemption for Canada from the IET was obviously going to cut in half the effectiveness of the measure for the US balance of payments. In order to get US agreement to exempt new Canadian issues from the tax, Canada had to agree to hold its borrowing in the United States to normal levels and not to allow borrowings that would increase its foreign exchange reserves. This meant, in short, a self-imposed ceiling on Canada's monetary reserves. Another part of the bargain was that Canada should manipulate its own interest rates structure with an eye to removing incentives to local borrowers to raise capital in the United States. Moreover, it agreed on behalf of the United States to police borrowing by nationals of third countries who might be tempted to use Canada as a backdoor to US markets. When IET was finally passed by Congress in August 1964, therefore, some important steps had been taken in the monetary integration of Canada with the United States.

The next time that US policy caused anxiety in Ottawa was in February 1965 with the voluntary guidelines on foreign investment and the extension of IET (see above, pp. 263–4). The Canadian exemption from the latter remained in force. In return, firm assurances were given by the Canadian government that it would maintain stability in its dollar holdings.[4] But among the investment guidelines, there was a request to US companies to expedite homeward remittance of profits, and they were also exhorted to 'Buy-American'. This stung the Canadian government to issue a set of counter-guidelines. The same US companies were urged to reinvest profits in Canada and to buy Canadian. This brought a reassurance from Washington that no major alteration was really intended in the practices of US companies operating in Canada. As Diebold concluded, 'the argument faded away, compromise presumably being helped by the fact that no formal action was necessary to reach an acceptable application of the guidelines'.[5]

On 16 January 1965, in fact, the two governments had reached an agreement of much greater long-term significance, the US-Canadian Automotive Products Agreement.[6] Though it was commercial in the sense that it set up a kind of free-trade area for the production of and trade in automobiles, trucks, buses and their parts, it had important consequences for the monetary relations between the two countries. The major US automotive companies—Ford, Chrysler, General Motors—agreed in 'letters of undertaking' to the Canadian government to increase the amount they spent on production in Canada (the Canadian value of their products added) by an amount equal to 60 per cent of the increase in value of their Canadian sales of cars, and 50 per cent of the increase in sales of commercial vehicles—and furthermore to supplement this by an additional $260m increase in Canadian value added over the next three years. The two governments reciprocally removed tariffs between them on new automotive products, although on the Canadian side the right of duty-free entry was limited to producing companies who in turn had to agree to maintain the market-share of Canadian automotive products. As Diebold points out, this highly innovative—and successful—tripartite agreement was made possible by the dominant position of US companies in the North American automobile industry and by the relatively small number of major producers who had to be induced to participate in an intergovernmental arrangement.[7] In two years US-Canadian trade in vehicles and parts tripled and by 1969, at $6 billion, was $8\frac{1}{2}$ times larger than it had been in 1964. The agreement also had important results for the balance of payments between the two countries; not only did it ensure that the US companies would expand their spending in Canada faster than they expanded their sales and would not in any case allow it to fall below 1964 levels, but it also changed the trade balance in automotive products between the two countries, cutting the US export surplus with Canada from $588·9m in 1964 to only $96·7m in 1969.

The price of these and other substantial benefits was, of course, much closer integration of a small, subordinate Canadian industry into a bigger North American one dominated by US companies. The integration had also extended to the labour markets, for the United Automobile Workers were then able to press for wage parity for their Canadian members. Canadian attitudes to the arrangement have understandably been somewhat mixed, for though such an arrangement gives Ottawa an important function as the guardian of Canadian interests, yet the area is correspondingly shrinking in which there can be said to be a visible national identity distinct from that of the United States.

Certainly towards the end of the decade the monetary integration of Canada with the United States had been taken several steps further, to the point where the relationship was more like that of Eire to Britain. As related earlier, the United States continued, as it came to use its administrative power in 1965 and 1966 to defend the dollar, to allow exemptions to Canada. But now and again the Canadians showed a spark of resistance to the integrative process. In 1967 a disagreement arose over a Canadian affiliate of the First National City Bank, the Mercantile Bank of Canada. The bank wished to increase its assets; the Canadian authorities thought its expansion should be limited. A compromise reached in February 1967 allowed the Mercantile Bank a free rein until the end of 1972 on condition that by then 75 per cent of its assets were in Canadian hands or the bank limited its assets to twenty times its capital.[8]

By about 1968 it seemed as though Canada had been brought ' almost within the US balance of payments in several major respects '.[9] Chief of these was undoubtedly the undertaking given by Canada in March 1968 to hold all its dollar reserves (apart from a minimal working balance) in US government securities. In this form they would not only be inconvertible into gold—as by then were Germany's—but inconvertible in any emergency into anything else. On its side the United States assured Canada that the total exemption from IET would remain in force indefinitely. These terms for maintaining the special monetary relationship were made explicit in an exchange of letters between the respective finance ministers, Henry Fowler for the United States and Mitchell Sharp for Canada.[10] Additionally, Canada had given further undertakings about the leakage of US capital to third countries via Canada which entailed in practice a standardization in certain respects of Canadian exchange controls with those of the United States. These controls had been extended by the mandatory restrictions imposed by President Johnson in January 1968 on foreign lending by banks and financial institutions, tightening the voluntary 1965 restrictions from the 109 per cent of 1964 levels to 103 per cent. Invoking a disused 1917 law, US companies were forbidden to invest at all in continental Western Europe. They could invest only up to 10 per cent above 1965–6 levels in the poor developing countries. Canada, Australia, Britain, Japan, and some oil states were put in an intermediate category in which US investment would be limited to 65 per cent of these levels. American officials later admitted that such exchange controls on companies operating internationally could not be enforced—so that the ' exemption ' of Canada from the foreign investment controls turned out to be more or less valueless.

By the end of the decade, both parties were beginning to have doubts about their bargain—but without any real intention on either side of unscrambling the association. In the United States it was questioned whether policy had been too generous to Canada. In Canada there was growing uneasiness about dependence on the United States. Could Canada continue to rely on the leniency of the Americans? Or, once having accepted monetary dependence and integration, were they stuck with it—even if the United States should prove more niggardly in future in handing out benefits?

These latent feelings gave the Canadian decision in May 1970 to return to a floating exchange rate something of an air of defiance. The Governor of Canada's central bank, Mr Louis Rasminsky, felt it necessary to warn the United States not to press Canada to repeg the rate. Later in 1970 US doubts also found expression. The Automotive Agreement had borne fruit in a record trade surplus with the United States. And Canadian borrowing in US markets, made possible by the IET exemption, swelled the capital inflow. Andrew Brimmer, a member of the Federal Reserve Board, made an ominously warning speech in Montreal on 18 November.[11] And when the United States decided on 15 August 1971 to impose the import surcharge (see below, p. 338), Canada was offered only partial exemption. Certain imports of Canadian primary products—newsprint, crude oil, iron ore, nickel, asbestos, wood pulp, etc.—were not surcharged, mainly because the 10 per cent tax would not have checked sales but would have immediately inflated production costs in the United States. Automotive products were also exempted under the terms of the 1965 agreement. Within a week of 15 August, a delegate from Ottawa appeared in Washington to plead for exemption of Canada's other exports, on the grounds that it must add to the country's already serious unemployment problem. But the request met with blank denial: US Treasury officials maintained that to make exceptions would destroy the credibility of their entire monetary strategy. In short, Canada had discovered the limits of US indulgence.

Besides Canada, the other major source of support for the United States in its defence of the dollar in the late 1960s was undoubtedly West Germany. (And a subsidiary beneficiary of this association was Britain, whose defence of sterling gained incidental support from Germany in the same period.)

As pointed out earlier (see ch. 2), this support rested on West Germany's perception of extreme dependence on US military protection and in particular on the presence of US armed forces in Germany. It had been expressed in the offset agreement of 1961 whereby, after some argument and acrimony, Germany had agreed to help offset the foreign exchange costs of these American troops by buying large quantities of US arms and by sharing with the United States the cost of military research and development. For the next three or four years German-American monetary relations were relatively undisturbed. The United States felt no need to make new demands upon Germany and was content that German representatives should show a general willingness to assist the United States in the development of international monetary co-operation in the Group of Ten, the IMF, and the OECD, and in the first tentative discussions of the liquidity question. The offset agreement of 1961 was renewed in 1963 for a further two years and the Bundesbank took a number of monetary measures to reinforce its defences against the inflow of hot short-term funds, by penalizing, restraining, and forbidding the acquisition of various types of German assets by non-residents. For example, in 1964 the Bundesbank levied a 25 per cent coupon tax on fixed-interest securities held by non-residents; reserve ratios for foreign held liabilities were increased to the top levels, and no interest at all could be paid on foreign deposit accounts. At this point, German and American monetary policies were working in the same, not opposite, directions. Indeed, the 1965 curbs on US investment made the Bundesbank's task marginally easier. The latter's criticism, at this stage, was directed more at the German than the American government—on the grounds that government spending was adding to the difficulties of controlling inflation by tight money and other measures.

But in 1966, just as the United States began to look for increased support from Germany, German resistance stiffened, precipitating the second major argument over the offset question. At this time increased US involvement in the Vietnam war was adding to government spending and putting renewed pressure on the dollar at the same time that Britain was running into renewed payments deficit. In Germany there was increasing anxiety over inflation, which continued at the rate of $3\frac{1}{2}$ per cent, accompanied in the latter part of the year by a downturn in the level of economic and industrial investment. For the first time for several years the German GNP failed to rise. There was a budget deficit of DM5,000m (quite apart from the DM3,600m due to the United States in offset payments). Such were the government's difficulties that it had to borrow DM1,000m from institutions to meet these offset commitments. Altogether, the prospects for a renewal of the offset agreement seemed poor when, in December 1966, the Erhard government was replaced by Chancellor Kiesinger's coalition government. This was committed to an economic policy of controlled expansion and easier credit, to cuts in defence spending and the termination of the offset agreement. Indeed, in February 1967 Finance Minister Strauss warned that no more funds would be available for offset payments to the United States until 1968. The State Department was told that the principle of exactly matching German arms purchases to the D-mark expenditure of forces in Germany would have to be abandoned.

Nevertheless, in spite of Germany's seeming recalcitrance, prolonged talks in the spring of 1967 ended in a tripartite agreement between Germany, the United Kingdom, and the United States signed on 2 May. It was for one year only but covered commercial and monetary as well as defence policies. The United States conceded the German government's right to decide unilaterally the precise amount of US arms it would buy. But in return Germany made much more important monetary concessions which were of very real value to the United States in its defence of the dollar. The most important of these was an assurance of indefinite duration by the President of the Bundesbank, Karl Blessing, that Germany would not seek to convert its dollar holdings into gold. This declaration was important even though it was only an assurance that Germany would continue with existing policy. For, apart from one conversion during the Italian crisis of 1964, no German-held dollars had been converted since 1960. But the written commitment was valuable because it helped allay fears in the exchange markets that Germany might be tempted to follow France's example of large-scale conversion. Perhaps significantly, although the correspondence was published by the US Treasury department,[12] no mention of it was made in the Bundesbank's annual report for 1967.

The other concession was that $500m of the Bundesbank's dollar holdings would be converted into medium-term US government securities. Substantial arms purchases would also continue—though decisions on these would henceforward be taken by the German government alone. These agreements were estimated to cover nearly all the $800m annual cost of keeping US troops in Germany.

Moreover, having given way to pressure from Washington, it was difficult for the Germans to resist British demands for similar offset agreements. The British Pink Book on the balance of payments for 1967 estimated that most of the £120m spent on British forces in Western Europe went to Germany, and this at a time when Britain was spending 6·4 per cent of national income on defence compared with 3·6 per cent by Germany. And whereas the German balance of payments in 1966 gained $1,240m on account of defence transactions, the British lost $762m.[13]

The 1967 agreement therefore offered Britain some assurance of German purchases to offset the foreign exchange costs of British troops in Germany. But as with the Americans, there was a natural tendency for British ministers to exaggerate the overall effect on the balance of payments, and to claim that German purchases fully covered these costs even when some of them would almost certainly have been made anyway.

When further talks were held in the spring of 1968, the monetary scene was still highly unsettled after the sterling devaluation and both the British and Americans were strongly urging the Germans to give all the help they could. They did agree to buy £21m British Treasury Bonds and to hold a total of £74·5m in sterling. The 1968 agreement with the United States, announced in June, promised that the Bundesbank would buy $500m in US Treasury bonds and would pursuade a consortium of German banks to buy $125m in US government bonds. Lufthansa would help with a purchase of US aircraft worth $60m and the German Defence Ministry with another worth $100m.

The next twelve months demonstrated, however, the ineffectiveness of such palliatives in face of the markets' perception of a structural imbalance in exchange rates. Foreign funds continued to flood into Germany even though subjected to a 100 per cent reserve requirement. By the end of the year the Bundesbank held DM3,700m in British and American bank notes and the United States agreed that an upper limit had been reached for finance supplied in this form.[14] But with so large a deficit, the Americans wanted their defence costs, which they estimated at $900m a year, fully offset. The Germans disagreed: the figure should be $625m a year and they offered to cover 80 per cent, not 100 per cent. Talks were begun in April and continued through May and June. The compromise finally reached in July 1968 was, as usual, nearer the Americans' than the Germans' bargaining position. The Germans had had to raise their first offer of $700m in offset purchases to $800m, plus a further $125m in non-military purchases. In addition, the German government would make a ten-year loan of $250m, at a modest $3\frac{1}{2}$ per cent, to the US government, and would buy Export-Import Bank and Marshall Plan claims on the United States amounting to $118·75m, would prepay $43·75m in debts to the United States; freeze $32·50m due in interest payments; and would transfer $150m of foreign exchange to the United States to encourage German investment.

Even greater concessions were given in the 1971 offset agreement which was finally concluded about the same time as the Pompidou-Nixon meeting in mid-December in the Azores that preceded the Smithsonian accord (see below, ch. 11).[15] This agreement was to cover a two-year period and provided for German purchases of US arms and military equipment, including a large order for Phantom fighter aircraft valued at $1,200m, and for a further contribution of $184m to the cost of modernizing US army barracks in Germany. A further $600m of official German reserve holdings in dollars would be used to buy US Treasury bonds.[16]

As with Canada, close association with the United States posed all sorts of political dilemmas for a series of German governments. And these sometimes proved, as in Canada, to be a fertile source of domestic, political, and administrative conflict. In Canada, the vulnerability had been economic and financial and quarrels had ensued from it in the Diefenbaker administration (for example) between Mr Coyne of the Canadian Reserve Bank and Mr Fleming at the Finance

Ministry. In Germany the vulnerability was military and strategic and the disagreements therefore tended to be between the Defence Ministry and the Finance Ministry or between the finance and economics ministers. Also, since the Bundesbank had a special statutory arrangement to preserve its immunity from direct political pressures, there were occasional conflicts between the Bundesbank and the government.

And although the arguments over offset agreements were often conducted on a highly technical level, involving the exchange between Bonn and Washington of complicated statistical calculations regarding the actual foreign exchange costs of US troops, the outcome was

Receipts from foreign troops and offset payments *

1. *West German Offset Agreements with the US, 1961–73*

	DMm	$m
1 July 1961–30 June 1963	5,700	1,375
1 July 1963–30 June 1965	5,600	1,375
1 July 1965–30 June 1967	5,400	1,350
1 July 1967–30 June 1968	2,000	500
1 July 1968–30 June 1969	2,900	725
1 July 1969–30 June 1971	6,080	1,650
1 July 1971–30 June 1973	6,650	2,065

Source: Information provided by West German Finance Ministry & Defence Ministry (Ulrich Schneider, ' Ein neues Abkommen über den Devisenausgleich ', in *Bundeswehrverwaltung*, 13, 1969).

2. *West German receipts from foreign troops, 1962–71* (DMm)

	1962	1963	1964	1965	1966	1967	1968	1969	1970	1971
USA	2,920	2,915	2,824	2,723	3,241	3,557	3,715	3,760	3,781	4,345
UK	732	848	853	907	953	949	946	981	1,094	1,386
France	252	256	276	277	410	386	284	343	410	373
Other countries	197	225	234	217	294	349	417	462	471	416
Total	4,101	4,244	4,187	4,124	4,898	5,241	5,362	5,546	5,756	6,520

Source: Bundesbank Annual Report 1968 (1970) and information provided by Bundesbank.

3. *Medium-term US & UK Treasury bonds* (DMm)

	1967	1968	1969	1970	1971
US	1,000	3,500	4,000	2,000	2,000
UK	—	200	200	200	—
Total	1,000	3,700	4,200	2,200	2,000

Source: Statistical supplements to Bundesbank Monthly Reports: series 3, Balance of Payments statistics.

* Tables taken from material in article by Gernot Volger, ' Devisenausgleich als militär-und zahlungsbilanzpolitisches Instrument ', *Konjunkturpolitik* 5/6 Heft, 1974, reproduced with permission.

decided by political circumstances and by the toughness with which each side was prepared to stick to its original bargaining position. Here the German government seemed to find extra resisting power when its government was in a very strong position—and also paradoxically, when it was teetering on the edge of electoral defeat. It lost resisting power when external events—such as the invasion of Czechoslovakia in August 1968—increased German awareness of military insecurity.[17] The United States, on the other hand, was unmoved by the problems of the German government but highly susceptible to pressures arising in Congress or elsewhere, especially from the state of the US balance of payments.

When it came to multilateral monetary negotiations, however (as will have been apparent from the account of the liquidity negotiations), German support for the United States was less dependable. If Germany had a special relationship with the United States, it also had one with France, and Bonn was particularly anxious at key points to strengthen this axis as a necessary foundation for a developing European Community.

The third bilateral relationship important to the United States within the general system was that with Japan. Japanese support was less openly visible than that given by Germany but, as the negotiations of 1971 were to show, was perhaps no less important in bolstering the weakening position of the dollar.

From 1964 onwards, except for one brief lapse in 1967–8, Japan's current account showed a consistent surplus, and Japanese reserves through the latter half of the 1960s mounted steadily (see table, p. 277). Yet the Japanese, unlike the Europeans, were content to hold ever-increasing dollar balances and showed little interest in acquiring gold for their national reserves. Indeed their gold holdings constituted only 15 per cent on average compared with about 50 per cent in West German reserves. In return for Japanese forbearance over the cashing of dollars for gold, the United States showed special forbearance towards the invasion of the US domestic economy by Japanese export industries. It also exercised its dominant power in multilateral organizations to give Japan special dispensation from the codes of behaviour demanded of other rich countries. Japan was allowed to preserve and to continue to use exchange and investment controls to keep severe limits on American direct investment in Japan, through the purchase of Japanese companies as affiliates and subsidiaries. The Japanese machinery of control over foreign direct investment, which had originally been introduced in 1950 (see above, p. 52), remained effective through the 1960s and although progressively liberalized, was so operated to show a marked preference for joint ventures which left at least 51 per cent and final control in Japanese hands.[18]

That the pressure on Japan to dismantle these controls was never fully applied owed a good deal to appreciation, especially in Washington, of the peculiar historical circumstances which accounted for them. Before World War II, foreign private credit had been used to finance Japanese rearmament and American opinion was opposed to a resumption of this practice for the same sort of emotional reasons that made Congress oppose sales of ' strategic ' exports to the Soviet bloc. The controls therefore started (from the American point of view) as a measure of economic disarmament corresponding to the provision in the Japanese Peace Treaty of 1951 that forbade Japan to rebuild its armed forces. Ten years later they were allowed (very largely) to remain because by then the US deficit made the United States hesitant to open the gates to another large and inviting field for foreign investment by US-based multinationals.

The Japanese government, meanwhile, was finding that the controls could usefully be operated as a conveniently adjustable tool of monetary and economic management. Since the culture and traditions of the country assumed that responsibility would be accepted and authority exercised by government over Japanese industry and enterprise of all kinds, it would have seemed unnatural for any Japanese government voluntarily to give up so effective a set of controls. And an additional reason why this was politically possible may have been that Japanese dependence on the United States had historically been more directly on the US government than (as in Canada) on private investors. What the American private sector had never had (or at least not to any marked degree) in Japan, it never missed.

Moreover throughout the 1960s Japan was never called upon by the United States to make any major overt financial contribution to the cost of the US alliance in Asia or to the Vietnam war. Defence expenditures in Japan even at the end of the decade were only 0·8 per cent of GNP, compared with Germany's 3·5 per cent. It was only in 1971 that for the first time the United States suggested to Japan something in the nature of an offset agreement on the German pattern. True, the foreign exchange costs of US troops in Japan was not so large an item in the balance of payments as US troops in Germany. But at an estimated $500m it was not negligible.

Various explanations can be given to account for the noticeably low profile adopted by Japan in international monetary diplomacy throughout the 1960s. One explanation would lay stress on the Japanese reaction to defeat in World War II and the natural desire to avoid conflict with the victorious power; another on Japanese recollection of the domestic consequences that followed the breakdown of the world market economy in the inter-war period. This, it will be remembered, had cut Japan's foreign trade by half in one

Japan's balance of payments, 1960–71 (US$m) [1]

	1960	1961	1962	1963	1964	1965	1966	1967	1968	1969	1970	1971
Trade balance	4	−558	402	−210	100	1,900	2,280	1,160	2,530	3,700	3,965	7,900
Services & transfers	−73	−424	−451	−365	−460	−970	−1,030	−1,350	−1,480	−1,580	−1,995	−2,000
Current balance	−69	−982	−49	−575	−360	930	1,250	−190	1,050	2,120	1,970	5,900
Long-term capital account	1	−10	172	470	380	−415	−820	−815	−250	−155	−1,590	−1,160
Basic balance	−68	−992	123	−105	20	515	430	−1,005	800	1,965	380	4,740
Short-term capital account [2]	704	40	113	140	−100	−105	−110	435	300	320	995	2,935
SDR allocation	—	—	—	—	—	—	—	—	—	—	120	130
Overall balance	636	−952	236	35	−80	410	320	−570	1,100	2,285	1,495	7,805

[1] On a transactions basis. [2] Incl. errors and omissions.

Source: BIS Reports (1963–71); OECD, *Economic Surveys of Japan.*

Japan's reserves, 1960–71 (US$m)

	1960	1961	1962	1963	1964	1965	1966	1967	1968	1969	1970	1971
Total reserves	1,949	1,666	2,022	2,058	2,019	2,152	2,119	2,030	2,906	3,654	4,840	14,148
of which gold reserves	247	287	289	289	304	328	329	338	356	413	532	738

Source: IMF, *International Financial Statistics.*

year and had set off a chain-reaction of political events that ended finally in war, privation, and national destruction and humiliation. Against such a background it would seem natural for Japan to take no initiative of any kind on monetary negotiations among the members of the affluent alliance in the 1960s, nor to oppose, save where its own direct domestic interests were involved, any policy or position taken by the United States, Japan did undertake commitments in the GAB in 1963, but did not until 1964 assume the full IMF obligations of convertibility under Article VIII of the Articles of Agreement. Even then Japan's quota was strikingly small ($725m in 1965),[19] in relation to the size of its GNP and to its involvement in international trade. Though its rank order on such indicators as these would already have put it in the top six or seven countries, Japan was in no hurry to move up to the top table. There was no exclusively Japanese Director (as there was even for Italy) on the Fund's Executive Board, and the Japanese were very poorly represented among the senior members of the Fund staff. And it was not until 1964 that Japan became a member of OECD.

Japan's association with the United States was therefore one which caused minimum embarrassment to the dollar through the 1960s. From the middle of the decade to past its end Japan was a great, quiet hole, silently and satisfactorily absorbing surplus dollars and causing no trouble. At the same time, Japanese governments nevertheless managed to run a relatively stable and extremely dynamic economy. They did this with the help of a more effective (because more thoroughly insulated) system of national monetary controls and policy weapons than was enjoyed by any other rich country government. A study by the OECD of monetary policy in Japan in the 1960s concluded 'the extent of economic adjustment induced by monetary policy has been large and the time lags required for the response of the economy have been relatively short in Japan '.[20] This close control within the country was undoubtedly a necessary condition for the extra dimension which Japan's silent and passive posture afforded the monetary diplomacy of the United States.

Crisis in the gold market

At first glance, there was much in the second major crisis in the international gold market that was the same as in the earlier one in 1960-1 leading to the organization of the Gold Pool. There was the same accelerating pace of speculation in the market; the same hastily arranged gatherings of central bankers and finance ministers to discuss and meet the challenge. Yet while all the contemporary accounts of the first crisis and its solution were much alike and were pitched in a rather low descriptive key, contemporary accounts of the second

crisis in 1967–8 have mostly been much more 'political' and therefore dramatic. The historian has to choose between a bewildering
variety of interpretations of the sequence of events.

Whether recounted in New York, London, Paris, Tokyo, or San-
tiago, the events of 1960–1 were seen as a straightforward response
by the members of the affluent alliance to the unruliness of market
speculation. Acting in collective self-defence against this common
danger, so the story went, they had confidently found, through extended inter-bank co-operation, the common-sense technical solution to
a tricky technical situation. Outside financial circles, public interest in
these earlier events was slight.

It was a measure of all the other changes on the international
monetary scene in the intervening six years that when it came to
recounting the second 'gold rush', many contemporary writers saw
it primarily as the outcome of an international political conflict; they
spoke of a 'gold war' between France and the United States and of
General de Gaulle's 'monetary offensive' in his all-azimuths strategy.
One account, for instance, by an informed British financial journalist,
Ian Davidson of the *Financial Times*, started with the sentence, 'The
French did not rest content with their performance over the sterling
devaluation'; and went on to say that the 'barrage' from the officially
inspired French press 'triggered off' a new wave of market speculation in the gold market.[21] Another British writer, Brian Johnson, in
The Politics of Money (1970), used an even more emphatically military
vocabulary. The gold rush of March 1968 'represented de Gaulle's
Austerlitz' (p. 204), and it was only two months after this apparent
'victory' that in the events of May 1968, the French students and
workers 'stepped in, or rather sat down, to relieve the pressure and
prepare the way for monetary truce. ... Just as it seemed that the
psychological ingredients of the monetary system must be ground to
powder by the Paris "rumour mills", de Gaulle's own monetary
breastwork began to give way' (p. 205).

The implication of this highly-coloured interpretation is that the
dissolution of the Gold Pool reflected primarily a conflict in international relations, the result of a jousting tournament between the
French and the Americans in which the fortunes of war favoured
first one side and then the other. It almost suggests that there would
have been no problem with the gold market in the 1960s if the
French government, instead of being awkward and non-co-operative,
had kept quiet.

An important concern of the present chapter, therefore, will be to
analyse the nature and impact of the French 'attack' and to assess its
importance in relation to various other developments which seem on
balance to have been much more decisive. One was the increasing

activity and power not only of the gold market but of parallel international money markets; the other was the declining monetary strength of the United States after six more years of deficit since the last gold market crisis in 1961.

Indeed, seen in a longer perspective of postwar history, the events of the 1960s fall into place as part of a much longer story in which the United States had been obliged, step by step, to retreat from the high point in 1934 of its power to dominate the world market and the world price of gold. In that year, Franklin Roosevelt and Henry Morgenthau had arbitrarily decided one morning—and without consulting anyone outside the United States—that the price of gold had risen high enough. A decade or so later, at Bretton Woods, the United States had decided that, in an orderly postwar world, this domination of the market would need the assent of the other governments. By joining together to set up the Fund and proclaim its rules, these other governments made the official dollar-gold price of $35 an ounce an international official edict and pledged their help to keep the black market in gold local and innocuous. The decision to organize the Gold Pool in 1961 was another step backward, in the sense that it acknowledged that the price of gold could no longer be held *only* by collective official edict. Active market intervention was necessary. In 1968 this too proved insufficient, and by the two-tier arrangement official transactions in gold were taken out of the market altogether. In 1971, when the dollar became totally inconvertible, the separation of the dollar from the gold market was complete.

Another difficult set of questions raised by the episode is why the two-tier arrangement proved so much more durable than many observers at the time expected. In the months that followed March 1968 a good many dire predictions were heard that it would break down the moment too large a gap appeared between the official gold price and the market price. They proved unfounded. Why? Was it that the separation of the official and the private market eliminated from the latter (at least in part) the destabilizing influence of official gold dealers? Or was the arrangement workable only because it effectively coincided with virtual non-convertibility of the dollar? Or did it reflect a restabilized balance of power—reflected at almost the same time in Stockholm by the SDR agreement between the United States and Europe in their exercise of political power over the management of the international monetary system? Perhaps no firm answers can be given. But the questions do emphasize the point that when the arrangement was made, it was something of a shot in the dark: the monetary authorities were not at the time quite sure what would happen next, or how the money and gold markets and the international economy generally would react.

It may first be helpful to recap the workings of the Gold Pool in the market in the years from 1962 onwards.

The Gold Pool and the market in the mid-60s

From 1962 until the middle of 1966 the Gold Pool arrangement instituted in 1961 proved remarkably successful. It will be recalled that under the Pool arrangement, the Bank of England acted as manager of an international buffer stock, fed by the central banks of the United States, Germany, France, Italy, Britain, Switzerland, Belgium, and the Netherlands, and used to stabilize prices in the London market. Because this was the largest international market, it dominated all others and it was unnecessary to use the Gold Pool to intervene elsewhere.

This success was more than a little due to good luck; the market itself kept rather well balanced at around the official gold price; supplies were steady and demand was moderate. A timely touch on the tiller was all that was needed for most of the time. The Pool's best years were 1963 and 1964. The Soviet Union sold heavily and so, it was thought, did some of the private holders who had bought gold in 1962. Confidence and overall stability were such that the assassination of President Kennedy in November 1963 caused hardly a tremor. Throughout that year the London price fluctuated by only 3 or 4 cents either side of $35·08 per ounce. This stability continued for most of 1964. For the first nine months the price stayed below $35·08, and even the pressure on sterling in the autumn brought it up (for the first time since March 1963) to only $35·10. Consequently, in both 1963 and 1964, the Bank of England managed to buy more gold in the market than it had to sell to maintain the price. The net gain to the Pool in 1963 was $600m, duly shared out between the participating central banks in proportion to their agreed contribution. Another $600m was gained in 1964. In both these years the Pool was serving the two main purposes sought by the participants. It was keeping the market price steady at the official price and it was also helping (by eliminating competitive bidding among central banks) to put more gold into official reserves.[22]

By 1965 the market was already, as the operators say, on the turn and the Pool was only saved from running into trouble by the Russians. During that year, gold sales by the Soviet Union reached the 1963 record of $550m. As Fred Hirsch observes:

Without the Russian sales of the mid-1960s, which were needed to pay for huge imports of North American grain to make up for the calamitous failure of Khrushchev's agricultural policy, gold reserves in Western official hands would have actually fallen. And on at least two occasions (autumn 1963 and again two years later) the prospect of these sales came at a critical time when private gold speculation might otherwise have burst out of control.[23]

In fact, thanks to the uneven global distribution of workable gold-fields, the domestic affairs and the political and economic management of the two major producers (the Soviet Union and South Africa) were always important underlying factors in any gold market situation. The supply situation would have become more quickly acute in the middle 1960s if the virgin lands had been as productive as Khrushchev had dreamed. It would also have become acute if the African revolution, predicted after Sharpeville, had actually broken out. As it was, South African gold production continued uninterrupted and the sale of gold abroad continued to be an important element in the country's balance of payments. Talk of a Commonwealth boycott came to nothing and the Rhodesian declaration of independence in November 1965 led to no open break between South Africa and the market in London. The parts played by both Russia and South Africa in feeding the market for new gold were determined at least as much by domestic political as by economic factors.

As always before, the other political factor capable of exerting a destabilizing influence on the market was the fear of war, revolution and political and social breakdown. Some staunching of the steady leak of illegal gold, eastward via the Persian Gulf and westward via Macao, into Asia might have followed if the Americans had accepted the North Vietnamese peace talks proposals in the mid-1960s and if, instead of escalating, the Vietnam war had ended. The first proposal made through U Thant to Adlai Stevenson (then US Ambassador at the UN) in the autumn of 1964, was for secret talks to be held in Rangoon. A second offer was made through Couve de Murville in Paris in May 1965. Both were at first denied by the State Department and both were rejected.[24] But as it was, the Vietnam situation, abetted by the continuing sterling situation, and the General's flamboyant press conference in February 1965 extolling the merits of gold over the gold exchange standard (see p. 285), all greatly encouraged private demand. The BIS estimated that this increased in 1965 by as much as $600m.[25] Because new gold supplies worth $2,000m came on the market, however, prices still kept within the $35·10 to $35·18 range and the Pool was even able to make a small net gain in gold purchases.[26]

This situation changed in 1966, and especially after July 1966 when demand sharpened just as new supplies dried up. For the first time since 1952, the Russians found it unnecessary in 1966 to sell gold in the world market. Western production also stopped rising, and for the first time since the war, *all* newly-mined gold went into private hands and, far from being able to add to their official reserves, the

Western central banks in the Gold Pool had to feed it with $95m in gold to keep the price down. Even so, in the second half of 1966, the price was never brought below $35·15 an ounce.

The next year, 1967, was even worse. The price in the London market repeatedly edged dangerously close to the top limit of $35·20 and after May 1967 seldom dropped far below it.[27] New production of gold was actually falling for the first time since 1953, while the private market (i.e. for non-monetary gold) was by now taking twice as much as in the mid-1950s. The June War in the Middle East certainly helped to quicken the rush into gold, but the market had much deeper-seated reasons for uneasiness. The first signs of dollar inconvertibility appeared in March 1967 when the Bundesbank, acceding to pressure from the United States, agreed as part of a deal on military support costs to present no more dollars accumulated in the German reserves for conversion into gold. Between 1 June and 21 November 1967, fourteen extensions were made to the Gold Pool arrangement, each of $50m.[28] The management of the market was getting difficult enough even before the sterling devaluation of 18 November. In the next month, between 17 November and 19 December, 660 tons worth $740m, changed hands in the London market and the Federal Reserve alone sold $1,000m from its gold reserves.

The French ' offensive '

Before continuing the account of events in the market, it would perhaps be as well to take a closer look at the part so far played in the story by French monetary diplomacy. Enough has already been said to make clear that the factors affecting market trends were complex and numerous. It seems most improbable, therefore, that market instability on the scale experienced in late 1967 and again in the spring of 1968 could possibly have been produced by the unaided efforts of any single government, however powerful or determined. Even so, several questions remain to be answered.

  i. Just how important a destabilizing agent was French policy, in deeds and in words?

 ii. What was the objective, precisely, of French intransigence in the gold question? Could this objective have been pursued any more relentlessly and ruthlessly than in fact it was?

iii. How much was this policy a personal decision of the General's? Or how much was it a continuation of traditional French attitudes?

 iv. What stopped the other European countries from supporting France in this offensive and on what points did they differ from the French?

One thing is very plain. The penchant in French policy towards gold as a necessary foundation of the international monetary system was of long standing, going back as far as the post-Revolution monetary policies of Napoleon. It had been very apparent in the unsettled period of the 1920s.[29] Nor had this penchant been dropped even when France's own gold holdings were at their lowest ebb towards the end of World War II. At Bretton Woods, for example, although it was never seriously discussed by the conference, there had also been a French Plan. Consistent with prewar French monetary diplomacy, this had expressed a firm preference for a gold-based system. The plan itself proposed a wider extension of the Tripartite Agreement of 1936 (see above, p. 54) and the equal acceptance of obligations to provide collateral against central bank holdings of foreign currency and to sterilize the inflow of foreign funds. More than that, however, it made a point of rejecting the idea of an artificial substitute for gold in settlement of international payments. ' Gold . . . has not ceased to be of valuable service for the settlement of balances of payment between countries. . . . The value of gold has thus become similar to the value of a fiduciary currency. . . Gold is the international currency of the future.' [30]

In the 1950s the attachment to gold had not been opposed by the Americans when the rules were drawn up for the EPU. In this the obligation to settle monthly accounts in gold increased with the size of the members' deficit in relation to its allotted tranche.

It was therefore perfectly consistent with established French attitudes that when, following the 1958 devaluation, French payments surpluses began to accumulate in the 1960s, they should seek to have them settled at least in part in gold. At the end of 1963, in fact, the Banque de France had begun to convert its dollar holdings so as to increase the gold reserves by 30 tons a month. A little over a year later, in January 1965, it announced that it would not only continue to do this but was immediately converting $150m and automatically would seek to convert any new accumulations of dollars. The action had thus begun well before the declaration of policy in the General's famous press conference on 14 February 1965. Moreover, as Triffin observed, France was by no means alone in presenting the United States with dollars for conversion to gold at this time. ' While France was widely denounced as the main culprit in this respect, its gold conversions [in the first half of 1965] accounted for less than one half of the total and its foreign exchange switches for little more than a third.' [31]

The press conference itself is mostly remembered for the General's eulogy of gold as an incorruptible standard of value. It is this which is most often quoted—usually by scoffing economists.

Nous tenons donc pour nécessaire que les échanges internationaux s'établissent, comme c'était le cas avant les grands malheurs du monde, sur une base monétaire indiscutable et qui ne porte la marque d'aucun pays en particulier.

Quelle base? En verité, on ne voit pas qu'à cet égard il puisse y avoir de critère, d'étalon autre que de l'or. Eh! oui, l'or, qui ne change pas de nature, qui se met, indifféremment, en barres, en lingots ou en pièces, qui n'a pas de nationalité, qui est tenu, éternellement et universellement, comme la valeur inaltérable et fiduciaire par excellence.

But the complete text was a broad statement of French objections to the dollar exchange standard which had developed since the first world war and the Genoa conference of 1922, and of the General's conviction that sooner or later the inconveniences involved in it would require the restoration of a better economic and political balance between Europe and America. All this led up to a carefully argued plea for negotiations on the long-term reform of the international monetary system—negotiations which the Group of Ten finally agreed to initiate at the Smithsonian meeting more than six years later (see below, p. 344). The argument closely reflected the views of Jacques Rueff, the veteran French economist, who had held and expounded these opinions for years—indeed had changed very few of his ideas about the role of reserve currencies since his official service in London in 1928. By his own account,[32] Rueff had managed by about mid-1964 to gain the ear of the General—already strongly disposed since the Nassau Agreement of 1962 on Polaris missiles to deplore certain aspects of US leadership in the world—with this new monetary stick with which to belabour Washington.

It is worth emphasizing though that while 1965 saw a sharp reversal of the French position on reserve asset creation (see below, ch. 11), on other matters concerning international monetary relations there was no sudden or violent change. It was not until the following year in fact that de Gaulle replaced Giscard d'Estaing as Finance Minister with Michel Debré, who was diplomatically more abrasive but personally more compliant. About this time too, the influence of the Quai d'Orsay was reduced by the dissolution of the foreign economic policy department, the Direction des Affaires Economiques. De Gaulle's personal contact with monetary diplomacy was further strengthened by the appointment of a financial adviser, M. Buron des Roziers, at the Elysée Palace, and incidentally by the delegation of discussions to the deputies of the Group of Ten. But though from 1965 onwards French criticism of both reserve currency countries, of Britain as well as of the United States, became sharper and more outspoken, it was not till more than two and a quarter years after February 1965 that France withdrew its support from the Gold

Pool—and even then did so in discreet secrecy. The policy may therefore justly be accused of not striving too officiously to keep the dollar-gold price alive. There is no evidence that the French government manipulated the market to bring about its downfall.

As to the belief that the international use of the dollar, and confidence in the security and stable value of dollar-denominated assets, were due at least in part to the dollar's unique relationship to gold, this was an opinion much more widely and deeply held in Europe than many Americans were ever prepared to admit. The rationale of this point of view had perhaps been most clearly and succinctly put many years earlier by one of the most famous of Europe's prewar central bankers and one whose shrewdness and technical brilliance were as generally acknowledged as his political associations were deplored.

'Governments,' Hjalmar Schacht had written in his old age in 1950,

are powerless against the influence of gold upon commerce and trade ... There are many currencies in this world, and in each country the man-in-the-street is calculating in his own currency. But world commerce is calculating exclusively in those currencies whose relation to gold has been stabilized and maintained. Today that currency is above all the American gold dollar. Whatever currencies are offered for goods in world trade, all are measured in terms of the dollar because it is essential currency possessing a firm gold parity ... We think in terms of gold whether we want to or not.[33]

Few Americans, perhaps, fully appreciated how closely linked the long economic history of Europe had been with gold—how the Dark Ages had coincided with the virtual disappearance of gold coins from Western Europe; how the renascence of European trade and the birth of international banking had concided with their reintroduction as florins and as ducats; how deeply European economic life had been affected by the influx of Spanish gold and silver; and how the general use of sterling and confidence in it had lasted just as long as its gold price had been held stable, while *assignats* and other currencies arbitrarily managed by governments had quickly been discredited.

In this long and often ill-articulated argument, each side charged the other with the heresy of fetishism. 'Is it possible,' asked Rueff on one side,

that the government and people of a great country, more conscious than any other of its responsibilities, national and international, which has assumed with such incomparable courage the duties imposed by its power and wealth, should pigheadedly expose the whole world to the burdens of another great depression, just because of its single desire to maintain with childish blindness the outdated fetish of a gold price arbitrarily fixed in 1934 in conditions utterly different from those of today?[34]

On the contrary, said most American economists, it was gold itself which was the fetish. As one of them put it, 'There is a mystique about gold deeply rooted in the human psyche; but there is no longer any rational argument for tying money to gold.' In this view it was the false, superstitious and tyrannical 'discipline' of gold that now threatened the security of the United States and it was the 'hegemony of gold in the field of international finance which, by instilling the fear that one may have to endure this type of discipline, forces mercantilist-type policies upon national governments '.[35]

The synthesis of the two points of view, as elegantly and concisely attempted by Robert Triffin, perhaps helps to explain both the official American reluctance to close the gold window or to dissipate the US gold reserves and the French and European concern, notwithstanding their doubts about the dollar, not to rock the general boat by actually abetting the gold speculators.

'The vulnerability of the key currencies to the functioning of the gold exchange standard ', Triffin had written at the beginning of the decade, 'is paralleled by a reverse vulnerability of the gold exchange standard itself to the fate of the key currencies upon which it rests.' [36]

By the winter of 1967–8 it was the vulnerability of the key currencies to the functioning of the gold exchange standard that was the root of the trouble. It was true that the onset of the crisis was hastened by the precarious balance of a private market in gold which could too easily be tipped into disequilibrium by the intervention of speculators and hoarders expressing their lack of confidence in the key currencies. And it is possible that the failure of confidence was exacerbated by the revelation (by Paul Fabra in *Le Monde* of 21 November 1967) that France had, the previous June, opted out of the Gold Pool arrangement.[37]

Secretary Fowler was thought by the market to be right, if unwise, when he remarked a few days after the sterling devaluation that the dollar was now 'in the front line '. Britain's deficit on the balance of payments in 1967 turned out to have been £637m—more than £200m worse than the two earlier crisis years, 1960 and 1964. And Britain had been forced in the end to devalue. By that time it was suspected that the United States also was going deeper than ever into deficit. And moreover that no new and more sophisticated method of calculating the overall payments picture would alter the fact.[38]

The Frankfurt meeting

On 26 November 1967, only eight days after the announcement of sterling's forced devaluation, the US Secretary of the Treasury called an emergency meeting of the remaining active members of the Gold

Pool. With the collaboration of the German Bundesbank, the meeting was arranged secretly at a hotel outside Frankfurt, presumably in the hope that this would attract less attention than a meeting in Washington, Paris, or London. Several measures to ease market pressure on the dollar were agreed, but not made public until later. According to the account given the following spring by the Federal Reserve Bank, these included a massive expansion of the Federal Reserve swap network and a ' co-ordinated launching of central bank operations in the forward market to induce reflows into the Eurodollar market '.[39] It was apparently also at the Frankfurt meeting that the finance ministers agreed to try and discourage the development of an active forward market in gold and to ' impede ' official gold purchases.[40]

These moves calmed the situation only briefly. In December frantic buying began again in the market. The acute anxiety of the US Treasury was revealed by the widely-publicized visit of Frederick Deming, Under Secretary of the Treasury, to Basle for one of the regular BIS meetings. This was most unusual as normally only central bankers attend, and was described in one report as a ' dramatic intrusion '.[41] The visit took place amid rumours (first published in *Le Monde* on 9 December) that the US was trying to persuade its Gold Pool colleagues to strengthen co-operation by depositing their gold with the US Treasury, presumably accepting gold certificates in its place. Deming denied this, but said that the Gold Pool countries had ' agreed upon an even closer coordination ' of their efforts to control the market.[42] However, anxieties were not allayed; the meeting at Basle failed to issue any communiqué and a subsequent statement a few days later on 16 December from the Federal Reserve Bank and the US Treasury failed to reassure the speculators. This statement contained another assurance that the price of gold would remain at $35, and said that no changes were to be made in the operation of the London market. But it still failed to give details of the measures said to have been agreed at Basle. Nor did it indicate that the administration was planning a big new attack on the problem of the US deficit.

The details of this massive balance-of-payments programme were announced by the President after Christmas. As if turning over a new leaf on New Year's day, President Johnson announced a long list of measures which, though in the event they turned out to be largely ineffective, at the time looked remarkably draconian. Seemingly very large cuts on American foreign investment were to be imposed. There was to be no more US investment in Western Europe; investment in Britain, Australia, Canada, Japan, and some of the oil states was to be cut to 65 per cent of 1965–6 levels and investment in any developing country was to be allowed only a 10 per cent maximum increase on 1965–6. Efforts would be made to reduce the foreign exchange costs of American military spending abroad. More credit and encouragement would be given to promote US exports. Restrictions on foreign lending by American banks and other financial institutions introduced in 1965 would be further tightened. Even American tourists were to be asked to defer for two years all non-essential trips outside the Western hemisphere.[43] On 17 January, in the State of the Union message,[44] the President announced that he would ask Congress to abolish the legal requirement which called for a gold backing for the American domestic currency issue. This would release another $10 billion of gold for the defence of the dollar and of the dollar-gold price if necessary.

The resultant calm lasted only till nearly the end of February, when the balance-of-payments figures for the year 1967 were announced revealing a payments deficit of $3·6 billion with a particularly rapid deterioration visible in the fourth quarter. This, together with a request from General Westmorland for yet more US troops to be sent to Vietnam, set off a new wave of gold market speculation. (At this time the conviction widely prevailed in the United States that the deficit on the balance of payments was very largely due to military spending in Vietnam and that it would disappear if and when the war came to an end.) Early in March speculation was further encouraged by the suggestion from Senator Javits of New York that the United States should ' close the gold window '.[45] The next day, on 10 March, the central bankers meeting at Basle issued another statement reaffirming the $35 gold price, but to no avail: the rush continued unabated, and the next four days saw a crescendo of speculative demand and private purchases totalling $850m. On 12 March the United States released $450m from its Fort Knox reserves to support the Gold Pool. Given only two more such shipments, the gold reserves of the United States would have fallen below the figure of $10 billion. This was not just a magical, totem figure; it was until 12 March the statutory gold backing for Federal Reserve notes. On that day the US Senate, after a long delay, had finally agreed to abolish this requirement. Thereafter the $10 billion minimum gold stock was available to meet the US international commitments to convert dollars accumulated by foreign central banks into gold.

On Thursday, 14 March, the private demand at $200m showed no sign of flagging. In Paris it was rumoured that other central banks might be following France in opting out of the Gold Pool arrangements. At the end of the day President Johnson appealed directly to Harold Wilson to close the London gold market while international consultations were conducted to decide what should be done. This the Wilson government—caught in the midst of a cabinet crisis which ended in George Brown's resignation—agreed to do even though it involved proclaiming an emergency bank holiday. The closure was made on condition that the Americans supported sterling on the New York foreign exchange market which would be staying open. After some delay, the Americans agreed to this.[46] In haste therefore the Governors of central banks involved in the Gold Pool (Germany, Britain, Italy, Belgium, the Netherlands, and Switzerland) and their finance ministers and officials were summoned to a weekend meeting in Washington.

Policy options

Caught by the pressures of the market, the US authorities (with whom the initiative clearly lay) were faced with several possible policy options.

First, they could hold the price but continue to lose gold and to operate the gold exchange standard by exchanging on demand any surplus dollars accumulated by other countries for gold drawn from the US gold reserves. Holding the gold price—given the mood of the market at the time—would certainly require heavy and continued intervention. And if other countries seemed inclined to follow France out of the commitment to help operate the collective buffer stock, the United States would either have to offer them extra inducements to do so or else be prepared in the last resort to feed the Pool alone, thus increasing the probable drain on the US gold reserves.

The prospect of such substantial gold losses, however, was one which no American administration was likely to find acceptable. No matter what academic economists might think, large and politically influential sections of American public opinion remained strongly convinced of the virtues of providing the currency with a substantial gold backing. The $10 billion figure was widely regarded in the United States as a dangerous low watermark, any lower figure being thought to be inconsistent with national security. As one American economist put it: ' The preference for gold basically reflects the deeply anchored views of those responsible for a nation's monetary reserves that there are times and circumstances where no other money will do '.[47]

The second main option was to give in to the pressure of the market and raise—perhaps even double—the official dollar price of gold. This would certainly end the market's speculative fever. But there were several serious objections to such a course—not least the humiliation of accepting defeat at the hands of the speculators. Every private buyer of gold in the market which the Gold Pool had so expensively fed with subsidies would reap an unearned reward and every central bank would feel its authority as a market manager seriously impaired. Among governments, the chief beneficiaries of such a policy choice would be the gold-producing states, especially the Republic of South Africa and the Soviet Union. It was true that their consequent capability in monetary and economic diplomacy might not be so substantially changed by the value added to an important export. Yet any United States administration (and especially a Democratic one) was highly conscious of the political risks involved in simultaneously alienating support from the black left and the white right. For once, the monetary managers and the party managers were likely to see eye to eye politically. Moreover, increasing the gold price would most likely be ill received by those closest associates of the United States— especially Canada, Germany, and Japan—who had helpfully agreed to hold dollars and not to ask for gold. They would find that their loyalty to the United States had left them a great deal less well off in the purchasing power of their monetary reserves, compared with such heavy gold holders as France and Italy.

The third possible option was to ' come off ' gold, to ' close the gold window '—in other words, unilaterally to announce that dollars were no longer freely convertible into gold at any price. This too would represent in some measure a capitulation to the forces of the market and moreover would most probably exacerbate the failing confidence in the value of the dollar felt by public and private holders alike. It would seem difficult to hold the market price unchanged and to close the gold window.

A possible alternative, but a risky one, would have been to try taking the heat off the gold market by allowing some realignment of par values in respect of other currencies—in other words, to devalue the dollar not in terms of gold necessarily but in terms of other currencies, as was eventually done in December 1971. The Americans, however, could not but be aware of the dangers of attempting to do this in a hurry and in a crisis situation. They were afraid that if they tried devaluing the dollar, others would simply ' follow the dollar down ', thus leading to a profitless game of competitive currency depreciation. To avoid this the Americans would have to prepare a broad strategy that would effectively force others to revalue their currencies and allow them to do so unequally in response to the dictates of the market. It was also by no means certain that such appeal to the verdict of the market on exchange rates would necessarily and entirely remove the speculative pressure on the gold market.

On balance, therefore, rejecting the first and second options and finding the last-mentioned option of currency realignment unduly risky, at least in the short term—though increasingly attractive in the longer term—left the final compromise alternative of maintaining the official dollar-gold price unchanged for official transactions while allowing the private dollar-gold price to float. Calling this a two-tier arrangement would also have the political advantage of distracting attention from the fact that the dollar would henceforth become virtually inconvertible and official gold holdings more or less petrified in their respective positions.

An ancillary political consideration recommending this course of action was that it would weaken French opposition at the final and forthcoming Stockholm discussions on the SDR scheme. If the gold window was already closed and all official dollars were inconvertible, the French threat not to accept SDRs as a substitute for gold (which could have been quite dangerous if gold were still being used in international monetary transactions) would seem rather empty all of a sudden. And in fact, since SDRs would have a gold guarantee, would make little sense in terms of French national interest.

Altogether, this was the policy option which seemed mainly on political grounds to have most to recommend it.[48]

The Two-Tier Agreement

The communiqué [49] finally issued in Washington on Sunday evening, 17 March 1968, is worth quoting in full to show its overriding concern to maintain the confidence of the market in the continued stability of the system even though some of the rules for its conduct had been revised. Its first concern seemed to be to reassure everyone that nothing important had changed, that no really serious step had been taken, and to present the collective decision as more technical than political. In particular, the fourth paragraph pronouncing the continued willingness of the United States to buy and sell official gold at $35 an ounce could be called in retrospect definitely misleading.

The Governors of the Central Banks of Belgium, Germany, Italy, the Netherlands, Switzerland, the United Kingdom and the United States met in Washington on March 16 and 17, 1968 to examine operations of the gold pool, to which they are active contributors. The Managing Director of the International Monetary Fund and the General Manager of the Bank for International Settlements also attended the meeting.

The Governors noted that it is the determined policy of the United States Government to defend the value of the dollar through appropriate fiscal and monetary measures and that substantial improvement of the US balance of payments is a high priority objective.

They also noted that legislation approved by Congress makes the whole of the gold stock of the nation available for defending the value of the dollar.

They noted that the US Government will continue to buy and sell gold at the existing price of $35 an ounce in transactions with monetary authorities. The Governors support this policy and believe it contributes to the maintenance of exchange stability.

The Governors noted the determination of the UK authorities to do all that is necessary to eliminate the deficit in the UK balance of payments as soon as possible and to move to a position of large and sustained surplus.

Finally, they noted that the Governments of most European countries intend to pursue monetary and fiscal policies that encourage domestic expansion consistent with economic stability, avoid as far as possible increases in interest rates or a tightening of money markets, and thus contribute to conditions that will help all countries move toward payments equilibrium.

The Governors agreed to cooperate fully to maintain the existing parities as well as orderly conditions in their exchange markets in accordance with their obligations under the Articles of Agreement of the International Monetary Fund. The Governors believe that henceforth officially-held gold should be used only to effect transfers among monetary authorities, and, therefore, they decided no longer to supply gold to the London gold market or any other gold market. Moreover, as the existing stock of monetary gold is sufficient in view of the prospective establishment of the facility for Special Drawing Rights, they no longer feel it necessary to buy the gold from the market. Finally, they agreed that henceforth they will not sell gold to monetary authorities to replace gold sold in private markets.

The Governors agreed to cooperate even more closely than in the past to minimize flows of funds contributing to instability in the exchange markets, and to offset as necessary any such flows that may arise.

In view of the importance of the pound sterling in the international monetary system the Governors have agreed to provide further facilities which will bring the total of credits immediately available to the UK authorities (including the IMF standby) to $4 billion.

The Governors invite the cooperation of other central banks in the policies set forth above.

Clearly there lurked some important ambiguities behind the text of this communiqué. For example, the statement that the existing stock of monetary gold was 'sufficient' left it unclear in what sense it was sufficient. And although it was stated that it was no longer 'necessary' to buy gold from the market, it did not say it was not desirable.

The communiqué also made some large unstated assumptions. One was that there was nothing basically wrong with the distribution of gold reserves among the countries in the international economy. Those countries which had little or no gold did not, it assumed, need any. Those that wanted more, were not going to find it easy to come by.

Secondly, it was assumed that with the introduction of SDRs in the fairly near future, there would be enough liquidity to finance world trade. Most of the liquidity debate had been conducted in terms of 'trend liquidity'. It was the growing volume of trade which had been treated as the major determinant of the world's liquidity needs, ignoring the fact that payments imbalances were often due to panic-stricken movements of capital at times of financial crisis. The amount of 'crisis liquidity' that might be needed to preserve the system had not been taken into consideration.

Thirdly, it was assumed that there would be no major changes in the supply and demand conditions for gold. This was also rather doubtful, since in 1968 for the first time, the consumption of fabricated gold equalled annual production.[50]

The communiqué invited the 'cooperation of other central banks' in the policies it set forth and much clearly depended on whether this would be forthcoming. This co-operation was solicited by the Americans in particular for their interpretation of a point not specifically made in the communiqué. This was that central banks would not seek to add gold to their reserves by buying newly-mined gold from South Africa, the source at that time of 75 per cent of Western supplies. This became a vital point in the dispute that was to follow (see below, ch. 10) but in the weeks following the Two-Tier Agreement the United States claimed to have got support from as many as sixty central banks. The only central banks actually known to have refused to observe it were Portugal, Algeria, and Congo (Kinshasa).[51]

The new system was vulnerable at several points. First, it was not known what would happen on the private market. One technical change may have had some importance: from April 1968 forward operations in gold in the London market could take place only with prior permission from the Bank of England. Previously, although there had been no organized or regular market for forward dealing, and it had been discouraged by the central banks, it had in fact taken place, often for large amounts.[52]

During 1968 and 1969 a major attempt to supersede London as the major gold market was made by Zurich bankers. Three of the big Swiss banks set up a pool type operation, with a daily fixing. During 1969 South Africa sold substantially via Zurich rather than London and the daily turnover almost tripled.

How this private 'free' market would develop was obviously a matter of guesswork. So was the behaviour of the speculators. The previous November they had ceased to believe the statements put out by the central bankers that the price would remain at $35 per ounce. The expectation of a rise had in some sense been fulfilled by the separation of the two markets—and they expected that the price in the free market would rise to a substantial premium over the official price, which would make the system still more unstable. The root of the problem remained the US deficit and it remained to be seen whether President Johnson's New Year programme would be effective.

Secondly, there was the question of the behaviour of the central banks. If those countries which had accepted the Two-Tier Agreement maintained their solidarity, so the official thinking went, the speculators could be beaten and the United States would win its battle to keep the dollar price of gold at $35. But the danger was that the price of gold on the free market would rise temptingly high and some banks might succumb to the temptation to sell their reserves of gold on the free market, making a considerable profit compared with what they could get by selling gold to other monetary authorities.

Once again, in short, the United States had made an arrangement to deal with the gold market which depended particularly on the co-operation and solidarity of the members of the affluent alliance. It gradually became clear from the immobility of gold movements between official monetary authorities that behind the formal communiqué lay an unwritten 'gentlemen's agreement' of considerable complexity, and based on assumptions which might not turn out to be well founded. If the US deficit proved resistant to the package of measures announced by President Johnson earlier in 1968; if large amounts of surplus dollars accumulated once more in European and Japanese hands; if the gold market or the foreign exchange market once again showed a failure of confidence in the arrangements made by governments; and if those countries which had not been consulted and were not bound by the Washington agreement proved able to disrupt it, then this would not prove to be the end of the gold story.

World gold production, 1940–70 ($m) [1]

	1940	1950	1960	1970
South Africa	492	408	748	1,128
Canada	186	156	162	82
USA	170	80	59	63
Australia	57	30	38	22
Ghana	31	24	31	25
Rhodesia	29	18	20	18e
Japan	30	5	12	25
Philippines	39	12	14	21
Colombia	22	13	15	7
Mexico	31	14	11	7
Congo	20	12	11	6
Other	157	74	57	46
TOTAL	1,264	846	1,178	1,450

[1] Excluding Sino-Soviet countries.
e = estimated.
Source : IMF.

Gold holdings, 1960–70 ($m)

	1960	1961	1962	1963	1964	1965	1966	1967	1968	1969	1970
USA	17,804	16,947	16,057	15,596	15,471	14,065	13,235	12,065	10,892	11,889	11,072
UK	2,801	2,267	2,581	2,484	2,136	2,265	1,940	1,291	1,474	1,471	1,349
France	1,641	2,121	2,587	3,175	3,729	4,706	5,238	5,234	3,877	3,547	3,532
Germany	2,971	3,664	3,699	3,843	4,248	4,410	4,292	4,228	4,539	4,079	3,980
Industrial Europe (excl. the above)	7,617	8,242	8,601	8,982	8,889	8,769	9,546	9,715	9,851	9,899	9,883
Canada	885	946	708	817	1,026	1,151	1,046	1,015	863	872	791
Japan	247	287	289	289	304	328	329	338	356	413	532
LDCs	2,905	2,660	2,740	2,750	2,715	2,705	2,565	2,895	3,430	3,455	3,290
Total world holdings	38,030	38,860	39,275	40,225	40,840	41,855	40,910	39,505	38,940	39,125	37,185

Source: IMF, *International Financial Statistics.*

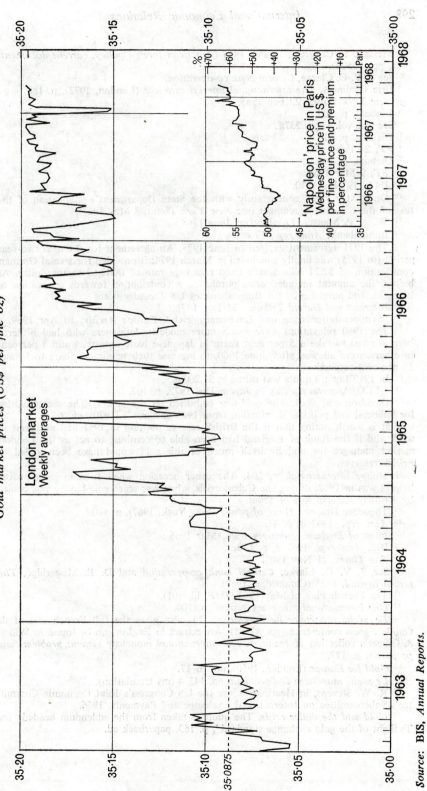

Gold market prices (US$ per fine oz)

London market
Weekly averages

'Napoleon' price in Paris
Wednesday price in US $
per fine ounce and premium
in percentage

Source: **BIS,** *Annual Reports.*

[1] Message to Congress, 10 Feb 1965 (*American foreign policy, current documents 1965*, pp. 1050ff).

[2] See S. V. O. Clarke, *Central bank co-operation.*

[3] Eric Chalmers, *The international interest rate war* (London, 1972), p. 188.

[4] *New York Times*, 22 Feb 1965.

[5] Diebold, p. 105.

[6] See also vol. 1, pp. 237ff.

[7] Diebold, p. 91.

[8] *FT*, 28 Feb 1967.

[9] Diebold, p. 106.

[10] *FT*, 9 Mar 1968.

[11] Ibid., 19 Nov 1970.

[12] On 2 May 1967, concurrently with the State Department's publication of the text of the tripartite agreement (see *New York Times*, 3 May 1967).

[13] W. A. P. Manser, *The Banker*, June 1968.

[14] Bundesbank, *Ann. rep.*, 1968.

[15] The 1971 agreement expired in June 1973. An agreement for the next two-year period (to 1975) was finally concluded in March 1974; it provided for a total German contribution of $2.24 billion at a fixed exchange rate of DM2.69 to the dollar. As before, the amount included arms purchases, a contribution towards renovation of barracks, and purchase by the Bundesbank of US Treasury notes.

[16] *International Herald Tribune*, 11 Dec 1971.

[17] 'Truppenstationerung und Devisenausgleich', *Europa Archiv*, 10 Apr 1969.

[18] The 1960 relaxations were much more modest: foreigners who had hitherto been allowed to take a 5 per cent share in Japanese basic industries and 8 per cent in others, were allowed after June 1960, to increase their maximum share to 10 and 15 per cent respectively.

[19] In 1969 Japan's quota was raised to $1,200m.

[20] OECD, *Monetary policy in Japan*, Dec 1972, p. 105.

[21] Davidson and Weil, *The gold war* (subtitled on the jacket 'The secret battles for financial and political domination from 1945 onwards') (1970), ch. 6.

[22] It is worth noting that if the British reserve position in 1961 had not been so weak and if the Bank of England had been able to continue to act as the London market manager for and by itself much of this gold would have been added to *British* reserves.

[23] *Money international*, p. 204. The other occasion when Russian sales proved helpful was in 1962, during the Cuban crisis, when war scare gold-buying was cooled by a timely Russian sale of $50m.

[24] Theodore Draper, *Abuse of power* (New York, 1967), p. 170.

[25] *Ann. rep.*, 1967–8, p. 41.

[26] *Bank of England Quarterly Bull.*, Mar 1966.

[27] BIS, *Ann. rep.*, 1967–8, p. 110.

[28] *The Times*, 21 Nov 1967.

[29] See S. V. O. Clarke, *Central bank co-operation* and D. E. Moggridge, *The return to gold, 1925* (Cambridge, 1969).

[30] The French Plan of May 1943 (*IMF*, iii. 101).

[31] *Our international monetary system*, p. 100.

[32] *Le péché monétaire de l'occident*. This also gives the full French text of de Gaulle's press conference (pp. 87–95). An extract in English can be found in Willett & Officer's collection of readings, *The international monetary system: problems and proposals*, p. 177.

[33] *Gold for Europe* (London, 1950), pp. 16–17.

[34] *Le péché monétaire de l'occident*, pp. 143–4 (my translation).

[35] R. W. Stevens, in Hearings before the US Congress's Joint Economic Committee's Subcommittee on International Exchange and Payments, 1966.

[36] *Gold and the dollar crisis*. The quote is taken from the addendum headed 'the Twilight of the gold exchange standard', p. 163, paperback ed.

[37] Confirmed the same day by French officials and by Henry Fowler, US Secretary of the Treasury, who agreed that the US had taken over the French share in the pool (*International Herald Tribune*, 22 Nov 1967).

[38] See vol. 1, table, p. 423.

[39] *FRBNY Monthly Review*, Mar 1968.

[40] BIS, *Ann. rep.*, 1967–8, p. 38.

[41] *The Economist*, 16 Dec 1967.

[42] *New York Times*, 12 Dec 1967.

[43] Action Program on the balance of payments statement by President Johnson (CFR, *Documents on American foreign relations*, 1968–9, pp. 498ff).

[44] Ibid., pp. 1ff.

[45] *The Economist*, 9 Mar 1968.

[46] Lord George Brown, *In my way* (London, 1971); Harold Wilson, *The Labour government*, 1964–70 (London, 1971), pp. 507, 509.

[47] Miroslav Kriz, *Gold: babarous relic of useful instrument?* (Princeton, 1967). See also *The Economist*, 2 Dec 1967, ' Still as good as gold? '

[48] Most of the discussion on this question which gathered momentum from 1966 onwards and continued to the end of the decade and after was conducted in the United States among American economists. The arguments put forward in this debate clearly departed rather far from the purely technical and were often frankly political. There accumulated a rather extensive literature to which the most notable contributors were as follows: Robert Z. Aliber, *Choices for the dollar* (Washington, 1969); Henry Aubrey, *Behind the veil of international money* (Princeton, 1969); C. Kindleberger & others, ' The dollar and world liquidity: a minority view ', *The Economist*, 5 Feb 1966.

[49] *Dept of State Bull.*, Mar 1968.

[50] *FT*, 10 Feb 1969.

[51] See Davidson & Weil, p. 136.

[52] See also *Bank of England Quarterly Bull.*, Mar 1964, p. 17.

10

SOUTH AFRICA AGAINST THE OLIGARCHY: THE NEGOTIATION OF NEW RULES ON THE SALE OF GOLD

There were four countries which dissented markedly from the American-led majority view that $35 an ounce was the right official price for gold, and who might therefore have been expected to disrupt the Two-Tier Gold Agreement of March 1968. Two of these were the world's major gold producers, the Soviet Union and the Republic of South Africa. The other two were Switzerland, who had never been a party to the Gold Pool agreement, and France who had withdrawn nine months before its dissolution.

What is perhaps most worth remarking is that although all four were united in favouring an increase in the price of gold, there was never any effective political alliance between them. Nor, so far as can be seen, was there any collusion between them. It would seem a reasonable hypothesis that this absence of collusion was *not* due (as was sometimes popularly supposed) to the ideological differences—concerning either the role of the state or of private profit-making enterprise in the management of the national economy, or concerning the political rights of Africans—which divided them, so much as to the low priority that any one of them accorded the gold price compared with other objectives of national policy. For France and for South Africa (to whose national economic welfare the price of gold was of much the greatest saliency) the stability of the system, however good, bad, or indifferent, was in the end a more important milieu goal than a change in the price of gold. And even the Soviet Union in the late 1960s could no longer be sure that an epidemic economic depression in the capitalist world, whether followed or not by widespread revolution, would be to its own political advantage. Rather, it must have seemed in Moscow that the *tertius gaudens* in such a situation was more likely to be China, the least politically involved with the international economy of the two and the least economically dependent on it. Marxist and New Left literature offers singularly little guidance on this question. It can explain what it calls ' the imperialist network ', based on the position of the United States as the world banker and of the dollar as the world reserve currency, and secured by the military and economic dependence on America of the other Western countries. What it does not satisfactorily explain is the failure of the Soviet Union to seek to exploit what Magdoff, for example, calls the centrifugal forces in ' the imperialist network '.[1] By contrast, the Ottoman Empire in the Middle Ages had been much quicker to exploit the dissensions and conflicts of interest in European Christendom than has been the Soviet Union those of Western capitalism in the twentieth century.

It is possible that the abrupt cessation of Soviet sales on the gold market in 1966 was not entirely due to a better harvest and a less pressing need for foreign exchange, but that the Soviet government was persuaded to stop selling gold by General de Gaulle when he visited Moscow in June 1966—and that the General's persuasion was followed up by M. Georges Pompidou, the Prime Minister, when he too went there in July 1967.[2] However, no evidence for this has yet appeared, and Russian disinterest in taking advantage of other opportunities to disrupt world markets (as in sugar or tin, for instance) seems to suggest that the stoppage of sales had economic rather than political causes.[3]

Indeed, taking the gold story as a whole, it looks much more as though each of the three main dissentients paddled its own canoe. As explained in the previous chapter, France in the person of de Gaulle had pronounced a view in 1965 that sooner or later the gold exchange standard would have to be reformed and the gold basis of international monetary relations restored. But apart from restating this opinion from time to time and sometimes, as M. Debré did in early 1967, thereby giving, inadvertently or otherwise, a downward nudge to a nervous market, France took no overt action that was not taken by other members of the Gold Pool. It is true that from 1965 on, France converted most of its dollar reserves into gold (and de Gaulle even insisted that instead of remaining alongside other European gold holdings in the vaults of Liberty Street in New York they should be brought home to Paris). But some other European governments in a position to do so were also converting dollars into gold or gold-convertible IMF claims at the US Treasury, as was the United States' most dependent ally, Japan.[4] Nor did France cancel her original liability to the Gold Pool until the midsummer of 1967 when the Pool upped the ante and began steadily increasing the liability of the shareholders (see above, ch. 9).[5]

From 1965 to 1968 the whole French posture towards the United States was negative, critical, non-co-operative, and obstructive—but never actually destructive. The aim was to limit US power and influence, not to disrupt the Western world. The distinction is important. In political terms, France was playing an opposition role in the Atlantic community, not a subversive or revolutionary one. This was as true of the monetary strategy to reduce American dominance in that community as it was of the various other strategies directed to the same end. There was, it will be recalled, the military withdrawal of French forces from NATO, and the enforced *démenagement* of the NATO secretariat from Paris to Brussels. And there were the attempts to exploit Latin American and French Canadian discontent. In each of these, however, the punch was pulled short of the point where the Western political and economic system would be seriously damaged or jeopardized. With each successive strategy, too, there was little attempt to recruit an operative anti-American alliance.

Not only, therefore, would a deliberately planned Paris-Pretoria axis have been out of character for the General, but the timing of events did not allow it. The capacity of South Africa to obstruct US designs only began with the ending of the Gold Pool and the *de facto* closing of the US gold window. But by the time this had become apparent, in May and June 1968, the French student riots had started a leakage from French reserves that in a period of three months lost $659m from French gold reserves and a total of $2,066m in gold and foreign exchange. The same *événements* rather changed the ideas of the Banque de France about the gold situation. Bourgeois nightmares in the summer of 1968 had boosted French gold hoarding to an estimated $7,000m. In 1969, with Pompidou firmly established in the Elysée Palace, and the gold price up to $43 an ounce, there was a distinct possibility that some of the 1968 hoarders might change theirs minds and take a quick profit on their gold. The inflationary effects on the French economy, coming on top of other forces, could be serious. At a BIS meeting in March 1969, therefore, the Banque de France let it be known that the French government no longer believed that there should be a rise in the gold price.[6]

This announcement put an end to the possibility—if indeed it had ever existed—of a Paris-Pretoria axis. It looked, more than ever, as if the South Africans were, once more, on their own in international monetary diplomacy.

South Africa and the Fund, 1948

It will be recalled that an important part of the Washington Two-Tier Agreement had been the collective decision to buy no more newly mined gold from South Africa. The idea behind this was that the speculative demand for gold would eventually subside, since the speculators had been denied the possibility of a rise in the official price; the free price would then fall as current production coming on the market exceeded industrial and hoarding demand. In other words, by taking the official floor price away the market price would tend to be brought sharply downwards.[7] It was assumed that South Africa would be forced to sell its current production on the free market (providing always that the central banks continued to refrain from buying newly mined South African gold).

But a week after the London gold market reopened, South Africa announced, on 8 April 1968, that it would not, at least for the present, sell any gold to the private market. Its strong balance-of-payments position, the result of a record maize crop and capital inflows, made sales of current production unnecessary. Some of this gold would therefore be put in the reserves. The oligarchy's challenge was thus taken up and the United States—clearly the main influence behind the stiff posture of the Fund—and South Africa faced each other, like the protagonists in a Western gun battle, across the market-place. Much was at stake on both sides, and the main requirement was for cool nerves.

The South Africans were well aware that they had played out this ' High Noon ' confrontation with the Fund once before—and had won, and that the Fund's position on the earlier occasion had been the exact reverse (see above, pp. 69–70). In 1948 it was the Fund which was forbidding the South African government to sell its new gold at a premium price on the private European market, and South Africa which had pressed its luck so hard as to bring the Fund's Managing Director flying to Pretoria. The Fund's Executive Board had taken the view that those buyers who were prepared to offer in May 1949 South Africa $38·20 could not be ' legitimate '. South Africa had claimed that the Fund had no legal *locus standi* in the matter anyway since Article IV (2) of the Fund Agreement only prohibited members from *buying* gold *above* the official price (plus a gold margin of 0·25 per cent plus handling charges). And Article IV (2) only prohibited members from *selling* gold *below* the official price. No legal prohibition existed against *selling above* the price. On that occasion, South Africa had unquestionably won on points. The sale had gone through and the South African government had met the Fund's objections only by making it the face-saving offer to request affidavits and import licences from the premium buyers.[8]

Now the Fund had come round to the point of view argued in 1948 by France's Executive Director, M. de Largentaye: that the best way of preventing the private market from putting pressure on the official gold price was to feed it with new supplies. And it was South Africa, hoping that the breakdown of the Gold Pool policy of market intervention was the first sign in twenty years of a crack in the $35 price, which was protesting its anxiety to leave the private market to its own devices. The intention, obviously, was to force the price of the free market up by withholding supplies from it, to break the two-tier system by creating an intolerable difference between the official and the 'real' gold price, and thus to force the Americans to accept a higher price for gold—perhaps even a doubling of the price to $70 an ounce.

As compared with the earlier situation, there were a number of differences. First, the United States had lost some of its dominant position in the Fund. Second, the forces of the market, which in 1948 had been hedged with innumerable postwar restrictions and difficulties, by the late 1960s had become very much more powerful. Thirdly, South Africa, though it had achieved a great advance in economic development since the war, was politically more isolated. It was the target of a numerous and vociferous group of Afro-Asian countries in the UN, it had been forced out of the Commonwealth and none of the old white Dominions—Canada, Australia, New Zealand—was anxious to be too closely associated with the exponent of apartheid. This isolation, allied to great dependence on foreign companies and investors for development capital, made South African governments keen to demonstrate their reliability as responsible participants in the world market economy. It was not forgotten that after Sharpeville there had been a disturbing net outflow of capital from the country. But by about 1964 this had been reversed, and from 1965 to 1969 the average annual net capital inflow was $312m or 9 per cent of gross domestic investment.[9]

Thus an understandable anxiety not to rock the boat inclined Pretoria—no less than Paris—to pull its punches and to use its disruptive power in the system less fully than it might conceivably have done. Moreover, the national economy was still almost as highly dependent for its foreign exchange income on exports of gold as it had been in the early postwar period. In fact, by comparison with 1948, South Africa's share of the world gold market had increased, while that of other minor gold producers (excluding the USSR) had shrunk. In spite of a great deal of investment and economic development, in 1971 gold was still accounting for 32·5 per cent of total South African exports, other minerals for 33 per cent, agricultural products for 18 per cent, manufactures for only 11 per cent.[10]

Gold mining also exerted a direct influence on the rate of capital inflow. Unusually for a semi-developed country, much of this was in the form of portfolio or indirect investment. For example, in the record year 1968, net private direct investment was $263m; net private indirect investment, including Stock Exchange transactions, was $204m. This portfolio investment was apt to rise sharply whenever stockbrokers and their clients in the bourses and stock exchanges of the world decided that new gold might be due for a price rise. As the ability of the managers of the international monetary system to

South African gold production, 1960–71

	US $m
1960	748·4
1961	802·9
1962	892·2
1963 [1]	960·6
1964	1,018·9
1965	1,069·0
1966	1,080·8
1967	1,061·6
1968 [2]	1,088·0
1969	1,090·8
1970	1,128·0
1971	1,098·7

[1] South Africa started to subsidize marginal mines.
[2] Effective increase in the subsidy to marginal mines.
Source: IMF, *International Financial Statistics*.

hold down the market price of gold against the speculators became subject to doubt, interest in investment in South African gold mining always tended to increase. But at the same time, this interdependence between South Africa and the international economy worked both ways. The South African Reserve Bank acted for the government as monopoly buyer of newly mined gold in the country. It thus was responsible for converting an export product into money and was consequently likely to encounter management difficulties if there was much variation in the amount of foreign exchange realized as a result of gold sales. This involvement of the state with gold mining also gave the government a special interest in the prevention of inflation. (This was because inflation caused a rapid drop in profits from gold mining as rising costs pushed against a rigid price; and falling profits would put the higher-cost mines out of production, with serious effects on exports, employment, and economic stability.) And since inflation was becoming increasingly an international problem which only international monetary management, and not merely national monetary management, could contain and control, the wish to get a better price for its main export had to be qualified by a wish not to see total disorder in the system.

One result of the buoyancy of the South African economy and the bullish view taken of investment in the country was that when Britain devalued sterling in November 1967, South Africa did not follow suit—indeed, with a balance of payments almost exactly in equilibrium, it would have found it difficult to justify a change in the parity of the Rand to the IMF—even though a devaluation would have increased the profitability of gold mining in terms of Rand.

In 1968, as the table below clearly shows, South Africa, in the wake of sterling devaluation and the troubles in the gold market, had a bonanza year. With foreign capital eagerly jostling its way into the country and export earnings in its important sterling markets increased by the British devaluation, there was no need to sell more than a small part of current gold production.

South African balance of payments, 1966–9 (US$m)

	1966	1967	1968	1969
Trade balance	−600	−864	−380	127
Goods, services, & unrequited transfers	−1,077	−1,335	−831	−475
Long-term capital	94	147	418	237
Short-term capital	75	110	127	19
Private mon. insts (increase)	41	−13	−8	39
Gold monetization	1,076	1,082	936	132
Total	209	−9	642	−48

Source: IMF, *Balance of Payments Yearbook, 1966–70.*

The legal tangle

Sooner or later, however, pressures on the balance of payments would force South Africa to sell some gold somewhere. It could not indefinitely be stored inside the country. If the strategy of starving the private market into raising the price was to be effectively pursued, as much gold as possible had to be unloaded on to the Fund and into official hands—hands which by the self-imposed discipline of the Two-Tier Agreement could not pass it on to the private market. The question was, under what circumstances and up to what limits could this be done?

There appeared to be three channels open to South Africa:

1. The rules of the Fund gave South Africa as a *bona fide* member the right to draw automatically and with conditions, from the gold and super-gold tranches of its quota (Art. v, sect. 7 (b)). It could draw foreign exchange in these tranches from the Fund but had the right to repay drawings on the Fund, in credit tranches, at least in gold rather than in currencies. This it did on two occasions, in July 1968 and again in April 1969. Whether the same right held good for repayments in the gold tranches was not clear.

2. If other members made drawings on the Fund and asked the Fund to include Rand in the package of other currencies drawn out of it, South Africa had to be consulted by the Fund. It was open to South Africa to demand, in return for its consent to the drawing, that

the Fund accord it the right to sell gold to the Fund to the value of the Rand drawn out, thus indirectly acquiring foreign exchange in return for gold. The Fund lawyers did not think this arrangement was a breach of the Two-Tier Agreement and allowed this to be done on the two occasions when major drawings—by Britain and by France—were arranged.[11]

3. Lastly, the South Africans believed that the rules gave them the right to offer gold to the Fund and to receive sterling (or other currencies) in exchange. It was this alleged right which proved the key point in the battle and which was the subject of so much involved dispute. The rule concerned was Article v, sect. 6. It reads: ' Any member desiring to obtain, directly or indirectly, the currency of another member for gold shall, provided that it can do so with equal advantage, acquire it by the sale of gold to the Fund '.

According to the Fund's own history, this provision had originally resulted from a difference of opinion on the extent to which the Fund should seek to divert gold into its own hands. The question had come up once before, in a discussion in March 1951 on voluntary re-purchases of currency from the Fund. The Board had then apparently assumed that the Fund had no discretion to refuse to buy gold offered to it. And the view that it could refuse to do so did not appear until after the institution of the two-tier arrangement.[12]

In June 1968 South Africa, in order to test the water, made its first request to the Fund to be allowed to sell gold for sterling. The Executive Board appeared uncertain how it should reply. It shelved the issue, feeling that the questions raised ' were too large for an immediate decision '.[13] And it was evident that this prevarication was the result of extreme pressure from the United States.[14] The Americans argued that because South Africa could get a higher price on the free market, the advantage was *not* equal to that obtained from the Fund in the words of Article v (6) and the Fund was not therefore obliged to sell South Africa foreign currency in return for its gold. At this point the Fund itself was ' an embarrassed referee '.[15]

The Emminger Plan

Soon after this, in the weeks before the annual Fund and Bank meeting in September 1968, a compromise plan began to emerge. This was the Emminger Plan, an Anglo-German attempt at mediation. The plan had first seen the light of day in an article by Dr Otmar Emminger of the Bundesbank in a Hamburg magazine, *Inter-economics*, in September 1968. The solution it proposed was apparently in line with the conclusions reached a few weeks earlier in talks between Emminger and Roy Jenkins, the British Chancellor, and

which were said to have been developed over the preceding months
' by leading central bank and Finance Ministry technicians '.[16] Both
Britain and Germany were anxious to reach a settlement of the gold
dispute—international currency upheavals affected both adversely,
though in different directions. Germany's promotion of the plan was
especially significant, since after Italy, it had been foremost in formulating the March 1968 Two-Tier Agreement. The Germans had now
decided that it was time the issue was settled.[17]

The Plan was based on a formula by which South Africa could sell
part of its newly mined gold to the IMF and to the central banks when
the free market price was near or below $35, if at the same time the
South African balance of payments was in deficit. The European
monetary authorities still showed what, to the Americans, was a
regrettably old-fashioned attachment to gold. They had had severe
doubts about the legality and wisdom of American obstructionism
over South African sales to the Fund. They were therefore beginning
to waver over the agreement not to buy gold from the South Africans.[18]
They argued that if South Africa could be certain of making *some*
sales to the central banks, it would also be encouraged to sell *some*
gold on the free market—because there would be greater certainty that
the free price would not go below $35, and therefore it would be able
to secure a higher average price without risking the upheavals which
would be the consequence of the breakdown of the two-tier system.
The Europeans, including the United Kingdom, liked the Emminger
Plan for several reasons: it would put an end to uncertainty; it
would minimize the spread between the two prices; it would provide
some prospect for Europe and Japan to add to the gold in their
reserves; and it would provide a floor price without prejudice to the
long-term issue of whether gold should or should not be demonetized.[19]

By the end of September, just before the Fund meeting, the US
had virtually accepted the Emminger formula and thus had moved
away from the original hard-line position of allowing no sales of
newly produced gold at all to monetary authorities. But Washington
still insisted that the private market should not be supported—although
(as the Europeans pointed out) this was not necessary; a guaranteed
price of $35 from the IMF for the South Africans would establish
a similar floor on the free market. The chief American obstacle to
an agreement was apparently the opposition of the White House and
the Treasury, which did not see eye to eye with the Federal Reserve
Board on this issue.[20] The compromise in the Emminger Plan heavily
favoured the United States, but the Americans were reluctant to commit themselves to it until it had been accepted by the South Africans.
In the event, during discussions at the time of the Fund meeting,
South Africa turned the proposals down; but the net result of the

talks was that the United States had virtually conceded a $35 floor price and the Europeans had succeeded in making their point that gold must continue to play an important role in the system.

One explanation for the failure to reach agreement on this occasion was that a wrecking amendment by Jelle Zjilstra (the Netherlands Director) and Karl Blessing had reopened the US-Europe split on the future of monetary gold. They had proposed that individual central banks should be able to buy gold direct from South Africa.[21]

The statement issued after the talks bore the name of the Federal Reserve Board rather than the Treasury,[22] but an American presidential election was imminent and the departure of Fowler, the hardest hard-liner of them all, from the Treasury, was assured. It was possible —or so the gold speculators (and probably the South Africans) hoped —that the new administration might, when it eventually took office, be more flexible than its predecessor on the question of the price of gold and on South African sales.

A statement by David Kennedy, the new Secretary to the Treasury, on 22 January somewhat dampened these hopes. He said that the United States would not seek a solution to its problems in a change in the official price of gold. A few weeks later, Dr Nicolaas Diederichs, the Finance Minister, in a budget debate in the South African Parliament, hinted, hopefully, that agreement would soon be forthcoming. He laid down four principles on which it would have to be based. These were (1) that South Africa had the legal right to sell gold to the Fund for foreign currency; (2) that the possibility of a further flow of newly mined gold to reserves must exist; (3) that South Africa could not undertake *not* to sell gold to monetary authorities at $35 per ounce; and (4) that the attempt to separate monetary from newly mined gold would have to be reviewed.[23]

These conditions were unacceptable to the United States, and over the next few months, as South Africa's position deteriorated, Diederichs became prepared to accept less favourable terms. Throughout 1968 there had been the hope that, once the new American President had been installed, agreement might be much easier to reach. But once Nixon was in the White House, it was not in South Africa's interests to stall indefinitely. All through 1969, therefore, Diederichs continued to drop hopeful hints about an approaching agreement.

Agreement was indeed becoming more urgent from the South African point of view. In the nine months following the crisis of March 1968, South Africa had added gold worth $500m (or 60 per cent of current production) to reserves. By contrast, in 1969, due to a worsening payments balance, South Africa sold the whole of current production plus $130m from reserves and from May 1969 onwards sales began to exceed production.[24] It has not yet been disclosed what part of these gold sales went into the private market and what proportion found its way into official reserves.

In August 1969 it was revealed that the country's payments were slipping into deficit on capital account; the capital inflows of the previous year or so had been reversed, and without gold sales the current account had never been in surplus. The amounts of foreign currency obtained through the IMF operations were not large enough. Moreover, South Africa's room for manoeuvre was further diminished by the falling price of gold on the free market.

What had dominated price fluctuations in the market for the first year of the two-tier system was the behaviour of the owners of speculative stocks of gold. The 'speculative overhang' was estimated to be about $3,000m.[25] For the first year, holders were optimistic that the official price would be raised. The free market price rose continually from November 1968 to May 1969. But by May 1969 a significant change in market expectations had occurred: in spite of yet another currency crisis, the chances of breaking the two-tier system seemed small. It was noticed that whenever the price touched $42, a large seller—which can only have been South Africa—appeared. In this way, the South Africans, who were selling substantially through Zurich, in fact stabilized the market and defeated the main purpose of their own policy.

Thereafter, in the late summer and autumn of 1969, the price of gold fell steadily. There were several reasons for this, but according to the BIS, sales on the market by South Africa was not one of them. The speculators were growing restive; there was no sign of South Africa breaking the system, and the enormously high Eurodollar rates to be earned in 1969 vastly increased the opportunity costs of holding gold. The increased strength of sterling, the calmer political situation in France, and the agreement on SDRs all served to reduce tensions and anxieties on the international markets and to give to the two-tier system an appearance of stability which it had lacked in 1968. In addition to this, two parity changes, that of the French franc in August and the D-mark in October, took some of the heat out of currency speculation. The price of gold began to drop sharply in October, reaching $35·50 on 24 November and $35·20 on 5 December.

Ever since the agreement in March 1968, European central bankers had been worried that the US policy might result not in a stable price but in a drastic fall in the free price of gold—a fall which would threaten the value of their very substantial gold reserves. Hence their enthusiasm for a $35 floor. The sharp fall in the autumn of 1969 was thus a cause of concern to them as well as to the South Africans. Several of the Group of Ten countries had been wanting to increase the gold element in their reserves, but had been prevented from doing so by the ban on purchases from South Africa. All along the Americans had been aware of the risk that if the free market price fell too near to $35, the principal central banks might regard themselves as no longer bound by the Washington agreement—and might go ahead and buy from South Africa. The Americans for their part would have been happy for the price to fall to $35 or even lower, as a demonstration that there was not and would not be any formal floor in the free market.[26]

The South African government was not only under pressure from a falling market and a weakening balance of payments. It was acutely aware of the approach of a general election scheduled for early 1970, and of the political risks of deflating the economy. Thus the sharp fall in the gold price completely changed the situation and made it imperative for them to come to an agreement soon. Their bargaining position weakened dramatically in November and December 1969 and they were therefore prepared to accept terms much the same as those they had rejected more than a year before.

On their side, the Americans were prepared to agree for several reasons. There was increasing pressure from European central bankers and from Japan—pressure which became more difficult to resist as the summer went on. There was also the matter of increased IMF quotas, for which some $2,000m was required in increased gold subscriptions.[27] In any case, as the price fell, the bottom dropped out of the ' equal advantage ' argument against South Africa selling gold to the Fund.

After some unproductive preparatory talks in Washington in October, Paul Volcker of the US Treasury and Gerald Browne from the South African Treasury, finally met for secret talks in Rome in mid-December. The next day the US Treasury announced that the basis for an agreement had been reached and that talks would now be continued in the framework of the IMF. (The terse communiqué issued after the meeting indicated that agreement had been reached on the conditions which should be satisfied before monetary authorities would consider buying South African gold.) At a press conference on 17 December, Volcker said that on an official settlements basis he could see only a moderate surplus on the US balance of payments for 1969, and that 1970 would be worse. In these circumstances, the Nixon administration evidently realized that they would need all the goodwill they could get from Europe, and that this was not the time for Americans to object strongly to European desires to buy gold from South Africa.[28]

The formal agreement between South Africa and the IMF was announced on 31 December 1969. This defined in broad terms the various circumstances in which South Africa might sell gold to the

IMF. First, when the free market price of gold fell to $35 or below, to the extent to which South Africa needed the sales to satisfy its foreign exchange needs. Secondly, South Africa could sell to the Fund, *regardless of the market price*, when its foreign exchange needs over six months could not be met from the sale of all newly mined gold. Thirdly, South Africa might also make regular sales of up to $35m per quarter from the stock of gold held on 17 March 1968. Fourthly, it might sell gold to the Fund in exchange for SDRs; and Rand purchased from the Fund by other member countries would continue to be convertible into gold.

Thus the agreement provided a means of channelling gold from South Africa via the IMF to those countries which wished to increase the gold proportion of their reserves. In this way, it provided the United States with extra protection against dollar conversions. Those countries said to have been becoming most rebellious over the Two-Tier Agreement were Belgium, the Netherlands, Switzerland, and France. The last of these, France, apparently abstained in late December in the Executive Board vote, arguing that the agreement was incompatible with the IMF Charter.[29]

South Africa was able to claim the outcome of its confrontation with the United States as a victory, although to the extent that its strategy had failed in the main objective of bringing about an increase in the official dollar-gold price, it had unquestionably failed. What it had achieved was to make sure, as Diederichs pointed out, that it would never be necessary for South Africa to sell *more* than its current production in the free market (as against none at all). South Africa had also accepted the commitment to sell its output of newly mined gold in the free market 'in an orderly manner'. The idea was to reduce the danger of South African exploitation of speculative movements in the market and thus further diminish threats to the $35 official price.[30]

At first, the details of how the agreement would work were not entirely clear. But by mid-January, it was becoming evident from the market that tight limits had in effect been put on South African sales to monetary authorities. These limits were set out in the formal letters from Diederichs and Volcker to Schweitzer [31]—yet another instance of an important monetary agreement expressed not by treaty or even executive agreement but by a simple exchange of letters. From these letters it emerged that sales of gold by South Africa to monetary authorities might be made on any day when both London fixing prices were $35 or less, in an amount reasonably commensurate with one-fifth of weekly sales of new production required to be marketed to meet balance-of-payments needs.

But at the same time, neither could the United States claim the outcome as an unqualified victory over South Africa. The Americans had had, in the end, to concede the right to sell *some* gold in *some* circumstances to the Fund. Another limit had been discovered to the power of the United States to redraw the rules to suit its perceived national interest, and/or its assessment of the perceived interest of the international community.

In retrospect, although the practical consequences of this comparatively minor episode in international monetary diplomacy were not so important, yet it is still of some academic and analytical interest for what it reveals about the working of the system and the changing behaviour of the actors in it. To begin with, the most remarkable thing about the confrontation was the way in which it was strictly confined to the monetary relationship. There was no mixing up of trade and defence or security questions with monetary ones. US trade policy towards South Africa was not used as a coercive weapon. Nor was the capacity of the United States to stop arms sales to South Africa or to apply discriminatory controls on US investment there. No extraneous weapons were brought to bear on the gold battle. It was as though Goliath had agreed to compete with David as to who could sling stones most accurately. The contrast with the subsequent Nixon-Connally strategy in the summer and autumn of 1971 (see below, pp. 336–44) could not be more striking. The explanation must be that in the dispute with South Africa, the Americans were trying to act within the system, to protect its future, and generally to stick to its rules, even while bending them slightly, whereas in 1971 Nixon and Connally had decided that the time had come to change the system by breaking the rules and acting outside it. The distinguishing feature, therefore, of American diplomacy in this episode was the conscious responsibility for the management of the international economy and the conscious dependence, derived from this responsibility, on the co-operation of the Europeans in this task. The second thing that is striking is the extent to which South African diplomacy was much affected by the government's political responsibility for the welfare and efficient management of the South African economy. The ' home front '—to borrow a metaphor from military crises (which in many ways more resemble monetary ones than do most diplomatic crises)— was Diederichs's Achilles' heel. Domestic political pressures and economic necessities—and practical politicians seldom distinguish the two—required the government to compromise with the Americans. At the same time, the South African capacity to shift the United States from its rigid position depended a great deal on the state of the market at any given time. The other constraining factor limiting South African influence was its conscious dependence on the international monetary system—that system of which the Fund was the legitimate authority and in which the United States, with its rooted attachment to the $35 an ounce price of gold, was the most powerful single influence.

Essentially, the argument concerned the interpretation of the rules of the system, and, unlike some other episodes in the history of international monetary relations in the 1960s which rather undermined the influence of the Fund by inventing new organizations or using new ad hoc diplomatic channels, this one appeared to increase the status and power of the IMF as the central source of legitimate authority in the system. Channelling gold into the Fund was the only acceptable compromise open to the United States and South Africa, and this left the Fund with the future prospect of holding more gold than before—and perhaps of feeling a greater attachment to it and maybe of exercising more independent power because of it.

What is unclear—and perhaps always will be since it is a chicken-and-egg question—is whether the episode coincided with a polarization of opinion on the normative question of the proper or desirable role of gold in the international monetary order and its relation (positive or negative) to the international welfare. Or, alternatively, whether the attention focused on gold by the altercation over the rules actually propelled opinion in two opposite directions. Did it produce or accidentally mirror a stiffening of attitudes in international political/ economic debate over the role of gold? Certain it is that official opinion and opinion among a great many American professional academic economists and those influenced by them was much more convinced by 1970 than it had been in 1967–8 that ultimately gold should be ' phased out ' of its place in the system and that this would be for the common good. Over the same period, the European politicians and officials and some economists by and large became more confidently doubtful that the dollar, especially if it became fully inconvertible into gold, could ever be regarded as an adequate substitute for gold, either as a numéraire or as a standard in the system—and indeed that some of the attractions of the SDRs as an alternative numéraire lay precisely in its comparatively fixed gold value.

Appendix : Arrangements for South African Gold Sales to Fund *

MINISTRY OF FINANCE
PRETORIA

23rd December, 1969

Dear Mr Schweitzer,

As you know, for some time the Republic of South Africa, has been discussing with the United States, with other members, and with you procedures for the orderly sale of newly-mined gold in the market and the sale of gold to the International Monetary Fund. I wish to inform you

---

* IMF, *International Financial News Survey*, 16 Jan 1970.

that as a result of these discussions, the South African authorities have adopted a policy with respect to gold sales and I would like to request that the Fund confirm that it will be prepared in the light of this statement of policy to buy gold from South Africa in the circumstances and under the conditions set forth below.

The following are the intentions of the South African authorities as to the handling of newly-mined gold and reserves.

(1) Without prejudice to the determination of the legal position under the Articles of Agreement of the Fund, the South African authorities may offer to sell gold to the Fund for the currencies of other members at the price of 35 Dollars per ounce, less a handling charge as follows:

(a) During periods when the market of gold falls to 35 Dollars per ounce or below, at which times offers to sell gold to the Fund under this paragraph (a) would be limited to amounts required to meet current foreign exchange needs, and

(b) regardless of the price in the private market, up to the extent that South Africa experiences needs for foreign exchange over semi-annual periods beyond those which can be satisfied by the sale of all current new gold production on the private market or by sales to the Fund under paragraph (1) (a) above.

(2) (a) The South African authorities intend to sell current production of newly-mined gold in an orderly manner on the private market to the full extent of current payments needs. It is anticipated that new production in excess of those needs during a semi-annual period may be added to reserves.

(b) When selling gold other than in the private market, the South African authorities intend in practice normally to offer such gold to the Fund.

(c) The South African authorities may use gold in normal Fund transactions, e.g. in repurchase of appropriate drawings from the Fund, and to cover the gold portion of any South African quota increase, and to obtain currency convertible in fact to exchange against special drawing rights for which South Africa is designated by the Fund. Rand drawn from the Fund by other members would generally be converted into gold when Rand are included in drawings under normal Fund procedures. These Fund-related transactions, which may take place without regard to the market price of gold, will be reflected by changes in the composition of South Africa's reserves but will not affect the volume of sales of newly-mined gold in the market.

(3) Notwithstanding paragraphs (1) (b) and (2) (a) above, the amount of gold held by South Africa on March 17, 1968, reduced by sales by South Africa to monetary authorities (including Fund-related transactions) after that date and further reduced by such future sales to monetary authorities as may be made to finance deficits

or as a result of Fund-related transactions, will be available for such additional monetary sales as the South African authorities may determine, up to 35 million Dollars quarterly beginning January 1, 1970. It is also contemplated that as an implementation of this understanding, the Fund would agree to purchase the amount of gold offered to it by South Africa in May 1968.

In order to determine whether South Africa has balance of payments surpluses or deficits as well as to indicate other operational and procedural points with respect to this policy, I enclose a memorandum which clarifies these particular matters.

It would be appreciated if, in the light of these policy intentions, the Fund were able to decide that it would purchase gold from South Africa in the circumstances outlined above. I would expect that the Fund would review the situation at any time if there were a major change in circumstances and in any event after five years.

The South African authorities will work out with the Managing Director consultation procedures on the currencies to be purchased from the Fund with gold.

I hope that this announced policy, the implementation of which I believe will be a contribution to the stability of the International Monetary System, and my suggestion meet with the concurrence of the Fund. A copy of this letter has been sent to the Secretary of the Treasury of the United States.

Your sincerely,
/s/ N. DIEDERICHS
Minister of Finance
Republic of South Africa

The Managing Director
International Monetary Fund

Operational and Procedural Points

A. For the present purposes, balance of payments deficits and surpluses will be equal to the change during the accounting period in the total of South African official gold and foreign exchange reserves, the net IMF position and changes in SDR holdings, and any foreign assets held by other South African banking institutions and public agencies under swap arrangements with the Reserve Bank. It is understood that changes in gold holdings outside the monetary reserves and in monetary banks' positions not covered by Reserve Bank swaps are normally not significant. If they should at any time become significant, further consideration will be given to their inclusion in the calculation. SDR allocations will not be considered as reducing a deficit or increasing a surplus as above defined. South Africa does not envisage unusual or non-traditional foreign borrowings or other special transactions that would affect the elements listed in this paragraph.

B. Addition of newly mined gold to South African reserves under paragraph 2 (*a*) will take place when there is a surplus for an accounting period. It is envisaged that all new gold production, less domestic consumption, during the accounting period will be treated as a balance of payments credit item and that it will, in fact, be sold currently under paragraph 1 (*a*) and paragraph 2 (*a*) to the full extent necessary to meet payments needs, except for the sales available under paragraph 3, apart from the Fund transaction initiated in May 1968.

C. Sales of gold by South Africa to monetary authorities under paragraph 1 (*a*) may be made for any day when both London fixing prices are $35·00 p.f.o or below, in an amount reasonably commensurate with one-fifth of weekly sales from new production required to be marketed to meet balance of payments needs.

D. Subject to paragraph 2 (*a*):

1. Should sales to monetary authorities under paragraph 1 (*b*), plus sales of SDRs and drawings from the IMF by South Africa, exceed the deficit defined under paragraph A of this memorandum, such excess will be deducted from the amount allowable for the first succeeding accounting period wherein a deficit is again encountered.

2. Should sales to monetary authorities under paragraph 1 (*b*), plus sales of SDRs and drawings from the IMF, fall short of the amount allowable for an accounting period in which South Africa aims to finance its entire deficit by these means, such shortfall will be added to the amount allowable for the next succeeding accounting period.

3. It is expected that any discrepancies under 1 and 2 above will be minimal.

4. Should sales to monetary authorities under paragraph 1 (*b*), plus sales of SDRs and drawings from the IMF, fall short of the amount allowable for an accounting period in which South Africa does not aim to finance its entire deficit by these means but chooses to sell more on the free market than it undertakes to do in paragraph 2 (*a*), no correction will be made for any succeeding accounting period.

E. When the price criterion is operative, sales of gold to the IMF shall be attributed to the total deficit, if any, during the accounting period. The balance of such sales, if any, will be attributed to newly mined gold to the extent of gold production during the accounting period.

F. Sales or payments under paragraph 2 (*c*) in connection with IMF-related transactions are expected to take place only within the criteria normally envisaged for IMF drawings by members, for use of members' currencies in drawings by other members and for SDR transactions.

G. Fundamentally, it is expected that the composition of South African reserves will not be greatly changed. In particular, it is understood that the ratio of gold to total reserves will remain relatively stable. If South Africa should desire to make additional sales of gold or otherwise exchange assets for the purpose of achieving a basic change in the composition of its reserve holdings, further discussion would be held with a view to clarifying intentions.

THE SECRETARY OF THE TREASURY

WASHINGTON

December 24, 1969

Dear Mr Schweitzer

I have received a copy of the letter dated December 23, 1969, sent to you by Mr Diederichs in which he sets forth the intentions which South Africa proposes to follow with respect to the handling of its newly-mined gold and reserves. This matter bears importantly on the continued effective functioning of the two-tier gold market which was initiated at a meeting on March 16–17, 1968, which you attended.

In view of the intentions of South Africa, and in view of discussions we have had with other fund members, I should like to inform you that I have instructed the US Executive Director to take the following position. The United States is prepared to support decisions of the International Monetary Fund to purchase gold offered for sale by South Africa in the circumstances and under the conditions described in that letter, assuming that there is an understanding among Fund members generally that they do not intend to initiate official gold purchases directly from South Africa. With this understanding, I believe that the policies to be followed will be consistent with the stability and proper functioning of the international monetary system.

Sincerely yours,

/s/ PAUL A. VOLCKER

Acting Secretary

The Managing Director
International Monetary Fund

Notes

[1] See Harry Magdoff, *The age of imperialism : the economics of US foreign economic policy* (1969) pp. 109–10.

[2] A suggestion made in Davidson & Weil, p. 128.

[3] Tibor Wilczynski, *The economics and politics of East-West trade*, gives no support to the suggestion of French influence on political motivation for Soviet gold sales policy.

[4] It is true that none of these conversions was on quite the same scale as France's. In the last six months of 1965, for instance, France converted $900m to gold or gold convertible IMF claims, Italy converted $475m, Germany $276m, Belgium $175m, and the Netherlands $132m (see Brian Johnson, *Politics of money*, p. 198).

[5] France in fact left the table some $50m in gold to the good, as a result of its part in the pool's transactions. Had it stayed in, it would have more than lost the gains made in 1963–4, since these amounted to little more than $1,200m, whereas the Gold Pool was reported to have involved the members in sales of $3,000m between the 1967 sterling devaluation and the Washington meeting in March 1968.

[6] Johnson, *Further essays*, p. 208.

⁷ This argument is explained by Harry Johnson, 'The future of gold and the dollar', *Journal of World Trade Law*, Mar/Apr 1969.

⁸ A full account of this incident is given by Mary Gumbart in *IMF*, ii, ch. 8; see also ibid., i. 252–6.

⁹ UN Unit on Apartheid, *Foreign investment in the Republic of South Africa* (New York, 1970), ST/PSCA/Ser. A/11, 1970.

¹⁰ The figures are for 1964 (D. Hobart Houghton, *The South African economy*, Cape Town, 1964).

¹¹ *The Economist*, 6 July 1968 & 11 Oct 1969.

¹² However, the last purchase under Art. V (6) took place as far back as November 1948 (*IMF*, ii. 244 & 562; see also Terence Higgins, *The World Today*, Feb 1970).

¹³ *FT*, 26 June 1968.

¹⁴ Ibid., 29 June 1968, spoke of 'intense lobbying' of Executive Directors of the Fund.

¹⁵ R. N. Brown, 'Gold: prospects for the two-tier system', *Journal of World Trade Law*, Jan–Feb 1971. See also Lombard in *FT*, 18 June 1968.

¹⁶ *The Times*, 6 Sept 1968.

¹⁷ *FT*, 12 Sept 1968.

¹⁸ *The Economist*, 13 July 1968, p. 61.

¹⁹ Peter Jay in *The Times*, 3 Oct 1968.

²⁰ *FT*, 18 Sept 1968.

²¹ Jay in *The Times*, 10 Oct 1968.

²² *The Economist*, 5 Oct 1968, p. 73.

²³ *The Times*, 17 Feb 1969.

²⁴ BIS, *Ann. rep.*, 1969–70.

²⁵ R. N. Brown, *Journal of World Trade Law*, Jan–Feb 1971.

²⁶ *The Times*, 8 Dec 1969.

²⁷ *FT*, 1 Jan 1970.

²⁸ Ibid., 18 Dec 1969.

²⁹ See *The Times*, 1–2 Jan 1970.

³⁰ Ibid., 5 Jan 1970.

³¹ The texts were made public in IMF Press Release No. 780, 13 Jan 1970, and reprinted in *International Financial News Survey*, 16 Jan 1970 (see appendix, p. 314).

11

THE UNSETTLED SYSTEM: STOCKHOLM
TO THE SMITHSONIAN, 1968–71

In an environment of increasing market stress, three broad topics dominated international monetary affairs in the closing years of the period—that is to say in the forty-five months between the agreement on the two-tier gold price arrangement in March 1968 and the conclusion of the Smithsonian Agreement in December 1971. All three reflected some aspect of the erosion and accelerating distintegration (under the pressures recounted earlier) of the so-called Bretton Woods system—that version of the gold exchange standard that centred on the dollar as the dominant or top currency, the main component of other countries' foreign exchange reserves, their chief medium for market intervention to maintain fixed exchange rates and the pivot of other par values.

One of the three topics was the viability (and desirability) of fixed exchange rates between the major currencies. Market pressures had already demonstrated to the British the high cost of maintaining a fixed rate when confidence in it once began to wane. Much academic opinion—in the United States particularly—was already convinced that more flexible rates were to be preferred for functional efficiency. But controversy continued about the political issues raised by the proposition.

Another topic was the role of the dollar and its relation to other international reserve assets, notably gold and SDRs. As dollars accumulated in the hands of surplus countries like Germany and Japan, the political asymmetries of a system that made it especially easy for American companies to acquire foreign subsidiaries and for US troops to live and fight abroad became more glaringly obvious. The same situation made the United States increasingly reluctant to convert foreign dollar balances into gold, and the market increasingly uneasy about the stability of the growing dollar ' overhang '.

Thirdly, there was the question mark over European monetary union. This period was one in which the European Community, having achieved the relatively easy first stage of ' negative ' integration through liberalization and the dismantling of national economic barriers, now had to screw up its courage to tackle the much more difficult first steps in ' positive ' integration [1]—harmonizing and co-ordinating national policies with the aim of converting a customs union into an economic and monetary union. Like a canoe emerging from some sheltered estuary to head into the choppy waters of the open sea, the European Community at this point ran into an environment in which it was much harder than it would have been in the early or middle 1960s to maintain a mutual balance and to hold stable intra-Community exchange rates, even though these were a necessary foundation for the common agricultural policy and an acknowledged *sine qua non* of further progress towards monetary union. The growing crisis of confidence in the dollar often showed up in increased and exaggerated market attitudes to individual European currencies. A pendulum pattern developed in Community affairs in which the taking of good resolutions to advance in step together alternated with the acknowledgement of setback at the hands of market forces. Succeeding moods of optimism and pessimism in turn affected European attitudes and bargaining postures on the other two questions of fixed versus flexible rates and on the relative status of the dollar, gold, and SDRs.

This was just one of a number of ways in which opinion and policy in each of these monetary issue areas closely interacted with the other two. Indeed, each was so intertwined with the other two that together they formed a plaited rope in which different angles of vision often gave rise to the conflicting views as to which strand was uppermost in importance. Although the arguments used and the proposals discussed often seemed impenetrably technical and esoteric, the underlying conflicts were increasingly recognized as political. They concerned the rules governing relations between national currencies and the distribution of power, of rights and duties, of costs and benefits, among the members of the affluent alliance. This was why international monetary negotiations and the resolution of international monetary crises came to be treated by the media and by international relations scholars at the end of the decade as matters of ' high ' politics where once they had been considered fairly unimportant ' low ' politics.

These closing years were also ones in which the spectre of inflation, not in any particular country but in the international monetary system generally, came increasingly under scrutiny. Inflation was a sort of backcloth to each of the three issue areas already mentioned. Diagnoses of its cause and prescriptions for its cure similarly differed somewhat with political and economic standpoints. For example, advocates both of flexible and of fixed exchange rates each accused the other system of carrying an inflationary bias. The advocates of flexible rates argued that rates were more stubbornly fixed when they should be moved up (i.e. currencies revalued) than when they should be devalued. The consequent devaluation bias in the system tended therefore—because imports then cost more—to produce an inflationary bias. Conversely, the opponents of flexible rates argued that 'taking the strain on the rate rather than the reserves' removed the only effective curb on national governments' propensity to solve their own financing problems in the time-honoured way by depreciating the currency (i.e. by inflation); and that with the United States thus enabled to conduct with impunity a continuing devaluation of the dollar while exporting some of the inflationary consequences, the flexible rate system would only accelerate the international process.

Similarly, the goal of European monetary union seemed the more desirable as Europeans grew more inclined to blame inflation on the Americans rather than on domestic culprits or on their European neighbours. And conversely, some doubt was cast on the claims of the dollar to provide an adequate and convenient international currency for use as reserve asset and numéraire. If the United States could not stop inflation at home, did this mean that other parts of the system when they accumulated dollars would be subjected to an 'inflation tax' from which only the US economy benefited?

Thus controversy continued on the main causes and the main consequences of inflation. The one thing that was certain was that the rate of inflation in the rich countries did show from 1968 on a marked and alarming acceleration.

Overall price developments in the OECD area*
(Percentage changes at annual rates)

	1960–5	1965–8	1969	1970
United States	1·5	3·3	4·7	5·1
Other major OECD countries	4·0	3·3	4·8	5·9
Smaller OECD North	4·3	4·4	4·1	5·1
Other	4·9	4·5	(3·5)	(4·8)
Total OECD	2·6	3·4	4·7	5·5

* GDP deflators at constant 1968 exchange rate.
Source: National Accounts of OECD countries and Secretariat estimates.

As the OECD report, which was written in 1971, observed, 'there has been an almost universal tendency to underestimate prospective price increases over the last few years'. The report concluded that there was an urgent need to bring about a significant reduction in inflationary expectations over the next twelve to eighteen months. And although usually tender towards the United States, the OECD did suggest mildly that 'For the OECD area as a whole the effects of a faster price rise in the United States are not just arithmetic; there are significant direct effects for our international trade, and also—possibly more important—indirect psychological effects on inflationary expectations on other countries'.[2]

The same allegation was more explicitly expounded by Professor Harry Johnson:

Inflation can and will go on quite happily at a moderate pace so long as the reserve currency country itself inflates at a reasonably modest pace. Adjustment problems will not occur too frequently or be too difficult and can be handled by changes in the exchange values of particular national currencies against the key currency... The situation changes however if the reserve currency country begins to inflate at an immodest pace; this was true of the United States from 1965 on and formed the background to the crisis of 1971. The reserve currency country then becomes an active source of inflation within the system, through the direct influence of its own prices on world prices, through the demand-injecting influence of a deterioration in its current account, and through the monetary implications for others of a vastly enlarged outflow of its currency.[3]

Overall, the consequence was a new measure of uncertainty among the actors concerning ends and means in the international monetary system, and an increasing incidence of stress and turbulence in it. To cope with this turbulence, the governments of the affluent alliance had evolved over the previous eight or ten years a versatile armoury of institutions, practices, and conventions for the conduct of monetary diplomacy. Would these now be adequate to stand up to increased pressures? Which parts of the system would prove most useful and which most vulnerable? Or would the machinery of international monetary co-operation prove less important (in the sense of influencing the outcome) than the relative constraints, emanating from domestic economic and political systems, to which different governments would be subject in their external monetary relations? These are some of the questions to bear in mind when considering the course of events.

The franc and the mark

The first part of the story focuses primarily on the exchange rates of the French franc and the D-mark. But it is misleading to consider them separately, for together they worked somewhat like a seesaw, in that anything pushing one side violently downwards tended to be involuntarily reflected in a sharp upswing on the other side. (The same seesaw effect had also been evident at the beginning of the period, before the 1961 revaluation of the D-mark. Then it had been sterling that occupied the lower end of the seesaw.) Yet the seesaw simile is imperfect, for the domestic influences in both cases were obviously very powerful, both economic and political. In the French case the first downward impetus was primarily political, in that it was set off by the consequences of the student riots of May 1968. In Germany, the impetus was more economic: after the recession of 1965–6, an economic revival started in the spring of 1967 with investment and employment both picking up again, encouraging the government to lower interest rates and otherwise pursue expansion. German exports, now very competitively priced, grew and the second quarter of 1967 showed a record surplus on current account. German confidence in foreign investment at last began to return and capital outflows to build up. When in March 1968 sterling came under market pressure (chiefly as a result of the decline in OSA sterling balances), there were sympathetic speculative inflows into D-marks. These continued despite revaluation denials from Finance Minister Strauss and Economics Minister Schiller, until the markets were calmed by the Washington meeting, the abandonment of the Gold Pool, and the institution of the Two-Tier Agreement for gold (see ch. 9).

After a summer of continued economic expansion in Germany, speculation returned in August 1968, anticipating the possibility of an arranged revaluation when the central bankers met at Basle in September. Nothing happened. But soon, about mid-October, the inflows of foreign funds began again, gathering speed until in the first three weeks of November 1968 DM9½ billion (nearly $2½ billion) entered Germany, of which DM5 billion was accounted for by foreign deposits with German banks.[4]

By this time of course, the franc-mark seesaw was working strongly. That is to say, the underlying doubts about the franc exchange rate were exacerbated and aroused by speculators' growing confidence that the mark would sooner or later have to be revalued. The November 1968 crisis therefore was properly speaking a franc-mark crisis—the first of several. The force of this mutual responsiveness via the foreign exchange and short-term credit markets can be seen by going back over the sequence of monetary developments affecting France after the start of the événements of May and June 1968. These, it will be recalled, had led to a loss of an estimated 750m working hours from strikes and lock-outs, and a consequent flight of French capital, some of it abroad, some into gold. The Banque de France acknowledged reserve losses of $307m in May and $203m in June. The first policy response was to impose controls and to seek supporting credit from the IMF. Fortunately, this could be drawn automatically without prior negotiation since France had an untouched gold tranche and a super-gold tranche allowing a total drawing of $885m. Following the British example of an import surcharge (see above, p. 124), de Gaulle arranged a similar quasi-devaluation by introducing both an export subsidy and an import tax. The discount rate was raised from 3½ to 5 per cent and a long-stop standby credit package of $1·3 billion was put together by the Group of Ten central banks in case it should be needed. These measures, reinforced by the massive victory of the General at the general election of 30 June, slowed down the capital outflow. But the price of victory was a round of wage increases in June under the 'Grenelle Agreement', a rise in hourly rates of as much as 12 per cent [5] and a consequent acceleration in the French inflation rate. This by itself might not have upset the market, for in September the French government went for growth and lifted exchange controls; there was a fighting chance, had the other end of the seesaw stayed still, that the speculators would be convinced—or at least would be content to wait and see.

But, as we have seen, it did not stay still. Speculation in favour of the D-mark hit the franc and the pound and obliged the Banque de France to reverse gear, raise discount rate to 6 per cent and reintroduce credit restrictions. But to no avail; 'the flight from the franc became first a rout and then a speculative orgy '.[6]

The result was a Franco-German political confrontation. De Gaulle's determination not to devalue was matched by an equal determination, then shared by all parties in the Kiesinger coalition government not to revalue. New German elections loomed in September 1969 and the coalition depended a good deal on the farm vote and on the support of export industries. A revaluation seemed to spell a check to export sales and a fall in farm incomes if the CAP intervention prices, fixed in units of account, were to lose internal purchasing power. If anyone had to budge, in German eyes, it should be the French. And for once the Germans refused to respond to American pressure, the Washington preference (on economic export-trade grounds) being for a D-mark revaluation. (A relevant complicating factor here being that November 1968 found the United States with a lame duck administration. In other circumstances the American bias might have favoured any outcome that humiliated the General.)

The first German tactic, at a special central bankers' meeting at Basle on 17 November, was to offer strong German support for the franc, but on brutally stiff conditions—which the French refused. The Germans then publicly—and unconventionally—advocated devaluation of the franc. A $2 billion central bank credit package was put together for the French and it was confidently expected by all that devaluation would follow, the deal reportedly being a 10 per cent devaluation in return for the credit. At the last moment, General de Gaulle stopped the devaluation and instead, cut public spending, increased bank reserve requirements, and slapped back the exchange and credit controls which the Banque de France had lifted only six weeks earlier.

On the other side of the looking glass, the Germans also opted for substitute measures rather than change the exchange rate: a 4 per cent tax concession on imports and a corresponding tax surcharge on exports—in short, an 8 per cent revaluation on the trade account. This was reinforced on 1 December by measures to inhibit capital inflows. Deposits by non-residents in German banks had to be matched 100 per cent by bank reserves with the Bundesbank. This very tough requirement was relaxed within a week, as large funds flowed out again.

During the ensuing winter, as the German economy continued to expand and exports to boom in spite of accelerating price rises, the semi-independent status of the Bundesbank within the German political economy—strongly contrasting with the dependence of the Banque de France in the French—began to show. It was perhaps the more marked as the German elections drew near. The constitutional statutes of the Bundesbank obliged it to carry out whatever measures the government chose. But equally they charged it with responsibility to defend the stability of the economy and the value of the currency. The trouble was that the Bundesbank could initiate certain monetary measures but not fiscal ones. If, in an election year, a German government rejected fiscal measures (other than self-cancelling discriminatory border taxes), then the Bundesbank had to fall back on monetary measures. With these, however, it encountered the recurrent dilemma (also encountered by the Americans and the British) that deflationary tight credit at home could be achieved or assisted by higher interest rates, but high interest rates attracted yet more inflows of inflationary foreign capital. (Indeed, in 1969 there was the odd spectacle of the French raising their discount rate (13 June) in order to keep capital at home while the Germans raised theirs (in April, and again in June) in order to curb the boom and discourage foreign capital from coming in. Neither was markedly effective.)

The second franc-mark confrontation in April–May 1969 was brought on by the exit of the General on 28 April after the defeat of his referendum proposals. The markets not unnaturally assumed that, with the General, the main obstruction to a franc devaluation had been removed. Anticipation was increased by what appeared to be a German move to smooth the way for France by offering, instead of confrontation, a compromise. Two days after de Gaulle resigned, Strauss had implied on two separate occasions that though Germany would not revalue alone, she might do so (and by 8 or 10 per cent) in the context of a general realignment of exchange rates.

Behind this move lay an internal political situation in which the Kiesinger coalition was—as coalitions are apt to do as elections approach—starting to crumble. Schiller, in particular, was having second thoughts about revaluation. Neither the border taxes nor capital controls were proving very effective; the choice (if continued surplus, inflow and inflation were to be avoided) was narrowing to revaluation or really very restrictive monetary policies indeed, threatening employment and wages. For the Social Democrats these were greater political deterrents than the risk of a cut in farm prices or a loss of export markets. Although Strauss opposed revaluation, the general realignment idea offered a chance of holding the coalition together a little longer. But it was rejected by the French—and, more important, by the Americans. Official opinion in Washington was still afraid that a dollar devaluation would be dangerously destabilizing and commercially self-defeating. On 5 May Emminger and Dr J. B. Schoellhorn, minister of state in the Economics Ministry, returned from Washington and reported this to a cabinet meeting of ministers and Bundesbank representatives. At this meeting Schiller's proposal for a 7 per cent revaluation was turned down by the Christian Democrat majority. In the next three days, money poured into Germany and the *Frankfurter Allgemeine Zeitung* described 9 May 1969 as 'the most chaotic Friday of the postwar era'. (Bundesbank figures later revealed that where the inflow in November 1968 had been DM9½ billion, this time it was DM16·7 billion or about $4·4 billion.) Late the same day, Kiesinger, his hand strengthened by an opinion poll giving 87 per cent against revaluation, called a second cabinet meeting. This time it produced an ultra-firm announcement that revaluation was ruled out 'immer und ewig', for all eternity. According to Davidson and Weil, who described these as 'hyperbolic terms', Kiesinger's resolution had been perversely strengthened by the advice given by the Bundesbank—perversely since the Bank, backed by academic opinion and the foreign exchange dealers' hunches, now believed that revaluation was the only solution.[7] But it told the government that Germany's trade surplus was chronic, based on the country's economic strength. Therefore, a moderate revaluation in 1969 would not reverse it but would have to be backed up by annual 'crawling peg' revaluations of 1 or 2 per cent a year.

Abroad, the French protested; the European Commission was relieved; and the central bankers moved at their next meeting to insist that Germany take some palliative measures to protect the system from the turbulence surrounding the mark. A rare BIS communiqué declared that though some foreign funds were expected to recede soon, the Bundesbank would at once take steps to recycle hot money traceable to other countries' reserves. However, this left untouched the largest flow which had come in, via the Eurodollar market. The other follow-up was domestic: a package of substitute measures including a 50 per cent reserve requirement for non-resident bank deposits which were received before 15 April, and 15 per cent on resident deposits. The market cynically interpreted ' immer und ewig ' to mean ' until after the elections on 24 September ' and meanwhile the Bundesbank, who did not believe in it, was left to defend the rate.

Its task was surely eased by the unilateral French decision to spring a surprise 11·11 per cent devaluation of the franc on 8 August, while the rest of Europe was away at the beaches. Disregarding legal obligations (or perhaps interpreting them very literally), France informed but did not consult its EEC partners and the IMF beforehand. The French view was that since this was the precise degree of devaluation discussed by the Group of Ten at Bonn the previous November and then found acceptable to the Fund, there was no further need to obtain their agreement. The practical justification for devaluing lay primarily in a reserve loss of $4,700m in twelve months since June 1968, leaving estimated reserves of under $2,000m.

The devaluation was accompanied by a short price freeze and followed by a September package of domestic measures aimed at flattening the J-curve [8] and reducing the inflationary effects of dearer imports. Before these were announced, it was made known that France would seek to draw nearly $1 billion from the IMF to back up the reserves (and to minimize any further gold losses) and Fund officials arrived in Paris in time to be consulted about the measures. What advice they proffered and whether it was accepted was never revealed. Probably the consultation was more symbolic than real; it drew the obvious comment, that for France to ' swallow the IMF pill ' was the biggest break yet with the age of de Gaulle.[9] The French press was at some pains to play down the element of surveillance involved as a mere formality. There is certainly no evidence that the unpublished Letter of Intent, which Finance Minister Giscard d'Estaing submitted to Working Party III, and some days later to the Fund's Executive Board, contained any commitments not already announced in the policy statement at the beginning of the month—i.e. reduced public spending and a balanced budget for 1970; a balance of trade by mid-1970; credit restrictions and price controls. It was examined at length and, according to *Le Monde* (17 September), accepted without enthusiasm by Working Party III. The Fund drawing, despite the manner of the devaluation, was unanimously approved by the Board. Its composition is shown in the table on p. 329.

Although it may have eased the pressure, the franc devaluation did not remove speculation on a D-mark revaluation once the elections of 28 September were out of the way. It was useless for a doomed cabinet to reiterate its determination not to revalue, to point to a basic payments deficit and to raise interest rates still higher. Like some voracious Moloch, the markets were not satisfied—still less so when the polls showed the pro-revaluation Social Democrats drawing ahead.

$m	From Fund's resources	Through the GAB	From gold sales
Total	410	375	200
United States	269	—	33
Germany	—	185	66
Japan	—	65	16
Italy	12	60	33
Canada	10	50	12
Netherland	—	15	14
S. Africa	45		
Others	74		

Note. In addition, France arranged a large supplementary line of central bank credits. These were: a Fed swap of $1,000m; and a further $44m from Germany, Italy, Belgium, and Holland; also $200m from the BIS.

What the markets perceived very clearly was that, notwithstanding the franc devaluation, the mark was still undervalued in relation to the dollar (or the dollar overvalued in terms of marks).

Another tide of foreign funds began to flow into Germany at the beginning of the pre-election week. In two days DM2·2 billion came in. Kiesinger then upset Schiller and the Social Democrats by ordering him to close the foreign exchange markets until after the election. What this meant was that dealing in D-marks could continue abroad, in London, Paris, and other centres, but free of central bank interference and with channels for foreign funds into Germany closed. But although some political fencing inevitably followed, it was clear that none of the German political leaders really wanted the exchange rate as an election issue. It was the anticipation of the markets which thrust it upon them, forcing the politicians to protect themselves.

When the election results came in, they indicated a Social Democrat-Free Democrat coalition government. But constitutionally Kiesinger had to remain in office for another three weeks. Thus, when the markets reopened, $250m (about DM1 billion) came in in the first two hours. This had been anticipated by Emminger and he and Schiller persuaded Kiesinger that it would be futile to close the market again and that the mark must be allowed to float.

The float continued for a month until 24 October when the new government had taken office. The market now knew that a revaluation would come; Blessing had practically told the IMF so in Washington. The question was by how much. Six per cent was a favoured figure, 7 per cent a rumoured maximum, but even with the Bundesbank buying dollars, the floating rate went up to 7·3 per cent before the government announced a change of 9·29 per cent. The ' overkill ' tactic at least succeeded in sending speculative funds home with prompt dispatch. In the last three months of 1969, Germany's reserves shrank by DM19·5 billion (about $5·4 billion) and it was possible, while keeping interest rates up, to ease up on the reserve requirements on foreign deposits in German banks.

The experiment, involuntarily undertaken in unique circumstances of suspended political authority, was nevertheless a turning point in the system at large. It demonstrated that the markets could be entrusted with deciding exchange rates without serious disruption of trade and international investment decisions; that other central banks could adjust to a floating currency and that ' dirty floating ' [10] (i.e. central bank intervention to blunt the sharp edges of market fluctuations) was a practicable halfway house. Academic advocates of floating were heartened to press for it harder, especially in the United States where, though the Council of Economic Advisors favoured it, it was still firmly opposed by the Federal Reserve Board. David Kennedy, Secretary of the US Treasury, spoke out against the crawling peg solution at the 1969 Fund meeting. Schweitzer saw it as a possible modification not incompatible with generally fixed rates and proposed the undertaking of a study.[11] At this stage, however, under American leadership and with British support, the Group of Ten still asserted that greater flexibility was out of the question.

Politically, by far the most important impact of the German float and subsequent revaluation was on the prospects for economic union in the European Community. These it almost literally set back by at least five years. In 1965 the EEC's Monetary Committee had been congratulating the Community that the use of the gold-dollar-based unit of account for fixing prices under the CAP was making it ' increasingly difficult and unlikely ' that individual governments would change their exchange rates.[12] Now, far from the CAP ushering in the first stages of monetary union, the French and German exchange rate changes of 1969 had shot great gaping holes in the CAP. French farm prices, in francs, should really have been raised—but the rise had to be deferred on anti-inflationary grounds. German farm prices, in marks, should have been brought down. But this, too, was politically awkward and deficiency payments—a British device—financed partly nationally and partly by the Community funds, were introduced. And while these running repairs were made to the CAP, the challenge on monetary union looked to the Six like a call to double or quits. Which was it to be?

The decision was complicated by continuing disagreement—which appeared to be technical but was really political—between the ' monetarists ' and the ' economists '. The monetarist argument held that, as with tariff reduction, the important thing was to decide to move towards a common currency, by stages if necessary, but to align currencies first and deal with economic consequences second. The 'economist' argument was that harmonization and synchronization of national economic management (e.g. on inflation) was a necessary precondition of monetary union and that tension and conflict between members would only be increased by unrealistic attempts to put the monetary cart before the economic horse. German opinion, predictably, inclined to the latter view; French opinion, unwilling (as in other matters) to compromise the autonomy of French national economic management, inclined to the monetarist solution. The Commission, in self-defence and to maintain the momentum of European integration, had naturally proposed a neat compromise. Instead of either/or, the answer was both—a hand-in-hand progression towards concerted economic policies *and* towards a common currency. This idea, put forward in February 1969, was better received than the original (monetarist) Barre Plan of a year earlier. And when the ministers of the Six met at The Hague a little over a month after the German revaluation, it encouraged them to take the plunge and declare for the first time their intention to create an economic and monetary union. A special committee headed by M. Pierre Werner, the Luxembourg Prime Minister—Luxembourg was united monetarily with Belgium and, having no central bank of its own, was inherently monetarist—was set up to lay plans and to study the Commission's idea for short- and medium-term credits between Community central banks. (The need for something like a European Reserve Fund had been pointed up by France's continuing dependence in the 1969 troubles on IMF credit and on the swap network organized by the Americans.)

The spinelessness of this Hague declaration, however, was all too soon apparent. When ministers came to discuss the Werner Report in February 1970, they refused to be bound by any firm commitment on economic union; agreed to try out the first experimental narrowing of inter-currency bands from mid-June 1971 but deferred a decision about moving on to the second phase to 1974. A medium-term support fund would be established in 1972, but if further progress could not be made, members would be free to withdraw altogether from the venture in 1976. The doubts and reservations implicit in this February compromise were evident.

Even before 1969, it had seemed to some observers of the effects of international economic interdependence that these made it more, not less, difficult for EEC countries to co-ordinate national monetary management and to liberalize monetary controls. A study by Samuel Katz, for example, had already concluded that European central banks, while seeking to maintain national economic growth and employment and to fight inflation, had actually been led to act more strongly and protectively against each other than they did previously. It was not that they were bad Europeans. It was just that ' Central bankers in our generation have not been prepared ', Katz concluded, ' to watch passively as international forces disturb the internal economy without regard to domestic priorities '.[13]

The events of 1969 would seem to have confirmed the truth of this conclusion and to have underlined the difficulty of any attempt to try and maintain fixed exchange rates between European countries against the powerful forces of the markets.

However, it is easier to see this with the benefit of hindsight than it was at the time. Then, some of the over-optimism of the Six can probably be ascribed partly to the political element that had apparently played so large a part in the franc and D-mark changes. With the French troubles and the German elections behind them, the way ahead naturally looked clearer. In part, too, the over-optimism arose out of an incomplete perception of the interdependence of the developed countries' economies, a consequent tendency still to see problems in terms of separate national currencies rather than as symptoms of a single international system labouring under increasing stress. The 1968–9 difficulties did not *look* like a dollar crisis, or even like the reflection in Europe of an underlying dollar crisis.

One strong contributory reason was undoubtedly the masking effect on the US balance of payments of international short-term monetary movements, mainly between Western Europe and the United States. Through most of 1969, the growing number of US banks operating abroad had massively increased their liabilities to their foreign branches, drawing, in effect, on the pool of Eurodollars in Europe to increase the volume of ' repatriated ' dollars at home. Between December 1968 and September 1969, these liabilities increased from $6·9 billion to $14·3 billion. This was reflected in a large positive figure for short-term capital movements in the balance-of-payments tables—without which the total for the year on a transactions basis would have looked very different.

This westward tide indicated the response—ingenious and not entirely anticipated—devised by American banks to US domestic policy measures. The Eurodollar market and their unrestricted freedom to borrow from their foreign branches offered the banks a means of maintaining their liquidity and lending capacity at home, thus frustrating the anti-inflationary intentions of the monetary authorities. It was a classic example of the increasing difficulty that the United States found in managing its domestic economy without doing something that had unforeseen and possibly disturbing consequences for the international system.

The May 1971 crisis

In due course, the Federal Reserve Board, in June 1969, put reserve requirements on the banks' Eurodollar borrowings, and this did somewhat reverse the movement. But much the stronger influence reversing the tide—and this time exaggerating, dramatizing, and amplifying the balance-of-payments deficit—was once again monetary measures taken in the United States for reasons of domestic politics and economic management.

First, in order to reassure Wall Street after the Penn-Central collapse, Dr Arthur Burns, the new chairman of the Federal Reserve Board, amended Regulation Q (see above, p. 180)—in effect de-restricting the banks' capacity to lend on the strength of term deposits. In nineteen weeks the American banks responded by massively increasing (by $10½ billion) their holdings of large denomination dollar certificates of deposit. This new source of funds relieved them of the need to borrow Eurodollars from their foreign branches, and by December 1970 this total, at $7½ billion, was almost back where it had been in December 1968.

Second, for political reasons and with an eye on the 1972 elections, President Nixon decided in the autumn of 1970 to ease up on interest rates in order to encourage investment and thus reduce unemployment. But the unity of capital markets, and the close interaction of Eurodollar and US interest rates, meant that this was very hard to do without aggravating the US deficit by turning short-term monetary movements into a strongly negative factor. But as before, the palliative measures that followed the initial policy change were too little and too late to quiet the nervousness of the market. For instance, on 15 January 1971 the US government, through the Export-Import Bank, offered special three-month bills paying 6 per cent or about 1½ per cent more than ordinary US Treasury bills. The foreign branches of American banks could hold these Export-Import bills instead of on-lending to the Eurodollar market and could count them towards maintenance of their reserve-free Eurodollar bases.[14] Another step that was taken about this time smacked of shutting the stable door when some, if not all, the horses had gone. This was the central bankers' agreement announced in June 1971 to stop reinvesting their dollar holdings in Eurocurrency markets—thus adding to the problem and, as Machlup put it, ' multiplying the rabbits ' (see above, p. 193). At least this decision arrested the pyramiding process and checked the multiplication of rabbits.

This move effectively immobilized $1 billion which otherwise would eventually have been deposited with European central banks, further swelling their dollar holdings and adding to the menace of the dollar overhang. Another issue of $500m of the high-interest bills was made in February. But by December 1970 Germany's reserves, at $13½ billion, were already higher than before the 1969 revaluation and about twice what they had been earlier in the year. No amount of fiddling with interest rates—an 'Operation Twist' at home and a collaborative reduction in Bundesbank discount rates (contrary to German tight-money policies) abroad—was of much avail.

By April 1971 the market had got to a point where any small thing could set off a speculative rush out of dollars and into D-marks. On Monday, 3 May, the signal was given when the chief economic institutes in Germany declared their united opinion that the only answer to the dollar inflow was another float. In the next two-and-a-half days until Wednesday morning, 5 May, $2 billion came in, half of it in the last forty minutes before, in desperation, the Bundesbank closed the market. The Dutch, Swiss, Belgians, and Austrians did likewise.

The true nature of this market panic—a loss of confidence in the dollar (or, to put it more broadly, in the dollar-based system)—was this time much more apparent. Although the main rush had been once again into marks, a good deal had gone into other European currencies—probably $6,000m into Switzerland, $3,000m into France, $240m into the Netherlands, and $100m each into Belgium and Britain. But the United States showed official indifference and Dr Burns, testifying to the Senate Committee on Banking and Currency, blamed European central banks and the disparity in the phasing of the business cycle in Europe and the United States. The more basic reasons why the Americans were standing by, hands in pockets, were explained much more frankly by Secretary of the Treasury John Connally when he addressed a conference in Munich of the American Bankers' Association. The United States, he explained, was tired of playing Atlas unaided. It was time the Europeans shared the burdens, paying more for their own defence, taking in more American imports, and co-operating more willingly on the monetary problem. If they would not do so, Connally gave fair warning, the United States would act unilaterally to force them. In American eyes the Europeans were acting as though the mounting US deficit was an American problem; the Americans believed it was everyone's problem.[15]

Thus when the Europeans, in the spring of 1971, began to press the United States to convert at least some of their dollars into gold, the Americans were both annoyed at the requests and embarrassed by a gold loss which brought gold stocks down to just over $10 billion—the lowest point since 1936. The 1968 Two-Tier Agreement had made the convertibility of officially held dollars into gold impossible through the market. But payments to the Fund were not covered by the agreement and in March 1971 France asked for $282m on the ground that it needed gold to pay the Fund. The Swiss, Dutch, and Belgians asked for smaller amounts—the latter having accumulated the maximum required of SDRs. These were requests the Americans could not refuse. (But a German request for repayment of $500m in gold lent in 1969 was hastily dropped when knowledge of it was leaked to the press.)

Once again the interdependence of the gold question and the weakness of the dollar was apparent. The real argument was over what solutions were acceptable and which unacceptable, about the reasonable parameters of action to deal with a clearly deteriorating situation. The Americans ruled out two solutions the Europeans would have not thought unthinkable—an increase in the gold price allowing further redistribution of gold stocks, and a reduction of US gold stocks at the old price below the $10 billion mark. The Europeans—less than enthusiastic in their support for the war in Vietnam—ruled out any major European contribution to US defence costs, and saw no special need, since the US still sold more to Europe than it bought, for any major alteration in the monetary terms of trade. In particular, there was deep conflict over the question of agricultural trade. The Europeans did not really believe that the United States was entitled, by the sacred law of comparative costs, to a share in the European market and held that protective agricultural policies that had social and political objectives considered important by European governments should be respected. If possible, they would like to have ruled out as unacceptable any action that either disrupted the CAP—and the first stages of monetary and economic union—or any that involved the abandonment of basic domestic objectives, such as controlling inflation or maintaining employment. That the argument had by now got down through the superficial layers of technicalities and expedients to this brutal political level of who pays, who bears the pain and discomfort of domestic adjustments, who sets the order of economic priorities, was an admission, part conscious and part unconscious, that the affluent alliance had come to the end of the road, the bottom of the barrel of palliatives and easements. By 1971 the disorder was getting too serious for aspirins.

The only possible escape that occurred to the Germans from what was otherwise a bitter dilemma was to take the Community with them on a concerted float—a jump, as it were, into Phase 2 of the Werner Plan.[16] This in effect the French rejected, partly because it conceded too much to the Americans and partly no doubt because floating with a strong mark would subordinate policy-making to German influence. This rejection, confirmed at a deadlocked meeting of EEC finance ministers on 8 May, decided the Germans that, if it was going to be a case of each for himself, then domestic national objectives could justifiably take priority over European ones. On 10 May the German government announced that the mark would be allowed to float, while banks would be forbidden to pay interest on non-resident deposits and foreigners would be barred from buying German commercial bills. The Dutch followed the German float, parting company from the Belgians, who held to the two-tier market separating financial and commercial transactions. Austria revalued the schilling by 5 per cent and the Swiss government (having recently changed the constitution so that National Assembly consent was no longer needed) revalued their franc by 7 per cent. Japan did nothing; neither did France, Britain, or Italy. None had been under serious pressure and their markets had kept open.

The main impact of the May crisis was obviously on the Community. It had postponed the planned advance to Phase 1 of the Werner Plan. This was the arrangement whereby the five currencies would keep within a narrower band, the famous ' snake in the tunnel '. This had been scheduled to begin in mid-June, and though the French at first hoped that the German float would be brief, the Germans were not prepared to take the risks of renewed market pressure if they turned out not to have picked the right rate at which to revalue. The experience had also demonstrated that, when faced with the choice, the Europeans were neither prepared to risk a joint float nor to erect a common external wall of monetary defences in the shape of exchange controls and restrictions on the short-term capital flows resulting from Eurocurrency and similar international financial dealing. It had also demonstrated the feasibility of floating as a prelude to revaluation. Although it had not been intended as such, the May crisis had thus turned out quite a useful dummy run for US monetary strategy later in the summer.

The August crisis

The important distinguishing feature about the August 1971 crisis when it came was that it was a manipulated crisis in which the US, foreseeing renewed market turbulence, resolved deliberately to use a weapon of economic diplomacy—rather as a naval strategist would use the combination of coastal reefs and an offshore wind to exert better mastery over the enemy.[17]

Such masterful tactics are only available to those who know their own mind. Behind the Connally ' offensive ' of 15 August 1971 was a new clarity in US policy about the nature of the dollar problem and the chief objectives to be gained in the national interest—though it is true that external pressures sharpened this appreciation. The American gold stock was reduced to the minimum still statutorily necessary as backing for the currency and by early August the United States had had to borrow all but $600m of its gold tranche from the IMF. When that was gone it could draw more only by submitting to Fund scrutiny. The conviction began to gain ground, that of all the alternative solutions available the best would be a devaluation of the dollar in terms of the other chief currencies. Losing gold or raising the gold price were both equally unpalatable; a drastic cut in US forces or a reduction in the US foreign investment both looked impracticable in the short run. At the same time, a number of economists, led by Paul Samuelson, had been arguing for some time that the dollar was over-valued and that the deficit could best be corrected by a realignment of parities. This view gained support in Washington, aided first by the Reuss Committee,[18] which reported in August, and later by the Williams Commission, which reported to the President[19] in the middle of September, although evidence had been heard and the debate conducted more or less in public through the summer.

Much more powerful, however, were the wider political considerations weighing with the President. To get himself re-elected in 1972, Richard Nixon needed to offset the retreat from Vietnam with improved and stabilized relations with both the Soviet Union and China; and at the same time so to manage to deal with the consequences of the US payments deficit that neither his personal prestige, nor his foreign diplomacy, nor the American domestic economy suffered thereby. In the circumstances, Connally's argument was persuasive that the President could afford neither to wait nor to leave the initiative with market forces, but must provoke a showdown—both to anticipate trouble in the foreign exchange markets and, as it were, to play a forcing bid that would compel the Japanese and the Europeans to help devalue the dollar, whether they liked it or not.

Signs of such impending trouble began to appear by July. A move out of dollars began in European markets and the Bundesbank found that to get rid of the unwanted dollars it had taken in the previous May, it had to lower the price (i.e. the mark-dollar rate) to $3·50. But to preserve the system against a new outburst from the market the US would need the co-operation of the rest of the Group of Ten. If this co-operation could not be obtained by persuasion, then it must be obtained by using such leverage as the wealth and military power of the United States gave it. The question was how susceptible the allies—and especially Japan—would prove to this leverage. For the other major point about the August crisis, as compared with the spring crisis, was that this time the market was equally if not more nervous about the fixity of the Japanese yen as it was about European parities. The US strategy was therefore more aimed at a redefinition of American economic relations with Japan than to adjusting its economic relations with Europe. Seventy per cent of the US trade deficit in the first half of 1971 was in trade with Japan, which also accounted for 40 per cent of the overall deficit. Between May and August Japanese reserves rose by $3 billion. Part of this was a 'genuine' surplus—imports, following flagging domestic demand, were well down—but part was a 'leads and lags' response by foreign customers trying to pay off their yen accounts before an anticipated revaluation. Although Japan's controls against capital inflows were much more effective than Europe's, they were not proof against this kind of market pressure. Meanwhile, American tolerance of Japanese invasion of the domestic market was wearing very thin and the administration was under growing Congressional pressure to take some protective action to maintain US employment.

The 15 August package was put together over a weekend at Camp David, primarily by the President and Mr Connally. Dr Henry Kissinger was not present and the State Department was not represented—perhaps the first time that a major step in US foreign relations was taken without some participation, however marginal, by the Department. Less surprisingly, M. Schweitzer of the Fund was kept completely in the dark until a bare half-hour before the President made the announcement on television. The package combined domestic measures with foreign policy: a 90-day freeze on rents, wages and prices—but not dividends—and a Cost of Living Council to back it up; tax cuts of $6·2 billion; government spending cuts of $4·6 billion, bringing a 5 per cent cut in Federal employment and a 10 per cent cut in foreign aid, and investment incentives in the shape of tax credits with a built-in 'Buy American' character. The chief foreign measure in the ultimatum was the 10 per cent import surcharge on 50 per cent of total US imports; only imports subject to nil duty or under mandatory quotas were to be exempted. This would add $2 billion to the cost of American imports and affect about half of them by value. It was, Nixon said, a temporary measure to compensate American exports for 'unfair exchange rates'; 'when the unfair treatment is ended, the import tax will end as well'.

On the monetary side, Mr Connally, directed by the President, formally suspended the gold convertibility of the dollar, announcing that under no circumstances would the Treasury exchange dollar holdings for gold, and making *de jure* a situation that had been *de facto* since 1968. Nor would the Treasury alter the official gold price. Furthermore, the Federal Reserve was to suspend the swap network through which dollars would be changed with other central banks for other currencies. Even the exchange of American holdings of SDRs for other assets would in future be strictly limited. An additional screw applied soon after was the US Treasury's refusal to roll over the $1½ billion of short-term interest-bearing bonds it had issued to foreign branches of US banks in the early summer. As these matured, a useful incentive was removed to hold these dollars in the branch banks, thus increasing the tendency for dollars to accumulate with foreign central banks.

To sum up, the United States, by suspending dollar convertibility unilaterally, obliged other governments either to accumulate and hold non-convertible dollars; or to sell them for whatever they would fetch on a free market thus effectively revaluing their currencies; or to steer some middle course of market intervention which traded a lower rate of revaluation for some increase in dollar holdings.

Even in the middle of a holiday month, the foreign exchange markets could not be kept closed for long. Yet when they reopened on 23 August, the Japanese—the main target of US strategy—refused to float the yen. In attempting to hold the old rate Japan was obliged to take in $4,000m in the fortnight after 15 August. Thereafter, the upward float was kept, with official intervention, to 6 per cent—and criticized by Washington as ' dirty ' floating. The D-mark, meanwhile, had appreciated by 8 per cent. Otherwise, there was relative calm, and this gave time for the governments to conduct a pavane of diplomatic bargaining to decide who was to budge, how much and how soon.

At the first of these negotiating sessions, the Group of Ten deputies' meeting in Paris on 2 and 3 September, no solution to the impasse could be seen, though Britain pointedly lined up with the EEC countries in agreeing that in any eventual settlement there would have to be an increase in the official gold price. For the first time in a major monetary negotiation, the United States could not count on the almost unquestioning public support (for whatever it was worth) of the British. The French and Germans remained divided in spite of EEC consultations and bilateral talks at the end of August, the Japanese— as Washington intended—totally isolated. A Japanese ministerial visit to Washington early in September was unproductive.

At the mid-September meeting of the Group of Ten in London, Mr Connally confirmed the full extent of the American demands—the full text of the ultimatum as it were. This was that measures should be taken to effect a turn-round within two years in the American deficit of the order of $13 billion—$5 billion on the trade account, $6 billion on the capital account, and $2 more billion to be on the safe side.[20] Connally called this ' a very conservative figure ' but it was $3 billion more than what the OECD thought was needed and $5 billion more than the Fund's figure. The tone of Texan-style diplomacy could be heard in Connally's ungrammatical explanation: ' We had a problem and we're sharing it with the world—just like we shared our prosperity. That's what friends are for '. The solidarity of the Nine [21] was confirmed and their readiness to realign parities (i.e. allow the dollar a substantial devaluation) only on condition that the surcharge was dropped and that, in the reconstructed international monetary order, the rules should be changed to modify the central role of the dollar in the system, especially its reserve role. Partly anticipating the British proposals, rather grandiloquently christened the Barber Plan, for substituting the SDR as the numéraire of a reformed system, Signor Mario Ferrari Aggradi, the Italian Finance Minister, proposed a four-point change in the rules that allowed wider bands for fluctuation in which the new fixed parities should be in terms of SDRs not dollars. The next week the Fund made a stab at acting as mediator, putting forward a plan it had worked out for realigning of parities, devaluing the dollar by 3 to 5 per cent and revaluing the yen by over 15 per cent and the D-mark by over 11 per cent. This fell flat. But it did correctly indicate that negative solidarity among the Nine was not enough. Before the United States could make a deal, there would have to be agreement among the Europeans on the relative values of their currencies and with the Japanese on the relations between the yen and the other currencies.

In the United States, meanwhile, criticism of the Nixon strategy began to mount from Congress, from the press, and, most important perhaps, from professional economists, including Galbraith, Roosa, Kenen, and notably Fred Bergsten, who until earlier in the summer had been on Kissinger's staff at the White House. Much of the objection was not to the main objective of the policy (a dollar devaluation) so much as to the manner in which it was being conducted. Was it really necessary, it was being asked in Washington as in Europe, to put the whole system in jeopardy just to show the world that the United States meant business?

Before the end of September the first relenting move had been conceded. In Washington Mr Connally admitted to the Group of Ten on the eve of the annual Fund meeting that he wanted to negotiate and he did not repeat his obdurate refusal to discuss the gold price. The communiqué [22] declared the collective belief that it was ' necessary to find prompt solutions in order to ensure the stability and the effective working of the international monetary system pending the adoption of longer-term reforms and in order to avoid the development of restrictions on trade and payments '.

The move towards a mutual understanding was confirmed at the Fund's annual meeting. The Executive Directors were asked to report on possible amendments to the Articles of Agreement. And the Barber Plan, which was really more of a declaration of principle that both reserve currencies—the dollar as well as the pound—should eventually be retired as major reserve assets, was warmly acclaimed just because it was felt to be a constructive contribution at a dark moment. On the interim settlement, however, the United States was less moved to be conciliatory.

Two months later, on the eve of the next Group of Ten meeting in Rome on 30 November, the United States still appeared not to have budged. The foreign exchange markets had been comparatively calm. Some of the commodity markets had taken a tumble but this mainly affected disfranchised developing countries. The big international companies were managing well enough, with their eggs well spread in all sorts of baskets. And trade had on the whole continued without serious hindrance, even though there was some tendency to revert to invoicing export deals in national currencies. The economic consequences of floating had proved less damaging than some had feared—at least in the short run.

Confidence in the long term was another matter. Here the two major contestants, the United States and Japan, had both begun to fear the political and economic consequences if the stalemate went on too long. Japanese industry had begun to press hard for an end to the float in October. By mid-October Japan was ready to accept a maximum revaluation of 9 per cent. By the end of November, however, political and market pressures brought the government to contemplate a much more substantial revaluation of perhaps 15–18 per cent. By now, the Americans were ready to start negotiating the terms on which they would lift the surcharge. It is not quite clear at what point the corner was turned. A very tough policy statement issued by the US Treasury on the eve of the Rome meeting made everybody threaten to go away if it was not withdrawn. But this could have been a deliberate piece of gamesmanship. For by this time Nixon had announced his plans to visit Peking early in 1972 [23] and possibly Moscow later on, and had arranged dates for a series of preliminary meetings with the heads of state of Canada, Japan, France, Britain, and West Germany, in that order. This was the main international political imperative. Another was the German argument that the Europeans were being pushed into readiness to build the EEC into a defensive monetary and trading bloc and therefore a later deal would be a worse one for the United States. Finally, on the trade side the EEC had made clear that (helped perhaps by the prospect of British entry) it was now prepared to stockpile grain rather than queer the market for the Americans by cheap surplus sales abroad. The importance attached to this bait demonstrated once more the disproportionate weight attached to agricultural interests, both in American domestic politics and in international bargaining.

The market was also working strongly for a settlement, in the sense that, in spite of dirty floating (i.e. market intervention to influence the free price), the average revaluation of the currencies of the Americans' fourteen chief trading partners had now reached over 7 per cent, thus substantially reducing the gap to be bridged by negotiation. The same market forces made it impossible for the 'stable Europeans'—France, Britain, and Italy—to pretend that they could follow the dollar down; the question was whether they would have to revalue a little or could stand pat.

The market turned the screw a second time when the dealers' appreciation that important factors were working for a settlement increased the expectation of one. Since any settlement would revalue other currencies by more than the current market rate, there were profits to be made and losses avoided by a quick shift out of the prospective devaluers' currencies. In the last week in November, therefore, official dollar holdings rose by $723m, the biggest weekly rise since August. (One possibly important effect of this market movement was on the French, who found the gap between the commercial franc and the financial franc rates widening to 3·3 per cent and costing some $250m to hold from widening further.)

By the time of the Rome meeting in November, therefore, Connally was ready to abandon the demand for a $13 billion turn-around in the balance of payments and declared that the United States was ready to settle for a deal which would produce a $9 billion turn-around, involving an average currency revaluation of 11 per cent. After a closed executive session, at which progress was clearly being made, Connally declared that, though no decisions had been taken and no communiqué was being issued, hypotheses were being discussed and assumptions were being made for the overall realignment between the dollar and other currencies and for the distribution of the necessary parity changes between countries.[24]

Before the package could be tied up, however, it was necessary that any remaining differences between the EEC countries should be settled. Britain, France, and Italy were already in broad agreement. Germany was the odd man out and Professor Schiller and Giscard d'Estaing got on badly. Hence the importance of the Paris meeting on 4–5 December between Chancellor Brandt and President Pompidou. It was necessary that they should agree not only on the figures but also that the EEC should concede some further readiness to talk to the Americans about trade. Reportedly, the two heads of state also agreed at this time that efforts towards closer monetary union in the EEC should be renewed and that EEC central banks should co-ordinate their interventions in the market in order to defend the new parties and to maintain intra-EEC rates within a closer range.

This was how it came about that President Pompidou, meeting

President Nixon in the Azores on 14 December, as arranged earlier, was able to act as the spokesman for Europe and to announce the broad lines of the deal with the United States.[25] This was, as expected, that the surcharge would be withdrawn at once in exchange for a package of revaluations, and that the President should ask Congress to agree to raise the official gold price to $38 an ounce. The Europeans also agreed, as part of the deal, to negotiate on various trade issues in which the Americans sought concessions.

The Group of Ten, meeting at the Smithsonian Institute in Washington three days later, on 17–18 December, was therefore able to wrap up the details in time for the foreign exchange markets to reopen on Monday morning on the basis of the new rates. The agreed percentage changes in central rates in terms of the dollar were announced as follows:

Belgian franc	+11·57
French franc	+ 8·57
Italian lira	+ 7·48
German mark	+13·58
Japanese yen	+16·88
Netherlands florin	+11·57
Swedish krona	+ 7·49
British pound	+ 8·57

Thus the franc and the pound retained their gold parities; the Dutch and the Belgians moved together again. The Canadian dollar continued to float and the Swiss franc, already revalued by 7·07 per cent in May, had now appreciated by a further 6·8 per cent, making a total appreciation of 13·9 per cent. (Weighted according to each country's trade without other members of the group, Japan's revaluation mounted to about a 14 per cent change; Germany's to about 6 per cent; the Swiss to just under 5 per cent, and the British to just under 3 per cent.)

The agreement was concerned only with the currencies of the affluent alliance. Other members of the Fund were to decide for themselves which course to choose: whether to float (like the Canadians); to keep in line with the British and the French—as did all the franc zone countries as well as the three North African ' old ' franc zone countries (Algeria, Tunisia, and Morocco); and the main holders of sterling (Libya, Kuwait, Hong Kong, Australia and New Zealand, Ireland, Nigeria, Malaysia and Singapore) and some minor old sterling area countries in Africa and the Caribbean. Alternatively, they could take a good opportunity to devalue (as did Israel, Yugoslavia, South Africa and her associates, Rhodesia, Lesotho, Swaziland, and Botswana). A third alternative was to take an intermediate line, revaluing in terms of the dollar but usually by less than Germany or Japan—as did the four Scandinavian countries, Norway, Sweden, Denmark, and Finland; Turkey, Portugal, and India: Malta, Venezuela, and Germany's monetary associates and neighbours, Belgium, Luxembourg, the Netherlands, and Austria. Finally, there were the countries which elected to keep their currency directly linked with the dollar. These were no longer an exclusively Latin American group. They also included the United States dependencies in the Far East (Vietnam, Thailand, Taiwan, and Korea) and Nepal, Pakistan, Ceylon, Iran, and the three East African states (Kenya, Tanzania, and Uganda), and Zambia.

The overall result was a marked increase in the diversity of monetary strategies chosen by countries all of whom were supposed to be acting according to a single IMF rule book; the open acknowledgement of no less than five currency groups grouped around the dollar, the pound, the franc, the D-mark and the Rand, as well as other less clearly defined groups like the Scandinavians and the East Africans.

The communiqué [26] issued after the Smithsonian meeting also confirmed the main points of agreement reached at the Azores. It further agreed in somewhat general—and therefore non-committal—terms that:

discussions should be promptly undertaken, particularly in the framework of the IMF, to consider reform of the international monetary system over the longer term. It was agreed that attention should be directed to the appropriate monetary means and division of responsibilities for defending stable exchange rates and for insuring a proper degree of convertibility of the system; to the proper role of gold, of reserve currencies, and of Special Drawing Rights in the operation of the system; to the appropriate volume of liquidity; to re-examination of the permissible margins of fluctuation around established exchange rates and other means of establishing a suitable degree of flexibility; and to other measures dealing with movements of liquid capital.

Pending agreement on these reforms, the Ten agreed to make provision for new and wider $2\frac{1}{4}$ per cent margins of exchange rate fluctuation above and below the new exchange rates.

Conclusions

But the agreement, though it was acclaimed with relief and satisfaction at the time, was not really a happy ending to the story. It was a truce not a peace settlement. The old order that, through the later 1960s, had alternatively crumbled and given way and been patched up and underpinned, was gone now. Unless the United States restored gold convertibility (which seemed increasingly unlikely) it could not be restored. To stop the conflict for fear of what might be destroyed if it went on was easier than to reach agreement on the entire structure of a new international monetary order. Recent political and military history had shown—after World War II in Europe and after the Arab-Israeli wars of 1948 and 1967, for instance—that there could be long intervals between the ceasefire and the peace treaty. It could be the same in international economic relations; and the risks involved, though different in kind, would be no less great.

In short, all that was resolved in December 1971 were the most immediate and pressing questions at issue, allowing calm to return to markets for the time being but without even any certainty that the change in relative currency values would be adequate or lasting.

The crisis had once more demonstrated the dominant role of the United States in the international monetary system. That system had been severely modified in 1971, but the American monopoly of the power to initiate monetary pressures on other governments and to make use of those pressures to gain ends believed consistent with the national interest of the United States was undiminished. Of the other members of the affluent alliance, Japan had played a central role for the first time. Indeed, the crisis would possibly never have been provoked by Mr Connally had the pattern of US-Japanese relations that had persisted through the 1960s remained unchanged—that is to say, if the United States had continued to be as indulgent towards Japan, or Japan as compliant to the wishes of the United States as it had been through most of the 1960s.

The other change of role was that of Britain. This was the first international monetary crisis in which the British had not stood firmly beside the United States (or vice versa). British help in bringing the Europeans round—which had still been quite useful in the early 1960s—was now shown to be easily dispensable. Nor did it make any difference to the balance of power in the negotiations that Britain had sided firmly with the Europeans. The latter were still unable in the autumn (as in the spring) of 1971 to pool their monetary sovereignty even to the extent of providing each other with the necessary credit support to maintain a joint float against the dollar.

In retrospect it is pretty clear therefore that the knell of European monetary union was rung in 1971 and not in 1974 with the floating of the French franc. By the latter step, the Community's snake was effectively reduced to an embryonic D-mark area. But it was the failures of 1971 that had first revealed the lack of political will behind the technical arrangements.

Indeed, far from the Europeans jeopardizing the restoration of a permanent international monetary order by their united opposition in an aggressive and unco-operative bloc, as some Americans feared,[27] they were much more likely, judging by their performance in 1971, to obstruct progress to that end by their lamentable indecision and disunity.

As a direct result of this disunity, the European Commission had been unable to play the essential and influential part in the drama that it would have liked. Its advice had been disregarded and its proposals ignored. Its elaborately laid plans for European monetary union had been postponed *sine die*. The growing impression was confirmed that it had filched nothing in real power from national governments. These remained the real decision-makers on any matters of importance, even including the external economic diplomacy of the Community.

Similarly, the fragile fiction of the authority of the Fund took a severe knock in 1971. From 1958 to the Stockholm meeting in 1968 ten years later (see above, p. 252), the importance of the Fund— even though it had been necessary to supplement it with additional mechanisms for credit and consultation—had seemed to grow continuously; from a shadowy presence in the wings it had become accustomed to playing from time to time right down stage before the footlights. Now the United States, which had designed and upheld it for so long, had most flagrantly flouted its authority. Now it was not at all certain that the damaged prestige of the Fund could be subsequently repaired or, alternatively, that the Group of Ten could fill the vital role of international monetary authority, making and interpreting the rules of the game.

Indeed, the crisis had dramatically exposed the weakness of all international economic organizations, the Fund, the OECD, the European Commission, and the BIS. The 1960s had been a decade of almost uninterrupted development and expansion in the tasks assigned to these agencies and in the number of experts employed by them. Yet none of these bureaucracies had been able to play an influential part in controlling the market or in mediating between governments. And no matter how mutual confidence had been built between the delegates who deliberated under their auspices, it was not these international bodies who were able to conduct the final negotiations but only the heads of state.

Unfinished business

But while the crisis showed up the impotence of institutions as such, it had paradoxically demonstrated the resilience of the system, both of the network of private financial and commercial transactions in the world market economy which had maintained throughout its vigorous activities; and of the intergovernmental network of understanding and mutual co-operation that had been built up between the officials of national finance ministries and central banks. Here there was apparently a tacit agreement that though confrontation would be tough, it would never become ruthlessly destructive. This was why some observers found that the popular use of the word ' crisis ' for the period after August 1971 was unwarranted in that it implied somehow that the gloves were right off and that the situation might conceivably become more than merely disturbing. It also confirmed the hypothesis that, in international monetary relations, the governments of developed countries repeatedly find it easier to agree *not* to act in a mutually destructive manner than positively to agree on international codes, rules, and regulatory mechanisms.

Thus, of the four main areas in which the basic questions concerning the running of the international monetary system were left unresolved by the Smithsonian Agreement, two concerned the management of relations between national monetary systems. These were the questions concerning the nature, management, and use of reserves and other aspects of what economists saw as the ' liquidity problem '; and the questions concerning the adjustment problem, i.e. the rules governing exchange rates between currencies, when and how they should be changed, when and how they should be supported. These matters, at least, were recognized as requiring discussion and, if possible, resolution.

The other two concerned the positive management of a financial system and a series of money markets that had so far outgrown the confines of any single state authority that they could truly be called an international or transnational system and international or transnational markets.[28] They were the questions of the money supply and therefore of the inflation of prices expressed in monetary terms treated as a world problem; and the question of stability and discipline among the market operators—that combination of basic regulations to restrain unwarranted risk-taking with intermittent intervention to correct undue oscillation. On the national scene, this function is performed by the central bank and by other public and semi-public agencies backed by the political authority of the state. They are held responsible for seeing that financial booms, bubbles, and crashes that would affect not only the monetary system but also the whole economy are, so far as possible, avoided or at least minimized.

Because among the developed countries in 1971 no single political authority existed to take this responsibility, and because there was no political ' constituency ' able to insist on its importance and hence on the need for action, these were questions that at least in the short term could be neglected with impunity. The results of the failure to set up such an international monetary authority (or to evolve one out of an existing organization such as the IMF) to control the money supply and to supervise the financial markets of the world could best be judged by analogy with the problems of international military security. In the absence of an overall international authority, whether for disarmament or for the development of atomic and nuclear energy, the responsibility automatically devolves upon the strongest single state. The most powerful national authority then has the power for good or for ill to provide for international security as best it can. And as, in matters of military strategy, the world learned to depend in the 1950s and 1960s on the prudence and sagacity of the US President, on the US National Security Council, and on the deterrent power of US armed forces, so in monetary matters it may, in the 1970s and 1980s, have to learn to depend on the sagacity of the US Secretary of the Treasury and the chairmen of the US Federal Reserve Board and perhaps of the US Securities and Exchange Commission. The military analogy is also helpful in that it suggests that the choice in such matters is not really—as some writers on international organization would have had us believe—a straight one between international government and international anarchy, but rather a narrower choice between the authority of an international body which would largely be directed by the choices of the most powerful state, and the authority of the latters' national institutions acting directly (even if not altogether effectively) on the international system.

The other two issue areas of liquidity and adjustment were really different aspects of the same question. In the absence of a single universally acceptable international currency, a single world monetary system and a central monetary authority, the international market economy had to make do with a collection of national currencies and monetary systems and national monetary authorities of different sizes, degrees of stability, and credibility. Their coexistence, given these differences, required both mutual adjustment through changes in the rates of exchange between currencies and the settlement of shorter-term deficits or surpluses in some mutually accepted monetary medium. Neither of these adjustment processes was totally dispensable. But the easier it was to make exchange rate changes, the more limited the need for a medium of settlement; and vice versa. The two questions were therefore closely interrelated though each comprised a number of subsidiary issues. In the context of a historical survey, there is room only to summarize the main questions under discussion without going into the complex arguments adduced on either side. This is necessary in order to indicate, however briefly, the agenda of unfinished business which remained to be settled by the affluent alliance at the end of our period. However, it will show only the substance of disagreement. The causes of disagreement can in these, as in earlier debates recounted in this survey, be easily discerned as being basically political rather than technical. Some of them were highly charged with emotion and centred on what constituted the proper order of priority in the management of the system as between efficiency, stability, and justice, or on what was a proper and fair apportionment of rights and duties within the system. None of these were matters on which any objective technical solution could be devised that would avoid conflict.

To take the adjustment question first, the Bretton Woods system had obviously been distorted in the 1960s by the reluctance of countries, usually for political reasons, either to devalue in good time or to revalue. The trouble had been compounded further by the excessive rigidity of the dollar parity in terms of other currencies. The Smithsonian Agreement, it is true, required an immediate amendment of the Fund rules, allowing a wider band of permitted divergence above or below a central rate. But it would soon be clear that this hardly rated even as a guideline, and that in practice countries would feel quite free to float their currencies or to observe much tighter rates with some countries than with others.

Yet without some rules there was a built-in inequity that allowed some countries—and especially the United States—greater freedom to avoid adjustment than others and that distributed the burden of internal economic adjustment not necessarily on those who needed to make the change as on those who were least able to insulate themselves. Lack of rules would risk either a general retreat into the defensive postures of economic nationalism or a submission of the weak economies and states to the domination of the strong. But as the IMF Committee of Twenty (the committee appointed to discuss reform of the international monetary system) was soon to discover it was by no means easy to devise a workable and universally applicable code of good behaviour for the adjustment of exchange rates. The United States especially was apt to change its mind from one year to the next on what rules best suited its national interest. Moreover a rule-book on exchange-rate change would also require some objective definition of what constituted clean and dirty exchange-rate management. This, in view of countries' very diverse financial institutions and practices and needs, was also going to be difficult. Moreover, the latitude in running a deficit, or in accumulating a surplus, which was open to different countries varied very widely and imposed very different constraints on their policy-making. An objectively 'fair' rule-book would also have to legislate on the access of countries to various forms of credit—to Eurodollar borrowing for instance, no less than to credit from the Fund and the network of inter-central bank swaps.

As for the question of reserve assets, here the Bretton Woods agreement had first been freely adapted and then largely discarded in the course of the 1960s. Instead of using gold and Fund credit for the settlement of inter-state payments debts, countries first accepted and then used dollars which became increasingly non-convertible in the later 1960s. The choice now lay between a series of options. The most ideal solution would be the total substitution of SDRs (or of internationally issued assets under a different name) for reserve assets denominated in any national currency (or for both gold *and* reserve assets denominated in national currency), and the exclusive management of international liquidity—the supply of reserves for inter-state settlement—by an international monetary authority. But although enthusiastically advocated by many economists, the transfer of monetary power involved was much greater than most of them were able or willing to appreciate. This solution in effect demanded the appointment of some sort of international monetary dictator or Supremo with a power to grant or to withhold reserve assets that would have to be at times both discriminatory and arbitrary. This much had been well demonstrated in the 1960s by the increasing flexibility of the Fund when practising credit creation on a much more limited scale.

Moreover, to be permanently effective, the substitution of SDRs (or some similar asset) for dollars would require international financial markets to use SDRs instead of dollars as an everyday international currency, because otherwise national central banks would inevitably find themselves the recipients of new dollar deposits alongside their SDR reserves. For this reason, the monetary Supremo would also have to be given the very sensitive task of managing international money and security markets, in just the same way as a national central bank Governor has to manage national markets. Inevitably, therefore he would find it necessary to take highly political decisions on when to deflate or inflate, when to support and when to discipline the whole world market economy. It would be a task that could only be carried out with the backing of overwhelming political (and in the last resort) military power.

Other problems would arise if the rule-book aimed at the predominant use of SDRs with some limited use of other assets, gold, and dollars. The practical limitation of the right to hold dollars would have to be denied in this case not only to central banks but also to other financial institutions which might be inclined to accumulate them. To leave the system dependent, as it was in 1971, on dollars inconvertible into gold but supplemented by SDRs, on the other hand, would leave the United States with an acute asymmetrical influence within the system which other countries were certain increasingly to resent and would give it an inequitable freedom to avoid exchange-rate adjustments according to any rule-book that might be devised.

The alternative option of using SDRs, gold, and dollars convertible into gold or into SDRs (possibly in a fixed or semi-fixed ratio to one another) would subject US policies and the monetary management of the US economy to constraints and difficulties that would make it unacceptable to any American President, let alone any Congress.

An associated (and unresolved) problem concerned the numéraire—the accepted international unit of account. The Bretton Woods system had worked well so long as confidence continued in the validity of the dollar-gold numéraire of $35 to one ounce. But once the United States would not convert dollar reserve assets into gold at any price, the system was deprived of an agreed and accepted medium for certain essential transactions and calculations. Such a unit of account, for example, was needed in order to quote or contract exchange rates with the IMF, to calculate IMF quotas, to make drawings from or repayments to the IMF, to cover the issue and repayment of World Bank and other international bank bonds, to calculate and fix salaries and pensions of international civil servants, national contributions to international agencies, and so forth. It was also indispensable to any coherent and consistent series of trade, financial, or national income statistics and highly convenient (if not absolutely vital) for the operation of forward exchange markets and international commercial and financial transactions. It was clear that for such purposes the use of the dollar as a unit of account, though once accepted by European currencies, for example, would now be convenient but inequitable and less than satisfactory. Gold at free market values would be potentially unstable as well as inequitable. Yet for everyone to use the SDR as a unit of account required prior agreement on how the value of the SDRs was to be assessed and, still more, maintained. Thus, the idea of a ' basket-of-currencies ' valuation for SDRs began to take hold, giving a numéraire which, though less than perfect technically, was acceptable and with goodwill, workable.

For on this as on the other unresolved questions of monetary reform the developed countries were probably going to have to compromise to reach some workable arrangement that was far short of ideal or technically perfect. Nor, possibly, would it be entirely rational, and certainly not expected or predictable. That was less important than that it should have the consent of the major parties concerned and should avert open conflict between them. If there was, after all, one sure lesson to be learned from both the liquidity negotiations and the negotiations that led up to the Smithsonian Agreement—indeed from all of the history of international monetary relations in the 1960s—it was that the bargaining process, however technical in its detail, was not in essence too different from other kinds of diplomacy. The bargaining strength of unequal powers, the non-quantifiable factor of the national will to use such power as was available, the way in which external factors could arbitrarily favour one side rather than the other—all these things were more likely than neat academic blueprints to decide (in the future as in the past) the sort of rules and customs by which the international monetary system would be managed. The best hope for the world market economy was still, as in other forms of international politics, the ability of those responsible for making policy and for conducting monetary diplomacy to discern and pursue an enlightened self-interest—the sort of wisdom and vision that saw the need sometimes to sacrifice the short-run national advantage for the sake not only of the international community but also of the long-term national welfare.

Notes

[1] The distinction which has now passed into general usage was first made by John Pinder, Director of Political and Economic Planning, in 1968 in a paper given to the eleventh Bailey Conference and later published in *The World Today*, Mar 1968. It was reprinted in Michael Hodges, ed., *European Integration: selected readings* (Penguin, 1973).

[2] OECD, *Inflation: the present problem* (Paris, Dec 1970), para. 62, p. 30.

[3] Harry G. Johnson, 'The Bretton Woods system, key currencies and the "Dollar Crisis" of 1971', *Three Banks Review*, June 1972, pp. 17 & 18.

[4] Bundesbank, *Ann. rep.*, 1968, p. 38.

[5] IMF, *Ann. rep.*, 1969, pp. 12 & 78.

[6] *The Banker*, Dec 1968.

[7] Weil & Davidson, p. 160.

[8] By which a country's import bill after devaluation is increased, before more competitive exports can expand, thus producing a perverse deterioration in the payments chart.

[9] e.g. from *The Economist*, 30 Aug, p. 46.

[10] The pejorative term—'Verschmutzten floating'—was first coined by Schiller in September 1971. But, ironically, it had been the Bundesbank, in October 1969, which had first practised it (see *Frankfurter Allgemeine Zeitung*, 20 Sept 1971).

[11] The subject had been exhaustively discussed in the course of 1969 at four meetings of economists, officials, and bankers organized by Fred Bergsten, George Halm, Fritz Machlup, and Robert Roosa. A statement known as the Burgenstock communiqué had been made on 30 June 1969: 'There was a consensus that such changes (in exchange rates) when appropriate should take place sooner and thus generally be smaller and more frequent than during the past two decades.' Discussion continued on alternative schemes for increasing the flexibility of fixed rates or ensuring the fixity of flexible rates (*New York Times*, 30 June 1969).

[12] *7th Ann. rep.*, para. 25. In fact, under Arts. 105 and 107 of the Rome Treaty members are supposed to consult and collaborate on balance-of-payments positions and to treat exchange rate policies as a matter of common interest.

[13] *External surpluses, capital flows and credit policies in the EEC, 1958–67* (Princeton, Feb 1969), p. 44.

[14] Charles Coombs, 'Treasury and Federal Reserve exchange operations', *FRBNY Monthly Review*, Mar 1971.

[15] USIS release, 1 June 1971.

[16] Communautés Européennes, *Rapport au Conseil et à la Commission concernant la réalisation par étapes de l'Union économique et monétaire dans la Communauté* (Brussels, Oct 1970).

[17] This feature was most clearly analysed by Ed. Morse, 'Crisis diplomacy, interdependence and the politics of international economic relations', *World Politics*, XXIV (1972), Suppl.

[18] After Rep. Henry Reuss, its chairman, properly called the Congressional Economic Subcommittee on International Exchange and Payments.

[19] Commission on International Trade and Investment Policy, *United States international economic policy in an interdependent world* (Washington, July 1971).

[20] FT, 16 Sept 1971.

[21] i.e. Canada, Japan, Britain, Germany, France, Italy, Netherlands, Belgium and Sweden.

[22] London Press Service, 16 Sept 1971.

[23] Dr Kissinger's interview with Chou En-lai had taken place in July, and he had later been sent on repeated visits to Paris.

[24] *The Times*, 2 Dec 1971.

[25] *Le Monde*, 16 Dec 1971.

[26] *Dept. of State Bull.* 10 Jan 1972.

[27] See, for example, Diebold, *The United States and the industrial world*.

[28] For a clear exposition see Lawrence Krause, ' Private international finance ', *International Organization*, Summer 1971 (also published as Brookings report 223, 1972).

12

CONCLUSIONS

Looking back over the story that has just been told, what changes stand out as the key developments in the monetary history of the 1960s? And what conclusions can we derive from contemplating those changes—conclusions, that is, of a broad and general nature about the international monetary system and the problems it presents?

There seem to me to be four key developments that stand out from the details; and three main conclusions, perhaps less obvious, that follow from them.

The first—and most obvious—key development of the decade was what some have labelled ' the politicization of money ' in international relations. The phrase in itself is a poor one. In my view, money is *always* political at any level of community from the family upwards. But when monetary arrangements are such, or a monetary system is so run that it does not obstruct prosperity, that it assures monetary stability and is believed to operate with justice, then it does not usually generate political criticism and conflict and will normally be supported by a tacit political consensus. The only other time when criticism is silent and when political conflict about money is suppressed is when a monetary system is maintained by such overwhelming tyrannical power that its shortcomings are only some of the many grievances which people are forced to endure. But between these two extreme situations—when either the monetary system is less than satisfactory or when the dominant political power is weak or less than ruthlessly tyrannical, then the subject of monetary management can be expected to generate political conflict.

In the 1960s the politicization of money simply meant that from being a matter of relatively minor importance in the relations between states it came to be seen, and treated, as a matter of major importance. This change from the *pianissimo* to the *fortissimo* seems to emerge strongly as one looks back over the years from 1971 (or later) to the end of the 1950s.

A corollary of this rise in political salience over the decade was that money matters could no longer be treated as technical and thus safely dealt with by experts without political supervision. Nor could they be treated in isolation from other political arenas. The result was that by the end of the 1960s trade, money and defence had all become aspects of one interrelated bargaining process, a process that took place mainly between the United States and the other developed countries.

The second key development was that of accelerating economic interdependence, especially between the developed countries. This meant not only that states became, as Richard Cooper has described,[1] more susceptible to each other's economic development and policies, but also in practical, everyday, terms, that people in these countries—and especially economic enterprises—became sensitized to and had to keep watch on events and developments throughout the world. National horizons were no longer sufficient. People had to be—and very soon became—ready to respond to innovations, stimuli, and market forces emanating from outside the national economy. What has been happening with the growth of economic interdependence, in short, is that while the political boundaries set by the state and the nation have remained intact, the economic boundaries have been dissolving under the impact of improved communications, increased international investment, international use of currencies and movement of people. This is a development still only very partially assimilated by conventional political theory or by conventional economic theory.[2] One aspect of this dissolution of national economic frontiers that was particularly important for the international monetary system was the development of arbitrage between parallel markets—especially for foreign exchange and short-term credit. This is only another way of saying that the market—that is, the body of potential buyers and sellers—of credit, of monetary assets and claims—was rapidly becoming a single world market with regional outlets rather than a series of national markets some of which had international channels of communication.

The third main development was surely the gradual erosion and abandonment of the monetary arrangements agreed at Bretton Woods. By the end of our period, most of the landmarks of the old monetary system had gone—the fixed gold price, dollar and gold convertibility, fixed exchange rates, the relative stability of value in the main currencies, the international use of sterling. After ten years of effort finding all sorts of palliative measures—unilateral, bilateral, and multilateral—to shore up the old system, the United States finally took the last prop away in August 1971.

Four years on, it was still not clear what new code of rules could replace the old ones and whether it would as successfully sustain a prosperous world economy. What was increasingly clear was that, just when the old system had started to give way under the pressures put upon it, all sorts of new problems relating to the international monetary system were demanding collective attention and concerted action—the problem of inflation, of international taxation, of the regulation of banking and the co-ordination of interest-rate policies, to mention only a few. Perhaps it was the perception of multiplying problems and disappearing solutions that accounted for the grave anxiety for the future which—despite the acceptance of managed floating—marks the end of the story.

The fourth item was a non-development: the continued, even accentuated predominance of the United States, in spite of the years of deficit and the chorus of doubts about the dollar. This surely was a remarkable feature of the 1960s: that the US should prove no less powerful a force in the operation of the system when it was seemingly monetarily weak than when it was monetarily strong. Indeed, because of its growing international involvement Washington was inclined increasingly to extend its *lex economica* beyond the frontiers of the state, regulating and restricting what its citizens and corporations could do in the world at large. Yet the control of the Congress and other legislatures over monetary edicts of all kinds was visibly weakening.

The three conclusions I would draw from these very broad developments can also be quite briefly put. From the politicization of money in the international system I would deduce the emergence, at an accelerating pace, of an international political economy. By this I mean an international economic system whose management, or mismanagement, or non-management, is a matter of international concern—or concern to the international community and not simply to the society of nation states. International businessmen, for example, now anxiously urge that 'someone' should decide how to recycle Arab oil money, should act to stop inflation, should safeguard them against sudden disruption of supply contracts. But now they no longer look exclusively to 'their' national governments. Not everyone may agree with their order of priorities. But the point is that they are coming increasingly these days to look for a political resolution of international economic problems, not necessarily or even optimally one decided or imposed by any single state. It follows that much thinking about the international system may need revision. It is not a political system plus an economic system. It is both together, one and indissoluble—a political economy.

It follows too that conflict in the system is of two distinct kinds. There is the conflict between states that may ultimately culminate in war; and there is the dissension between states that may be just as dangerous because it impedes international political action and invites disorder. One is disturbing; the other is disruptive. Much contemporary pessimism about the future of the world recalls the helplessness of many ancien régimes whose members could often perceive the problems facing their society but were unable to break out of long-established habits to do anything about it before disaster struck.

The accelerating process of economic interdependence is perhaps another aspect of the same thing. The conclusion I would draw from it, however, goes somewhat further. If the interdependence process is accelerating, so too must the political change to cope with it. Otherwise impossible economic, if not political, tension ensues. The degree of international co-operation, suspension, regulation, and co-ordination required to avoid disruption, to maintain order and stability—and (not by any means least) to dispense justice by the exercise of political will—is not, and cannot be static. Politically, we are trying to go up while standing on a down-escalator, not at the foot of a staircase. Each co-operative achievement therefore does not take us one step nearer heaven; it only saves us being taken downwards one step nearer hell. We are thus subject to an adaptative imperative in international economic relations, and especially in the management of the international monetary system.

The third and last conclusion follows from the third and fourth main developments of the decade—that is, from the conjunction of the vacuum left by the dissolution of the Bretton Woods rules with the continued dominance of the United States. It would seem logical to deduce that some new political framework must be devised to fill the vacuum and to take care of the neglected problems and that the United States must take the initiative in proposing it to its associates in the affluent alliance. It is clear to everyone by now that the present machinery of intergovernmental discussion—notably the Fund's Interim Committee—is quite inadequate to this task.

It is inadequate, not certainly for lack of sophistication and expertise, but for lack of power and (perhaps more important still) for lack of political legitimacy. Ministers have the power but lack both expertise and time to apply themselves to rather complex tasks. Moreover, all are to some extent constrained by prior loyalties—to ministerial colleagues and to political parties who have to submit to the test of national elections fought on national issues. Yet no alternative body that has too much power is likely to prove politically acceptable to national governments.

We are once again up against the recurrent dilemma of all international organizations. It may be, of course, that it is an insuperable problem. But if it is ever to be solved, it must surely be evident by now that it is more likely to be done by building small rather than big. To erect yet another vast bureaucracy of international officials such as the UN or the European Commission is asking for trouble—worse still, it is fostering dangerous illusions. The trick may be to do the opposite, and to see how finely power could be separated, spreading real but limited powers of financial regulation among a number of international boards or commissions. If each dealt only with a narrow issue-area, governments might find it easier to delegate decisions to it.

The make-up of these boards would also be important. They should somehow combine the expertise of officials (and perhaps of ex-practitioners such as bankers) with the political legitimacy of parliamentarians. The latter would supply the common sense and the political backbone—the readiness to defy Prime Ministers and financiers alike—that officials notably lack. The Fund in its time developed the habit of consulting with academic and non-official experts and this practice would be some precedent for going much further in the same direction. The nearest model for these international bodies would be Federal commissions and boards, which, in the US system, exercise independent judgement in special areas of government policy. The most powerful and best known of these is, of course, the Federal Reserve Board. It may be that no such single body responsible for whole areas of monetary management is feasible at present in the international system. But the other boards in the United States—those responsible, for instance, for tariffs, for the regulation of communications and of air transport as well as of stock exchanges and the market for securities, have more narrowly defined tasks and are less imposing. An essential feature of these Federal bodies is their immunity from electoral change, their well-defined, if limited, powers and their acknowledged authority as guardians of the general welfare. Our now extensive experience of international organizations suggests the importance of financial and budgetary independence for any such regulatory body. This both the Fund and the BIS have enjoyed and profited from, and some association with the latter might be found that would avoid the financial problems attendant on security and peace-keeping operations run by international organizations dependent on annual national subscriptions.

To some such new departure in international economic administration there are only two alternatives. One is to court, and ultimately probably to experience, financial and monetary anarchy and disorder, with political consequences to the security, self-confidence, and stability of the social fabric that can hardly be imagined. This is the alternative most to be feared, which any sane politician must surely seek to avoid at all costs. Yet it is perhaps, on present form, the most probable outcome.

The only other alternative is to submit to a measure of tyranny by the most powerful and ruthless member of the affluent alliance—the United States. In my view this might be unpleasant, painful, and humiliating for Europeans and Japanese. But it would still be infinitely preferable to chaos. Whether the political system of the United States is really capable of taking on the responsibility entailed is at present rather doubtful. Could it really take the necessary broad view of monetary objectives, and could it enforce its will, when necessary, on reluctant subjects? How far would the US Congress go in permitting the representation of its non-American associates in national decision-making institutions and processes? For the greater the dispersion of responsibility in such hegemonial arrangements, the greater the influence commonly exerted by the dominant partner—as witness the successful hegemonial domination of Prussia over the other German states after 1870 and the unsuccessful hegemonial domination of Britain over the white Commonwealth after 1926. Certainly, an element of flexibility in the political system of the hegemonial power is a vital requirement. It may be that if we are lucky, a financial equivalent of the Cuban crisis of 1962 will bring us near enough to the brink of disaster to sharpen our appreciation of the danger ahead and at the same time to strengthen our resolution to escape it.

Notes

[1] *Economics of interdependence.* For a more recent discussion of the political problems involved, see Miriam Camps, *The management of interdependence: a preliminary view* (New York, 1974).

[2] The unfilled gap between the two has been well explained by H. O. Schmitt, ' The national boundary in politics and economics ' in R. Merritt, ed., *Communications in international politics* (Urbana, Ill., 1972).

FINANCE FOR DEVELOPING COUNTRIES: AN ESSAY

by Christopher Prout

1

AID CLUBS

The financial relations of the Western world during the period under review were not entirely inbred. A particular set of problems arose from the provision of financial resources to the Third World which impinged upon the West in a novel fashion from the latter part of the 1950s eliciting a response which influenced the behaviour of Western countries towards one another in a sufficiently distinctive way to merit separate analysis. Those problems concern the extent to which efforts to co-ordinate the volume and harmonize the terms of such resources led the affluent nations to accept, or even seek, some limits to each other's autonomy. There was the growing endeavour to co-ordinate the terms on which budgetary finance was offered to the developing countries and to reach some agreement about the amount that ought to be provided. This is the subject of chapter 1. A parallel process took place in the field of public, or publicly guaranteed, commercial lending and this is investigated in chapter 2. Chapter 3 discusses co-ordination and harmonization not in the context of normal financial relations, as in chapters 1 and 2, but in that of financial crisis. Here the story is a very different one. Whereas co-operative ventures proved extremely difficult to mount, let alone to operate successfully, in normal times, they made remarkable headway in the white heat of crisis—a conclusion which adds some weight to the contention that whereas nation states are weak at contingency planning, they are rather effective at crisis management.

In at least one respect the degree of recognition and acceptance of limited autonomy is inadequately documented here because a description of developments within multilateral lending agencies during this period has been omitted. This is only partly for reasons of space. Multilateral aid forms a relatively modest proportion of the total volume of finance we have to consider and a detailed analysis of a major UN agency, such as the World Bank Group, would unbalance the presentation. It is also self-evident that to the extent that funds are handed over to be distributed by multilateral agencies, donors have already accepted a substantial curtailment of autonomy. Concern here is with tied investment finance and with the mechanisms that emerged to control its volume and terms and to attenuate the problems of debt accumulation that it generated.

The Development Assistance Committee

Long before the end of the 1950s the industrialized nations had opted for a bilateral system of financing economic development. Balance-of-payments difficulties, employment problems, the desire of governments to be fully associated with the projects they financed, protection against restrictions on the part of other donors—even the ability to marshal domestic opinion in support of aid—all these factors, to a greater or lesser degree, ensured the dominance of bilateral solutions. An alternative solution would have been to channel all budgetary funds through one, or several, multilateral lending agencies. Although by no means themselves free of defects, it would have avoided much of the waste and unfairness that the existing system exhibited. But the nature and strength of the commercial and political pressures on governments, far from favouring a multilateral approach, held scant hope of any form of co-operative behaviour between nation states. It comes as no surprise, therefore, that such efforts to co-ordinate and harmonize budgetary flows during the 1960s as did occur owed little to an enhanced perception by developed nations of a need for more order and justice in the system. They stemmed rather from the extension into the arena of development finance of a feature of American external policy which was already making itself strongly felt within NATO—the drive to persuade its allies to share the financial burden of allegedly common foreign policy objectives more equitably, and in particular in such a way that the United States paid relatively less.

For a number of reasons—the most important being the emergence of a group of young and politically uncommitted nation states, the entry of the Soviet Union into the development business, and a growing hostility towards its policies in Latin America—the United States, in the late 1950s, had both substantially increased the volume and widened the geographical application of its economic aid programme. Its motivation was unashamedly political. Americans believed that contributing to the economic and social development of the uncommitted nations would lead to the growth of societies sympathetic to their way of life. Development finance, although not used for military expenditure, was seen as directly furthering the aims of the alliance system. Accordingly, the United States felt no compunction about asking its allies to make substantial contributions to the aid drive, especially as most of them had been beneficiaries of American economic support on a massive scale less than a decade before. Indeed, the fact that the United States had initially sought to use NATO as the forum through which to develop a co-ordinated programme indicated how closely it associated aid with the aims of the alliance; though NATO proved so inappropriate for this purpose that it subsequently pursued its objective through the Organization for European Economic Co-operation (OEEC).

The establishment of the Development Assistance Group (DAG), as an informal group within the OEEC, in 1960 was the first tangible evidence of US pressure. When in 1961 the OEEC became the Organization for Economic Co-operation and Development (OECD), the DAG was succeeded by a formal group called the Development Assistance Committee (DAC). So closely related was it to its predecessor that its terms of reference were adopted from a DAG resolution of March 1961. In this resolution, the so-called Resolution of the Common Aid Effort, members agreed *both* to increase the aggregate volume of resources flowing to the less developed countries (LDCs) *and* to share the burden of such increases more fairly. Its adoption by the new Committee was substantially in accord with US objectives (the Americans were now, of course, members). The undertaking to increase was qualified by the agreement to share in some way not yet specified; and the United States believed strongly that, as the source of the biggest flow, it would be equitable if increases over the next few years should come from its allies.[1]

DAC GUIDELINES

The Americans were assisted in achieving their objectives in the early years of the decade by a feature of the DAC's approach to the measurement of burden-sharing which they themselves did much to foster. It never set its members the specific ' aid ' target of ' 1 per cent of GNP ' suggested by the UN for the first Development Decade. While using it as a guideline and as a basis upon which to compile its statistics, DAC adopted a more flexible means of assessing the capacity of an individual member to assist, qualifying the size of the percentage of GNP that it devoted to external aid by such matters as its additional responsibilities in the field of foreign affairs, its regional underdevelopment problems and the state of its balance of payments. A member would not be criticized for failing to facilitate a World Bank bond issue if it was undergoing a major balance-of-payments crisis—or for not increasing official grants if it were obliged to make heavy budgetary commitments elsewhere (unless, of course, such commitments were politically unacceptable to other members). As the member with the largest and most rapidly escalating responsibilities in the field of foreign affairs, the United States felt peculiarly able to take advantage of the ' other foreign responsibilities' qualification; both to justify a failure to increase its own lending more rapidly (a point of view given further weight by the fact that the adoption of such responsibilities involved in their opinion indirect or direct military aid to many other DAC members), and to cajole countries who were themselves falling short of the standards it felt they ought to be meeting. Even French aid which, in the early 1960s, exceeded 2 per cent of GNP, did not escape the American criticism that it tended to be discriminatingly concentrated in a rather limited area. But of those members that might best have been expected to make substantial contributions—the UK, France, West Germany, Japan, Italy—Germany and Japan were singled out for special pressure. Neither had, as a result of World War II, extensive foreign responsibilities; nor were they in balance-of-payments difficulties; nor did they spend a high proportion of their GNP on defence. Above all there was the feeling that these were the two countries that had principally benefited from US postwar aid and that now it was their turn to pay back some of this help.

However, the advantage to the United States of this approach was, at least to some degree, offset by the very broad definition of aid adopted by the Committee—the Net Flow of Resources to Developing Countries.[2] It was composed of a number of transactions which either could not be reasonably classified as assistance at all or which, though properly classifiable as assistance, involved little or no burden to the donor countries. Private flows, whether equity investment, commercial credits, or reparations payments, would be defended by few as aid; yet they were included in the Net Flow of Resources measure. Moreover, the burden of supplying much of the rest was considerably less than the statistical magnitudes implied. The contributions of many members were concentrated either in their former colonies, or in areas which were relatively well off, or in areas in which their commercial interests played a dominant role.[3] Much assistance in kind was drawn from surplus domestic stocks—the most important example in this category being US Public Law 480 lending which, far from being a burden to the United States, in some years was a positive benefit to the maintenance of orderly agricultural markets. Finally, most of the budgetary aid was tied contractually, though in this case it is only fair to add that, irrespective of legal obligation, other factors frequently combined to favour the donor country as a source of procurement. For example, Great Britain and France grant or lend much of their budgetary assistance to countries with which they had, for a number of historical reasons, strong financial and trading links; and the US PL480 food aid programme was tied by virtue of being in kind.

The United States undoubtedly benefited from this rather undemanding definition. However, the benefit was somewhat double-edged. It disguised the fact that the actual burden that it bore was considerably less than the size of the resource transfer it made—thus making it easier for Washington to defend itself against its critics in the UN Conference for Trade and Development (UNCTAD). Yet it constrained it from openly making the argument against the Germans and the Japanese that they transferred an even greater proportion than the Americans on non-concessional or territorially advantageous terms. Making such distinctions in public would draw the attention of the critics to similar, though perhaps less marked, inadequacies in its own programme.

Generally speaking, the rather unexacting definition of what comprised the 1 per cent was extremely useful to all the members of DAC in confronting their Third World critics. In the first place, it gave the maximum appearance of performance for the minimum amount of effort. Each was acutely aware that a given percentage of GNP for two or more of their number might conceal substantial differences in the real burdens incurred, and behind the closed doors of committee rooms they made that very clear to each other. But the proceedings of such meetings were never published, reflecting the convention that members should refrain from washing their dirty linen in public. Like gentlemen in clubs they discussed and settled their differences discreetly. Indeed, that the debate about burden-sharing was conducted in this way prevents the contemporary historian from getting to grips with it. He can but rely on hearsay, verbal at that, and most of it spoken a long time after the events in question. In the second place, the Net Flow of Resources measure had served to disguise important differences in the motivation of the donor countries. So long as every kind of financial transaction made with the Third World was called ' assistance ' nobody's motives for undertaking it needed to be called into question.[4] Statistically, the humanitarian drive ranked equally with the military, the political with the commercial. In fact, all four ingredients were present in the aid programme of most members but the mix varied from one to another. The preponderant motive of the US authorities has already been considered. Concessionary finance to former colonies by their erstwhile masters, particularly Britain and France, was both a means of sustaining a former commercial dominance and a reflection of benevolent interest in the continued progress of societies for which they were, after all, in large part responsible. And for the defeated nations in World War II, Germany, Italy, and Japan, it was both a means of repairing broken commercial links and of re-establishing themselves as a force in international economic affairs.

From the middle of the 1960s the influence of the United States declined. There was growing disenchantment in Congress about the effectiveness of aid as a foreign policy weapon. Criticism of American policy in UNCTAD in 1964 and the outbreak of the Indo-Pakistan war in 1965 contributed to and confirmed this view. Then the competing claim of the Vietnam war and the sharp deterioration in the balance of payments placed a high premium on reducing non-military foreign expenditure. Consequently, the Agency for International Development (AID) became growingly involved in defending the level of its own programmes and less willing (and able) to influence the programmes of others. At the same time, because of declining American interest in aid and because of the experience it had gained in the first part of the decade the DAC secretariat, composed of members of the permanent staff of the OECD, emerged as an independent force in the work of the Committee. In particular, it redefined 'assistance', developing a set of statistical measures which more accurately reflected the real burdens borne by members and bringing into sharper focus their differences in motivation. By the end of the decade Net Flow of Resources was replaced by three categories: Official Development Assistance (ODA), Other Official Flows, and Private Flows.

OFFICIAL DEVELOPMENT ASSISTANCE

The new ODA category was of cardinal importance; it was introduced into the official statistics of the DAC in 1969 and in private meeting and discussions long before. It consisted of transactions made 'with the primary purpose of promoting the economic and social development of developing countries'. To qualify, flows must have been 'administered with the promotion of the economic development and welfare of developing countries as their main objective' and their terms must have been 'intended to be concessional in character'. Henceforth motive mattered. The constituents of ODA emerged as Contributions to Multilateral Agencies (excluding bond purchases), Food Aid, Technical Assistance, Budgetary Assistance, and Project and Programme Lending. Other Official Flows comprised official transactions which 'even though they have concessional elements, are primarily export facilitating in purpose' [5] and included official buyers' and suppliers' credits, the rediscounting of guaranteed private export credits, and government purchases of bonds issued by multilateral development banks at market rates.

DAC worked through a system of Recommendations and Review. Its broad policy objectives, formulated in Resolutions or Recommendations, were not binding. Yet they were expected to be met by members to the best of their abilities and the Committee conducted an annual review of each member to monitor its progress towards doing so. Its conclusions were presented in the annual OECD publication *Development Assistance*.[6] Although ODA did not emerge until the end of the decade as the critical component in financial flows to the Third World, it was, throughout, the only flow over whose level members had real control. Other Official Flows and Private Flows responded passively to the propensity and ability of commercial enterprises to export and invest abroad. It is, therefore, worth considering the movements in GNP/ODA ratios throughout the decade both to see how governments actually performed and to indicate some of the difficulties in trying to assess the reasons for their performance.

Changes in the ratios were as follows:

	1960		1970	
	Per cent	*Rank*	*Per cent*	*Rank*
Portugal	1·55	1	0·45	5
France	1·38	2	0·65	1
Belgium	0·88	3	0·48	4
United Kingdom	0·56	4	0·37	7–9
United States	0·53	5	0·59	12
Australia	0·38	6	0·59	3
Germany	0·31	7–8	0·32	11
Netherlands	0·31	7–8	0·63	2
Japan	0·24	9	0·23	13
Italy	0·22	10	0·16	14
Canada	0·19	11	0·43	6
Norway	0·11	12	0·33	10
Denmark	0·09	13	0·38	7–9
Sweden	0·05	14	0·37	7–9
Switzerland	0·04	15	0·14	15
Austria	—	16	0·13	16
Total	0·52		0·34	

Source : OECD/DAC, *Development assistance, 1971 review*, p. 174.

Admirable in monitoring and recording the statistical progress of members *Development Assistance*, from which these statistics derive, gives no clues as to the motives behind the changes in performance. Thus members who apparently conformed to the DAC Recommendations may have done so for reasons which had nothing to do with their influence. Equally, members who appeared not to have responded might have performed far worse in their absence. It is therefore extremely difficult, if not impossible, to measure the impact of the Recommendation/Review procedure—in effect to decide whether the performance of any donor would have been different in its absence. The most interesting feature of these statistics lies in the record of the smaller industrialized countries—Australia, Canada, Sweden, Norway, and Denmark—which were hardly involved in the aid business in 1960. It is true that throughout the decade their steadily increasing ODA/ GNP ratios took place at the same time as DAC was emphasizing, with growing authority, that they should do so. It is also clear that these countries were not participants in the traditional burden-sharing game that was being conducted between the larger and more established donors: had they been, their programmes would have levelled out long before the end of the decade in harmony with the decline in American effort. But can this consistent and sustained improvement in the ratio be attributed to the DAC? An equally plausible, if not more probable, explanation is that during the 1960s most of the industrialized nations, for a number of purely domestic reasons, wanted a meaningful aid programme as a permanent part of their foreign policy. Given this objective, it was likely that those whose contributions were marginal at the beginning of the decade would rapidly increase their budgetary appropriations for this purpose, irrespective of DAC pressures. All that can be said with certainty is that here was a distinct group marked out by its members' newness on the aid scene, their modesty in size, their relative degree of uncommittedness to the American dogmas and their lack of any traditional ' captive ' markets. It is equally difficult to assess the part played by the DAC in the case of the traditional donors. The pattern here, with the exception of the Netherlands, is of sharp decline over the period. Yet it may well have been that in the absence of DAC, the decline would have been even more marked. Moreover their performance must be judged in the light of the fact that they divested themselves of a major part of their imperial possessions during the early 1960s. Germany and Japan, who do not fall easily into either category and on whom most pressure was put by the United States in the early part of the decade, kept their ratios about level.

While the overall ODA/GNP ratio declined over the decade, the net flow of ODA from DAC members during the same period increased from $4,665m to $6,805m. Of the large donors the United States increased the flow of its aid from $2,702m to $3,050m, after reaching a peak of $3,592m in 1964; the United Kingdom from $407m to $447m, after reaching a peak of $493m in 1964; and the French from $823m to $952m (they reached a peak of $955m in 1969 although it was not until 1968 that they surpassed their 1964 figure). The three of them contributed an extra $516m, or one-quarter of the total increase over the decade. Germany increased its aid from $223m in 1960 to $599m in 1970 and Japan from $105m to $458m—between them providing an extra $729m over the decade, or about one-third of the total increase. In both relative and absolute terms therefore the Germans and the Japanese out-performed the big three. Between 1960 and 1964 the Germans doubled their ODA from $223m to $459m; thereafter it increased much more slowly. Evidence, it might be said, of the rise and decline of American influence. Yet between 1960 and 1964 Japanese ODA rose from $105m to a mere $116m—and thereafter quadrupled to $458 in 1970.

What can be said with some degree of confidence is that by the end of the decade aid had become an accepted and established budgetary heading in the finance bills of most OECD countries. It became part of the domestic budgetary process and, like any other item of budgetary expenditure, had to take its chance along with the rest in the hurly burly of the great annual domestic financial debates. More aid meant greater fiscal sacrifices by member governments (and the electorates upon whom they depended for office); and the size and shape of an official assistance programme reflected the degree of commercial, parliamentary, and, ultimately, public support that individual governments received in pursuing a positive aid programme. Not surprisingly, members differed in the priorities accorded to aid or to concessionary finance in the light of competing fiscal demands. But if the influence of the DAC upon the performance of individual members is uncertain, there can be little doubt that its secretariat became more independent of them.

Although *Development Assistance* does not apportion criticism in so many words, the accuracy of its statistical judgements repeatedly exposed the inadequate performance of certain members. Having begun as the servant of American policy, the Committee had now become its conscience. But despite a sharpened perception of what was what in development finance and a willingness by the end of the 1960s to assess members on the basis of their motivation for lending as well as on the total volume of resources actually transferred, the DAC was still unwilling to require members to meet a specific target. There was, quite simply, insufficient political consensus to make that type of commitment. At the end of the decade the Pearson Commission, the UN Committee for Development Planning, the Capacity Study of the UN, and the Presidential Task Force on International Development all, in turn, considered the question. The best publicized report was that of the Pearson Commission [7] which recommended that a new disbursement target for ODA of 0·7 per cent of GNP should be reached by the middle of the 1970s. However, the DAC pointedly declined to commit itself to a specific target. Its statistical reformulation had brought a more realistic analysis of real burdens borne. But it could not compel nations to change their ways.

THE TERMS OF AID

Co-operation on terms of aid was a different matter. Here there proved to be a greater sense of urgency about the need for some form of co-ordinated policy because the cost of not softening was to increase the danger of borrowers declaring insolvency—a condition which, as we shall see in chapter 3, presented as many problems to the creditor as to the debtor. And a greater capacity to provide for that need because the additional resources transferred by softening their terms did not have immediate budgetary costs. Members knew that, whatever their differing motivations for aid, they could only go on transacting if terms were softer. Between 1960 and 1970 the volume of official grants and grant-like flows fell from $3,692 to $3,298. Hence the entire increase in the volume of ODA during the 1960s was in the form of loans and there was strong pressure upon donors throughout the decade to soften their terms in order to compensate for the stagnation in grants.

As early as 1962 the Committee formed a working party to examine the conditions of aid. It set in motion a process of conceptual and statistical refinement with respect to terms similar to that noted in the case of volume. The working party submitted an Interim Report to a DAC meeting in April 1963, which passed a resolution recommending to members ' that they seek to achieve a significant degree of comparability in the terms and conditions of aid '. This was followed by the Recommendation on Financial Terms and Conditions of July 1965,[8] which included quantitative targets against which a member's progress in softening its terms could be measured. Members not already providing 70 per cent or more of their official assistance in grant form were urged to increase to 80 per cent the proportion of assistance given either as grants or as highly concessionary loans (viz. at interest rates of 3 per cent or less, with a maturity of twenty-five years or better, and an average grace period of seven years). Countries were asked to meet the recommendation within three years, although it was recognized that harder lending members might find it difficult to keep to this timetable.[9] The Recommendation bound the Committee to review the targets set after three years had elapsed. The working party duly started the review at the beginning of 1968. In February 1969 the Committee agreed upon a ' Supplement ' to the 1965 Recommendation establishing new and more stringent quantitative-term targets.[10]

The DAC secretariat met with some visible success in its efforts to soften terms. Interest-free loans with fifty years' maturity were introduced by the Canadian authorities in 1964. In 1966 the UK Ministry of Overseas Development was permitted to set interest rates at whatever level it felt was appropriate—though the maturities for these loans were limited to twenty-five years. Sweden and Denmark introduced similar programmes in the mid-1960s. Following the 1965 Recommendation a number of members, such as Germany, the Netherlands, and Belgium, deliberately adopted its quantitative recommendations. However, while some members consciously tried to adapt themselves to the DAC policy on terms, others ignored it. And it is noticeable that those that chose to soften after 1964, with the significant exception of the United States, were also the softest lenders before 1964, raising the same question as was raised about volume: would they have softened anyway? The United States is a special case. Its lending became progressively harder during the period under review. In 1961 nearly 80 per cent of total US lending was repayable on a local currency basis. Since the Foreign Assistance Act of 1961 most development loans became dollar repayable and interest rates increased. The terms of PL480 assistance also hardened. From 1964 the local currency cost was raised and from 1967 proceeds of commodity sales were gradually changed to a dollar repayable basis. In this the Americans were reacting to their balance-of-payments difficulties. But as traditionally soft lenders they were also demonstrating their unwillingness to go on pumping hard cash into the Third World when much of it was simply going out again to pay the rates of interest that harder-headed lenders were charging.

Apart from the difficulty of getting a uniform response to the DAC Recommendations, the technique of global softening was a rather undiscriminating instrument to solve the problem that it purported to confront. For it took no account of the debt-servicing capacity of the recipient country. The Committee discussed in some detail proposals for ' banding ' countries into categories according to their debt-servicing capacity and level of development—the idea being that, along the lines of the International Development Association (IDA), countries with the lowest debt-servicing capacity should receive the softest terms. Members have been reluctant to adopt any form of banding arrangements on the grounds that distinguishing between the more and the less credit-worthy would reduce the chances of the less credit-worthy from getting funds from other sources. This is not, however, a very respectable argument because IDA category countries rely to a very limited extent on private funds.

Consortia and consultative groups [11]

CONSORTIA

DAC was very much concerned about the wide disparities in the volume and terms of finance forthcoming from members to individual borrowers. It repeatedly complained that the lending programmes of certain members, while globally impressive, were marred by heavy concentrations in a few areas to the marked exclusion of others; or of the likely unwillingness of soft lenders to go on lending to a particular recipient if much of the money was going out again to defray the commercial interest rates of hard lenders. It did not, however, attempt to develop an institutional framework to confront such problems. This was partly because it felt itself ill-equipped to do so,[12] but mainly because, at the time it was established, one had already emerged.

In 1958 India, midway through its ambitious second Five-Year Plan (beginning in 1956), underwent a major balance-of-payments crisis. Such was the cost of importing the capital equipment required to meet its production targets that by the end of 1957 not even payments on existing loan obligations could be met. Accordingly the World Bank convened in August 1958 a meeting of the principal creditor countries —the United States, Britain, Germany, Canada, and Japan. At first the group met on an ad hoc basis to consider how best to lighten the burden of repayments on loans already made—rather along the lines of the debt rescheduling clubs discussed in chapter 3. Subsequently meetings became more regular and the group of countries involved became known as the Aid India Consortium. At the end of 1960 the consortium reviewed the foreign exchange implications of the third Five-Year Plan and assessed what foreign reserves would be required to enable India to place overseas orders in respect of it. Later its members agreed to make available $2,225m in grants and loans for that purpose. In effect they committed themselves to finance a resources gap that had not yet arisen—a substantial departure from the mere rearrangement of the repayment profiles of loans already made. In October 1960 similar arrangements were made for Pakistan. Unlike the Indian consortium, the Pakistan consortium did not emerge out of a debt rescheduling but began with the objective of raising long-term money, in the face of a threatened crisis, for economic development purposes.

The purpose of the Indian and Pakistan consortia meetings was, therefore, to review an economic development plan and to secure future commitments of aid, ' pledges ' as they came to be called, in order to assist in financing the external resources required to fulfil it. The central members of both operations were the United States and the Bank. The former because it was the biggest lender; the latter because it was the only lender which made a comprehensive and ongoing survey of the plans and enjoyed a relatively detached position. However, membership of a consortium was open to any potential aid-giver, whatever amount it was prepared to contribute and whatever its motives for joining. None of the founder members was prepared to look gift horses in the mouth. Borrowers, however, were not allowed to participate on the ground that their presence would inhibit frankness of discussion between members. Turkey, as a member of NATO, was particularly offended at being excluded from its consortium deliberations.

To the extent that the United States regarded the Indian and Pakistani consortia as useful adjuncts to its politics of burden-sharing it was to be disappointed. In 1962–3 the new members of the Indian consortium pledged 11 per cent of total requirements; by 1964 they were offering only 7 per cent—in absolute terms, half of the figure of two years earlier. Moreover, Germany and the UK also reduced their contributions on the ground that their pledges in 1961–2 were intended to cover projects for several years ahead. In each case the Bank and the United States were left to provide the rest.[13] The Pakistan case was similar. Having reached 9 per cent of total requirements in 1963, pledges of the new members fell away to 6 per cent of the total a year later, leaving the Bank and the United States to provide over 70 per cent of total requirements in 1964. To the extent that it was supposed to operate, burden-sharing wasn't working. In normal circumstances countries were unwilling to don the kind of open-ended financial obligations that a consortium implied. Indeed, it is likely that the pledging process was never seen as a long-term commitment. It emerged because the United States, the Bank, and those other countries that were substantially committed recognized that the only way to retain any momentum in the economic development of the subcontinent without a perpetual state of financial crisis was to undertake an exercise of this sort. But once the immediate pressure of financial crisis had gone and the permanent machinery of the consortium was established with the World Bank and the United States fully committed, the incentive to pledge disappeared.

CONSULTATIVE GROUPS

The distinguishing feature of the consultative group, as it was originally conceived in the early 1960s, was that it undertook the collective review of economic plans in the absence of an obligation to pledge. During 1962 and 1963 the World Bank established so-called consultative groups for Nigeria, Tunisia, Colombia, and the Sudan. All four countries wanted a consortium but, apart from the United States, there was no support for the proposal amongst donor countries. Moreover the Bank was determined to avoid an arrangement in which it would be liable as a lender of last resort. In the event a compromise was reached which involved a degree of co-ordination but no ' gap financing '. Members co-ordinated aid on the basis of specific projects by first jointly reviewing the national or relevant sectoral development programme and then negotiating the financing of industrial proposals amongst themselves. Like the consortium, there would be a group evaluation; but unlike the consortium, there would be no group commitment. With the partial exception of Colombia, these four groups met with little success. The recipients saw no reason to modify their domestic policies until they were assured that such a modification would result in an increase in aid, and the donors saw little reason to increase aid until there had been at least some degree of policy modification. Consequently the Bank set up a working party in 1964 to reconsider its whole approach to consultative groups. While not disposed to re-adopt the consortium, it did, as a result of its review, allocate to itself a far more positive role involving, *inter alia*, a continuing review of development policy and the identification of viable projects through regular missions from its own staff.

Largely as a result of this new initiative by the Bank, a new style of group now emerged which exhibited some of the features of both the consortium and the consultative group but which did not fall neatly into either category. An example of the greater range and flexibility of the new arrangements is provided by a sample of the range of topics considered at the meeting of the Nigerian group in February 1966. The group, among other things, discussed and endorsed the Nigerian development programme to the end of 1968; recommended that aid should not be given on terms harder than those laid down in the DAC Recommendation of 1965 (see above, p. 369); urged the government to limit its short-term borrowing, and assisted in the convening of export credit guarantee organizations to discuss the implications of such a limitation. Moreover, it specifically asked the Nigerian government to give a precise estimate of the gap between projected expenditure and available resources as an indication of the amount of aid required. The intergovernmental groups for Indonesia and Ghana, discussed in chapter 3, considered an equally wide range of issues.

As the decade progressed, the distinction between consortia and consultative groups became increasingly less sharp. This was partly due to the Bank's decision to broaden the scope of and play a more active role in the operation of consultative groups as a result of its working party's report; and partly to the abandonment of pledging by members of the Indian and Pakistan consortia. Both consortia were suspended in 1965 because of the war, and the practice of pledging was not resumed when they reconvened. Nevertheless, although pledging is officially a thing of the past, in certain cases—for example, India and Pakistan and the Intergovernmental Group for Indonesia (see below, p. 393)—donors still come ' prepared to state in fairly specific terms their intentions and commitments with respect to aid for the coming years '.[14] Despite the failure of pledging, rather similar to the failure of DAC to get agreement in OECD on global ODA targets, the World Bank had, by the end of the 1960s, succeeded in evolving a rather sophisticated instrument of economic co-operation which felt it within its remit to consider all the main development finance issues.

The limits of co-ordination

Some support for the view that the Bank made a substantial contribution to the evolution of a viable co-operative style may be gleaned from the story of the Turkish consortium established by the OECD in 1962.[15] Early in that year, in the wake of a series of balance-of-payments crises (see below, p. 392), Turkey formally requested NATO to set up a consortium. NATO transferred the request to the OECD which, in July 1962, passed the necessary enabling resolution. The fact that it did so owed much to the pressure of the United States, anxious to involve other members of the alliance in the financial health of one of their number. The World Bank, however, was not originally involved. (From 1954–64 it conducted no lending operations in Turkey on the ground of Turkey's default on foreign obligations.) Britain, West Germany, Belgium, Canada, France, Italy, and the Netherlands were the other members, later to be joined by Austria, Denmark, Norway, Sweden, Switzerland, and in 1964 by the World Bank.

There was considerable vagueness in the consortium's terms of reference. Although it was intended to mobilize an adequate flow of resources in support of the development plan, members understood that their participation did not imply any specific financial obligation. The United States tried to keep the consortium to the spirit of its original resolution but its efforts were regarded with deep suspicion. Its policy was regarded as another exercise in floating off part of the US aid programme. Indeed, there were moments when the consortium is reported to have become a simple confrontation between the United States and other aid givers. A further problem was the attitude of the Turks themselves. They interpreted any inquiry into their economic performance as an infringement of their sovereignty—a reaction which was aggravated by the consortium's failure to set any clear limits to the scope of its discussions. This inability to set such limits emphasized what was probably the consortium's main limitation. It had a weak secretariat. Neither its part-time chairman nor its executive secretary were members of the OECD staff. The OECD as such was not even a member. But even if it had been, it is highly unlikely that it would have carried the authority of an autonomous lending agency like the

Bank. Moreover, to the extent that the OECD itself had any influence, it was negative, for it was decided that the consortium should be the responsibility not of the DAC but of the Trade and Payments Department. Obsessed with short-term balance-of-trade fluctuations, the Department looked unkindly on any economic policy which gave rise to short-run strain.

As a result of the successful rescheduling of Turkey's debts in 1964 the World Bank re-entered the scene after a ten-year gap, both by sending a large economic mission to Turkey and by involving itself in the intergovernmental project syndicate established to finance the Keban Dam. (Intergovernmental project syndicates were normally set up for very large projects which occupied a central position in a developing country's economy—the Kainji Dam in Nigeria is another example.) In the same year a regular cycle of meetings was established and the post of executive secretary went to an OECD official. However, by the end of the decade the fundamental problems had not changed. The Bank certainly became increasingly involved, but the origins of the consortium itself and the nature of the Turkish attitude to it suggested that it would never gain the position it had in India and Pakistan.

The Turkish case points towards one tentative observation. The co-operative ventures in which the Bank was involved enjoyed a much greater degree of success than those in which it was not involved. Despite the failure of pledging, by the end of the decade groups such as that established for Indonesia were engaged in a very elaborate process of forward planning for, and finance on behalf of, the recipient. It is true that the most comprehensive arrangements were reserved for those countries that had grave external debt problems—and there is little doubt that the prospect of insolvency encouraged the lenders to co-operate (see ch. 3 below). Nevertheless, without the help of the Bank, as the Turkish case shows, co-operation even in the face of sovereign insolvency is likely to have proved hard to arrange. There are many characteristics of the Bank that suggest themselves as reasons for its ability so to influence events, such as its financial independence, its relative impartiality, and its formidable technical expertise. To discuss the relative weight of these factors would be to go beyond the purpose of this essay. It suffices to say that the coincidence of the Bank's presence with the few success stories in the 1960s cannot pass unnoted.

A further, equally tentative, observation is that not surprisingly co-ordination worked better when it was the servant of self-interest. In the case of intergovernmental project syndicates, the advantages to be gained for both sides were fairly clear cut. The Western members of the syndicate were able to exclude outside competition and share out the procurement amongst themselves; and their respective industrial interests were provided with a guaranteed market. Equally, the bargaining among these members was very tough, ensuring that the terms of the overall package were realistic. Moreover, the World Bank's participation in such syndicates ensured that the recipient countries' interests were properly guarded. A similar coincidence of self-interest working in favour of co-ordination may also help to explain the modest success that the DAC achieved with its terms recommendations. Lenders were aware that some softening was a condition of further lending. Here an additional factor may be that it is rarely in the interests of a donor to soften aid unilaterally since the extra resources transferred merely go to service the debt of harder lenders. In this sense some form of international arrangement would seem a necessary accompaniment to a nation's potential decision to soften, since it must be assured that other nations will follow suit. The fact that the 1965 and 1969 DAC terms recommendations were the subject of extensive debate behind the scenes and were drafted to allow as many members as possible to comply with them goes some way to support this contention.

Perhaps the most reassuring thing that can be said about the co-operative ventures that took place during the decade is that they survived, and even in some cases prospered, despite the fact that their chief instigator and proponent, the United States, took little interest in them, or was on the defensive within them, from the middle of the 1960s. The achievement was particularly remarkable in the case of the DAC which, unlike the consortia and consultative groups, did not have the support of a strong, autonomous international agency. This is not so surprising as it might at first appear. Throughout the decade, despite a number of attempts to change the situation, the majority of financial resources going to LDCs were transferred bilaterally. In the 1950s this did not have important implications because there were few lenders of any size, but by the early 1960s not only the UK and France, but also Japan, West Germany, and certain other OECD countries, had begun tied aid programmes on a worldwide basis. Simultaneously there was a dramatic increase in the number of new economically under-developed independent nation states, each committed to a development policy that could only be achieved given substantial increases in Western aid. In this changed environment, the potential for conflict of interest and the pressure to share burdens inevitably grew, and some attempts were bound to be made to construct co-ordinating mechanisms. In this sense the DAC and the other institutions had more enduring foundations than the political ambitions of any one state, however large and powerful.

Notes

[1] For a more detailed treatment of the reasons for the changes in US policy and for the origins of the DAC see, in particular, John White, *The politics of foreign aid* (London, 1974), pp. 203–17. See also S. J. Rubin, *The conscience of the rich* (New York, 1966).

[2] In early reports official aid was defined to include 'the flow of government grants and official lending exceeding five years'. The basis for the definition was that equivalent purchasing power would not have been made available through existing commercial channels on 'the same terms and conditions and for the same purposes'.

[3] It is true, that the less developed the country is the less capacity it has to absorb new investment. In this sense, therefore, distribution was bound to be uneven.

[4] See, on this point, White, *The politics of foreign aid*, p. 220.

[5] OECD/DAC, *Development assistance, 1969 review*, pp. 241–2.

[6] The documentary basis for the review was typically in three parts: a report prepared by the member; a report prepared by the DAC secretariat; and a list of interrogatories prepared, after reading the member's report, by the secretariat in conjunction with a number of other members elected as Examiners. In addition to the written questions, oral supplementaries were permitted during the review meeting.

[7] *Partners in development* (London, 1969).

[8] Made at a so-called High Level meeting of the DAC held in Paris on 22 and 23 July 1965.

[9] Members were also asked to extend concessionary terms to as many countries as possible and to endeavour to promote a number of other financial techniques.

[10] The new terms test, unlike that of 1965, relates only to ODA and excludes other official flows. It required that ODA must either contain a grant percentage of 70 per cent or more: or a minimum of 85 per cent of its individual constituent transactions must be at least as soft as a loan of 30 years' maturity with an 8 years' grace period at 2·5 per cent interest; or its softest 85 per cent must contain an average grant element of 85 per cent.

[11] See generally John White, *Pledged to development* (London, 1967) and E. S. Mason & R. E. Asher, *The World Bank since Bretton Woods* (Washington, 1973).

[12] The one institutional innovation that DAC did make was in the field of technical assistance. DAC groups were established for Thailand and East Africa which sought to assist in co-ordinating the provision of technical assistance from different donors. The East Africa group effectively ended when prospects for an East African Federation disappeared. The groups were not, however, concerned with project or programme financing.

[13] White, *Pledged to development*, p. 39 & table 1.

[14] Mason & Asher, p. 511.

[15] For detailed treatment see White, *Pledged to development*.

2

COMMERCIAL LENDING [1]

The problem of maintaining and increasing the flow of ODA and simultaneously keeping debt-servicing obligations within manageable limits was complicated by the fact that the public debt obligations of the recipient countries arose also from official export institutions and officially guaranteed supplier credit transactions. The uninhibited growth of these sources of credit during the 1960s, despite a marked softening of their terms, posed a real threat to the financial stability of a number of LDCs. Although the DAC fully recognized this danger, it declined to set guidelines for the rate of expansion of commercial finance because it considered it largely beyond the control of governments. Nor did it consider mounting an institutional solution because three other institutions were already, or were soon to be, in the field.

The oldest of these, the Union d'Assureurs des Crédits Internationaux (the Berne Union), was established in 1934. Its members are private and public export credit institutions. Until the 1960s it was the only international institution charged with the responsibility of regulating export credit competition. The Co-ordinating Group for Policies of Credit Insurance, Guarantee and Financial Credits of the EEC (the Co-ordinating Group), set up on 27 September 1960, consists of representatives from the Treasuries as well as from the export insurance companies of the Common Market countries. Although it only meets about six times a year, it maintains close communications informally. The High Level Group on Export Credits and Export Credit Guarantees (the OECD Group), created by the Trade Committee of the OECD in 1963, like the Co-ordinating Group in the EEC, is attended by both Treasury and credit insurance officials.

It is arguable that to distinguish budgetary loans from publicly funded or insured commercial loans is artificial. Both categories are tied and government supervised; both create an identical problem for the borrower—a heavier external debt-servicing burden; and both induce the same response—pressures for more credit on softer terms. But there are good reasons for making the distinction. One is that different institutions are involved. Another is that the developed countries perceived the distinction as being of importance; while DAC devoted all its energies to extending maturities, reducing interest rates, and increasing volume, the Berne Union used its limited powers to pursue precisely the opposite policy in each case, though by the end of the period so soft had the terms of commercial transactions become that they were practically indistinguishable from some official budgetary transactions. But the vital distinction between budgetary and other commercial loans was that the process of softening materially differed. Where funds were allocated from a budget, the domestic political process intervened to constrain their availability and the terms upon which they were disbursed. In the absence of a market mechanism to soften and equate terms, international political pressure was the means utilized to lower interest rates and lengthen maturities in a uniform manner. In contrast, the cost of commercial credit, whether its source was public or private, was determined by the balance of supply and demand for it in the international capital goods markets. In fact increasingly intense competition between the commercial interests in industrialized nations to sell capital equipment to the developing countries and a willingness by government-backed credit institutions to support them led to a lengthening of commercial maturities during the 1960s. That such pressures were subjected to any kind of control was due to the operation of the so-called ' matching procedure ' (discussed below), which ensured that the softening of terms between lender and borrower and the equation of terms between lenders themselves was orderly and reasonably equitable.

The Berne Union

Harmonization of terms first became a problem in the mid-1950s. During the early 50s Germany, France, Belgium, Britain, and, finally, Italy all inaugurated some form of medium-term export finance.[2] These developments were complemented by the extension of credit insurance schemes (first introduced in the UK just after World War I for short-term transactions) to medium-term financing, thus endowing suppliers' credit with its real potential as a major international financing technique. (Suppliers' credits are granted by the exporter in the developed country, the credit being guaranteed against default by an official institution.) Competing domestic credit requirements, together with a belief that a process of unco-ordinated softening could lead to substantial distortions in trade, led in 1953 to an Understanding being reached in the Berne Union that for sales of heavy capital goods insurance should not be extended beyond a period of five years. Since the permitted duration of insurance effectively determined the length of export credit maturities, the Understanding—had it remained effective—would have had a crucial influence on future financing patterns.

However, pressures soon built up to threaten the Understanding. From the mid-1950s exporters in all the West European countries began to demand that their governments should permit the insurance agreements to exceed the five-year limit. This movement appears to have been influenced to some extent by the slowly emerging ' buyers' market ' in the world market for capital goods, replacing the predominantly ' sellers' market ' which prevailed for the years immediately after the war. But two other factors seem to have been of greater significance. First, there was the increasing pressure for softer terms from the governments of developing countries eager to elicit credit maturities more in the line with their development requirements and debt-servicing capacities. Second, and from a political point of view of more weight, the Export-Import Bank, through its long-term project loans, was enabling American exporters to sell on terms which the Europeans could only offer if they could get insurance arrangements to cover bank refinancing for substantially more than five years. The difficulties intensified when in 1957 the UK decided to expand the volume of long-term financial assistance granted under the Export Guarantee Act of 1949. This situation, together with the slackening of world trade in 1957–8, which encouraged exporters to check the fall in their sales by offering more generous credits, led increasingly to breaches of the Understanding. In 1957 three were reported and in 1958 four more. This compelled the Union in 1958 to reaffirm its position that the terms of export credit should not exceed a maximum of five years. However, during 1959 a further six breaches were reported and it is probably fair to say that by 1960 the Understanding was a dead letter.[3]

The Berne Union was further hampered in regulating competition in export credit by limitations in its own powers. It did not operate through binding rules but through the issue of a recommendatory Understanding. However, members had some recourse in the face of a violation of an Understanding by one or more of their number. Pressure to comply was exerted through the so-called matching procedure, intiated at the 1958 Union meeting in Venice and subsequently expanded and elaborated at the Berne meeting in January 1960 and at the Management Committee meeting in Paris in April 1965. By this procedure members were entitled to interrogate each other on the terms of a proposed insurance contract that was being negotiated. If the interrogated member was found to be in breach of an Understanding, his inquisitor was entitled to offer similar terms in any negotiations relating to the same transaction, even though these were themselves in breach.

The matching principle permitted individual reprisals but it did not provide for collective enforcement. Nevertheless, it was a deterrent to those threatening to breach the Understanding. The penalties of price cutting between oligopolists spring to mind as a parallel. Members could, of course, respond to interrogation evasively or untruth-fully. However, it is unlikely that in the commercial world their breach would survive undiscovered for very long after the negotiations were complete. And discovery of a dishonesty of this sort would have proved of considerable embarrassment to a member of the Union—particularly since, after the meeting of June 1961, all members were obliged to report to the Union the issue of any insurance policy con-taining a term in breach of an Understanding.

It is worth noting that the absence of mandatory rules in the Union follows logically from the lack of sovereign membership. Membership was confined to institutions, whether privately or publicly owned, which insured export credit transactions. Sovereign states were neither members themselves, nor were they represented by their insurers, who belonged in their own capacity. Thus even if the Union Under-standings were binding, individual governments would not be obliged under public international law to recognize them; and, in the last resort, could compel institutions within their representative jurisdic-tion to act in breach of their private international obligations. Mem-bers would then have no alternative but to resort to a plea of *force majeure* when in breach of binding obligations to each other. It is to avoid such a situation that agreements amongst members have no force in law, public or private. As a matter of fact members have found themselves unable to resist official directives to insure trans-actions where terms are in breach of an Understanding. At the meet-ing of June 1959 a number of members stated that they contravened the 1953 Understanding precisely because of intense pressure from their respective governments. There is no reason to believe that their willingness or ability to resist the directives of their respective govern-ments would have been enhanced by the fact that they were legally bound to do so.

Two further limitations on the Union's powers were its inability to compel membership and its limited jurisdiction. Export credit institu-tions from Japan, Italy, and the United States, countries whose manu-facturing industries accounted for an important and rapidly growing slice of international trade in capital goods, were unwilling to join the Union for a long time. The Japanese Export Credit Insurance Depart-ment never applied for membership and the Instituto Nazionale della Assicurazione of Italy and the US Foreign Credit Insurance Associa-tion became full members only in 1962 and 1963 respectively. The Union was established to provide a forum for an *exchange of views* on export credit insurance matters. In its early years its aim was seen as improving co-ordination on technical matters. However, what seemed technical in the 1930s had become highly political in the late 1950s and 1960s. The Union was never intended to play the role of policeman in an international credit war. Moreover, its original terms of reference could not have envisaged the growth of new techniques.

By the 1960s a number of new credit instruments had been developed which fell outside its terms of reference. It was, for example, agreed that while the Understanding covered suppliers' credits, it did not cover buyers' credits. (Buyers' credits are granted to the importer in the LDC to purchase capital goods from the developed country.) In 1958 the German government authorized the granting of guarantees for credits direct to foreign buyers of German capital equipment if the sum involved exceeded a certain minimum price. Similar arrangements were subsequently introduced in France, Italy, the Netherlands, and the UK; thus in April 1961 the UK introduced a financial guarantee scheme which enabled British credit institutions to lend directly to overseas buyers if the sum involved was $5·6m or more. The Understanding was more crudely avoided by counting the period of five years from the delivery date of the last piece of equipment provided, or by suppliers accepting smaller downpayments.

The OECD Group

Generally speaking, too much was asked of the Berne Union in the late 1950s and early 1960s because it was the only relevant institution in the international arena and therefore the natural focus for attempts at regulation. Moreover, the record of the two more powerfully constituted institutions established in the early 1960s suggests that the failure of the Union had little to do with its institutional inadequacies. Institutionally, the OECD Group, established in 1963, had two advantages over the Union: its members were governments and its terms of reference were explicitly aimed at co-ordinating export insurance policy. Nevertheless it could do little to stem the propensity to soften the terms of export credits to the LDCs, to the point in some cases where they become practically indistinguishable from aid. For example, there was much discussion in the mid-1960s of the Dutch proposal to establish a ceiling for commercial credits of ten years and a floor for aid credits of fifteen years. The proposal received little support: partly because it was felt that it would lead to a reduction in the total volume of resources flowing to the less developed world but mainly because members were not willing to have their autonomy limited in this way. Difficulty in making any headway on global approaches, such as the Dutch proposal, persuaded the Group to pursue more limited objectives. In the late 1960s attention shifted to attempts to get agreements on credit terms for specific commodities. Here some progress was made. In June 1969 the thirteen principal ship-exporting countries agreed that credits should not exceed eight years, that there should be a minimum down-payment of 20 per cent and a minimum interest rate of 6 per cent.

In short, there existed no political will to accept mandatory limits. This is exemplified by the Group's attitude to the Matching Principle. In 1965 the Berne Union decided to hand over the responsibility for improvements in the procedure to the OECD on the grounds that its governmental composition and terms of reference made it better qualified to achieve progress. Although it considered at great length schemes for strengthening the procedure so as to give it ' teeth ', no agreement was reached to implement any of them. The industrialized nations were unwilling to establish an institutional regime with real authority to police maturity and rate changes because all the exporting countries tacitly agreed that lengthening of maturities and stability or reduction of rates were essential to the preservation of an overall market growth for capital goods exports—which seemed a far more important collective interest than the ironing out of any trade distortions that might result from an individual nation autonomously cutting the price of its own credit. The beauty of the ' matching ' mechanism, in its limited ' reprisal ' form, was that it achieved softening with the minimum amount of distortion: because one member was entitled, automatically, to ' level down ' to, or ' match ' the terms of another. It provided in effect a surrogate market mechanism whereby price changes by one supplier were transmitted smoothly to another, accommodating economic realities to the requirements of free market dogma that rates and terms had to be uniform.

The EEC Co-ordinating Group

This view receives some confirmation from the kind of progress that was made by the corresponding EEC institution. On 27 September 1960, in pursuit of its obligations set out in Article 112 of the Treaty of Rome, the Council of Ministers established the Co-ordinating Group for Policies on Credit Insurance Guarantees and Financial Credits. By the end of the decade no binding agreement had been reached upon the fundamental question of harmonization of supplier credit practices, although in 1965 agreed ' principles ' were submitted to the Co-ordinating Group's Technical Committee for detailed drafting, and in October 1970 a sufficient degree of compromise was reached for the Council of Ministers to issue two Directives—1970/ 509 and 1970/510—making the introduction of a standard Community policy for suppliers' credits depend upon a corresponding acceptance of an agreed and uniform system of insurance premia. However, in striving to attain such an ambitious target the Co-ordinating Group did make one significant advance on the arrangements developed within the Berne Union and the OECD Group. In May

1962 the Council of Ministers agreed to a system of advance notification for all proposed export credit transactions involving private funds guaranteed by a government institution which contravened either Berne Union Understandings or EEC Regulations; and in January 1965 they widened the system to include financial credits granted from public funds or mixed sources. The procedure adopted required that any member proposing to enter into such a transaction must telex certain prescribed information about it to its partners and wait seven days before acting further. Its partners have this interval of time from the receipt of the information within which to request further information or to convene a consultative meeting. Refusal to submit to the procedure obliges member governments to adhere to the relevant Understanding or Regulation in its entirety for that particular transaction.

Both the principle asserted, that of advance notification, and the procedure involved, that of prior consultation, represented a marked advance on Berne Union procedure. But the member in question could ignore a request if it considered the transaction concerned to be of ' importance '—unless reservations are lodged by all, or all but one, of the remaining partners. And in fact the procedure has not been allowed to become any more onerous than that of the Understanding; partly because it was in the collective interest to soften, and partly because it placed a heavier burden upon EEC members than on its industrial competitors outside.

A cartel for credit?

The importance of export credits as a component in the flow of financial resources from developed to developing countries increased beyond all anticipation during the 1960s. Since 1960 the greatest increase has been in credits whose maturity exceeds five years. In 1960 the total net insured credits extended to developing countries by member countries of DAC was $570·9m, of which $419·5m were from one to five years and $151·4m over five years. Of the total net insured credits in 1968, the figure for one to five years had increased only to $471·0m, whereas that for over five years had increased to $1,272·3m. Such credits were rare in the 1950s and even in 1959 accounted for less than 5 per cent of the net flow of guaranteed export credits. By 1961 they made up 50 per cent of the total and by 1967, according to the Pearson Commission, almost the entire net flow of export credits had maturities of more than five years. Part of the growth may be explained by the increase in world trade. But a greater proportion of world export sales was financed by export credits. This is partly explained by the higher proportion of engineering goods in world exports, which increased from 19·1 per cent in 1955 to 57·8 per cent in 1966. (Between 1955 and 1966 engineering exports to developing countries increased from $6·1 billion to $13·3 billion, 95 per cent of which came from the OECD countries.) [4]

However, the growth of credits was at a rate even faster than the rate of growth of exports of capital goods during that same period. The traditional techniques for financing capital transactions between developed and developing countries were proving inadequate to meet the unprecedented demand for capital goods that resulted from the drive by the developing countries to pursue policies of economic development through industrialization; particularly in circumstances where export earnings from primary commodities were hardly growing. Direct private investment was limited to countries having either mineral resources or close associations with metropolitan capital markets. Access to bond markets was restricted by many developed countries even after convertibility on current transactions was restored in the late 1950s and the capacity to provide long-term funds at low rates of interest was limited. Moreover, many developing countries were new and their credit-worthiness was not established. In any case long-term bond issues are better suited to finance goods for infra-structural than for industrial purposes. This last point is also true of multilateral institutional lending, such as through the World Bank, which had until the early 1960s concentrated upon power and transport projects. What took the place of these techniques, except of course for World Bank lending, to a very large extent was export credits. This occurred because the enthusiasm of the developed nations to sell was as great as that of the LDCs to buy, governments placing a high priority on the development of export markets and being prepared to give their exporters financial support through insurance and other schemes.

The suppliers' credit system induced a substantial transfer of real resources from developed to developing countries. But there were a number of ways in which the system, as it operated in the 1960s, proved counter-productive. First, private export credits were a high-cost form of finance. Despite the stability of interest rates and the lengthening of maturities during the decade, the prices of the equipment purchased with these credits were often inflated. Second, the lack of international co-operation and agreement on credit and insurance terms meant that capital investment decisions depended as much on the repayment maturity attached to a good as its price or quality. Third, the apparent lack of concern by all lenders and many borrowers with the economic soundness and foreign exchange earning/saving potential of projects contributed to the accumulation of excessive foreign exchange debts without a corresponding accumulation of foreign exchange earnings assets.

ANTICIPATING CRISES

It was the third factor which presented the critical threat to the system. Certain borrowers were accumulating an inordinate amount of debt from guaranteed export credits. In a World Bank study made in 1969,[5] out of thirty-nine countries surveyed, six accounted for 80 per cent of the total outstanding debt from guaranteed export credits. The question was, therefore, to what extent the lenders were willing or able to take the initiative in limiting flows to, or anticipating and overruling a crisis in, borrowing countries unwilling or unable to impose their own limits.

Three solutions were mooted. First, the World Bank, the International Monetary Fund (IMF), and the DAC all studied the possibility of establishing an ' early warning system '—a way of anticipating a debt crisis. There were two difficulties. One was technical. While there was good information on all forms of public debt, information on private non-guaranteed export credits and short-term debt was poor. It was not possible, therefore, to measure the burden of debt sufficiently accurately. The other and more intractable problem was political. A declaration of insolvency by a sovereign state is really a statement that it is no longer prepared to apply its limited foreign exchange resources to meet obligations on loan contracts in which its liabilities are denominated in hard currencies. It prefers, rather, to sacrifice its financial standing with its creditors in order to spend its foreign exchange on other international transactions which have greater utility for it. The propensity to default will depend upon a judgement by the government of the debtor state as to the political repercussions of squeezing the domestic economy even further, on the one hand, and displeasing its foreign creditors on the other. In this sense the authorities have a choice, unlike their directorial counterparts in a domestic corporation that cannot pay its creditors; and to this extent therefore sovereign default is a ' political ' decision. Insolvency will occur at or around a point at which the government of the day becomes politically indifferent between bowing to foreign or to domestic pressures. In some cases, such as India in 1968, the point of indifference was reached when it became practically impossible to squeeze further exchange resources out of the economy; in others, such as Egypt in 1966, the point was reached much earlier: Nasser cared for and depended upon the Western creditors much less than did the Indian authorities. Even if a satisfactory solution could have been found to both these problems, it could still have been a subject of extended debate among creditors as to whether more lenient terms or fewer loans should have been introduced well in advance of, or not until the moment of, crisis.

The second approach, devised to avoid this difficulty, was to seek a mechanism which provided a continuous dialogue between creditors and debtors and encouraged the adoption of policies on both sides to prevent the emergence of a crisis. To a limited extent the annual IMF consultations provided such a forum. But the institution was unattractive to the LDCs since it was its policy to place the burden of adjustment squarely on the debtor. There is nothing in the IMF system to encourage the creditor to increase his loans, or soften his terms. For example, there is none of the ' mutuality ' that is found in a consortium. But consortia were rare and principally confined to co-ordinating ODA. Moreover, while the export credit guarantee agencies compared information within the Berne Union on the credit-worthiness of debtor countries, there was no machinery to ensure that they received a clear warning of prospective acute debt-servicing difficulties or to oblige them to do anything about it even if in fact they did.

A different solution which was mooted was to introduce a rationing system for export credit operated by the lenders. However, there were formidable objections. It would have been as difficult technically and politically to establish ceilings for individual recipient countries as it was to try to institute an early warning system. Also there was a general feeling amongst the lenders that rationing was not their responsibility but that of the recipient countries. As creditors facing a debtor in default they were prepared, as we shall see in the following chapter, to reschedule accumulated debt, adjusting its burden *after* a crisis to the debtor's capacity to pay; yet somehow they did not see themselves as having any responsibility as lenders *before* the crisis to make a similar adjustment. Moreover a system of rationing would have involved partitioning of international markets which would, in the opinion of many Western countries, have been in restraint of competition, jeopardizing the LDCs' chances of getting the best terms available and, therefore, likely to provoke much opposition from them. (Generally speaking the LDCs were no more in favour of credit rationing than the creditors themselves.) And in addition the inter-lender political problems of dividing up the market threatened to be extremely complicated, especially in circumstances where certain markets were dominated by one or two countries.

DAC, which wrote increasingly about the implications for the burden of debt of untrammelled rises in export credits, was pessimistic about the possibility of control:

Donors in general tend to oppose any system of universal rationing or setting of ceilings for export credits, and are equally sceptical about the practicality of establishing general criteria governing the extension of such credits to developing countries, preferring to deal with the problem on a case-by-case basis.[6]

In fact, not only were governments unwilling to develop any co-ordinated regime for the control of the volume of export credits, they seemed unable to introduce controls individually in the face of the most blatant irresponsibility on behalf of the recipient authorities. In the case of Ghana, for example, industrialized nations continued to insure in a period when it was clear that Ghana's debt problem had become totally unmanageable—with the consequence that debt mounted as before. Thus, for instance, in each of the years from 1962 to 1964 the IMF called for a drastic curtailment of suppliers' credits to Ghana. These calls went unheeded, lenders only taking action when Ghana started to delay some of its repayments. Moreover during this period of financial deterioration the governments made their guarantees more expensive, contributing even further to the inevitable declaration of insolvency.

Frequently terms were made tougher as risk increased, but the inelasticity of demand for external finance in developing countries together with the fact that owing to the operation of the grace period the additional debt-servicing costs in the early years were inconsiderable made the effect of this toughening process on the behaviour of the borrower marginal. Moreover, however tough lenders were prepared to get about terms, even when faced with a possible default, they were reluctant to limit volume. This reluctance reflected the enormous power of commercial lobbies for capital goods exports in Western countries (represented by such giants as Krupp, Siemens, Phillips, and General Electric) in conjunction with their governments' need to sustain a strong export performance. The strength of these forces made the occurrence of some insolvencies during the decade inevitable.

Notes

[1] See generally, IBRD, *Supplies' credits from industrialized to developing countries* (Washington, 1967), and UN, Dept of Economic and Social Affairs, *Export credits and development financing*, pt 1: *Current practices and problems* (New York, 1966).

[2] For example, in 1952 the UK government extended the maximum export credit period for transactions with non-sterling purchasers to three years, and exceptionally to five. Similar arrangements were made in Germany and France in 1950, in Belgium in 1951, and in Italy in 1953.

[3] The same pressures that brought lengthening maturities also brought some lowering of interest rates. Examples of techniques employed were mixed credits combining public and private funds, subsidized institutional lending, and preferential rediscounting by central banks.

[4] See IMF, *Staff papers*, Mar 1970, p. 37.

[5] Ibid.

[6] *Annual report*, 1969.

3

CONSPIRING TO PREVENT DEFAULT

One common factor seems to emerge from the variety of attempts at co-operation amongst the lending countries in the context of both budgetary and commercial finance that have been examined in the last two chapters. The political and commercial forces working against co-ordination and harmonization generally proved stronger than those working in their favour. Even when catastrophe stared them in the face, as it did in the case of Ghana, the combined influence of commercial pressures, balance-of-payments considerations, and political interest overrode any impulse towards financial sagacity. The weakness of the forces working for co-operation was particularly marked in those institutions responsible for establishing global arrangements. But even attempts at mandatory arrangements at the recipient country level, except in the heat of financial crises, got nowhere.[1] It is argued in the following pages that when the same nations were presented with actual default during our period they were to react with a reasonable degree of uniformity and sense of common purpose; moreover, it will be demonstrated that they developed an effective burden-sharing technique called debt rescheduling—and that certain conventions have grown up with this procedure for it to work properly.

Perhaps the most striking contrast between what follows and what has gone before is the totally different attitude of nations when they cease to become lenders and become creditors—when the balance sheet replaces the profit and loss statement as the reflection of financial reality for them. In the previous chapter the industrialized nations *as lenders* were behaving like highly speculative fringe bankers devoted entirely to profit considerations and mindless of asset security. In this chapter, *as creditors*, they establish elaborate and lengthy procedures to salvage a financial disaster which need never have happened if even a fraction of the co-operation they demonstrated ex post the insolvency had been demonstrated ex ante the insolvency.

Debt rescheduling clubs

The multilateral arrangements which will be considered in this chapter are consortia and debt rescheduling clubs. The character of consortia has already been outlined in a different context (see p. 370) and, for present purposes, that description will suffice. A debt rescheduling club is an informal meeting of creditor governments convened at short notice to deal with a particular financial crisis. It is best suited to a short-term debt-servicing crisis engendered by excessive borrowing on hard terms, usually in circumstances of lax or inappropriate policies by the debtor government. The club refinances a portion of the short- and medium-term commercial credits—usually government guaranteed suppliers' credits—replacing them with new liabilities themselves of a fairly short-term nature; and requires that the offender undergo a dose of fiscal and monetary discipline policed by the IMF. Roughly, it is not unlike a ' composition of creditors ', familiar to English lawyers, in which two or more creditors of an individual jointly agree to forgo a portion of their contractual rights and to share out this forbearance in a particular manner. Although there is no consideration (in the legal sense) for their sacrifice the agreement is binding.

The typical *terms* of a ' club ' rescheduling in the 1950s and 1960s have been first to establish a consolidation period of two to five years during which something of the order of 50–75 per cent of the service payments falling due are deferred; and second, a repayment period lasting for a further five years. The *procedure* is that the ' club ' arrives at a ' General Agreement ' between the creditor and the debtor governments. The ' General Agreement ' is then worked out in detail through a series of bilateral agreements between individual creditor governments and the debtor government. Private creditors will form ' Protective Associations ' to negotiate arrangements for the rescheduling of purely private loans (the governmental agreements relate only to official loans and public guaranteed supplier credits). In addition the ' General Agreements ' will usually contain a so-called ' IMF clause '. This normally requires that the IMF is to monitor a stabilization programme; it sometimes establishes a specific limit on future borrowing on short- or medium-term supplier credit terms; occasionally it has required that the debtor adhere to strict performance targets specifically laid down in the Agreement.

The earliest clubs (apart from an arrangement for Cuba in 1949) were the Hague Club for Brazil and the Paris Club for Argentina, both convened in the 1950s. The initial purpose of the Hague Club, formed by the UK, Germany, France, Sweden, Belgium, and Holland in 1955, was to enable Brazil to reduce the bilateral character of its trade and monetary relations with the European countries. However, in the same year Brazil succeeded in getting its IMF purchases postponed and its debt rescheduled. The Paris Club operated in a tentative way from the summer of 1956 just after the fall of the Perón regime in Argentina; although its chief motivation was transparently political—to save the new regime by lightening the repayment burden of the vast accumulation of Peronist debt—it emerged, almost casually, from an Argentine initiative at an ad hoc meeting of European Treasury representatives. The club was placed on a more formal footing in November 1957 and received its name because meetings invariably took place at the French Ministry of Finance. The Hague and Paris Clubs are the first examples of a multilateral financial technique that was to be employed on several occasions during the 1960s to assist Chile, Turkey, Indonesia, India, Ghana, Peru, as well as Brazil and Argentina again. Yugoslavia, Liberia, and Egypt also rescheduled their external debt during the same period on a bilateral basis. In some cases, notably Argentina and Brazil, agreement has been reached fairly swiftly and relatively painlessly. In these cases the issues were clear and the procedures already well established. In others, in particular Ghana and Indonesia, where the political and economic issues were more complex, negotiations were complicated and protracted by issues such as the history of corruption, the change in regime, the amount and terms of the relief and, in particular, disagreements amongst the creditors themselves.

We are concerned here with three aspects of club and consortia: their respective roles in the rescheduling process; the behavioural conventions usually observed by members of debt rescheduling clubs (those relating to consortia have already been outlined above, p. 371); and reason why clubs have become the preferred response to sovereign insolvency in the face of competing behavioural options such as the use of force, remedies in the courts, and economic or financial embargo.

Club and Consortium: the common factors

The second half of the 1950s and the decade of the 1960s were characterized by two kinds of sovereign insolvency. One occurred because certain national authorities unwisely permitted their business communities to finance their industrial investments on terms which were too short. In these cases, mostly Latin American, the solution was a dose of traditional creditor discipline imposed by means of a multilateral debt rescheduling club. The other emerged where either the minimum development requirements of the nations concerned were such that even a strongly concessionary debt profile would have been insufficient to prevent insolvency, for example in India; or where majestic accumulations of short-term debt were incurred by public authorities to defray the cost of over-ambitious development programmes which had no hope of yielding sufficient foreign exchange to meet the added burden of external debt even in the medium term, for example, in Ghana. Here the solution was to prove more complex, creditors perceiving that more than rescheduling was required to restore financial stability.

The scale of India's debt and development problem and the evolution of the group of creditors from a club to a fully fledged consortium has been outlined elsewhere (see above, p. 371). In this case the club was transformed, exchanging its informal and temporary character for something more permanent and institutionalized, and its function from rescheduling past debt to guaranteeing future loans. The Pakistan consortium, established two years later, benefited from the experience of its neighbour by immediately considering Pakistan's second Five Year Plan and the implications that it had for external financing. Given the magnitude of India's actual and potential deficit, the creditors saw as essential some form of permanent collective external finance planning to avoid a recurrence of short-term debt crises which were not only disruptive of trade and time-consuming of diplomatic staff but also tended to erode the sanctity of public debt. Moreover, pledging seemed a logical development of rescheduling. Both filled an external resource gap, the distinction being that the gap was filled, in the case of the club, by an attenuation of a burden already accrued and, in the case of the consortium, by relating the volume and terms of future lending to what was required to make a sensible programme of economic development financially viable.

The origins of the Turkish consortium [2] were likewise connected with a debt crisis. By 1958 Turkey's external indebtedness had reached $371m, an amount greater than its total export earnings in the previous year. Debt repayments were partially suspended and rescheduling negotiations with creditor governments were begun under the auspices of the OEEC. The process was protracted, lasting from April 1958 to May 1959, as there was little willingness to underwrite the economic policies of the Menderes regime. At that time the OEEC, the European Payments Union (EPU), the International Monetary Fund (IMF), and the USA together made a fresh commitment of $223m and Turkey's commercial debts, by now exceeding $400m, were consolidated. The arrangement, an ad hoc rescue operation, fell squarely in the club category. Although the consortium, established in July 1962 (see above, p. 374), did not emerge directly from the debt rescheduling meetings, resulting as it did from a new initiative by the Turkish government, it operated with the same chairman, within the same framework, and was served by the same permanent missions. Its work was carried on by a series of working parties within the normal OECD structure, allowing its members to enter into discussion at any level at very short notice to handle either rescheduling or aid procurement. As a consequence the operations and purpose of the two institutions became confused, to the detriment of both.

Consortia were also established to deal with the Ghanaian and Indonesian debt crises. Unlike the Indian and Turkish cases, they neither replaced nor became enmeshed with the club operations functioning simultaneously and independently. The Intergovernmental Group for Indonesia (IGGI) first met under the chairmanship of the Netherlands in February 1967 and continued to meet regularly throughout the remainder of the 1960s. Although chaired by a member nation rather than by an international institution, in effect it observed the practice of mandatory pledging. Following the establishment of the IGGI, the Ghanaians succeeded in persuading the Fund to organize a meeting of potential donors, the first meeting taking place in Paris in April 1967. Further meetings were held in May 1969 and December 1970, by which time the Fund had handed over to the World Bank as chairman. In both these cases, creditors were at considerable pains to keep the two operations distinct—despite the fact that it was almost impossible to disentangle external solvency and development planning issues. When the crisis was perceived to require something more than a straightforward club exercise, rather than extend the terms of reference of the club to suit the particular occasion, creditors rigidly preserved its limited purpose, preferring to establish a separate institution to deal with the new financial requirements. The reason for this rather artificial distinction was to prevent potential debtors from connecting default with increased aid. The danger, which originally seemed remote in the cases of India and Pakistan, was considered more immediate in the light of the Turkish, Ghanaian, and Indonesian crises. *Creditors* wanted to keep their role as *lenders* entirely distinct.

That the distinction was, at the beginning of the Indonesian and Ghanaian crises, unclear is borne out by the respective roles of the Bank and Fund in these two crises. It is sometimes said that the Fund is to the club as the Bank is to the consortium, the Fund being concerned with balance-of-payments problems and the Bank with development problems. But in those countries where debt problems did not fall into a clear category—that is to say into neither short-term balance-of-payments problems (e.g. the Hague and Paris Clubs) in which the IMF was exclusively involved, nor long-term development problems (e.g. the Indian and Pakistan consortia), in which the Bank was exclusively involved—the respective roles of the Fund and the Bank in restoring financial stability were less clearly defined. In the case of Ghana, almost immediately after the coup deposing Nkrumah in February 1966, teams from both the Bank and the Fund went to Accra. In May 1966 a standby (of $36·4m) was approved, as is customary in any rescheduling. However, the Ghanaians also persuaded the Fund to organize a meeting of potential donors for balance-of-payments support for 1967 and 1968 on the grounds that a similar arrangement had been undertaken for Indonesia (the IGGI) in February 1967. The first meeting was held in Paris on 11–12 April 1967. These early meetings, in both cases, were a hybrid form. In the sense that the task they performed was to agree to fill a gap that had not yet arisen they were consortia. But their horizons were not, in the early stages, developmental, being limited to solving an immediate and pressing balance-of-payments crisis. By the third meeting of the Ghanaian inter-governmental group, the World Bank had taken over as chairman, and the developmental role began to assert itself.

At first blush it might seem that the degree of influence and control over domestic economic policy exerted by the creditors is considerably greater through consortia; partly because the creditors in the club have a declared short-term interest, having no desire to make rescheduling an easy matter for the debtor countries by institutionalizing the process; and partly because the consortium technique leads to involvement in the long-term planning and investment process. However, this view needs qualifying in two respects. First, the informality in organization and arm's length posture that clubs adopt towards the debtor are deceptive. Creditors' reluctance to involve themselves in debtor internal policy must be read in conjunction with the negotiation of the IMF standby (see above, p. 390). Indeed, the degree of involvement of the Fund was such that further interference by the creditors in the domestic affairs of the debtor would have been otiose. Moreover, as Douglas Dillon said of the IMF in a statement before the US House of Representatives Banking and Currency Committee on 4 March 1959:

As an international organization it is better able to advise sovereign governments on sensitive matters of financial policy, or to insist on appropriate corrective measures in return for credits, than are other sovereign governments.... In the delicate area of fiscal and monetary policy, governments find it much easier to accept the counsel of an objective, impartial, and highly competent international organization than the advice of other governments, no matter how good or well intentioned.[3]

Secondly, although the consortium technique does involve investigation of the long-term planning and investment process, lenders, because they do not possess the investigating resources themselves and for the reason given by Secretary Dillon, prefer to leave the task of monitoring to the World Bank staff. In each case it is the international institution that is relied upon to do the internal policing, leaving the creditors to concentrate upon the intricate and sometimes intractable problems of sharing the burden of rescheduling (see below, p. 396) or pledging (see above, p. 371).

Intermediation by the IMF and the World Bank is one of the main reasons why the main conflicts in clubs and consortia were not between creditor and debtor but between creditor and creditor. It was, as we shall see, the 'burden-sharing' rather than the 'creditor-debtor' issues that provoked the gravest differences imperilling rescheduling and destroying pledging. A good example of the effect of such intermediation is the Egyptian rescheduling. At the end of 1966 Nasser approached Egypt's main creditors individually with a view to obtaining a five-year grace period for debts repayable during that year. The creditors agreed on condition that Nasser adopted a stabilization programme approved by the Fund. Nasser, whose previous relations with the Fund had not been good, rejected its suggestions for budgetary cuts and the Fund countered by refusing further assistance. In March 1967 Nasser refused to make further payments on past debt unless he got more help from the Fund. It was a further year before Egypt moved its entrenched position and a compromise was reached. In these circumstances the Fund, in effect an agent of the creditors, bore the full weight of criticism and ill will which should, more accurately if not more justly, have been directed against the creditors. Equally the Bank's role as an intermediary in the Indian consortium at the time of the Indian devaluation in 1966 drew much of the sting that consortium members would otherwise have drawn on themselves.

It is worth adding that the experience of intermediation rather changed the relationship of both Fund and Bank with their major shareholders. In the case of Egypt, the Fund might have pursued the Cuban precedent and expelled it on grounds of default. It did not. Nor did it react when Nasser refused its advice to devalue. Moreover, in March 1968 it permitted two further drawings amounting to $63m to allay an acute balance-of-payments position, though at this stage little progress had been achieved in rescheduling. Once agreement was reached on the rescheduling, the Fund was swift to act very positively, the Managing Director visiting Cairo in November of that year and the 1969 mission publicly praising Egypt for its efforts to repay the foreign debt. The Bank, too, much maligned on occasions by the Indians (particularly on the devaluation issue), has proved India's warmest proponent. Indeed, the influence of the World Bank and the IMF, while repeatedly calling for greater restraint and self-discipline on the part of the debtor, was equally if not more powerfully brought to bear upon the creditor governments to show tolerance and consideration. They were, at almost any cost, concerned to avoid open default which would involve the resignation of the debtor from both institutions. But a number of other factors contributed to the attitude, among them the fact that rich as well as poor countries were members of both institutions and, still more, an awareness of the heavy responsibility that the creditor countries must bear for the debtors' insolvency.

The conventions of burden-sharing

When creditor countries were faced in the 1960s with the reality of a country with an unmanageable debt problem, they chose, or were obliged, to share the limited repayment capacity of that country amongst themselves in some equitable way. Before considering the reasons why creditors settled, repeatedly, for the club option—rather than other alternatives—it is worth illustrating that rescheduling proved to be a very real 'burden-sharing' operation in which strict attention was paid to the principle of 'non-discrimination.'

The principle is most forcefully demonstrated by the fact that it was rigorously extended to apply to creditors who either were not invited or did not wish to become members of the club. Taking over from President Sukarno in March 1966, General Suharto inherited a total debt of some $2,000m. The Tokyo Club was quickly organized on the initiative of Japan, but the USSR was not invited to send a representative to its first meeting in July 1966 even though Russia was owed over half the amount outstanding. Yet it became clear at the second meeting of the club in September 1966 that consent by the Russians to reschedule their portion was an essential pre-condition for agreement amongst the members. Nobody was prepared to defer if the Russians received on schedule. The Indonesian Finance Minister, Adam Malik, paid a visit to Eastern Europe in November 1966, but the Russians refused to take part in multilateral talks and it looked for a time as if they were going to insist on immediate repayment. As Malik was on his way back to Jakarta, however, they relented, and agreement was reached on the postponement of payments of $800m of the total $1,200m and a moratorium on interest. With this settled, the Western creditors were able to agree to the rescheduling of $357m of their portion at the third meeting of the club in December—less than a month after the reversal of Soviet policy.

One month earlier, in February 1966, Nkrumah was ousted in a coup d'état. Only the day before the Soviet bloc countries had agreed to a moratorium on the repayment of suppliers' credits and short-term loans. But after the coup they turned down the IMF request to participate in a multilateral rescheduling operation—influenced no doubt by the decision of the new regime to expel Soviet technicians. During the following years relations, if anything, worsened as the suspicion grew (especially after the arrest of Air Marshall Otu in 1969) that the USSR was actively assisting Nkrumah. The Ghanaians therefore unilaterally rescheduled the Russian debt along the same lines as the multilateral arrangements with the West agreed in 1968. There was little that Russia could do in the face of this action since the threat to halt further credit was of no use in circumstances where Ghana was rehabilitated in the eyes of her Western creditors. The decision of the Czechs and Poles in 1967 and the Romanians in 1968 to reopen negotiations was doubtless influenced by Ghana's threat to act unilaterally in their direction.

The protracted rescheduling negotiations in the case of both Indonesia and Ghana—the Indonesian arrangements were finally settled in March 1971 and provisional agreement for a Ghana settlement was arrived at in February 1974—were almost wholly the result of disagreements between the major Western creditors. The history of negotiations in both these cases illustrates a common feature of club exercises: that the more heavily committed the creditor and the more commercial his terms, the more intractable he is in his opposition to those who wish for a soft settlement. Equally, the less he is owed and the softer his terms, the more willing he is to concede and the more persuasive he is with others to do likewise; for he has more to lose from a lengthy interruption of commerce than from a liberal rescheduling agreement, the main burden of which will be borne by the harder lenders. Indeed, he may lose nothing from the rescheduling procedure at all. In corporate bankruptcies each is expected to bear the burden in direct proportion to the amount of money he is owed. This makes good sense in the case of a nation where the terms upon which creditors lend are more or less uniform. The same cannot be said, however, for the international market in development credits in which there are substantial differences in the terms of different lenders. Historically soft lenders like the United States have been affected rather less than most by rescheduling arrangements. Moreover a precedent was set in the case of India in 1968 which may be adopted in future. An assessment of what proportion of estimated exports India could devote to external debt servicing was divided by the total debt outstanding, which came to 6 per cent. Only creditors with service payments which exceeded 6 per cent were obliged to reschedule. The fundamental tension, therefore, in the club is between the hard/heavily committed and the soft/lightly committed creditor. The hand of the former is somewhat strengthened by the club convention that the biggest creditor, the man with the most to lose, should chair the club.

In Ghana, for example, Britain had the most to lose by a soft settlement—it was owed about half the outstanding debt [4]—and adopted the toughest stance. An initial agreement at the end of 1966 covering 80 per cent of the medium-term supplier's credits due between 1 June 1966 and 31 December 1968, was reached, which involved their repayment over eight years starting in July 1971. In 1968 a similar agreement was reached on those credits due between 1969–72. The negotiations in each case were characterized by hard bargaining by the British over the rate of interest. With the exception of the United States, which had almost no supplier credit exposure, the other creditors supported the British line and rates were finally settled at 6 per cent and 5·82 per cent respectively. Apart from its low commercial profile, the United States had two other reasons for advocating leniency. First, it approved of the new regime, wished it a long innings, and demonstrated these feelings by providing immediate military aid and access to PL480 and AID loans. Secondly, having responded to the new regime in this positive and concessionary manner, in strong contrast to its co-creditors, it found it hard to swallow the fact that the unbending policy of its more heavily committed colleagues in the club meant that its new assistance programme was in effect a transfer payment to them to the extent that it led to foreign exchange savings which were used to service debt.

By the time of the Marlborough House talks in July 1970 between Ghana and twelve western creditor nations the situation had changed in important respects in favour of the American position. Despite rescheduling in 1966 and 1968 on considerably more favourable terms than the classic Hague/Paris models, and despite the establishment of an intergovernmental consortium, the size of the total medium-term debt had actually increased due to the payments of moratorium interest. Moreover, even though as a result of the 1966 and 1968 renegotiations Ghana was paying only 10 per cent annually of the original amount due on medium-term debt, the burden was generally recognized as being, practically speaking, intolerable. In addition, the Pearson Report, published in 1969, had urged a policy of greater leniency among creditors in confronting the plight of developing countries with external debt problems. Indeed, the Ghanaians used this report as a leitmotif for their proposed rescheduling scheme, which was in line with its recommendations.[5] On this occasion, with the single and important exception of Britain, the main medium-term creditors were much more disposed to be sympathetic. However, the British had what was tantamount to a veto since at least half the outstanding medium-term debt was still owed to them. After stiff bargaining a provisional agreement was initialled in mid-July, but talks between Britain and Ghana on its details broke down in December 1970,[6] the British offer being rejected as insufficiently concessionary.

But for the attitude of the British, a final settlement would probably have been reached at the Marlborough House talks. In this case the pressure to share the burden imposed first by the United States and then progressively by the other creditors was insufficient to sway the adamantine position of the UK. Such behaviour by the most heavily committed creditor flies in the face of the view expressed by Herbert Feis when discussing increasing French involvement in Russian government securities in the 1890s: ' Once the sums loaned had grown great, they strengthened the necessity of making French foreign policy conform to Russian aims. Debtor and creditor were firmly bound to each other. . . .' [7] Or at least the more generally held view that a co-operative response is likely to be forthcoming from those who have lent so much that they cannot afford to see the debtor go broke. However, whatever the lesson in this respect (and it should be recognized that in the end Britain was the only non-compliant party), the military government of Acheampong, which took over in January 1972, immediately announced its intention to repudiate $95m of debt owed to four British companies and the moratorium interest charges established by the debt-rescheduling conferences, and to reschedule the remainder on IDA terms. It also stated that it would not discuss debts independently of development. The UK responded by suspending its export credit guarantee programme. No US debt was repudiated, and generally speaking the Americans were sympathetic. [8]

Avoiding insolvency

The Ghana story serves as a good antidote to those inclined to subscribe to the theory that the debtor is in a weak position, or equally, to those who believe that toughness of some degree or another will force a recalcitrant debtor to heel. In theory there are a number of tougher options open to the creditor or creditors: in particular those of force, the courts, or financial embargo. Yet another alternative open to the authorities in the nineteenth century was to do nothing at all; this was quite feasible since they themselves were rarely financially involved in any significant way. It is not difficult to see why such an option is no longer open to a creditor government today which, as donor or guarantor, is in effect the only creditor.

There is a popular misconception that ' the gunboat ' was much used in the nineteenth century to encourage recalcitrant debtors to pay up. In fact, in proportion to the number of defaults that actually occurred at that time, force of any sort was rarely employed. The Venezuelan blockade of 1902, the odd incursion of the United States into the Central American customs houses, the involvements of Britain in Egypt from 1883 and France in Morocco in 1911 were dramatic events by the standards of their own time; most unusual, and only possible either because, as in the case of Venezuela, all the great powers agreed that blockade was the right policy; or in most other cases because the debtor in question was accepted by the powers as being firmly within the sphere of influence of the creditor in question.

Generally speaking, however, balance-of-power considerations made it impossible to employ this option. Other reasons apart, the greater delicacy and immediacy of the contemporary balance of terror is a sufficient argument to dismiss the possibility of force as an option in the post-World War II era.

On the legal option, the law is clear that the public debt obligations of a state must be honoured [9] even—as was the case in Indonesia and Ghana—where there has been a change in the leadership or in the form of government of that state.[10] The capacity of a government to represent and bind the state depends in no degree whatever on the legitimacy of its origins. All that matters is that, on a change of government, the identity of the state is preserved.[11] However, in practice default is usually a genuine expression of a lack of capacity as opposed to a lack of intention to honour obligations. The expression of a lack of intention to pay would be, more properly, referred to as repudiation. Thus in 1966 both Indonesia and Ghana defaulted; at the same time both the new regimes accepted full responsibility for the debts contracted on behalf of the state by their predecessors. However, in 1972 the Acheampong government in Ghana repudiated $94m worth of debts incurred in relation to contracts with four British companies. (The ultimate settlement that Britain made with Ghana in February 1974 agreed that if, as a result of arbitration, some of the contracts for the sale of capital goods were found to have been concluded corruptly, then at least part of the obligation to pay for the goods involved could be avoided.) It is only in the, so far, rare circumstances of repudiation that legal action would be appropriate, if at all.[12] But nations generally prefer to settle such matters by diplomatic negotiation rather than by submission to an international tribunal.

In effect, the only practical alternative to rescheduling would be the imposition of a financial embargo by the creditor nations. But as for the strategic or economic embargo, so for the financial—as long as one substantial donor or insurer is prepared to forgo the principle of the sanctity of public contract and continue to transact, the debtor will get most of the goods he wants (either directly from the truant creditor or indirectly from other creditors who sell via the truant creditor) and the commercial pressures on the others from their export lobbies to do likewise is likely to be irresistible. Enough has already been witnessed both of allied disagreement in Cocom [13] as well as creditor disagreements within clubs to see the difficulties of presenting a united front in circumstances where national self-interest is perceived to matter more. Usually there is a spectrum of opinion amongst creditors at the time of a default ranging from those who are prepared to be very lenient in order to get on with selling and those who are very tough. Whereas in the rather fluid context of a club arrangement creditors believe, mainly because of their conviction of the need to sustain the principle of the inviolability of public debt, that the importance of maintaining a united front outweighs the advantages to be gleaned by breaking ranks, the rigidities of an embargo arrangement are likely to prove too much for those who are owed relatively little, especially if it is on soft terms.[14] The Americans, who had strong political and commercial reasons to co-operate with India, and with Ghana after the coup d'état, nevertheless, supported the principle of the club while urging a liberal policy within it. Since the United States was the major creditor country in the world, flouting a general principle of such central importance to them for the sake of relatively short-term political and commercial advantage was an unattractive option. It might be argued that the heavily committed creditors adopt the club route from the beginning in the knowledge that in this way they will get a better deal than by going through the charade of financial embargo to a situation where creditors break ranks and the most intransigent of them is finally forced to renegotiate its terms in isolation from the others. Indeed, these were in essence the facts of the Ghana case. Because of British obstinacy vis-à-vis both other creditors (and the debtor), the club lost its cardinal virtue, its fluidity, the essential condition for maintaining a united front and preventing small creditors from making separate deals. By maintaining an ' embargo ' mentality, Britain broke the fundamental convention.

In this context it is most significant that debtors where possible, prefer to reschedule bilaterally: something that Egypt, Yugoslavia, and Liberia managed to achieve during our period. It is significant that in Acheampong's ultimatum to the Ghana club on 15 February 1972, one of the principal assertions was that henceforth he would deal with creditors only on a bilateral basis. By making separate deals debtors can settle with the small creditors quickly and normalize trade, giving themselves time and resources to hold out against the large creditors for a soft settlement. It would not be possible for them to do so in face of the united front of a multilateral rescheduling operation. However, there is little merit in avoiding bilateral arrangements at the beginning by establishing a club if, by ignoring the rules of intercreditor compromise that the club mechanism implies, you end up deserted by your co-creditors and are obliged to make the best deal you can in the circumstances. Although, contrary to Acheampong's wishes, the façade of multilateralism was retained until the final settlement, in effect Britain had lost the initiative to keep the other creditors in line and really was negotiating bilaterally.

In principle the problem of operating a financial embargo would seem to be complicated as a result of the existence of the Soviet bloc as an alternative source of credit. Yet in many cases, notably Indonesia, the USSR is itself a large creditor and to that extent has an interest in the sanctity of public debt and in striking the best possible rescheduling deal. As with its adversary, the United States, the principles of financial order and the sanctity of public debt seem to transcend immediate political and/or commercial advantage.[15] This policy is further strengthened by the fact that the USSR is an unattractive alternative to a Western supplier. Besides the political cadres that frequently accompany the physical consignments, the quality of the plant often falls short of Western standards.

At the end of the 1960s a further factor emerged to make a policy of credit embargo even less feasible. The Eurodollar market, hitherto confined to borrowers from the OECD countries, began to reach out to the richer developing nations, many of which, such as Brazil, Yugoslavia, and Argentina, had had a series of rescheduling problems. Even, therefore, if agreement between creditors was forthcoming with respect to the behaviour of their respective national credit agencies, the Eurodollar market represented an alternative. Hence by the end of the period the argument against embargo had acquired a new dimension. Not only was there a political or commercial barrier to its control—there was in addition a technical and legal one. A much more sophisticated system of multilateral surveillance would be required to ration the allocation of non-secured Eurodollar loans to nations on the periphery of the international financial system than would be required for the control of public agencies operated by governments.

It has been argued above that in any single instance of default, nations that have little to lose from it have been prepared, provided certain conventions were observed, to club together with the bigger creditors in order to preserve a wider principle—that principle being the sanctity of public debt. Sovereign default on loan contracts threatens the whole fabric of international financial relations. At the heart of any market economy, national or international, lies the freedom to contract or not to contract—entirely without coercion—and the corresponding responsibility of honouring an obligation freely incurred. In terms of the volume of transactions affected, default in any one instance would be insufficient to lead to bankruptcy or even serious embarrassment among the creditors. But once a nation is seen to default with impunity, the example is unlikely to be lost on others. This is the creditor's nightmare. For it goes without saying that a large number of defaults could not be accommodated by the financial system as we know it today.

In the final analysis, then, the debt rescheduling club was designed to perpetuate the principle that whatever their financial position, debtor nations never default. During the 1960s, despite the strains of the Ghanaian and Indonesian negotiations, it served its purpose reasonably well. By the beginning of the 1970s, however, certain factors had emerged which suggest that clubs might have some difficulty in sustaining the principle. In particular, the sudden appearance and rapid growth of Eurodollar lending direct to developing countries by Western banks raises the possibility of a debt crisis in which the obligations defaulted upon were partly, or even mainly, uninsured. In the event of such a crisis, would the Western governments be prepared to represent the rights of such lenders in a multilateral intergovernmental setting or even adopt them as if they were their own? Or would they adopt the position frequently taken by nineteenth-century governments and choose to ignore the plight of the private banking system on the grounds that governments are not in business to bail out institutions which entered into commercial transactions with full knowledge of the kind of risks they were taking? Certainly the connection of national interest with Eurodollar lending is less strong than with supplier credit arrangements, because the former are untied.

More generally, the increasing restrictions which the burden of external debt is imposing upon the freedom of the LDCs to conduct a sensible domestic policy may lead some of them to consider the use of a number of short cuts to try to ensure solvency. The Ghana settlement, by introducing the concept of the ' tainted ' or ' corruptly made ' contract and succeeding in getting the British to acknowledge the possibility of the existence of such an animal in international law, provides a route for any nation wishing to endow repudiation with a degree of legal respectability. But this is only one of a number of possible routes. For example, the LDCs might be led to regard a whole range of issues, such as penal oil prices, high interest rates, or Western inflation of capital goods prices as constituting *force majeure*, thereby entitling them to avoid the binding effect of many of their contractual undertakings. Or the enhanced use and power of raw material cartels might so improve the terms of trade of certain LDCs that their burden of debt would be substantially diminished. Whether the debt rescheduling clubs will have a role in such a new environment must be a matter for conjecture.

Notes

[1] Some may wish to argue that Pakistan is an exception, but in the absence of the consortium some form of rescheduling would seem to have been inevitable.

[2] For a detailed account of the origins and operation of the Turkish consortium see White, *Pledged to development*, pp. 90–163.

[3] Quoted in Cheryl Payer, *The debt trap* (Harmondsworth, 1974), p. 31.

[4] The new government claimed that it had inherited £400m of debts (though the true figure was nearer £250m). Service charges on the total debt already amounted to £25m annually. *The new government pledged itself to repay the whole lot.*

THE AUTHORS OF THIS VOLUME

SUSAN STRANGE is Senior Research Specialist in international economic relations at the Royal Institute of International Affairs, and a visiting lecturer at the London School of Economics. She is author of *Sterling and British Policy* (1971).

CHRISTOPHER PROUT, formerly on the staff of the World Bank Group, is a Lecturer in Law at the University of Sussex.

INDEX